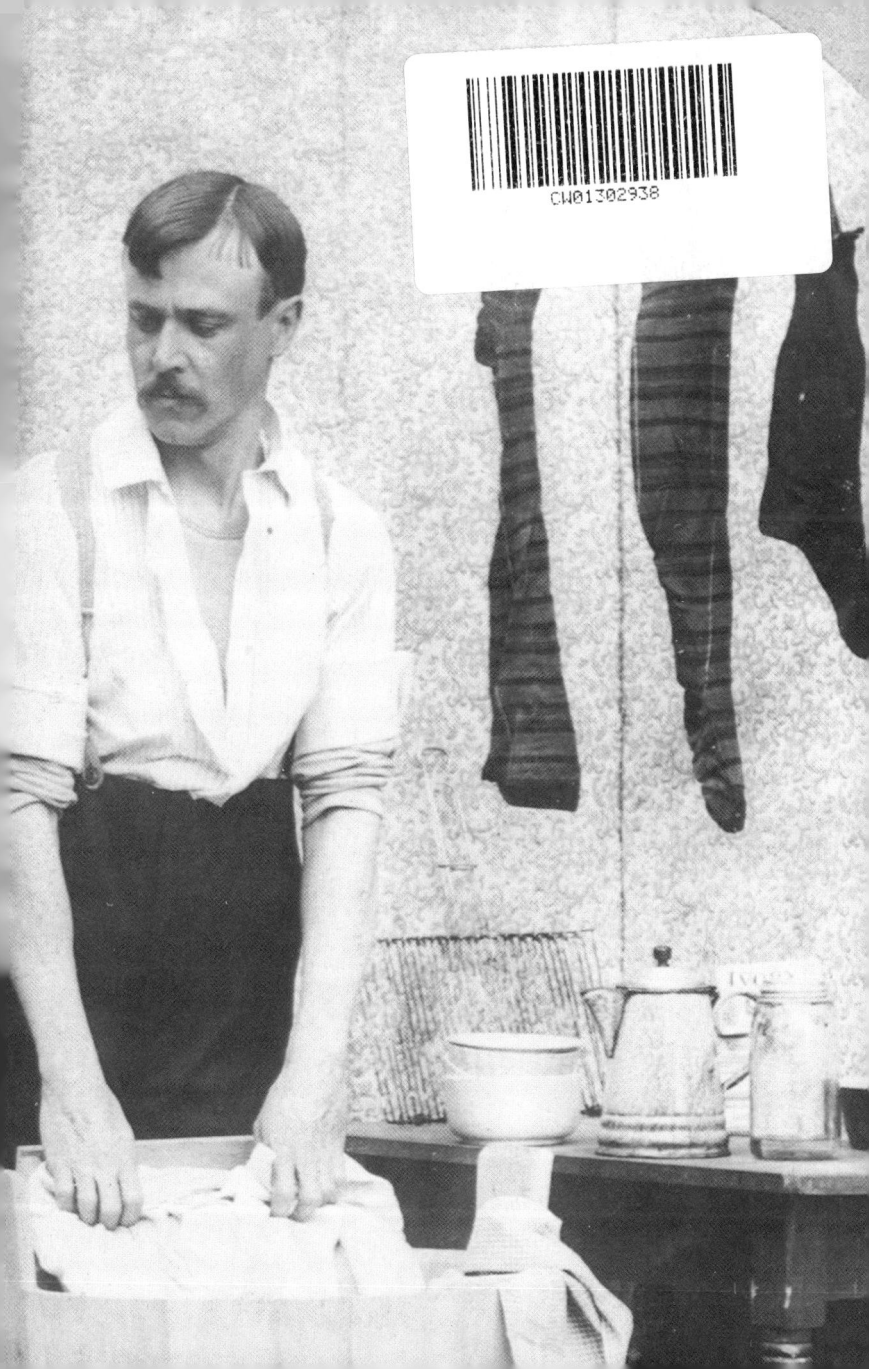

*Completely
Spotless*

Titles by
Shannon Lush and Jennifer Fleming
Spotless
Spotless 2
Speedcleaning
How to be Comfy
Save

Titles by
Shannon and Erin Lush
Kids Can Clean

Titles by
Shannon Lush and Trent Hayes
Stainless

Titles by
Jennifer Fleming and Anna-Louise Bouvier
The Feel Good Body

DISCLAIMER: While this book is intended as a general information resource and all care has been taken in compiling the contents, this book does not take account of individual circumstances and is not intended as a substitute for professional advice. The author and the publisher cannot be held responsible for any claim or action that may arise from reliance on the information contained in this book. Please follow instructions and measurements carefully as use of different quantities may have unintended consequences.

Completely Spotless

**SHANNON LUSH
& JENNIFER FLEMING**

ABC Books

The ABC 'Wave' device is a trademark of the Australian Broadcasting Corporation and is used under licence by HarperCollins*Publishers* Australia.

First published as *Spotless* in 2005 and *Spotless 2* in 2009
by ABC Books for the Australian Broadcasting Corporation
This combined edition published in Australia in 2011
by HarperCollins*Publishers* Australia Pty Limited
ABN 36 009 913 517
harpercollins.com.au

Copyright © Shannon Lush & Jennifer Fleming 2005, 2009, 2011

The right of Shannon Lush and Jennifer Fleming to be identified as the authors of this work has been asserted by them in accordance with the *Copyright Amendment (Moral Rights) Act 2000*.

This work is copyright. Apart from any use as permitted under the *Copyright Act 1968*, no part may be reproduced, copied, scanned, stored in a retrieval system, recorded, or transmitted, in any form or by any means, without the prior written permission of the publisher.

HarperCollins*Publishers*
Level 13, 201 Elizabeth Street, Sydney, NSW 2000, Australia
31 View Road, Glenfield, Auckland 0627, New Zealand
A 53, Sector 57, Noida, UP, India
77–85 Fulham Palace Road, London W6 8JB, United Kingdom
2 Bloor Street East, 20th floor, Toronto, Ontario M4W 1A8, Canada
10 East 53rd Street, New York NY 10022, USA

National Library of Australia Cataloguing-in-Publication entry:

Lush, Shannon.
Completely spotless / Shannon Lush and Jennifer Fleming.
ISBN: 978 0 7333 2988 3 (hbk.)
Includes index.
House cleaning. Spotting (Cleaning)
Other Authors/Contributors: Fleming, Jennifer.
Australian Broadcasting Corporation.
648.5

Cover design by Jenny Grigg, adapted by HarperCollins Design Studio
Internal design by Mark Thacker
Typeset in Adobe Jenson Pro Regular by Kirby Jones
Printed in China by RR Donnelley on 100gsm Yulong Pure Cream

6 5 4 3   11 12 13 14

Contents

Introduction	1
How to use this book	5
Useful Ingredients	7
The Kitchen	21
The Bathroom	103
Lounge, Dining and Family Rooms	135
Floors, Walls and Windows	213
The Bedroom	339
Clothing and Shoes	377
Kids' Stuff	447
The Laundry	471
Quick stain removal guide for fabrics	479
Outside	511
Formulas	567
Stain Diagnosis	577
Uses for Essential Oils	581
Index	584

Introduction

Have you ever accidentally put a jumper in the washing machine and found it will now only fit a twelve-year-old? Do you know what to do if you burn a pan, aside from chucking it out? What do you do if your lovable pooch has a mishap on your white wool carpet? How do you remove bird droppings on your deck or grease on your driveway? It doesn't matter how careful you are, at some stage you'll have to deal with stains and other problems in and around the home.

The good news is that there are solutions to these and many other household dilemmas, and this book will show you how to fix them. It also offers guidance on the correct way to do all those things you're not really quite sure how to do. Things like how to vacuum properly, how to organise your wardrobe, and the best way to wash dishes.

This book will also give you the confidence to walk past those expensive cleaning products in the supermarket. Because we know less and less about cleaning, advertisers can play on our fears of not being quite clean or hygienic enough. We will buy an overpriced product that promises instant cleaning because we think it could rescue us from becoming a social pariah. Well, there's no need to be seduced any longer. You will learn to love bicarbonate of soda. Vinegar won't just be part of a salad dressing. And here's something you won't hear about in one of those gleaming white ads on TV: the best cleaners are water and sunshine.

The advice in this room-by-room guide is set out like a cookbook so you can see which 'ingredients' or cleaning products you'll need before following the 'recipe' or cleaning process. There's information on how to care for and fix just about anything that can go wrong in each room. You'll also find real-life questions from people who've called Shannon when she's appeared on radio. If you have a problem that isn't covered in this book, contact Shannon through her website: www.shannonlush.com or www.homepalette.com.au

There are a couple of tricks with stain removal. First, don't panic and put something on the stain that could make it worse. Work out what's in the stain. Then work out what the solvent is. If there are several components to the stain, you must remove the protein part first, then fats, then any chemical or biological dyes, and then any resins or glues. The way to work this out is to remember that proteins are anything animal or seed based, fats are greasy between your fingers, and resins and glues are not water-soluble. If you're not sure, clean with cold water first, then use hot water, then any solvents.

You'll read a lot about 'blood-heat water' in the book. This is lukewarm or warm water. The way to test the temperature is to put the water on your wrist: if you can't feel it—if it's not too hot or too cold—it's blood heat.

When using vinegar, you'll get a better result if you use cider vinegar on hard surfaces and white vinegar on fabrics or white marble.

Dry-cleaning fluid is the same thing as white spirits or *Murlex*, which is a brand of dry-cleaning fluid.

When you come across the two-sponge method for bicarb and white vinegar, it means that you dip one damp sponge in bicarb and another in vinegar, then lay the vinegar sponge over the top of the bicarb sponge and squeeze the two together as you clean. As an alternative, if you're working with an intricate surface, make a paste of bicarb and water to the consistency of soft butter. Paint it over the surface with a cloth, leave it to dry and then polish off with a rag dipped in white vinegar.

And if you're feeling disheartened while cleaning or tackling that stubborn stain that just won't shift, just think about the Exxon Valdez disaster when thousands of litres of oil spilled into an Alaskan harbour. Your disaster will never be that bad!

This book is the household companion you've been waiting for. It combines all the stains, updates and revisions from *Spotless 2* with the tried-and-tested solutions from *Spotless*. It includes some *Spotless* classics, real-life questions from people who've called ABC radio from all over Australia. Other questions have come through our 'Stain Clinics', our website www.homepalette.com.au and Shannon's magazine and newspaper columns. There's a whole chapter devoted to common clothing stains and an extended chapter on carpet stains. There's even a chapter of cleaning formulas with a stain diagnosis guide to help you work out what is in the stain.

    We hope this book helps you solve all your domestic disasters. Whatever you do, don't stress about it. Stains happen! And so does stain removal.

How to use this book

Completely Spotless is set out a bit like a cookbook. It has lists of 'ingredients' or cleaning items followed by stain removal 'recipes', and these methods need to be followed exactly. You can't substitute one cleaning ingredient for another, just as you can't replace sugar with salt, or add extra eggs to a cake batter and expect the texture to be the same. Stain removal solutions are not interchangeable. Each chapter has an overview of various surfaces and materials and we strongly recommend that you read these before attempting any stain removal.

There are other guidelines to keep in mind. More is not better. You don't want to create a ski-field with bicarb; use it sparingly, the way you would dust icing sugar on a cake. Don't tip a whole container of white vinegar over your carpet or it will create another stain. If in doubt about a stain removal technique, first do a test on an area that no one can see. And don't throw just anything on a stain and wonder why it's worse than ever. Each thing you add changes the chemical signature of the stain and has to be removed before the right solvent can be applied. Work out what the stain is, what the surface is made of, determine the correct solvent and then apply just enough to remove the stain. Even though you're using less toxic cleaning items, because they're undiluted they can be very strong, so never overdo it!

Useful Ingredients

ACETONE is a volatile, flammable ketone. It's a liquid solvent for resins, primers, nail polish, superglue, acrylics and heavy plastics. It's available at the supermarket and hardware stores.

AQUADHERE is a wood glue and sealant available from hardware stores.

BABY OIL also known as mineral oil. It's a lubricant, skin ointment and dilutes dark oils. It's available at the supermarket or chemist.

BAY LEAVES are a moth and weevil deterrent. They're available at the supermarket.

BEESWAX is the wax produced by bees when making honeycomb and is used as a polishing, lubricating and sealing agent. It's available at hardware stores, chemists and some supermarkets.

BICARB (BICARBONATE OF SODA OR BAKING SODA) is a salt and alkaline that neutralises acid. When added to an acid (such as white vinegar) it releases carbon dioxide and water. It penetrates stains and dissolves grease. It's available at the supermarket in the cake baking section.

BLEACH is a whitening agent. It doesn't kill mould, just whitens it. Use with care and don't breathe the fumes. It's available at the supermarket.

BLOOD-HEAT WATER water at body temperature.

BORAX is crystalline sodium borate and is used as a fungicide, insecticide and detergent booster. It's mildly toxic and should be used with care. Avoid contact with skin and avoid ingestion. It's available at the supermarket.

BRAN or unprocessed bran is the ground husk of wheat or other grain. It's absorbent and a scourer and good for cleaning fabrics and furs.

BRASSO is a proprietary abrasive product that partially melts polyurethane. It's available at the supermarket.

BROOM there are many sizes and varieties available. It's used to sweep over floors and access out-of-reach areas. It's available at the supermarket and hardware store.

BUCKET these are available in various sizes—9 litres is most common. It's available at the supermarket and hardware stores.

CAKE OF BATHROOM SOAP a regular white cake of soap (not laundry soap)—the less fragrance it has, the better it is to clean with. Use it to remove protein stains. It's available at the supermarket.

CAMPHOR is a ketone from the camphor laurel tree. It has a strong vapour which most insects, particularly moths, don't like. Cats and possums are also deterred by camphor. It's flammable so don't heat it. It's found in mothballs, naphthalene flakes and *Vicks VapoRub*. It's available at the supermarket.

Useful Ingredients   9

CARNAUBA WAX is a hard, fine wax used in furniture and timber polish. It's available at the hardware store.

CARPET CLEANERS come in many varieties. They can be soap-based, bicarb-based, detergent-based or alcohol-based.

CARPET STEAM CLEANER is used for DIY carpet cleaning. It comes with a bottle of chemicals and Shannon adds her own concoction (see page 233). It's available for hire at the supermarket.

CEDAR CHIPS moth deterrent. They're available at the supermarket.

CERA WAX proprietary product used to wax marble surfaces. It's available through the internet.

CHALK STICKS normally used to write on blackboards but they're also very absorbent. You can tie white chalk sticks together and place them in areas that have a lot of moisture. They can be dried in sunshine and used again.

Chalk is also handy to mark around urine stains. It's available at the supermarket, craft stores, newsagents and toy stores.

CIGARETTE ASH from cigarettes, used to clean smoke stains. Get some from your local club or hotel.

CLINGWRAP plastic wrap. It's available from supermarkets.

CLR stands for Calcium, Lime and Rust. It removes calcium deposits from glass and kettles, lime scale from coffee machines, toilets and sinks, and rust from cement, porcelain, chrome and fabric. It can burn so wear protective gloves when using it and don't get it on your skin. It's available at the supermarket and hardware stores.

CLOTH old cotton T-shirts make great lint-free cloths.

CLOVES are a spice from the dried flower bud of the clove tree. They can be used to deter silverfish. Clove oil is extracted from the clove flower bud and used to inhibit mould. It's available from chemists (see also 'Oil of Cloves').

COLD WATER the coldest tap water. Use when removing protein stains.

COLOUR RUN REMOVER (formerly called *Runaway*)—there are two varieties: *Colour Run Remover: Whites* and *Colour Run Remover: Coloursafe* used to remove dye and colour run in fabrics and carpet. Place in a bucket with water and soak item overnight (unless wool). It's available at the supermarket in the laundry aisle.

CORNFLOUR is a starch of maize, rice and other grains. It's absorbent and a very fine abrasive. It's available at the supermarket.

COTTON BALL use over specific areas. They're available at the supermarket.

COTTON BUD use to wipe over and absorb stains. They're available at the supermarket.

CREOSOTE A liquid, oily wood tar distillation used as a preservative and antiseptic. Available from hardware shops.

DAMP CLOTH means a cloth that's been run under water and then very well-wrung or a cloth just dabbed with water.

DECK SCRUBBER a stiff bristled brush.

DENTURE TABLETS used to clean dentures but also useful to whiten porcelain and ceramic surfaces. They're available at the chemist.

DISHWASHING LIQUID removes grease. Add a couple of drops to your fingers and massage into oil and grease stains. They're available at the supermarket.

DISPOSABLE RUBBER GLOVES use to protect your skin from harsh chemicals. They're available from the supermarket.

DRY-CLEANING FLUID is a mixture of petroleum hydrocarbons. It's a solvent and also known as white spirits or *Murlex*.

EPSOM SALTS are hydrated magnesium sulphate and named because they were found at Epsom in the UK. They are good as a bath soaker and for unshrinking jumpers and other woollens.

ERASER (pencil and biro) made of rubber and removes lead pencil and biro marks on some surfaces. They're available at the supermarket or newsagency.

EUCALYPTUS OIL an essential oil distilled from the leaves of certain eucalyptus trees. It's a paint and dye stripper, solvent for adhesives and some resins, and releases vapours that inhibit some insects. It's available at the supermarket and chemist.

- **FULLER'S EARTH** is a calcium clay with bleaching agent and is very absorbent. It's a wool relaxant and used to shrink and unshrink woollens. It's available at the chemist.
- **GLYCERINE** is a clear liquid used as an agent in cosmetics, toothpaste and shampoos. It's water and alcohol soluble. Glycerine helps loosen stains, particularly tannin stains. It's available at the supermarket or chemist.
- **GOANNA OIL** is an oil made from goanna fat. It's used as a lubricant and liniment. It's available from chemists.
- **GROUT RAKE** a hand-held device with a flat tungsten tip which is run against grout to remove it, making it powdery. It's available at the hardware store.
- *GUMPTION* is a greyish cleaning paste with many uses. It contains a mild bleaching agent and is an abrasive. It's available at the supermarket.
- **HAIRBRUSH** use to fluff sheepskin as it's drying. It's available at the supermarket.
- **HAIR CONDITIONER (CHEAP)** cheap hair conditioners have fewer perfumes and additives. Use to soften woollens. It's available at the supermarket.
- **HAIR DRYER** speeds drying time and helps melt wax and crayon. It's available from department stores.
- **HYDROGEN PEROXIDE (3%)** an oxidising liquid used as an antiseptic and bleaching agent. It's available at the supermarket.

IRON is a regular, household iron. It's available from department stores.

KEROSENE is a combustible liquid hydrocarbon used as a solvent. It's available at the hardware store and some supermarkets.

KITTY LITTER absorbs moisture. It's available at the supermarket and pet stores.

LAUNDRY DETERGENT used in the washing machine to lift dirt and stains from fabric. It's available at the supermarket.

LAVENDER OIL is from lavender flowers and has many uses including insect repellent, dog inhibitor and air freshener. It's available at the supermarket, chemist and health food stores.

LEATHER CONDITIONER/LEATHER DEW used to treat leather. It's available at shoe repairers and hardware stores.

LEMON JUICE is the juice from lemons. It's used to remove rust stains and to lighten or bleach colour. It's available at supermarkets.

LEMON OIL is the oil in lemon peel and is used to deter spiders, polish pale timbers and provide a fresh fragrance. It's available at health stores.

MARBLE FLOOR WAX (such as *Cera Wax*) used to wax and seal marble. It's available from hardware stores and through the internet.

METAL LICE COMB used to remove nail polish from carpet. It's available at chemists.

METHYLATED SPIRITS is a raw alcohol with menthol. It's a solvent for some paint and marker inks, and helps release stains and smells in synthetic materials. It's available at the supermarket and hardware stores.

NAPISAN PLUS is a chlorine-based soaker and bleach. Not advised to use on leather, silk, wool, chiffon, satin or embroidered garments. It's available at the supermarket.

NAPISAN OXYACTION MAX its active ingredient is sodium percarbonate, a detergent and bleaching agent which removes some stains. It's available at the supermarket.

NON-IODISED SALT salt that doesn't contain iodine. The iodine in salt can stain some fabrics. It's available at the supermarket.

NYLON BRUSH regular dishwashing scrubbing brush. It's available at the supermarket.

OIL OF CLOVES cold-pressed oil from the dried flower bud of the clove tree. It's a mould inhibitor, insecticide, toothache soother and an ingredient in cooking. It's available at the chemist.

OIL OF PENNYROYAL is oil from a small-leafed mint. It deters moths, bed bugs and fleas, but is harmful to pregnant women and pregnant pets. Note that oil of pennyroyal should only be used as directed as it can be harmful to pregnant women and pets. Remember one drop means one drop.

PANTYHOSE/STOCKINGS normally worn over your legs. The weave and fibre make a great scrubber and polisher. They're available at the supermarket.

PAPER TOWEL used to polish glass, and absorb stains and excess moisture. It's available at the supermarket.

PETROLEUM JELLY (VASELINE) is a mixture of mineral oils, paraffin and microcrystalline waxes. It acts as a water barrier and inhibits snails. It's available at the supermarket and chemist.

PILLOWCASE used to cover pillows. Use them to hold items and protect delicates in the washing machine. They're available at department stores.

PLASTIC BAG protects items being placed in the freezer. Reuse shopping bags. Don't store clothes in them for an extended time because plastic sweats and fumes.

PLASTIC WRAP clingwrap. It's available from supermarkets.

POTTER'S PLASTER/PLASTER OF PARIS white powder made of calcium sulphate which forms a paste when mixed with water and has absorbent properties. It's available from art supplies and hardware stores.

RANEX removes calcium, lime and rust. It's available at hardware stores.

ROTTEN MILK milk left in the sun to rot until it forms solids. Absorbs ink stains. Buy milk from the supermarket.

SADDLE SOAP used to clean leather. It's available through the internet.

SALINE SOLUTION for contact lenses—used to clean contact lenses. It's available at the chemist.

SALT table or pool salt. It's available at the supermarket.

SCRAPER triangle-shaped metal device with a handle. It's available from the hardware store.

SHAMPOO (CHEAP) cheaper shampoos have fewer fragrances and are better for cleaning. Use to wash woollens. It's available at the supermarket.

SHELLAC is a varnish made of a resinous substance secreted through the pores of the carapace of the *Coccus lacca* scale insect. This substance is then dissolved in alcohol or a similar solvent. It's used for making varnish, polish and sealing wax.

SILICONE liquid gel that hardens once applied. It's used as a join sealant and is water impermeable. It's available at hardware stores.

SLURPEX is a fine-grade, chamois-like block. It is a very absorbent sponge that removes moisture from carpet and other surfaces. It is only available directly from the company, *Slurpex*. www.slurpex.com.au

SPRAY PACK plastic bottle with removable nozzle head. Can have many concoctions added to it. It's available at the supermarket or hardware stores.

SQUEEGEE implement with a rubber blade on one side used to wipe moisture from surfaces. It's available at the supermarket or hardware store.

STIFF BRUSH brush with strong bristles. It's available from the supermarket.

SUGAR SOAP is a highly caustic soap. It comes in powder or liquid form. The powder has a mild abrasive. It's available at the supermarket and hardware stores.

SWEET ALMOND OIL is the oil from almond nuts. Use it to clean bone, ivory, *Bakelite* and plastics. It's available from the supermarket or chemist.

TALCUM POWDER is a mineral powder. It's a superfine abrasive, lubricant and also absorbent. It's available at the supermarket and chemist.

TEA BAG used to make a cup of tea. Hang on to old ones to use when cleaning timber and aluminium and restoring tannins. It's available at the supermarket.

TEA TREE OIL is an oil extracted from the tea tree bush. It's an antibacterial and removes glues and resins including chewing gum. It's available at the supermarket and chemist.

TISSUES fine, soft paper. Use to absorb stains and moisture and protect surfaces. It's available at the supermarket and chemist.

TOOTHBRUSH used to clean teeth but also makes a great mini scrubbing brush. Keep old ones to clean in difficult-to-access areas and over grout. It's available at the supermarket and chemist.

- **TURPENTINE** is a volatile oil and resin distilled from trees and is a solvent for oil-based paints. It's available at hardware stores.
- **ULTRAVIOLET LIGHT** is used to fade stains. It's available from electronics stores, lighting stores or from ABC Shops in the form of the 'Dr Who' sonic screwdriver.
- **UNPROCESSED WHEAT BRAN (NOT JUST ANY BRAN)** is the ground husk of wheat. It can be used as a scourer and absorbent to clean fabrics and furs. It's available at the supermarket.
- **VACUUM CLEANER** sucks up dirt. It's available at department stores and specialist vacuum cleaning stores.
- **VANILLA ESSENCE** is extracted from vanilla beans. It is combined with alcohol and provides fragrance and flavour to food. Also a deodoriser. Available from supermarkets.
- **VINEGAR** is an acid. It's a preservative, condiment, beverage and, for our purposes, cleaner and sanitiser. Cider vinegar is best on hard surfaces and white vinegar is better on fabrics and white marble. It's available from the supermarket.
- *VIRACLEAN* is a hospital-grade antibacterial and antiseptic used for cleaning bodily fluids.
- **WASHING SODA** is sodium carbonate and an alkaline. Use to clean dirt and grease. It's available at the supermarket.
- *WD-40* stands for Water Displacement, 40th attempt. It's a high-grade penetrating oil and stops corrosion.

WET-AND-DRY is a very fine (2000 grade) abrasive paper. Available from paint supply and car accessory shops.

WHITE SPIRITS is a mixture of petroleum hydrocarbons and a solvent. It's also known as dry-cleaning fluid or *Murlex*. It's available at hardware stores.

WHITE VINEGAR is an acid and used to clean and sanitise. It's available at the supermarket.

WHITING is a powder used in cleaning and polishing glass. It's available from leadlight stores.

WITCH-HAZEL is extracted from the bark and leaves of a shrub, *Hamamelis virginiana*: witch-hazel or spotted alder. Used as a soothing and mildly astringent lotion. Available at supermarkets and chemists.

WOOLWASH is a mild soap combined with eucalyptus oil and bicarb soda or detergent. As the name suggests, it's useful in washing woollens. Buy it at the supermarket.

ZIP-LOCK BAG is a plastic bag with a top that clicks open and shut. It's handy to store items. It's available at the supermarket.

The Kitchen

The kitchen is the centre of the home. It's the room we gravitate to, particularly when we're hungry. Food is stored here, prepared here, served here and often eaten here. It's where the dirty plates and cutlery return, and where scraps and rubbish are dealt with. It's a zone of constant cleaning and also the space for creative culinary expression. Keep it clean and hygienic but don't overdo it.

We're all taught about the dangers of germs but for some this can become an obsession. For years, advertising has told us we must get rid of these disease-carrying microbes with antibacterial cleaners. Now we discover their overuse has led to the development of antibiotic-resistant bacteria. Rather than using harsh and harmful sprays, maintain a clean kitchen by wiping surfaces with a damp soapy cloth or sprinkle on bicarb, spray on a little white vinegar and wipe with a clean cloth. Simple! These days the modern kitchen is often part of the living area so there's an extra incentive to keep it clean as it's on display when visitors pop over.

A hot pot on laminate: *John's story*
INCIDENT: *'I'm living in a rental property at the moment that has a very 1970s yellow laminate benchtop. And I don't know how, but I managed to put a hot pot on the laminate and it's left a scald mark. I've tried all the usual cleaners and nothing has worked. How can I fix it so I get my bond back?'*
SOLUTION: What to do will depend on how deep the burn is. Either way, warm the laminate first with a cloth that's been run under hot water, then wrung out and placed over the affected area. If it's a shallow burn, put white spirits on a cotton ball and rub it over the scald. Then rinse it off with a damp cloth. If the scald is deep, put white spirits onto a cotton ball, add a dab of *Gumption* and apply the mixture to the scald. Then rinse it off with a damp cloth. If the burn is really bad, you may have to replace a section of the laminate and you'll need a restorer or other professional to help with this.

Not-so-fantastic plastic: *Sonia's story*
INCIDENT: *'I have an electric stove but the hotplates no longer light up, so you can't tell when they're on. I keep my plastic water filter jug near the stove and you can guess what happened. I ended up resting the jug on top of the hotplate and it melted. My husband turned the element back on to re-melt the plastic but that didn't work and it smelt awful. Now I'm left with a plastic ring on the hotplate which I can't remove.*

What can I do?'

SOLUTION: When you heat plastic it spreads and is more difficult to remove. Make sure the electric stove is turned off and is cold. Put ice-cubes in a zip-lock bag and place over the stain. When the ice has almost melted, remove and sprinkle the stain with a little bicarb. Spray with a little white vinegar and, while it's fizzing, rub with a rolled up pair of pantyhose. If any stain remains, mix equal parts glycerine and talcum powder and rub with pantyhose. To make sure you've removed all the burnt plastic, wipe with a little vegetable oil and shine a torch over the area. If the light beam shows an irregularity in the surface, it means some plastic is still there. If so, repeat until all the plastic is removed.

Oven

Shannon can still picture her grandmother cleaning the oven. She used to wrap a tea towel over her face in an attempt to block the fumes created by the cleaning agent, caustic soda. It used to stink the kitchen out for a couple of hours. Methods aren't as drastic now, though Shannon prefers to use bicarb and white vinegar and a rolled up pair of pantyhose to clean the oven rather than proprietary products. Shannon's niece saw her clean the stove using this method, and couldn't believe the result. She said it looked really easy. You don't need expensive cleaners to make your oven sparkle. Yes, you'll need to rub while the mixture is fizzing but this is far preferable to breathing nasty fumes.

Be careful when cleaning ovens because most are made of enamel and steel. Enamel is essentially very tough glass fired onto a steel base and will scratch if you use abrasives and scourers. If you can, wipe the oven every time you use it and clean it properly every couple of uses. Just make sure it's cool enough that you don't burn yourself! Remove the oven racks, rack supports, element and light cover and sprinkle the surface with bicarb, then splash some white vinegar over the top. There will be a fizzing when the two come into contact. Scrub with a sponge or nylon brush as soon as this happens. To clean the sides of the oven, use one damp sponge dipped in bicarb, and another sponge dipped in white vinegar. Apply the bicarb sponge first, then place the vinegar sponge over the top of the bicarb sponge and press the vinegar through both sponges. Once you've cleaned, rinse with water. If there are stubborn stains or burns, reapply the bicarb and vinegar several times and use a nylon brush to scrub. In order to see what you're cleaning on the oven roof, place a small mirror at the bottom of the oven.

Clean all the bits you removed with bicarb and white vinegar. Let them stand before washing in the sink with dishwashing liquid and water.

If you inherit a very scratchy oven, sand it gently with damp 2000-grade wet-and-dry or have it re-enamelled.

TIP

To avoid warping and discolouration in your cupboards, install a heat-resistant metal panel between the oven and the surrounding cupboards.

Q 'I've got a huge scorch mark on the oven glass,' says Natalie. 'Is there anything I can do?'

PROBLEM: Scorch marks on the oven glass.
WHAT TO USE: Bicarb, white vinegar, nylon brush.
HOW TO APPLY: Sprinkle bicarb onto the scorch mark at about the same thickness as you would sprinkle icing sugar onto the top of a cake. Then splash it with an equal amount of white vinegar. While it's fizzing, rub it with a nylon brush then rinse. You may need to repeat this several times.

Q 'My white oven door handle and surrounds are yellowing,' says Sue. 'What can I do?'

PROBLEM: Yellowing oven door.
WHAT TO USE: Glycerine, talcum powder, cloth, pantyhose, bicarb, white vinegar.
HOW TO APPLY: Plastic heat-resistant door handles can become yellow from heat, sunlight or the bleach in cleaning products. Mix a paste of glycerine and talcum powder to

the consistency of thickened cream and polish on with a cloth. Leave for 10 minutes and polish off with a pair of pantyhose. If the burn is deep, this will only lighten the yellow. The oven surround is usually made of baked enamel and can be cleaned with bicarb and white vinegar. If you can't fix it, you can replace the handle or have the doors re-enamelled.

TIP

Your oven will work more efficiently and food will cook more evenly if the hinges and seals are in good working order. If damaged, have them professionally refitted. If your sponge cakes are flat or uneven, it could be from poorly fitted oven seals.

Q 'I left the stove on and returned an hour later to find my house full of smoke,' admits Jim. 'Fortunately, the house didn't burn to the ground. Is there a way to remove the smell of smoke throughout the house?'

PROBLEM: Smoky smell in house.
WHAT TO USE: Bicarb, tennis racquet (or similar item to whack cushions), vacuum cleaner (upholstery); bicarb, white vinegar (hard surfaces); cigarette ash, bicarb, white

vinegar, disposable rubber gloves, stiff brush (brickwork), warm water, soft broom.

HOW TO APPLY: Smoke travels throughout the house and gets trapped in the soft furnishings so everything in the house needs to be cleaned. For upholstered items and soft furnishings, scatter with bicarb and give them a good whack with a tennis racquet. Leave for half an hour, then vacuum thoroughly. If you have air conditioning, clean the filters. Wash curtains and other removable fabric.
For hard surfaces including painted walls (except marble), clean with bicarb and white vinegar. To clean brickwork, mix 1 part cigarette ash (you can get cigarette ash from your local pub or club), 1 part bicarb and 1 part white vinegar. Wear disposable rubber gloves (because this mixture can burn skin) and scrub the mixture over the bricks with a stiff brush. Leave for 5 minutes and scrub off with warm water on a soft broom. To clean wallpaper, rub over with slices of stale bread.

TIP

Clean the grill after each use as you would the oven.

Grill

The grill is really just a small oven and should be cleaned the same way. For day to day cleaning, take the removable parts of the grill out and wash with dishwashing liquid and water.

Most stains should come off. For any stubborn stains, use bicarb and white vinegar as described for the oven.

Cooktop

Shannon almost burned the house down when she was fourteen. It was just like that ad on TV when the woman leaves some chips cooking on the stove while she answers the phone. The pan ignites in flames and she exclaims, 'Oh my goodness, the chips!' It was a bit like that with Shannon, who was making choko chips and answered the door. She was only gone for about two minutes but in that time the plastic on the extractor fan was in flames and the wiring in the brick wall was also alight. Never leave a cooking fry pan!

Wipe the area every time you use it with either bicarb and white vinegar or hot water and dishwashing liquid. Gas jets should be removed and cleaned in water and dishwashing liquid. Don't use a scourer because it will scratch the surface. Make sure all the jets are clear before putting them back.

PROBLEM: Candle wax on the cooktop.
WHAT TO USE: Ice cube, flat-bladed knife; or plastic/wooden spatula, dishwashing liquid, cloth; old stockings.
HOW TO APPLY: Chill the wax by placing ice on it, then scrape as much of it away as possible with a flat-bladed knife. If you're removing wax from an enamel stovetop, use a plastic

or wooden spatula. Then mix cold water and dishwashing liquid on a cloth to remove any remaining wax. You must use cold water because hot water will soften the wax, spread it and make it harder to remove. If it's really hard to get off, rub the wax with an old pair of stockings or pantyhose. If you are melting candle wax on the stovetop, use a double boiler and always heat and stir slowly.

PROBLEM: Chocolate on the cooktop.
WHAT TO USE: Hair dryer, wet cloth.
HOW TO APPLY: Always use a double boiler if you're cooking chocolate on the cooktop. Burnt chocolate sets like cement and can only be removed with a hair dryer and wet cloth. Lay the wet cloth over the chocolate. Then hold up one edge of the cloth and apply the hair dryer so that the chocolate melts into the cloth. Shannon learned this trick when she was training to be a chocolate chef and had plenty of spillages. It also turned her off the smell of chocolate for years.

CERAMIC/INDUCTION

If you have this type of cooktop, our advice is to clean it thoroughly after each use because it can become permanently etched and marked. Wipe with a damp soft cloth or pantyhose when it's cold (don't use dishwashing liquid because it discolours the surface). If there's any food or gunk on the surface, carefully use a scraper (they are often supplied when you buy the cooktop) or a single-sided razor blade at a low angle to remove it.

ELECTRIC

Never use strong chemicals to clean coil elements because it damages them. When cold, wipe with a pair of pantyhose wrung out in white vinegar, then follow with a clean, damp cloth.

Q 'My electric cooktop has rings around the hotplates,' says Sue. 'How can I remove them?'

PROBLEM: Rings on electric cooktop.
WHAT TO USE: Bicarb, white vinegar, pantyhose; or single-sided razor blade.
HOW TO APPLY: When it's cold, sprinkle the cooktop with a little bicarb followed by a little white vinegar and, while fizzing, scrub with pantyhose. Because the cooktop is made of glass, it etches easily so don't use caustic cleaners. Many come with scrapers to remove gunk. If you don't have a scraper, use a razor blade at a low angle under the caked-on muck. Don't hack into the glass surface.

GAS

If you can see yellow in the flame, or if some spots have no flame at all, it means the jets are dirty. Gas jets are designed to be pulled apart and cleaned. Simply wash in warm soapy water and scrub with a nylon brush. If there's any baked-on char, sprinkle with bicarb followed by a little white vinegar and scrub with a nylon brush or a rolled up pair of pantyhose. Allow to dry.

If the jets are clogged, clear them with a needle or opened paperclip.

Knobs and dials are also designed to be removed so you can clean under them.

Splashback

There are many types of splashback. Some common ones include:

Glass—clean with equal parts white vinegar and water in a spray pack applied with a pair of pantyhose.

Tiles—clean with bicarb and white vinegar. Scrub the grout with an old toothbrush.

Stone and stainless steel—clean with a damp cloth or a pair of pantyhose.

PROBLEM: Smoke marks on the splashback.
WHAT TO USE: Ash, bicarb, white vinegar, cloth.
HOW TO APPLY: Use ash from a cigarette or from the fireplace. You need enough ash to make a thin covering over the smoke mark. Rub the ash over the mark and then clean it off with bicarb and white vinegar on a cloth.

PROBLEM: Scratches on the splashback.
WHAT TO USE: Bicarb, sponge, white vinegar; or whiting, cloth.
HOW TO APPLY: Put bicarb on a sponge and wipe it over the scratch, then wipe over it with a sponge soaked in white vinegar. If this doesn't work, use a chalk product called whiting, which is available at leadlight stores. Sprinkle whiting over the scratch as though you're icing a cake and rub the area with a damp cloth.

Range Hood and Extractor Fan

If you think about all the fumes and particles sucked up by these workhorses, it's no wonder they need to be cleaned. Get into the habit of cleaning the range hood each week—it will keep your kitchen much cleaner and use less power. The more time you leave before cleaning, the more work you'll have to do. Most range hoods can be pulled apart and put in the dishwasher or scrubbed in the sink with warm soapy water and a nylon brush. Use bicarb and white vinegar if the build-up is really stubborn. Charcoal filters should be washed backwards—that is, where the smoke comes out—and need to be replaced from time to time. Check the manufacturer's instructions.

Using the extractor fan is the best way to minimise stains on cupboards and odours in your house.

The cupboard above the stove always ends up greasy.

Store canned goods here instead of plates or glasses that need to be washed to get all the grease off. And don't leave boxed goods here because heat and grease affect cardboard and can penetrate the packaging.

Pots and Pans

Pots and pans can be made of stainless steel, aluminium, *Teflon*, enamel, copper, cast iron, tin or glass. The best way to wash them is with dishwashing liduid and water. Don't put pots and pans in the dishwasher if the handle is wooden, plastic or *Bakelite* because it will fade and crack. Instead of using scourers to clean pots and pans, use a pair of pantyhose. Simply roll the pantyhose into a ball and scrub. And as with most cleaning, the easiest way to keep your pots and pans sparkling is to clean them thoroughly after each use. If you don't, the next time you use the pot, the heat will make the charred remnants stick to it more stubbornly. Stains will come off more easily if you put a small amount of water and a drop of white vinegar in your pots straight after using them.

If you have cast-iron pots, never put them in the dishwasher because they will rust. Instead, wash them by hand and dry them in the oven. Set the oven on its lowest temperature and allow it to warm, then turn it off and leave the cast-iron pot inside until it dries. Re-season cast iron with a little olive oil rubbed around the base with a paper towel, then let it heat through on the stove for a couple of minutes before wiping again with the same paper towel.

Shannon has a very strong grip so she's always breaking the plastic handle on lids. And there's nothing trickier than trying to remove a hot lid without a handle. An easy replacement is a brass or ceramic cupboard doorknob with a screw-and-nut back.

SPOTLESS CLASSIC
Burnt pan

There are a couple of options when cleaning a burnt pan. One is to sprinkle with a little bicarb followed by a little white vinegar and, when the mixture fizzes, scrub with a nylon brush. If the burn is caked on, you've got quite a task ahead of you. One suggestion is to half fill the pot or pan with water and add 1 cup of white vinegar. Heat on the stove until the mixture boils. Remove, allow to cool and scrub with a scraper or nylon brush. Sprinkle with bicarb, add white vinegar and, when the mixture fizzes, scrub with a nylon brush.

Another way to clean a burnt pan is to add white vinegar to a cold pan until 5 mm deep and place in the freezer. When frozen, remove the pan and allow to thaw. Sprinkle bicarb on top and, when fizzing, scrub with a nylon brush.

Q 'We had Indian the other night,' reports Bill, 'but I burnt the rice and it's stained the frying pan. What can I do?'

PROBLEM: Burnt rice on frying pan.
WHAT TO USE: White vinegar, freezer, bicarb, nylon brush.
HOW TO APPLY: Add white vinegar to a cold pan until 5 mm deep and place in the freezer until the vinegar freezes. Remove from the freezer and allow to thaw. Sprinkle with bicarb and vigorously scrub with a brush as it's fizzing. If the pan won't fit in the freezer, sprinkle with bicarb followed by white vinegar and scrub with a brush. Repeat until clean.

Q 'I've got some cast-iron cooking pots,' says Wally. 'And they've gone rusty. Can I fix them?'

PROBLEM: Rusty cast-iron.
WHAT TO USE: Cheap vegetable oil, paper towel.
HOW TO APPLY: Add enough vegetable oil to the pot to cover the bottom and wipe around the inside with paper towel. Put the pot over low heat and when the oil starts to fume, turn off the heat and allow to cool. When it's cooled, rub with paper towel.

Q 'I cook everything in my old wok,' says Graeme. 'It's got to the point that if I can't cook something in the wok, I won't eat it! But it's accumulated all this build-up which, despite some concerted scrubbing on my behalf, just won't shift. Is there anything I can do?'

PROBLEM: Burnt pan.
WHAT TO USE: Bicarb, white vinegar, nylon brush.
HOW TO APPLY: Sprinkle bicarb into the pan then sprinkle white vinegar over it. This will make it fizz. Scrub with a nylon brush while it's fizzing. You may need to repeat this two or three times for bad burns.

PROBLEM: Egg stains in the pan.
WHAT TO USE: Rubber gloves, eggshell, aluminium foil, white vinegar.
HOW TO APPLY: Put on rubber gloves. Then place half an eggshell together with a strip of aluminium foil and 1 cup of white vinegar into the stained saucepan. Leave for half an hour and the egg stain will wipe off. The reason this works is that the calcium in the eggshell leaves a chalky deposit that absorbs the egg. Shannon learned this from her great-aunt Letitia's wonderful notebook.

PROBLEM: Rust in the pot/pan.
WHAT TO USE: Potato, bicarb.
HOW TO APPLY: Cut a potato in half and dip the cut surface in some bicarb. Rub it over the rust and then rinse the pot or pan in water. The starch and iodine in the potato remove the rust. The salt reacts with the starch and iodine and forms a mild caustic.

PROBLEM: Dent in a pan.
WHAT TO USE: Wooden spoon, hammer.
HOW TO APPLY: Place the edge of a wooden spoon on the pointed side of the dent, then tap a hammer lightly onto the other edge of the wooden spoon until the dent smoothes out. If the bottom of the pan has a dent, place one block inside and another block underneath the pan, then hammer the blocks and it will smooth out so you can cook evenly again. This technique can also be used for *Teflon* pans.

> **Q** 'I picked up some old *Bakelite* canisters at a second-hand store,' says Jane, 'but they've got some scratches on them. Is there anything to be done?'

PROBLEM: Scratches in old *Bakelite* canisters/handles.
WHAT TO USE: Sweet almond oil, paper towel or cotton ball; or whiting, glycerine, cloth.

HOW TO APPLY: Apply a small quantity of sweet almond oil with a paper towel or cotton ball. Then wipe it off. If you have deep scratches, use whiting and glycerine. Mix ½ teaspoon of whiting with 2½ tablespoons of glycerine to the consistency of runny cream. Rub the mixture around and around in circles with a cloth until the scratches have rubbed out, then wipe it off.

PROBLEM: A glued pot handle has cracked and come loose.
WHAT TO USE: Butcher's twine, heat-resistant superglue.
HOW TO APPLY: Strap the handle with butcher's twine then cover the strapped handle with heat-resistant superglue. This forms a seal that is hygienic and non-toxic. It can loosen again if washed repeatedly in a dishwasher or if it's left soaking in boiling water.

Appliances

Whether it's grinding coffee or making bread, there's an appliance for everything! Most appliances can be cleaned with dishwashing liquid and water either in the sink or with a sponge. Clean them as soon as you can because when food sets it becomes much more difficult to remove. Pull the appliance apart as much as possible but never put electrics in water. If there's staining on plastic surfaces, wipe with glycerine first, then use bicarb and white vinegar. To remove rust marks on plastic, use a paste of glycerine and talcum powder.

KETTLE/ELECTRIC JUG

Shannon drinks massive amounts of tea every day so she's very used to cleaning the kettle. For general cleaning on the outside, use bicarb and white vinegar. Apply with two sponges, one with bicarb on it, the other with white vinegar on it. Start with the bicarb sponge then rub the white vinegar sponge over the surface.

One of the main problems with kettles and electric jugs is lime scale or tartar build-up. To remove, empty the kettle or jug of water and add 2 tablespoons of uncooked rice, 2 tablespoons of bicarb and 2 tablespoons of white vinegar. Cover the openings with your hands and shake for 1 minute. Rinse thoroughly. The rice gets into all the corners and acts as a scourer.

TIP

Cockroaches are attracted to the heat and magnetic field of electrical appliances. Wipe with a cloth dipped in salt and water. Just make sure the appliance is switched off and you don't get water on the plugs.

To protect items such as portable phone bases from cockroaches, stand them on a salt covered plate but don't allow the salt to contact metal parts. Instead, elevate with rubber stoppers or cork (slice an old wine cork).

Another option is to place 2 chopped lemons inside the kettle, fill with water and bring to the boil. Pour everything out and rinse thoroughly before making your next cuppa.

Thanks to Sam for suggesting this: add 1 teaspoon of citric acid powder to the kettle and boil. She adds that citric acid is an ingredient of sherbet and is completely edible!

Q '**My stainless steel electric jug has a build up of gunk from years of use,**' says Cecily. '**What should I do?**'

PROBLEM: Scaling in the kettle.
WHAT TO USE: CLR; or bicarb, white vinegar, nylon brush.
HOW TO APPLY: Put 1 teaspoon of CLR in a kettle full of water. Leave it for an hour, then rinse out with water. Make sure you clean it out well or your next cup of tea will taste a bit funny. You could also try bicarb and white vinegar scrubbed with a nylon brush if the area is accessible, but generally the build-up happens under the element so CLR is the best option.

ESPRESSO/COFFEE MACHINES

Some espresso machines can cost thousands of dollars so it's important to care for them. Clean according to the type of material from which it's made (check the manual). Any areas that have contact with coffee should be rinsed with a salt solution, which also makes the coffee taste better. Flush through with 1 tablespoon of non-iodised salt per litre of water. The areas that come into contact with milk need to be cleaned with cold water first to remove proteins and then cleaned with hot water to remove fats. It's not a good idea to use dishwashing liquid because it curdles milk and makes the curds stick to the surface, encouraging bacterial growth.

Q 'My espresso machine has white scale/calcium around the rim where the water is placed,' reports Deborah. 'Can you suggest a cleaning solution for this?'

PROBLEM: Lime scale on coffee machine.
WHAT TO USE: White vinegar, cloth, non-iodised salt, water, cheap vegetable oil, dishwashing liquid, warm water.
HOW TO APPLY: Rub the exposed surfaces with white vinegar on a cloth. To clean the steam pipes, flush through with 1 tablespoon of salt per litre of water. If smaller metallic parts are corroded (such as strainer sections), place them in a pot of vegetable oil and slowly heat until the oil starts to fume. Remove from the heat and allow to cool. Wash in a little dishwashing liquid and warm water and dry well.

MIXERS AND BLENDERS

Clean the inside of blenders by adding 2 teaspoons of bicarb and ½ cup of white vinegar and then switching the blender on. Make sure you cover the blender first or you'll be cleaning the whole kitchen. Then rinse out with water. Shannon used to make pâté for restaurants, and one time she forgot to put the lid on the blender. It was like a volcano spewing hot liver around the kitchen. She was cleaning it up for weeks afterwards. If you're blending anything hot, place a clean tea towel over the blender before you put the lid on. It protects the plastic in the lid from melting, stretching or shrinking and will lessen mess in the kitchen if the lid takes off because of too much heat inside. If the fit is poor, hold the lid with your hand while blending.

Q 'The aluminium strainer-like blade on my mixer has corroded,' says Gillian. 'What can I do?'

PROBLEM: Corroded aluminium.
WHAT TO USE: Saucepan, cooking oil, dishwashing liquid, warm water.
HOW TO APPLY: Place the corroded items in a saucepan, cover with cooking oil and heat until the oil starts to fume. Remove from the heat and allow to cool. Remove the items and wash in dishwashing liquid and warm water. Dry well.
PREVENTION: Store clean mixer parts in greaseproof paper.

SANDWICH MAKER

Sandwich makers create great snacks and light meals but cleaning them can be complicated because they can't be immersed in water. The easiest cleaning method is to half fill the inside of the sandwich maker with equal parts water and white vinegar (straight after cooking the sambo) and close the lid. If needed, turn the sandwich maker on for a short time so the steaming mixture cleans top and bottom. Wipe with a paper towel or cloth. All done!

TOASTER

Clean the outside of a toaster with bicarb on one sponge and white vinegar on another sponge. Wipe with the bicarb sponge first, then the white vinegar sponge. For the interior, sprinkle coarse salt in the top of the toaster, cover the slots with your hand and shake it up and down a few times. This cleans it and helps prevent vermin. When you've finished, shake the contents into the bin. Make sure you get all the salt out or it may cause corrosion.

TIP

To clean an old stained flask or thermos, put 2 teaspoons of bicarb and ½ cup of white vinegar inside. Put the lid on and give it a shake, but not for too long or it will explode. Take the lid off, let it sit for half an hour, top it up with hot water and leave overnight. The next morning, give it a shake and rinse.

BENCHTOP OVENS

If you don't clean benchtop ovens after each use, nasty odours can develop. Before cleaning, unplug the oven and remove the grills. Wash the racks in the sink in dishwashing liquid and wipe the interior with a damp soapy cloth. If needed, add white vinegar to the cleaning cloth. Don't use sharp implements to remove gunk or you could damage the surface.

BARBECUE GRILL

To clean a dirty barbecue grill, sprinkle with bicarb, splash with white vinegar and, while it's fizzing, scrub with a nylon brush. To remove rust, heat the grill, sprinkle with a little sugar and splash a little white vinegar on top. Together, the vinegar and sugar create a toffee which bonds to the old char, making it easier to remove with a scraper. While the grill is still hot, cover with cheap vegetable oil and continue heating until the oil starts to fume. Rub the grill with a handful of paper towel. The oil seasons the grill, leaving a non-stick surface that won't rust as easily.

MICROWAVE

Shannon loves the microwave and it's much easier to clean than the oven. The glass or china turntable can be removed and cleaned in the sink with dishwashing liquid. Make sure it's dry before you replace it or your rollers will rust.

Remove the nylon turning ring and wheels and clean in dishwashing liquid, then dry them.

For the interior, sprinkle bicarb over first, then add white vinegar and wipe with a sponge. For the sides and top, use the two-sponge method: wipe with the bicarb one first, then the vinegar one.

Shannon thinks it's worthwhile learning how to operate the microwave properly because there is an art to good microwave cooking. All microwaves come with an instruction manual and cookbook. If you don't have one, contact the manufacturer and generally they'll send you one free of charge. Also be aware that microwaves have different power settings so each machine will be different.

Q 'How can I remove the smell of burnt popcorn from my microwave?' asks Christina.

PROBLEM: Burnt popcorn in microwave.
WHAT TO USE: Bicarb, white vinegar, water, microwave-safe bowl, damp cloth.
HOW TO APPLY: Mix 2 tablespoons of bicarb, 2 tablespoons of white vinegar and 1 cup of water in a microwave-safe bowl. Place the bowl in the microwave and heat until the water just comes to the boil and the interior is covered in steam. Wipe every surface of the microwave, including the back grille, with a cloth wrung out in the mixture. If

the smell remains, you may need to wash the filter pad behind the perforated grille at the back of the microwave. If this grille has a catch for easy opening, remove the pad and rinse in bicarb and white vinegar. If the grille is screwed down, have it professionally treated or you will risk losing your warranty.

PROBLEM: Food splattered inside the microwave.
WHAT TO USE: White vinegar, water, bicarb, large microwave-proof bowl.
HOW TO APPLY: Mix ½ cup of white vinegar, 1 cup of water and 1 tablespoon of bicarb in a large bowl. Put the bowl in the microwave without a lid on and cook on high for a few minutes, allowing the mixture to boil, but not boil over, for around 1 minute. While the microwave is warm and steamy, wipe the interior down with a cloth.

DISHWASHER

Dishwashers may have saved many relationships, but they've ruined plenty of crockery, cutlery and glassware. Shannon hates them because dishwashers clean by flinging small particles of soap, food and water at high speed, which virtually sandblasts your plates and cutlery. Bear this in mind when putting things in. Never put fine china, crystal, items with gold edging or good cutlery in the dishwasher. Some of the damage won't be fixable, even by us. For other items, always rinse before putting them in. Heat-sensitive items should sit at the top; saucepans should sit at an angle towards the bottom centre of the dishwasher. And don't overpack the dishwasher because china and glass can break if they bang together. Don't put electrical parts in. And always use a good-quality dishwashing liquid and a rinse agent that dissolves well.

We know it's a bit annoying to have to clean the filter each time you use the dishwasher but it's necessary. If you don't, nasty smells may develop. If there's an odour, put bicarb in the detergent compartment and white vinegar in the rinse-aid compartment and run empty on a short cycle. This will clean the drainpipes at the same time. If the dishwasher really stinks, wipe the rubbers and interiors with vanilla essence. This removes the smell and acts as an antibacterial. If the rubbers become perished, they harbour bacteria. To help prevent perishing, rub the surfaces with dry salt and then vanilla essence.

Don't forget to check and clear the jets in the arm. If needed, unblock them with a needle or opened paperclip. Clean the seals with bicarb and white vinegar on a butter knife wrapped in a tea towel. If the water in your area has a high mineral content, you're more likely to get lime scale, so fill the wash slot with bicarb and the rinse slot with white vinegar and run empty on the short cycle every 10 washes.

TIP

Most new appliances have sticky labels on them and some are harder to remove than others. Put a drop of dishwashing liquid and a little water on some plastic wrap, mix together and place the plastic wrap over the label. Leave for 10 minutes. The label should come off when you remove the plastic wrap. For stickier labels, apply a couple of drops of tea tree oil along the top edge of the label and leave for about 15 minutes. It should peel off easily. Stronger still is eucalyptus oil applied with a cotton ball but use sparingly because it can remove paint. If none of these techniques work, run a hair dryer backwards and forwards over the label to melt the glue.

REFRIGERATOR

Shannon will never forget the state of her friend's fridge when she helped him move house. It had been switched off for a few weeks and the door had been left closed tightly. When they opened it, mould was all the way to the door and filled every cavity. They ended up hosing it clean in the backyard.

Most fridges are easy to look after, especially those with auto-defrost. New fridges have solid shelves which are really easy to clean. Just wipe with a damp pair of pantyhose or a cloth. Clean the fridge once a month with bicarb and white vinegar. The best time to clean is just before you do your shopping because it'll be fairly empty. Pull the shelves and compartments out and wash them with bicarb and white vinegar. If you have an older fridge and the plastic has come away from the wire shelves, spray the steel with heat-resistant engine paint (available from hardware stores). Leave to dry and return to the fridge. To clean the sides of the fridge, put bicarb on one sponge and white vinegar on another and press the vinegar sponge through the bicarb sponge when cleaning.

To cut back on cleaning, put a thin foam rubber sheet in the bottom of the crispers. This stops food getting caught in the ridges and slows the rotting process because air circulates around the food. The foam can be washed as well.

Clean the rubber seal around the fridge door with a tea towel soaked in white vinegar and bicarb. Then wrap the tea towel over a plastic knife and clean inside all the little grooves. If you can slide a piece of cardboard between the fridge and the seal, it's time to get a new seal. You can buy seals at most hardware stores either sized to fit your model or by the metre. Put them on yourself with an appropriate adhesive.

The exterior of fridges, including stainless steel ones, should be cleaned with bicarb and white vinegar. Cockroaches are attracted to the warm motor in the fridge so scatter salt underneath. If you use cockroach baits, put one behind the microwave, one on either side of the bottom of the stove and one behind the fridge.

Q 'I have a stainless steel fridge with a water filter and ice-maker,' says Caroline. 'But the black plastic drip tray has white stains on it. I have tried many cleaners and they won't shift. Any help?'

PROBLEM: White marks on plastic.
WHAT TO USE: Glycerine, talcum powder, cloth.
HOW TO APPLY: The marks could be from harsh cleaning products or minerals salts from the water. Mix equal parts glycerine and talcum powder and polish with a cloth. If this doesn't work, the plastic is permanently damaged.

Q 'Our power went off while we were away,' reports Diana. 'And the freezer section of the fridge really smells. What can I do?'

PROBLEM: Smelly fridge.
WHAT TO USE: Sugar, bicarb, white vinegar, nylon brush or pantyhose, cloth, butter knife.
HOW TO APPLY: Turn the fridge off and sprinkle sugar over the base of the freezer to speed up defrosting. Sprinkle with bicarb and white vinegar and, while it's fizzing, scrub with a nylon brush or pantyhose. Dip a cloth in white vinegar and

wrap it over the end of a blunt butter knife to clean in all the grooves and creases in the seals.

TIP

Shannon cleaned an old freezer with fine-grade steel wool and accidentally left the steel wool inside the freezer. When she discovered it, it didn't have any rust on it. She now stores steel wool in a plastic bag in the freezer to prevent rust.

PROBLEM: Odour in the fridge.
WHAT TO USE: Small divided dish, vanilla essence, bicarb.
HOW TO APPLY: Try to locate the source of the smell and remove it. Then fill each side of a small divided dish with vanilla essence on one side and bicarb on the other. Sushi condiment dishes work well for this. Place the dish in the fridge and it will absorb the nasty smells and deodorise the fridge.

PROBLEM: Defrosting the freezer more quickly.
WHAT TO USE: Sugar, rubber gloves, rubber spatula.
HOW TO APPLY: After turning the fridge off, sprinkle sugar over the base of the freezer. This speeds up the defrosting process. Use gloved hands or a rubber spatula to remove the ice. Never use a hair dryer or heater because it could

crack the coils. Never use a sharp knife or you could pierce the coils and release the gas.

Wine coolers with a difference

An unglazed terracotta tile makes a great cooler. Soak one in water then put it in the freezer ready to use in wine coolers or eskies. It also helps the ice last longer. Make your own wine cooler with a clean unglazed terracotta flowerpot. Soak it in water and put it in the freezer until you need to use it. The evaporation keeps the wine chilly. Or create a disposable wine cooler from an old cask wine bladder. Fill the bladder with water and, with the tap on the outside, wrap it around an empty wine bottle. Then put it in the freezer. It's great for picnics because you'll have iced water on tap when it melts as well as chilled wine.

WATER FILTER

When it's time to change the water filter cartridge, add ½ cup of salt to 1 litre of water, pour it into the top reservoir and allow it to work through the filter. While you're waiting, wipe the outside of the reservoir with salt and water on a cloth. Once the salt water has worked through, fill with clean water and replace the cartridge. For stand-alone water containers, add a pinch of salt and ½ teaspoon of white vinegar when refilling with water. This stops the water from becoming brackish but won't affect the taste.

JUICER

Q 'I have a stainless steel and plastic juicer and wash it after each use,' reports Margaret. 'But brown stains are beginning to mark it. What can I do?'

PROBLEM: Brown stains on juicer.
WHAT TO USE: Glycerine, warm water, bicarb, white vinegar, nylon brush or pantyhose, water.
HOW TO APPLY: When some fruit is exposed to oxygen, it goes brown (think of a cut apple). Over time, this builds up and stains. Right after using the juicer, put ½ teaspoon of glycerine in 1 cup of warm water and pour it into the juicer. Turn the machine on for 1 minute. To clean the exterior, sprinkle with bicarb, followed by white vinegar and, while it's fizzing, scrub with a nylon brush or pair of pantyhose. Rinse thoroughly with water. In some cases the staining will have penetrated into the plastic and you'll just have to live with it. It's still safe to use.

Benchtops

Just as you can age a tree by counting its rings, you can age a kitchen by the kind of benchtop it has. Flecked laminate suggests the 1950s. If it's mission brown, burnt orange or avocado green it's likely to be from the 1970s. And stainless steel screams 1990s! No matter the fashion, all of them need cleaning and maintenance. If your kitchen is well ventilated but you have persistent smells, it means you have a build-up on your surfaces or in your plumbing. Wipe the benchtop thoroughly each time you prepare food.

Benchtops can be made of laminate, *Formica*, quartz (such as *CaesarStone*, *Quantum Quartz*, *Silestone*), acrylic compounds (such as *Corian*), marble, granite, timber or stainless steel. When cleaning, first work out if they're sealed and with what. For marble and granite, put your eye level with the surface and shine a torch along the top. If the light shines in an uninterrupted beam, the benchtop is coated in polyurethane. If the beam has lights and dots, it's not sealed. To work out the sealant for other benchtops, see page 572. If the polyurethane is damaged, you have to reseal the entire surface, which is a big job. Seek professional help with this. To remove scratches, apply a small amount of *Brasso* to a cloth and polish using speed rather than pressure. This partially melts the polyurethane. It will look worse before it looks better.

The best polishing cloths for benchtops are pantyhose and they can be used on most surfaces. They're excellent for removing those ever-present fingermarks but there is a technique to using them. Have two pairs—one damp and one dry. Rub the damp pair over the surface and follow right away with the dry pair. This technique will even make stainless steel streak-free and gleaming.

LAMINATE/*FORMICA*

Laminate and *Formica* benchtops are very popular and can be cleaned with a damp cloth and the rinse water from the washing up or a sprinkle of a little bicarb followed by a little white vinegar (rub while it's fizzing). Wipe clean with a damp cloth. If you get heavy staining with tea or scorch marks, put glycerine on the stain for about 5 minutes then use bicarb and white vinegar. Avoid abrasive cleaners because they can scratch the surface.

Q 'I've spilt coffee on my laminate benchtop,' complains Mike. 'What's the easiest way to get it out?'

PROBLEM: Coffee on laminate.
WHAT TO USE: *Gumption*, glycerine, pantyhose, damp cloth.
HOW TO APPLY: Mix equal parts *Gumption* and glycerine and polish with a pair of rolled up pantyhose. Remove with a damp cloth.

Q 'I've got a big blob of superglue on my laminate benchtop,' reports Kamahl. 'Any ideas?'

PROBLEM: Superglue on laminate.
WHAT TO USE: Superglue remover, pantyhose, white vinegar, cloth; or steam, pantyhose.

HOW TO APPLY: Apply superglue remover only over the superglue and it will melt. Rub off with pantyhose and neutralise the remover by wiping with white vinegar on a cloth. Alternatively, apply steam to the superglue and rub with a pair of pantyhose.

TIP

To make superglue set more quickly, breathe on it (but don't inhale!). The humidity helps superglue to set more quickly.

Q 'The colour from a plastic bread wrapper has stuck to my laminate benchtop,' reports Nigel. 'Can it be removed?'

PROBLEM: Coloured plastic on laminate.
WHAT TO USE: Hair dryer, glycerine, talcum powder, pantyhose, damp cloth.
HOW TO APPLY: Gently warm the laminate with a hair dryer. Mix equal parts glycerine and talcum powder to form a paste the consistency of runny cream, place on the mark and rub with pantyhose—it takes a bit of elbow grease. Wipe clean with a damp cloth.

Q 'How do you get burn marks off laminate?' asks Tom.

PROBLEM: Burn marks on laminate.
WHAT TO USE: Cigarette ash, toothpaste, pantyhose; or *Gumption*, white spirits, cloth.
HOW TO APPLY: Mix equal parts cigarette ash and toothpaste and polish with pantyhose. Alternatively, mix equal parts *Gumption* and white spirits and polish with a cloth. If the burn has penetrated, it will need to be repaired professionally.

Q 'I've got mould on my laminate benchtop,' says George. 'Can it be removed?'

PROBLEM: Mould on laminate.
WHAT TO USE: Oil of cloves, warm water, 1 litre spray pack, pantyhose.
HOW TO APPLY: Mix ¼ teaspoon of oil of cloves with warm water in a spray pack (the warm water makes it easier for the oil of cloves to penetrate the surface). Spray over the mould, leave for 20 minutes and scrub with pantyhose. If needed, spray the mixture again and leave for 24 hours to allow the oil of cloves to kill the mould spore.

Q 'I've got a hair-dye stain on my laminate benchtop,' reports Alice. 'What's the solution?'

PROBLEM: Hair dye on laminate.
WHAT TO USE: Same brand hair dye, cloth, cheap shampoo, damp cloth.
HOW TO APPLY: Use the same brand and colour hair dye and rub a dab over the mark with a cloth until the stain begins to loosen and spread. Add a little shampoo and continue rubbing until the stain starts to loosen even more, then wipe with a damp cloth. Repeat the shampoo step if necessary.

Q 'I was on a health kick and decided to make beetroot soup,' says Lisa, 'but the lid flew off the blender and beetroot landed all over the laminate bench. What can I do?'

PROBLEM: Beetroot stains on laminate.
WHAT TO USE: White vinegar; or glycerine, cotton bud or cotton ball.
HOW TO APPLY: If you are dealing with the stain while it's fresh, clean the area with white vinegar. If the stain has set, apply glycerine to the stain with a cotton bud or cotton ball; leave for a few minutes then remove. To prevent the problem, put a tea towel over the blender before putting the lid on. If the lid comes off, the tea towel will contain the mess. If the fit is poor, hold the lid on with your hand.

PROBLEM: Laminate has come away from chipboard backing or the chipboard is breaking down behind the laminate.
WHAT TO USE: Water, oil of cloves, *Aquadhere*, paintbrush, clingwrap, clamp.
HOW TO APPLY: Into ¼ cup of warm water, mix 1 drop of oil of cloves and stir thoroughly. Then mix 1 tablespoon of this mixture into 1 tablespoon of *Aquadhere*. Paint this over the chipboard, then wrap the entire join in clingwrap and clamp it, making sure you have something between the clamp and the bench, such as a magazine or small piece of wood. The mixture will seal the chipboard and the oil of cloves prevents mildew. Shannon learned this after living in some pretty revolting rental properties.

CAESARSTONE/QUANTUM QUARTZ/*SILESTONE*

Many modern kitchens have quartz-based benchtops which are not porous, so they don't need sealants such as polyurethane. Clean with a damp cloth and remove glues or resins with a single-sided razor blade held at a low angle. Fill chips with a malleable epoxy resin.

Q 'I had a new kitchen installed and chose a dark blue *Silestone* benchtop,' says Louise. 'But it never looks clean. It shows every fingerprint, watermark and cloth mark. Can you suggest anything that would help the benchtop look clean and shiny?'

PROBLEM: Streaky *Silestone*.
WHAT TO USE: White vinegar, pantyhose, damp cloth.
HOW TO APPLY: *Silestone* is a great benchtop but when it's brand new the high-gloss surface shows dirt, oil and dust. Clean with a little white vinegar on a rolled up pair of pantyhose and wipe with a damp cloth. Polish with a dry pair of pantyhose.

CORIAN

Corian is a composite of many different materials including quartz, marble, granite, mica, feldspar and synthetics such as polycarbonate, epoxys or cement blends. Clean with bicarb and white vinegar. If it has a polyurethane finish, use dishwashing liquid and water.

MARBLE

Marble is often regarded as the glamour benchtop. But care should be taken when cleaning it because it's porous. The best way to clean marble is by sprinkling bicarb over it and then splashing 1 part white vinegar to 4 parts water on top. It's important to dilute the vinegar because full-strength vinegar can react with the lime in the marble and create holes or a rough surface. Marble is often coated in polyurethane to give a slick finish and provide protection. Be careful not to damage the polyurethane because it's difficult to repair. If the surface isn't sealed with polyurethane or other sealant, make it less porous and less likely to absorb stains by using a good quality, liquid hard wax for marble flooring (follow the instructions on the pack). The way to tell if marble is covered in polyurethane is to put your eye level with the marble and shine a light along the surface. If the light shines in one uninterrupted beam, it's sealed with polyurethane. If the beam of light has lines and dots, it's unsealed.

Q **'I've got tea stains under my sealed marble benchtop,' says Fran. 'Can I get them out?'**

PROBLEM: Tea stains on polyurethane-sealed marble.
WHAT TO USE: Cloth, acetone, plastic wrap, pantyhose, warm water, plaster of Paris, glycerine, plastic scraper, marble floor wax.
HOW TO APPLY: This is a big job and you may decide to live with the stain rather than go through this tricky process. It's likely the tea has penetrated through a tiny hole in the polyurethane but you'll need to remove a relatively large area of polyurethane to remove the stain. Seek professional help or, if you're handy, remove the polyurethane coating by tightly wringing a cloth in acetone and placing it over the stained area. Cover the cloth with plastic wrap so the acetone doesn't evaporate and leave for 20 minutes. Remove the plastic wrap and the cloth and rub with a pair

of rolled up pantyhose dampened in warm water. To remove the tea stains, mix plaster of Paris with water to form a paste the consistency of peanut butter. For each cup of mixture, add ½ teaspoon of glycerine. Apply a 1 cm thick layer of the mixture on the stain and leave to dry. When it's completely dry, remove with a plastic scraper. Have the polyurethane replaced by a professional or seal with marble floor wax.

PREVENTION: To prevent staining on marble, apply marble floor wax every month.

TIP

You can repair chips in marble with crayon wax, candle wax or surfboard wax in a matching colour. Melt the wax into the chip with a hair dryer and buff with pantyhose until it's level with the surface.

Q 'I've got rust marks on unsealed marble,' says Pat. 'What do you suggest?'

PROBLEM: Rust on unsealed marble.
WHAT TO USE: Plaster of Paris, water, stiff brush; or bicarb, white vinegar, nylon brush.
HOW TO APPLY: Mix plaster of Paris and water to form a paste the consistency of peanut butter. Paint a 1 cm thick

layer of the mixture over the stains and leave until dry. Brush off with a stiff brush. You may need to repeat this several times. If the marble is sealed, sprinkle with bicarb and white vinegar. Scrub with a nylon brush and rinse quickly because vinegar can make holes in marble.

PROBLEM: Stain in the marble.
WHAT TO USE: Bicarb, white vinegar, water, clingwrap; or glycerine, cotton ball; or salt, lemon.
HOW TO APPLY: To remove fat and oil stains, mix 1 dessertspoon of bicarb, 1 dessertspoon of white vinegar and 4 dessertspoons of water into a light paste. Place the paste on the stain then put clingwrap over the top of it for no more than 15 minutes. Then remove the mix. The stain should come out as well. For fruit stains, first apply glycerine with a cotton ball then use the above method. For rust stains, place a small mountain of salt over the stain then squeeze enough lemon juice to wet the salt. Scrub and repeat. Do not use CLR on marble because it will dissolve it.

PROBLEM: White, chalky-looking chips in the marble.
WHAT TO USE: Candle wax, hair dryer, soft cloth, marble floor wax.
HOW TO APPLY: Match the candle colour to the marble. Place a small piece of wax over the chip then use a hair

dryer to slightly melt the wax into the marble. Buff it with a soft cloth until it's the same height as the rest of the bench. Then use a marble floor wax to treat the whole area.

GRANITE

Even though many granite benchtops are sealed, the surface is still porous so if there's a spill, wipe it up as soon as possible. The best way to clean granite is with bicarb and white vinegar. If it has a polyurethane finish, keep the surface clean because it can bubble. If you do get bubbles, mix 1 part *Aquadhere* to 20 parts water and inject with a syringe. Do this with each bubble and then place a flat weight over them. A heavy book should do the job but make sure you have clingwrap underneath the book so that it doesn't stick. Check the drying time of the glue on its packet. When it's dried, wipe off the excess with warm water.

For spills that have penetrated, mix plaster of Paris and water to form a paste the consistency of peanut butter. To each cup of mixture, add 1 teaspoon of dishwashing liquid (to remove oils) or 1 teaspoon of white vinegar (to remove coffee and tea stains) and place over the stain. When the plaster is completely dry, brush away. The plaster of Paris absorbs the stain.

Q 'A bottle of dishwashing liquid leaked onto our granite benchtop and penetrated under the sealed surface,' reports Jenny. 'How can I get it out?'

PROBLEM: Dishwashing liquid on sealed granite.
WHAT TO USE: Acetone, cloth, plastic wrap, plaster of Paris, water, white vinegar, stiff brush.
HOW TO APPLY: If it is a small area, mix plaster of Paris and water to form a paste to the consistency of peanut butter. For each cup of mixture add 1 teaspoon of white vinegar. Apply a 1 cm thick layer to the stain and leave to dry. Brush away with a stiff brush. If it is a large area you may need to remove the polyurethane. This can be done by a professional or if you wish to attempt it yourself, soak a cloth in acetone and place it over the stained area. Cover with plastic and leave for 20 minutes. Clean the melted polyurethane off with a white vinegar-soaked cloth, then rinse with clean water and leave to dry before using the plaster of Paris mix above. When the stain is clean, replace the polyurethane. This is often better done by a professional as it can be tricky to get a nice smooth finish. If you don't wish to replace the polyurethane you can use a quality marble flooring wax.

PROBLEM: Grease stains in granite.
WHAT TO USE: Dishwashing liquid, water; or bicarb, white vinegar, clingwrap; or potter's plaster or plaster of Paris, paint brush, plastic/wooden tool, damp cloth.

HOW TO APPLY: Try cleaning the stain with dishwashing liquid and water first. If this doesn't work, make a paste of bicarb and white vinegar and apply the paste to the stain. Cover it with clingwrap until it's almost dry. The grease should scrub out with dishwashing liquid and water. You can also use potter's plaster or plaster of Paris. Mix to the consistency of peanut butter, then paint the paste over the stain and leave it until it goes hard. Remove the mixture with a plastic or wooden tool so you don't scratch the surface. Rub the rest off with a damp cloth. The plaster pulls the stains out because it's very absorbent.

STAINLESS STEEL

The best way to clean stainless steel is with bicarb and white vinegar. Dust with bicarb, then splash some white vinegar and wipe with a sponge. Rinse with water and wipe with a cloth to remove any smears. Repeat if necessary.

Stainless steel can discolour if left in contact with harsh chemicals, including acidic food, for extended periods so clean regularly with damp pantyhose. If it is very dirty, damp the pantyhose with white vinegar. Always rub in the direction of the grain or it will lose its shine. Never use steel wool, scourers or stainless steel wool because they will cause rust marks. And don't use baby oil because it creates a build-up that attracts dust and dirt.

Q 'How do you remove a rust mark from a stainless steel benchtop?' asks Andy.

PROBLEM: Rust on stainless steel.
WHAT TO USE: Non-iodised salt, lemon juice/lemon, pantyhose, damp cloth.
HOW TO APPLY: Place salt over the mark, add lemon juice and scrub with pantyhose. Alternatively, sprinkle salt over the top of a cut lemon and scrub. Wipe clean with a damp cloth.

PROBLEM: Scratches in stainless steel.
WHAT TO USE: *Gumption*, sponge, bicarb, white vinegar, cloth.
HOW TO APPLY: Apply a dab of *Gumption* to a sponge and rub it over the scratch. This will smooth the surface. Then sprinkle bicarb over the scratch and splash a little white vinegar. Remove with a cloth.

TILES AND GROUT

Tiled benchtops need particular care because bacteria can thrive in the grout. Clean tiles and grout by sprinkling bicarb over the surface then splashing white vinegar over the top. Wipe with a cloth then rinse. I'd recommend cleaning tiles more often than other surfaces because grout is very porous and will stain, particularly in the area behind your cooktop. Use an old toothbrush to get into tricky areas.

Q 'The kitchen tiles surrounding my stovetop are stained with grease that's accumulated over the years,' says Thelma. 'I've tried everything to remove it without success and have been told by experts that the grease has penetrated into the glaze of the tiles and the only solution is to replace them. As this is an expensive and messy job, and I love the colour of my wall tiles which have now gone out-of-date, it means I would need to have my whole kitchen redone. Is there any solution at all?'

PROBLEM: Grease on tiles.
WHAT TO USE: Grout rake, plaster of Paris, water, dishwashing liquid, stiff brush.
HOW TO APPLY: Remove the grout with a grout rake (available at hardware stores). Mix plaster of Paris and water to form a paste the consistency of peanut butter. For each cup of mixture, add 1 teaspoon of dishwashing liquid. Apply a 1 cm thick layer to the entire side of the tile. Leave it to dry completely and remove with a stiff brush. If any oil or grease remains, repeat. When all the staining is removed, replace the grout.

TIMBER

If the timber is unsealed, clean it with dishwashing liquid and water then dry. Then wipe it with good quality furniture oil. For surfaces that come into contact with food, use a small quantity of warm olive oil. Some olive oils contain vegetable sediment, which can attract fruit fly, so make sure you spread it thinly and wipe off all the excess. Only use olive oil on surfaces in the kitchen. Bicarb and white vinegar will remove any stains but remember to reapply the olive oil. If you prefer, keep the timber moist and splinter-free by rubbing it with the skin of a lemon. For sealed timber, clean with bicarb and white vinegar. Be very careful with polyurethane surfaces because if you scratch them you'll have to reseal them. If you do scratch polyurethane, wipe it with glycerine.

PROBLEM: Dents in timber.
WHAT TO USE: Hot wet sponge, hair dryer.
HOW TO APPLY: Cut a sponge to the size of the dent, wet it in hot water and place it over the dented area only. Leave the sponge for 5 minutes, take it off and dry the spot with a hair dryer. The timber should have swelled back into place. Don't put hot sponges on any other part of the timber or it will expand it as well.

PROBLEM: Gap between timber bench and splashback.
WHAT TO USE: Disposable rubber gloves, mineral turpentine, silicone sealer; or water, matches, candle wax.
HOW TO APPLY: There are a couple of ways you can fix this. Put on disposable rubber gloves and dip the tip of your

finger in mineral turpentine. Then feed silicone with your finger into the gap. Another way is to wear disposable rubber gloves, wet the tip of your finger with water, then light a candle and feed the dripping wax in between the bench and splashback with your finger. Candle wax doesn't last as long as silicone and would need to be replaced every six months but it has the added bonus of being easy to replace if needed.

Q 'I left a rockmelon on a timber benchtop and it went off,' says Steve. 'It's left a green stain on the bench and eaten through the varnish!'

PROBLEM: Rotten rockmelon on timber benchtop.
WHAT TO USE: Bicarb, white vinegar, nylon brush, varnish.
HOW TO APPLY: Clean the excess oxide by sprinkling bicarb over the area, add white vinegar and scrub with a nylon brush. Then rinse with water. Allow it to dry and then re-varnish.

Chopping Boards

A clean chopping board is a hygienic chopping board! They can be made of timber, plastic or glass and Shannon reckons the bigger the better. Timber should be scrubbed thoroughly after each use with dishwashing liquid and water and stood up to dry. To prevent splintering, scrub with olive oil and steel wool once a week. Timber has the added benefit of containing a natural antibacterial. Plastic should be cleaned with dishwashiing liquid and water. As soon as it's scuffed, throw it out because scratches harbour bacteria. Clean glass with bicarb and white vinegar. To make cleaning around the chopping board easier, put a tea towel underneath it to collect crumbs and food spills. It also makes chopping quieter and there's less chance you'll mark the benchtop.

Q 'I was chopping some raw meat on my timber chopping board and it's left blood stains,' complains Natalie. 'What's the best way to get it out?'

PROBLEM: Blood on timber.
WHAT TO USE: Cake of bathroom soap, cold water, white vinegar, cloth, sawdust.
HOW TO APPLY: Scribble over the stain with a cake of bathroom soap dipped in cold water and scrub with a dish brush. Rinse with white vinegar on a cloth, sprinkle with sawdust (available at hardware stores) and leave in the sun to dry. Brush the sawdust into the garden (it's great mulch).

Sink

Most kitchen sinks are made of stainless steel or enamel although some are now made of polycarbonate or cement. The best cleaning combination is bicarb and white vinegar. If the sink is heavily stained use *Gumption*, but be aware that it contains a mild bleaching agent and abrasive. Avoid using borax in the sink because it's quite toxic and, no matter how well you wash it down, you'll have some residue. Don't use abrasives on polycarbonate and always put the cold tap on before the hot tap or it will craze.

Be mindful what you put down the sink. Not only can it be bad for the environment, but you'll also end up creating more work when the sink becomes clogged. Don't put oil, fats, eggs, proteins or starch-based products down it. For fats and oils, re-use an old tin, put a paper towel on the bottom to stop splatter, and collect the waste. When it's full, throw it in the bin.

If you have mildew or bugs under your sink, place some whole cloves and salt inside the cupboard. You could also rub some oil of cloves around the cupboard door edges under the sink. Apply with a cloth.

Q 'How do you remove tobacco burns from a white sink?' asks Rebecca.

PROBLEM: Cigarette stain on white plastic sink.
WHAT TO USE: Talcum powder, glycerine, pantyhose, damp cloth.
HOW TO APPLY: Mix equal parts talcum powder and glycerine, place on the stain and scrub with pantyhose. Wipe clean with a damp cloth.

TIP

To clean along silicone joins, use equal parts white vinegar and water on a cloth.

PROBLEM: Scratches in stainless steel sink.
WHAT TO USE: *Gumption*, sponge, bicarb, white vinegar, cloth.
HOW TO APPLY: Apply a dab of *Gumption* to a sponge and rub it over the scratch. This will smooth the surface. Then sprinkle bicarb over the scratch and splash on a little white vinegar. Polish with a cloth.

PROBLEM: Tarnished brass sink ring.
WHAT TO USE: Bicarb, white vinegar, sponge or brush; or toothpaste, old toothbrush.
HOW TO APPLY: If the sink is discoloured, apply bicarb and white vinegar with a sponge or brush and scrub. If the ring is badly corroded, put a dab of toothpaste on an old toothbrush and scrub it over the sink ring as though you're cleaning your teeth. Rinse with water.

PROBLEM: Leaking pipes under the sink.
WHAT TO USE: Hemp rope.
HOW TO APPLY: Untwist some hemp rope so that you have about six threads or fibres. Then undo the nut and wind

the hemp fibres around the thread on the pipe to seal it. Screw the nut back on over the hemp fibres. The fibres expand as soon as they become wet and this creates a really good seal. This was the technique used before plumber's tape was invented. Hemp rope is also good for leaks at the bottom of the tap and sink.

PROBLEM: Smells in the sink drain.
WHAT TO USE: Bicarb, white vinegar.
HOW TO APPLY: Put 1 tablespoon of bicarb down the drain, followed immediately by ½ cup of white vinegar. Leave for half an hour. If it's still smelly, do it again. If you have copper or brass pipes, it will smell worse for about half an hour before it gets better. Once it's rinsed through the smell will dissipate.

PROBLEM: Black mould in the silicone behind the sink.
WHAT TO USE: Bicarb, white vinegar, old toothbrush; or silicone remover, sharp knife, silicone or candle wax.
HOW TO APPLY: First, try sprinkling bicarb over the mould and then splash with white vinegar. Scrub with an old toothbrush then rinse off with water. If this doesn't work, you may need to remove the silicone with a special silicone remover or a very sharp knife. Then replace with new silicone or candle wax.

Washing up by hand

The first rule of washing up is to rinse as much food as possible from plates and cutlery. Rather than leaving the tap running, use a small bucket to rinse items. You can also use paper towels to wipe food off. Put a little hot water in your dirty pots to soak them. Then stack everything needing washing on one side of the sink and have your drying rack on the other side of the sink.

The washing water should be hot, but not too hot. Use a small amount of dishwashing liquid and wear rubber gloves to prevent slippage. The order to wash things up in is:

1. glassware
2. plastics
3. china
4. cutlery
5. serving dishes
6. pots, pans and cooking utensils.

If you have a second sink, keep hot water in it and rinse the item after it's been scrubbed. Then stack the item on the drying rack to air dry or be dried with a tea towel. Air drying is more hygienic.

- To avoid streaking, glassware is best drained on a tea towel that has been laid out on the benchtop.
- Don't put good china or good glassware in water hotter than you could leave your hand in.
- Never use steel wool on porcelain or china no matter how

dirty it is. It will scratch the surface, making it porous and vulnerable to dirt and bacteria. If there are ingrained marks, clean them with bicarb and white vinegar.
- Never use a scourer or abrasives on polycarbonate glasses because they will scratch the surface. Instead, soak them in warm water with a little dishwashing liquid. For bad staining, apply glycerine first then wash in dishwashing liquid.
- To clean your washing gloves, turn them inside out, put them on and wash your hands in soap. Then leave them inside out to dry.

TAPS

Taps can be made of stainless steel, chrome, brass or powder coated. Except for powder-coated taps, clean with bicarb and white vinegar. To clean the back of taps, use an old pair of pantyhose. Wrap the leg around the tap and move it in a sawing motion backwards and forwards. Powder coating is a form of plastic that is heat sealed onto the surface of metal to colour it. Powder-coated taps are often cream, white or black. Don't use any abrasives on them, just wash with soap and water and always turn your cold tap on first or the powder coating will chip and discolour.

Drains

Drains are designed to take things away but they can also provide an entry for other things, such as insects. To stop insects gaining entry, put flyscreen material behind the drain grill. This will prevent blockages as well.

To keep cockroaches away, wipe a solution of salt and water around the drain.

If your drain is blocked, put ½ cup of bicarb down, then add ½ cup of white vinegar and leave for half an hour. You can also use a proprietary caustic cleaner. However, if your pipes are old and made of iron, using a caustic cleaner could pit the surface of the pipe (caustic is an oxidising agent and eats into iron), which also means it will hold bacteria.

Garbage Disposal Unit

The easy way to clean and freshen a garbage disposal unit is to place ½ raw potato and ½ lemon inside the unit and turn it on. Add hot water until it stops making a noise. The starch from the potato attracts dirt and the acid from the lemon helps break down grease. The lemon also leaves a clean, fresh smell.

Cupboards

The more often you wipe your cupboards, the cleaner they will stay. If you can, give them a quick clean every day with equal parts white vinegar and water in a 1 litre spray pack. If you have an issue with cockroaches, spray with ½ cup of salt combined with 1 litre of water in a spray pack and wipe with a cloth. And don't forget about the surface on

The Kitchen 79

top of the cupboard. As much as you'd like to adopt the 'out of mind, out of sight' approach, the dust which settles here will gradually spread around the rest of the kitchen. Try this homemade solution which Shannon developed through trial and error and which really cuts through the grime.

In a jar, mix ½ cup of grated soap, 2 tablespoons of methylated spirits, ½ cup of white vinegar and 2 tablespoons of bicarb. Seal the jar and shake it until all the ingredients are dissolved. Then clean the tops of your cupboards with a cloth. It's a very strong solution and could eat into other surfaces so only use it on this not-for-public-viewing area. To cut back on future cleaning, put paper—even newspaper will do—on top of cupboards and change it regularly.

The best time to clean the underside of wall-mounted cupboards is after making soup or boiling the kettle because the steam softens the grease and grime.

The easiest way to clean inside your kitchen drawers is to vacuum them every couple of weeks, then wipe with a damp cloth. If you haven't cleaned them in a while, use bicarb and white vinegar, then wipe with a cloth that has been soaked in hot water.

If strips of veneer are coming away from the edges of your cupboards, hold the strip in place and put a dripping wet towel on top. Iron on a cool setting and the steam will soften the adhesive and hold the strip in place. Don't add extra glue because the cupboard doors won't close properly. Specialist irons are available at electrical and plant hire.

Q '**I spilt a bottle of pure cinnamon oil from India and it splashed onto the vinyl-wrap white kitchen cupboard doors,' reports Sandy. 'What should I do?'**

PROBLEM: Cinnamon oil on vinyl wrap.
WHAT TO USE: Plaster of Paris, water, dishwashing liquid, stiff brush; or car polish, cloth.
HOW TO APPLY: This is a tricky job because cinnamon oil penetrates and permanently damages surfaces. To try to remove the stain, mix plaster of Paris and water to form a paste the consistency of peanut butter. For each cup of mixture, add 1 teaspoon of dishwashing liquid and mix well. Place over the stain. When dry, brush away.

Alternatively, use a dab of car polish and rub over the area. This will remove a fine layer from the vinyl. If the surface is permanently damaged, you may have to repaint, resurface or replace it.

Q '**The melamine edging on the cupboards around my stove has yellowed,' says Rob. 'Can this be fixed or will I need to replace the strips with new ones?'**

PROBLEM: Yellowed melamine.
WHAT TO USE: Glycerine, talcum powder, pantyhose; or melamine spray finish.
HOW TO APPLY: Try to remove the yellow stain with a paste of equal parts glycerine and talcum powder and polish with pantyhose. If this doesn't work, replace or recoat the surface with a melamine spray finish (available from hardware stores and specialist paint stores) or consult a professional.

Q 'A mouse died in my kitchen cupboard,' says Kate. 'That was bad enough, but there's still an awful smell. What do you suggest?'

PROBLEM: Dead mouse smell in cupboard.
WHAT TO USE: Cloth, white vinegar.
HOW TO APPLY: The smell is probably from mouse urine. Scrub every surface with a cloth dampened with white vinegar. Don't forget to clean the tops of the cupboards as well. Mice are particularly clever at peeing on the ceiling areas of cupboards.

Crockery

Most people have plates for everyday use and another set for special occasions. Crockery can be made of china, porcelain, pottery, glass or polycarbonate resin. Those in everyday use can be washed in dishwashing liquid and water. Never soak pottery as it can lift the glaze. To prevent your good china chipping and cracking in cupboards, put a small piece of paper towel in between the plates. This also helps prevent wear and tear on them. Never put gold-rimmed china in the microwave or dishwasher.

To keep crockery and china in top condition, don't wash in the dishwasher. Instead, hand wash in a little dishwashing liquid and warm water and rinse in clean warm water. For extra sparkle, add 1 tablespoon of white vinegar to the rinse water.

If you keep special china in a 'good cabinet', wash it every 6 months to prevent crazing or at least put a glass of water in with it. If the crockery is crazed or discoloured, add 2 denture tablets to a sinkful of warm water and soak the items overnight, then dry them in the sunshine.

Q 'How do you get tannin stains off fine English bone china mugs?' asks Timothy.

PROBLEM: Tannin stains on china.
WHAT TO USE: Methylated spirits, cotton bud, bicarb, white vinegar, pantyhose.
HOW TO APPLY: If the mugs have a metallic trim (including gold, white gold and platinum), wipe the trim with methylated spirits on a cotton bud. Clean the rest of the

mug with ½ teaspoon of bicarb and 1 teaspoon of white vinegar and rub with pantyhose. Don't get the mixture on the trim (it's very delicate).

Q 'I've got two crystal bowls that are stuck together,' says Anna. 'How can I get them apart without scratching them?'

PROBLEM: Crystal bowls stuck together.
WHAT TO USE: Hot water, iced water.
HOW TO APPLY: Run hot (but not boiling) water into your kitchen sink. Place the bowls in the water so the bottom one floats. Slowly add iced water in the top bowl. The top bowl will contract and the bottom bowl will swell and they'll pop apart.

Q 'I have some stained and scratched *Bessemer* plates,' reports Morag. 'What can I do?'

PROBLEM: Stained *Bessemer* plates.
WHAT TO USE: Glycerine, talcum powder, pantyhose or cloth.
HOW TO APPLY: *Bessemer* is a type of melamine. To remove stains, mix equal parts glycerine and talcum powder and polish over the stain with pantyhose or a cloth. If there's extensive scratching, replace the plates because bacteria can

get into the scratches. Turn the scratched ones into pot-plant saucers or paper plate supports at a picnic.

PROBLEM: Plates with discoloured crazing.
WHAT TO USE: Effervescing overnight denture soaker.
HOW TO APPLY: Add 2 tablets of denture soaker to a sink full of hot water. Put the plates in the sink and leave overnight. Rinse them off in clean water then leave them in the sun, if possible. Dry them very well. No matter what anyone tells you, do not soak china in bleach. The bleach can lift the glaze and cause a white powdery coating that won't go away.

PROBLEM: Stained teacups/teapots.
WHAT TO USE: Bicarb, white vinegar, nylon brush; or methylated spirits, cotton ball, cotton bud or cloth.
HOW TO APPLY: Mix 1 teaspoon of bicarb with 1 tablespoon of white vinegar. Rub it inside the teacup or teapot with a nylon brush. Rinse in clean water. If you have gold edging on cups, the tannin in tea builds up a scum over the gilding. Remove it with methylated spirits applied with a cotton ball, cotton bud or cloth.

PROBLEM: Chips in crockery.
WHAT TO USE: Denture soaker, glycerine; or sapphire nail file, glycerine or heat-resistant superglue.

HOW TO APPLY: This is only a temporary solution. Clean the plate in a sinkful of hot water with 2 tablets of denture soaker added to it. Allow the plate to dry thoroughly in sunlight. Then soak the chip with glycerine to seal it. It's best to throw chipped crockery away because bacteria can get into the porous surface. For special pieces, see a professional restorer. If you have a sharp chip, file with a sapphire nail file (a file which contains ground sapphire and will grind glass) around the edge of the chip, not down or across the chip. Then treat with glycerine. You can also use heat-resistant superglue to seal the chip. If you have grey lines across a plate, it means the seal has gone and dirt has penetrated into the plate. Rather than throw it away, add it to your recycle box to use as a pot plant saucer or something else. See a restorer for valuable pieces.

SALT AND PEPPER

To keep your salt shaker loose, add rice to it. To keep pepper loose, use dried peas. Adding dried peas also keeps parmesan cheese loose.

Teapot

Q 'How do you remove tea stains from a teapot?' asks Roland.

PROBLEM: Tea on crockery.
WHAT TO USE: Bicarb, white vinegar, nylon brush or pantyhose.
HOW TO APPLY: Sprinkle with bicarb followed by white vinegar. When the mixture fizzes, scrub with a nylon brush or pantyhose. Wash and dry normally.

TIP

To remove tannin build-up on strainers, dip pantyhose in methylated spirits and rub over the surface. Allow to dry, then rinse well.

Q 'How do you clean a silver teapot?' asks William.

PROBLEM: Dirty silver.
WHAT TO USE: Bicarb, white vinegar, cloth; or unprocessed wheat bran, bowl, white vinegar, pantyhose, cotton socks/gloves.
HOW TO APPLY: To remove heavy tarnish on solid silver or silver plating, sprinkle with bicarb followed by a sprinkle of white vinegar and, while it's fizzing, polish with a clean cloth. With regular cleaning, place 1 cup of unprocessed wheat bran in a bowl and add white vinegar drop by drop, stirring as you go. It's ready when the mixture is clumpy like brown sugar. Either put the mixture into the toe of a pair of

pantyhose, tie it off and scrub over the pieces or apply the mixture directly wearing a pair of old cotton socks on your hands to prevent sweat from your hands tarnishing the silver.

Jars

Q 'What's the best way to get rid of garlic odour from a jar lid?' asks Jo.

PROBLEM: Garlic odour in jar lid.
WHAT TO USE: Coarse salt, chopped fresh parsley, cloth.
HOW TO APPLY: Rub the lid with a mixture of 1 tablespoon of coarse salt and 1 teaspoon of finely chopped parsley. Wipe with a dry cloth.

TIP

Many glass jars have plastic or rubber linings inside the lid which absorb smells and oils and can contaminate your preserves. Put a film of beeswax or paraffin wax (available at the hardware or craft store and some supermarkets) over the preserves before securing the lid. The easiest way is to place 2 tablespoons of wax into a microwave-safe dish and heat in 10-second bursts in the microwave until just melted. Hold a warm teaspoon face down over the preserve and trickle the wax over the back of the warmed spoon. This allows a thin, even layer of wax to settle over the preserve that's easy to remove.

Plastic Containers

At a Stain Clinic in Perth, Harold brought along a white plastic bowl with a red ring circling the middle of the inside edge. Shannon said the red mark was from reheating tomato soup in the microwave. This can be a tough stain to fix if the tomato dye has been absorbed into the plastic. The solution is to scrub the stain with a paste of equal parts glycerine and talcum powder on a nylon brush. Alternatively, sprinkle coarse salt over the cut face of half a lemon, scrub over the stain and leave in the sunshine to dry.

Q 'I have a couple of old *Tupperware* containers that are quite sticky to touch,' says Sonia. 'What can I do?'

PROBLEM: Sticky *Tupperware*.
HOW TO APPLY: *Tupperware* has a lifetime guarantee and the company will replace the item. It's best not to use containers that are sticky because bacteria can stick to it.

TIP

To get rid of greasiness on plastic containers, add 1 teaspoon of white vinegar to the rinse water.

Lunch Bags

Q 'I've got salmon juice all over a cloth-insulated lunch bag,' says Louise. 'It stinks!'

PROBLEM: Salmon juice on cotton.
WHAT TO USE: Cake of bathroom soap, cold water, sunshine.
HOW TO APPLY: Run a cake of bathroom soap under cold water and scribble over the stain. Massage the stain with your fingers, including into the creases, and rinse in plenty of cold water. Hang it in the sunshine to dry. If the stitching along the edge rots, smells or becomes rough, it's time to throw the bag away because it's vulnerable to bacteria. A plastic lunch box is sturdier.

Cutlery

Most cutlery is fairly robust. If it has plastic handles, it won't last as long but they're generally cheaper to buy. Buy the best quality you can afford.

Wash cutlery in dishwashing liquid and water. If it's very dirty, stained or has rust spots, use bicarb and white vinegar first. Gold cutlery should only be cleaned with bicarb and white vinegar.

Brass, copper, silver and pewter cutlery can also be cleaned in an old aluminium saucepan with ½ cup of baking soda dissolved in 4 cups of hot water. Put the cutlery in and leave it for a few minutes. Don't put your bare hands into the water because they will burn! Wear rubber gloves or use wooden kitchen tools or skewers to manipulate the pieces. Then rinse the cutlery with water and white vinegar. Never add water to the aluminium pot after cleaning. Pour the solution out first as it can boil over because of the reaction between the aluminium, baking soda and hot water.

An old-fashioned way to get a glass-like polish on silverware is to rub it with a paste of unprocessed wheat bran and white vinegar. Put cotton gloves or a pair of old cotton socks on your hands to stop acid from your hands affecting the silver. Clean the paste off, then polish with a cloth. Remove scratches from silverware by rubbing a handful of bran over it with your hand. Don't use proprietary sprays that contain silicone. Clean pewter with bran and white vinegar but be careful not to overpolish it or you'll remove the patina of age and devalue the piece.

To clean, polish and seal bone handles on cutlery, mix 20 parts sweet almond oil to 1 part oil of cloves and mix thoroughly. Then rub this mixture over the handles. If the handles have become dry and cracked, leave them soaking in the mixture. After soaking, polish with a clean cloth. If the bone is very dirty, clean it first with bicarb and a little water. Never use heat with bone because it will discolour and crack.

Q 'Is there a way I can rejuvenate our 30-year-old everyday cutlery?' asks Mary. 'It's made of stainless steel and has fine scratches on the handles and blades.'

PROBLEM: Scratches on stainless steel cutlery.
WHAT TO USE: *Gumption*, cloth, bicarb, white vinegar, tea towel.
HOW TO APPLY: Stainless steel is a wonderful material because it's extremely tough and doesn't damage easily. On the downside, it's difficult to polish out scratches. To ameliorate the scratches, apply a dab of *Gumption* to a cloth, rub over the scratch, sprinkle with bicarb and splash with a little white vinegar and rub as it's fizzing. Polish with dry tea towel.

Q 'I'd like to know how to stop the dishwasher leaving rust on my stainless steel cutlery,' says Nicole.

PROBLEM: Rust on cutlery.
WHAT TO USE: Bicarb, white vinegar.
HOW TO APPLY: The dishwasher sandblasts your cutlery and creates rust marks. Polish the cutlery by hand with a paste of white vinegar and bicarb, wipe, then rinse off in water.

Q 'I've got green marks on my Thai copper cutlery,' says Susan. 'Do they come off?'

PROBLEM: Green marks on copper cutlery.
WHAT TO USE: Bicarb, white vinegar, nylon brush.
HOW TO APPLY: Lay the cutlery in the sink and sprinkle bicarb over it, then splash white vinegar on top. Scrub with a nylon brush and rinse. The reason Thais use copper cutlery is because curries taste sweeter when eaten with copper. Silver gives curries an acidic tang.

Knives

When Shannon was young, she remembers seeing a Chinese chef creating sculptures out of vegetables with his Chinese chopper. It was a fantastic sight to witness. She later learned that half the skill lies in having a good knife! Choose the best you can afford. Shannon suggests having a Chinese chopper, a large carving knife, a carving knife with a curved blade, a serrated bread knife, a serrated vegetable knife and a paring knife. Choose high-quality steel and ensure handles are solid and well secured.

If you use the wrong tools to sharpen knives, they'll rust. Only sharpen them with a steel and a whetstone. Never use cheap wheel sharpeners or you'll demagnetise the blades and get rust spots. If in doubt, use a professional knife sharpener. Shannon suggests asking your local restaurant when their knife sharpener is coming and arranging to have yours sharpened at the same time. Never use steel wool to clean a knife because it'll rust.

Hand wash your knives or you could get rust marks on them. If this happens, wipe with bicarb on a damp cloth. To help a knife retain its edge, try Shannon's trick. Keep a glass of water next to you when chopping onions and garlic and dip the knife in the water while you chop. Onion and garlic blunt knives!

Glassware

The worst things for glass are extreme heat, extreme cold, chemicals and abrasives. To protect your good glassware, avoid putting it in the dishwasher. As we've said before, Shannon hates dishwashers, particularly when it comes to glass because it becomes scratched and cloudy-looking and this damage is permanent. Don't soak glassware in dishwashing liquids or use strong bleach products. Just use water.

To prevent crystal becoming cloudy, only wash it in water no hotter than you can leave your hands in. Add a small amount of white vinegar to the wash to prevent spotting and fogging.

To clean dirt out of champagne glasses or glassware that has narrow apertures, put a little olive oil in the glass first and leave for a few minutes. The oil collects and lifts the dust. Then get a thin, long-handled paintbrush, wrap sticky tape around the ferrule, or silver part, and rub it around the difficult-to-reach area. Wash the glasses in dishwashing liquid and water. If it's too narrow for a thin paintbrush, use a bamboo skewer and chew the end of it until it's like a brush.

To make glasses sparkle, add 1 cup of white vinegar to a sink of warm rinse water. This removes streaking and detergent residue from glass. To dry, stand the glasses upside down on a clean tea towel.

To remove scratches in glass, make a paste of equal parts glycerine and whiting (available from leadlighting stores) and polish the scratches out. If the scratches are deep, this can take a long time. Wash in warm water and polish with a clean tea towel.

If glass is etched, wipe with sweet almond oil on a cloth. It won't clean the glass but removes the cloudy appearance.

- Always put a tea towel in the bottom of the sink in case you drop a piece while your hands are wet. The tea towel will cushion the impact.
- Never leave wine sitting in glasses because it will leave a mark.
- To remove lipstick on the edge of glasses, dip a small cotton ball in white vinegar and wipe over the lipstick.
- Never twist a tea towel through a stemmed glass as the glass could snap.

PROBLEM: Soap scum on glass.
WHAT TO USE: White vinegar, water, cloth.
HOW TO APPLY: Mix 1 tablespoon of white vinegar with 1 cup of water. Place the glass in the mixture. Then polish dry with a cloth.

Q Gabrielle puts everything in the dishwasher. 'But I've noticed I'm getting white marks on my glasses. What can I do about this?'

PROBLEM: Whiteness on glass.
WHAT TO USE: Goanna oil or sweel almond oil.
HOW TO APPLY: If it's soap scum, see above. If it's been scratched, the damage is permanent. You may be able to alleviate the problem by soaking it in goanna oil or sweet almond oil; however, this only works on some pieces and you don't know which ones will respond until you do it. Leave the goanna oil or sweet almond oil on for a week.

PROBLEM: Tiny chips on the edge of your glass.
WHAT TO USE: Sapphire manicure nail file.
HOW TO APPLY: Place the nail file horizontally and flat to the rim of the glass and slowly buff along the chips. Never go across or down the glass.

How to remove sticky labels

Shannon comes from a family that always removed labels from jars before putting them on the table because it was considered the polite thing to do. And, because it was the era before *Tupperware* and takeaway containers, glass jars were used for everything! There are several ways to remove sticky labels from glass and plastic containers. One method is to fill them with hot water, close the lid tightly and leave for a few minutes. Then lift the edge of the sticker slowly with a blunt knife. If any adhesive remains, wipe it with tea tree oil. Another way is to lay down a piece of clingwrap just bigger than the sticker. Mix one drop of dishwashing liquid with a small quantity of water in a spray pack, spray it over the clingwrap then place the clingwrap over the sticker. Leave for five minutes, or longer if the glue is very strong. The sticker will come off with the clingwrap. Rubbing white spirits or eucalyptus oil over the label, then rubbing off again, are other alternatives. Just make sure you neutralise them afterwards with methylated spirits. Don't try to remove the label by placing the jar itself into hot water—even though the paper will dissolve, the glue won't and you'll be left with a sticky mess that you'll have to rub and rub and rub!

The Pantry

Because Shannon was one of five children she learned to cook from an early age. The first thing she ever cooked was baked apples and cinnamon. She's always enjoyed cooking and experimenting with flavours and this is much easier to do if your pantry is organised.

If you organise your pantry by keeping similar items together, you won't waste time searching for things. If you don't have enough room in your pantry, think about putting another shelf in. Or get some free-standing wire shelves that are stackable.

Keep grain foods separately because bugs are attracted to them. Once you open any packet, put the contents in an air-tight container and mark the contents and use-by date on it. Shannon likes to cut the relevant information from the packet and sticky tape or glue it to the jar. You can also seal a packet with an old bread clip or bulldog clip. Putting a bay leaf in containers will help keep moths and weevils away. Another way to prevent weevils in grain food is to make a small clingwrap bag, fill it full of salt, seal the top and prick the bag with pin holes. Place this inside the containers. Shannon always removes cereals from the cardboard box because insects are attracted to cardboard. Seal the plastic liner with a peg or old bread clip.

Most canned food will last from two to four years, but the earlier you consume it, the better. Most cans have a use-by date on them. If they don't, write the date of purchase on the side. Shannon learned the hard way when a can exploded in the pantry. It's an experience she doesn't want to repeat any time soon!

Refrigerate jars such as mayonnaise and mustard after opening.

Oils will go off and become rancid. You should only store them for about six months. Rather than buying expensive oil sprays, put oil in your own spray pack. Oils react differently when heated and some leave more grease than others on your kitchen cupboards. Rapeseed oil is the worst for leaving oily scum as it seems to fume more. Shannon bought a cheap drum of it once thinking it was a bargain but it was costly in cleaning-up terms! However, it's great as a salad oil or for low-temperature cooking. As a rule, the better the quality of oil, the less splattering you're likely to get. Have a range of oils available so you use the right oil for the job. For example, don't use olive oil for chips because the oil will burn before the chips are cooked.

Place a layer of paper towel in the bottom of a sugar container to prevent lumping and clumping. If you put a piece of terracotta in your brown sugar it won't clot.

Always keep your dried herbs tightly sealed in glass or plastic and out of strong sunlight. Buy them in small quantities because they lose their flavour after about six months. Even better, grow them fresh on your windowsill.

Keep the pantry clean by regularly wiping surfaces with a damp cloth. Get into the habit of putting newer cans and packaging at the back, rather than at the front, of the pantry. That way you'll get to things before the expiry date (hopefully!). After opening a packet of food, store the food in an airtight container or you could get moths flying about in your pantry. If this happens, place bay leaves along the shelves or wipe over them with no more than 2 drops of bay oil or oil of pennyroyal on a cloth. Note that oil of pennyroyal should only be used as directed as it can be harmful to pregnant women and pets. Remember one drop means one drop.

PROBLEM: Ants.
WHAT TO USE: Powdered borax, cornflour, icing sugar; or powdered borax, finely grated parmesan cheese; or boiling water.
HOW TO APPLY: Work out whether the ants are attracted to sweet or savoury flavours. For those with a sweet tooth, mix ½ teaspoon of borax, ½ teaspoon of cornflour and ¼ teaspoon of icing sugar and place along the ant trail. For savoury eaters, mix equal parts borax and parmesan and scatter along the ant trail. The ants will take the mixture back to the nest and die. Be careful using borax around pets and children—it is mildly toxic! Alternatively, a non-toxic option is to go nest hunting by sprinkling cornflour on an

ant trail so that the ants walk it back to the nest, making a visible track for you to follow. When you find it, pour boiling water down the ant nest.

PREVENTION: Keep benchtops spotless.

Q 'We've got these pesky moths in the pantry that seem to breed in anything and everything,' says Michael. 'Can we get rid of them?'

PROBLEM: Moths in the pantry.
WHAT TO USE: Oil of pennyroyal or bay oil or mint tea, cloth.
HOW TO APPLY: Put 1 drop of oil of pennyroyal in a bucket of water, then wipe the shelves with a cloth. Note that oil of pennyroyal should only be used as directed as it can be harmful to pregnant women and pets. Remember one drop means one drop. Pregnant women can apply bay oil to a cloth and then wipe over the shelves or they can wipe the shelves with a very strong mint tea. These methods aren't as effective as oil of pennyroyal and have to be reapplied more often but they will work.

RECYCLING CONTAINERS

Nearly everything we buy comes in a container. Hang onto these because there are plenty of other ways you can use them. For example, plastic takeaway containers can be reused for leftovers. To get rid of the greasy feel, put a little white vinegar in the water when you're rinsing. Even cereal boxes can be converted into files for paperwork. Plastic bags can be washed, hung out and reused. Reuse tins to store nails and other things. Hold on to jars as well, as they're good for storing liquids.

SWEET-SMELLING HANDS

Rubbing your hands with bicarb and white vinegar removes smells, especially after working with onions, garlic or chilli. An alternative is to wear disposable gloves when chopping.

The Bathroom

There's nothing more relaxing than sinking into a hot bath! But this blissful state can be ruined if, as you lie back, you notice mould on the ceiling or mildew on the walls. The green and black stuff is the bane of many a bathroom cleaner, particularly in older bathrooms, as Jennifer knows only too well. Shannon loves cleaning the bathroom because she ends up with plenty of sparkling surfaces.

Bathrooms seem to be multiplying as fast as cane toads. The absolute minimum now appears to be two, master bedrooms must have an en suite and larger homes have as many bathrooms as bedrooms. And let's not forget the toilet and shower recess out by the pool! We want all of these to be immaculate. And not just for us; no one wants guests discovering something worse than dirty tiles.

Grab the right cleaning items, put on a favourite CD and in no time your bathroom surfaces will be gleaming. Remember: always work from top to bottom.

Tacky timber: *Reg's story*

INCIDENT: *'I've got sealed timber walls in my bathroom but there are numerous toothpaste and soap stains around the vanity area. It ruins the clean Swedish image. What do you suggest?'*

SOLUTION: Roll pantyhose into a ball, dampen with water and rub over the stains. It's likely the toothpaste will have bleached the timber. If this is the case, wipe with a damp tea bag. The tannins in the tea draw out the tannins in the timber and replace the lost colour. Always remove toothpaste marks as soon as possible.

Be careful where you put spray cans: *Deborah's story*

INCIDENT: *'I've got a beautiful old marble vanity top. But the look of it is marred by some circles of rust that I can't remove. It's such a pity because the marble is so beautiful. Is there any way of removing them?'*

SOLUTION: Put a circle of bicarb over the rust mark, add diluted white vinegar and rub it off with a sponge. The rust stains were probably caused by the bottom of a hairspray can. Most cans are unsealed, and when they interact with water, they rust. One way to prevent this is to paint clear nail polish on the bottom of any cans that sit on the vanity. You could also keep a small wooden tray on your vanity for storing unsealed cans, or go old-fashioned and use doilies.

Q 'We've got a problem with millipedes,' says Helen. 'They head for the bathroom and create a massive black mess.'

PROBLEM: Millipedes in the bathroom.
WHAT TO USE: Oil of pennyroyal, cloth.
HOW TO APPLY: Put no more than 2 drops of oil of pennyroyal on a cloth and wipe it over the areas where the millipedes crawl. Note that oil of pennyroyal should only be used as directed as it can be harmful to pregnant women and pets. Remember one drop means one drop.

Q 'I've got these little black flying bugs in my bathroom,' reports Sam. 'They gravitate towards the roof. Is there anything I can do?'

PROBLEM: Black bugs in bathroom.
WHAT TO USE: Salt, water, sponge.
HOW TO APPLY: These could be a variety of fruit bug. Many shampoos have fruit oil in them, which attracts some bugs. Make sure your shampoo is sealed and keep the tops of the containers clean. If the bugs are beetles, make a solution of salt and water and paint it around your drains and windowsills with a sponge.

Toilet

Cleaning the toilet is easier if you don't allow grime to accumulate—and, besides, most toilets are easy to clean.

Has anyone shown you how to clean the toilet properly? We'll assume 'no' was the answer to that question. This is Shannon's approach using bicarb and white vinegar, but feel free to substitute the cleaning product of your choice.

Tools: Bicarb, sponges, white vinegar, toilet brush.

Technique:
1. Flush the toilet to wet the sides of the bowl.
2. Sprinkle bicarb over the inside of the bowl.
3. Wipe the top of the cistern using the two-sponge technique with bicarb and white vinegar.
4. Wipe the top of the lid, under the lid, the top of the seat and under the seat using the same technique.
5. Splash white vinegar over the bicarb in the bowl, then use a toilet brush to scrub, including up and around the rim.
6. Wipe the top of the rim with a sponge.
7. Wash the sponge in hot water and wipe again.
8. Flush.
9. Rinse the sponge and wipe the outside of the toilet bowl right to the floor, including the plumbing at the back.
10. Congratulations, you're done!

One of the most common toilet stains is urine. Now, how do we put this delicately? There are often 'spray' issues that not only stain but leave a noxious smell as well. Fix by wiping the area with white vinegar or lemon juice on a cloth, making sure you also wipe the pipes at the back and the floor area around the toilet. If your floor is unsealed marble, dilute white vinegar and rinse with clean water when you have finished or the vinegar could damage the surface.

Shannon isn't keen on the 'if it's yellow, let it mellow' approach to water saving. She thinks it's okay to leave urine in the bowl for a few hours but says it can remove the surface from the porcelain, leaving a rougher surface for bacteria to stick to. To neutralise acid in urine, sprinkle bicarb into the toilet bowl after peeing (½ teaspoon should do the job) and flush every 24 hours. You'll add a layer of protection to the surface of the toilet bowl if you lightly spray with a mix of 1 teaspoon of lavender oil to a 1 litre spray pack of water after cleaning.

For a super-duper clean, scoop the water out of the toilet bowl with a paper cup (you don't want to chip your good china) and lightly sprinkle the entire bowl with a little bicarb, followed by an equal amount of white vinegar and, as it's fizzing, scrub with a toilet brush. Repeat if needed. If there are very grotty stains, flush first with hot water (pour it straight from the kettle) to dissolve fats and oils that build up on the surface. And there's always the *Coke* solution! Many people swear that adding *Coke* to the toilet bowl gives a great clean; however, it can damage the ceramic glaze, leaving a greater surface area for bacteria to stick to. (If *Coke* does that to a toilet, imagine what it does to your stomach.)

THE PING-PONG BALL TECHNIQUE

If you have a young boy who's having difficulty getting all his pee in the bowl, put a ping-pong ball at the bottom of the toilet and tell him to aim for it. The ping-pong ball won't flush because it's too light and you'll be surprised at how much better his aim becomes.

PROBLEM: Bad stains on the inside of the toilet bowl.
WHAT TO USE: Small plastic cup, bicarb, white vinegar, nylon brush.
HOW TO APPLY: Turn the tap off at the cistern. Drain the bottom of the bowl with a small plastic cup. Then sprinkle bicarb over the bowl and splash some white vinegar over the bicarb. Scrub with a nylon brush. Turn the water back on at the cistern.

Q 'We've got orange rust stains on our toilet bowl from bore water,' says Sue. 'How can we remove them?'

PROBLEM: Rust stains/hard-water fur.
WHAT TO USE: *CLR/Ranex*, rubber gloves, mask.
HOW TO APPLY: Put half a cap of *CLR* into the cistern, leave it for an hour, then flush the toilet. This will help prevent the bowl staining as it cleans the fur out of the cistern. For heavy stains, clean the bowl with *CLR* but make sure you use rubber gloves and a mask. Note that *CLR* should only be used to remove staining and not as a regular cleaner.

Q 'We have a septic tank and live near a stream and are therefore careful about the cleaning products we use,' says Melanie. 'The toilets have marks on the bottom inside the bowl (below the water level) and I'd like to remove them. What do you suggest?'

PROBLEM: Cleaning a septic toilet.
WHAT TO USE: Paper cup, bicarb, white vinegar, toilet brush.
HOW TO APPLY: Use a paper cup (to avoid scratches) to remove the water from the toilet bowl. Sprinkle the bowl with a light dusting of bicarb followed by an equal amount of white vinegar and, as the mixture fizzes, scrub with a toilet brush. Because the quantities of bicarb and vinegar are equal, it creates salt water which isn't damaging for septic systems.

The Bathroom 111

Q 'I've got a pale blue stain (water stain, I think) at the back of the toilet,' says Joan. 'The house is near the coast with a lot of limestone in the ground which probably affects the water quality. What do you suggest?'

PROBLEM: Water stain on back of toilet.
WHAT TO USE: Talcum powder, disposable rubber gloves, *CLR/Ranex*.
HOW TO APPLY: The blue line running down the back of the toilet is likely to be from mineral deposit in the water. Flush the toilet, lightly dust the bowl with talcum powder and allow to dry. Put on rubber gloves and apply *CLR* or *Ranex* to the talcum powder. The talcum powder holds the *CLR* or *Ranex* in place, allowing it to soak in. To prevent the problem, add 1 capful of *CLR* or *Ranex* to your cistern when you do a regular clean of your toilet.

PROBLEM: Dirty seat.
WHAT TO USE: Bicarb, white vinegar, sponge; or *Gumption*; and sweet almond oil or glycerine.
HOW TO APPLY: For plastic seats, sprinkle bicarb then wipe a white vinegar-soaked sponge over the top. For *Bakelite* seats, put a dab of *Gumption* on a sponge and wipe it over the seat. Then rinse with water. If you've lost that glossy

look on your *Bakelite* toilet seat, rub a drop of sweet almond oil on it. If it's plastic, rub it with glycerine.

PROBLEM: Urine smell.
WHAT TO USE: A lemon, ice-cream container, water; or white vinegar, water.
HOW TO APPLY: Wash surfaces with the juice from half a lemon added to an ice-cream container of water. Alternatively, use white vinegar and water. Lemon is preferable because it leaves a nice smell. It's particularly important to wipe the pipes at the back of the toilet.

PROBLEM: Rubber beginning to perish.
WHAT TO USE: Salt, glycerine, talcum powder, cloth.
HOW TO APPLY: Rub the perish marks with salt, wipe over with glycerine and then sprinkle with talcum powder. When dry, remove the talcum powder with a cloth. If the rubber has perished too much, you'll need to replace it.

CUTTING BACK ON TOILET PAPER

Shannon grew up in a house with more girls than boys and they went through loads of toilet paper. If you have the same problem, squash the roll before you put it on the roller. This slows the spin down and stops little fingers making paper trails through the house.

NON-TOXIC AIR FRESHENER

Shannon suffers from asthma and proprietary sprays make her wheeze so she created this non-toxic bathroom air freshener. Fill a 1 litre spray pack with water and add 2 drops of dishwashing liquid and 5 drops of lavender oil. You can substitute other essential oils except those with high colouring levels, such as stone fruits. Eucalyptus oil should be used sparingly because it will mark painted surfaces. Spray as needed.

Bath

Taking a bath is one of life's great luxuries. Shannon's Mother's Day treat is taking a bath with a glass of champagne, her favourite book and no one bothering her.

Most baths are made of vitreous china although new ones are made of acrylic, fibreglass or polycarbonate. You may also encounter stainless steel, metal or cast-iron baths. Use bicarb and white vinegar to clean them or, if they're very dirty, *Gumption*. An old pair of pantyhose rolled into a ball is great to clean with because it cuts through soap scum really well without scratching. Never use steel wool to clean baths or you'll leave scratch marks.

If you have a cast-iron bath, don't put hot water in first. Cast iron shrinks and expands at a different rate to the enamel covering and if the water is too hot you'll get chips and cracks. Put a little cold water in cast-iron and polycarbonate baths first.

When cleaning the bath, clean the tiles above the bath first, then the taps, then the sides and bottom of the bath. Then rinse. Never use abrasives on polycarbonate baths. Use glycerine to remove stains.

To clean your bath, lightly dust with bicarb, add equal parts white vinegar and, while it's fizzing, give a good scrub with a cloth or soft broom. That's all your bath should need to be clean and gleaming. If you have a build-up of dirt and it's difficult to shift, try the denture tablet trick. Fill your bath with hot water, add 12 denture tablets and leave overnight. When you pull out the plug and give it a rub, the dirt will wash down the drain. If you've got seriously ingrained dirt in your bath (old ones are susceptible to this), commercial sponge products are available where you just add water and scrub over the muck. Be aware that these products actually remove the top surface of the bath. It might be necessary to try one of these if you have a century-old bath but use the sponges sparingly in other cases. An alternative method is to cut a lemon in half, sprinkle the cut surface with non-iodised salt and scrub the lemon over the surface of the bath. It's abrasive but the salt crystals break down so it's not damaging to the surface of your bath.

If the surface is badly scratched or you want an update, you can have baths professionally resurfaced for around

$500.00 (depending on the size). If yours has been renovated in this way, be careful when adding hot water because the new surface will expand at a different rate to the base surface and may crack. Protect the new surface by putting a little cold water in the bath before adding hot water.

TIP

Reduce your cleaning time by wiping the bath with a rolled up pair of pantyhose immediately after using it. You won't get dirt rings and it will minimise any etching.

Q 'I have a fibreglass bath with stains from essential oils,' reports Jodie. 'The stains look like tiny little brown marks. Can you help me?'

PROBLEM: Essential oil on fibreglass.
WHAT TO USE: Dishwashing liquid, glycerine, talcum powder, pantyhose, soft cloth.
HOW TO APPLY: Mix 1 teaspoon of dishwashing liquid, 1 teaspoon of glycerine and 1 teaspoon of talcum powder and scrub over the stain with pantyhose. Leave for 20 minutes and polish off with a soft cloth. Repeat if necessary.

Q 'I've spilt liquid shoe polish onto a white enamel bath,' admits Anne. 'What can I do?'

PROBLEM: Liquid shoe polish on enamel.
WHAT TO USE: Tea tree oil, cloth.
HOW TO APPLY: Wipe the stain with a dab of tea tree oil on a cloth. It should come away easily.

Q 'We have bore water,' reports Frances. 'And it's left a stain on the ceramic bath. What do you suggest?'

PROBLEM: Bore water stain on ceramic.
WHAT TO USE: Disposable rubber gloves, water, *CLR/Ranex*, nylon brush.
HOW TO APPLY: Put on rubber gloves, fill the bath with water and add 2 capfuls of *CLR* or *Ranex*. Leave for 2 hours, drain the bath and scrub with a brush. Don't get *CLR* or *Ranex* on your skin because it can cause irritation.

PROBLEM: Rust stains on the sink ring.
WHAT TO USE: Disposable rubber gloves, *CLR/Ranex*, cloth.
HOW TO APPLY: Put on rubber gloves then wipe *CLR* or *Ranex* on the sink ring with a cloth. Wipe it off then rinse.

PROBLEM: Scratches in fibreglass.
WHAT TO USE: Glycerine, 2000-grade wet-and-dry.
HOW TO APPLY: Put glycerine on the wet-and-dry and rub over the scratch.

SPA BATH

At the press of a button, a bath is transformed into a bubbling comfort zone. When you're sitting back enjoying a jet-filled soak, don't use soap because it gets into the filter and creates a cloggy mess. Instead, use shower gel or liquid soap.

To clean a spa bath, put 1 cup of bicarb in a full tub of water, run the spa bath for 5 minutes and allow the bicarb to circulate. Add 2 cups of white vinegar and run for a further 5 minutes. Drain and rinse with clean water. As you clean, look out for chalk deposits, body fat and skin cell build-up. Chalk deposits come about because soap and water is flushed backwards and forwards at different temperatures. Remove with white vinegar and clean the nozzle regularly with *CLR/Ranex*. After every couple of uses, run white vinegar and water through the spa.

Shower

It might be okay to wear thongs in the shower at a caravan park but do you really want to do this in your own home? Keep the area clean with bicarb and white vinegar. Sprinkle bicarb over the surfaces then splash some white vinegar over the top and wipe with a sponge or brush. Then rinse with water. For vertical surfaces, have a tray with some bicarb in it and a bucket with white vinegar in it and use two separate sponges. Begin with the bicarb sponge then press the vinegar sponge over the bicarb sponge and wipe. Then rinse with water. If you have particularly grimy surfaces, use *Gumption*. If you like fragrance, add a couple of drops of tea tree oil, lavender oil or eucalyptus oil to the rinse water. Don't use eucalyptus oil on anything plastic or painted.

In these water-saving times, we're encouraged to spend only 3 minutes taking a shower—and it's a lovely 3 minutes. One of the most common problems with showers is mould, particularly in the silicone. The reason mould grows is from a combination of moisture and lack of ventilation, so get into the habit of wiping up any water in the shower area and allow air to circulate in the room. You could even leave a squeegee in the shower area and encourage users to wipe over the area after each shower. If your shower is vulnerable to mould, spray with ¼ teaspoon of oil of cloves in a 1 litre spray pack of water.

If your shower includes polymarble, clean it with a rolled up pair of pantyhose after each use. It doesn't react well to soaps or shampoos left on the surface. Don't clean with bicarb or white vinegar or it will damage the polymarble.

Some modern bathrooms are designed as wet rooms that are completely open with nothing separating the water spray from the shower from the rest of the bathroom. If this is the case in your home, you'll know it's important to have a protected area for your towels!

PROBLEM: Rust marks on shower tiles.
WHAT TO USE: Water, talcum powder, disposable rubber gloves, *CLR/Ranex*, white vinegar, cloth.
HOW TO APPLY: Wet the affected area with water and sprinkle with talcum powder, to help with absorption. Put on rubber gloves, apply *CLR* or *Ranex* and leave for 10 minutes. The rust should be gone. Neutralise the chemicals by wiping with white vinegar on a cloth.

Q 'My shower recess has a fancy border tile along the wall which is made of marble and runs right around the bathroom,' reports Kerry. 'The tiles in the shower (that get wet) are turning white-ish and have lost their shine. What can I do?'

PROBLEM: Dull marble in shower.
WHAT TO USE: Glycerine, talcum powder, pantyhose or cloth, marble wax.
HOW TO APPLY: The marble is reacting to the caustic properties in soap. Polish with a paste of equal parts

glycerine and talcum powder on a pair of pantyhose or cloth. Finish by polishing with a quality marble wax, such as *Cera Wax*. In high-traffic areas such as the shower, marble needs to be cleaned after every use, even if it's only a wipe down. Marble should be waxed once a week if used regularly.

Q 'I've had a rubber suction mat on the bathroom floor,' reports Dawn. 'And it's left marks. What can I do?'

PROBLEM: Rubber on tiles.
WHAT TO USE: Water, coarse salt, stiff scrubbing brush or broom, damp cloth.
HOW TO APPLY: Damp the tiles with water and scrub salt over the marks with a brush or broom. Remove the salt with a damp cloth.

TIP

To remove make-up and dead skin cells, place unprocessed wheat bran in the toe of a pair of pantyhose, tie to enclose, dampen with water and gently rub over your skin. It's a great exfoliator.

PROBLEM: Soap scum build-up in soap holder.
WHAT TO USE: Old pair of pantyhose, warm water.

HOW TO APPLY: Scrub the soap scum with an old pair of pantyhose rolled into a ball and warm water.

SHOWER SCREEN

As a general rule, it's best not to use abrasives or strong chemicals on any shower screens. If you have a glass shower screen, clean it with white vinegar or methylated spirits on a cloth. Some shower screens have nylon and wire in between two layers of glass, and problems occur because air cavities are created. This allows moisture to get in and causes either mould or glass cancer on the inside of the screen. It often looks as though you've got soap scum on the screen. Shannon has seen this many times and unfortunately there's not much you can do about it. You can alleviate the scratchiness with goanna oil or sweet almond oil, which you rub over the surface and edges. If you can't live with the scratchiness, you'll have to buy a new screen or get some glass-etching cream and make the clouds a feature. The other common type of shower screen is made of polycarbonate and should only be cleaned with white vinegar.

If you clean shower screens regularly, you won't get stain build-up. To tackle mould, combine ¼ teaspoon of oil of cloves with 1 litre of water in a spray pack, lightly spray the solution over the affected area and leave for 24 hours. If mould has formed behind the silicone join, combine

¼ teaspoon of oil of cloves with 1 litre of water in a spray pack and after spraying, scrub with an old toothbrush. If the mould is ingrained in the silicone, you'll need to replace the silicone. You can replace it yourself or seek professional help.

SPOTLESS CLASSIC
Cloudy shower screen

We get many questions about how to fix streaky marks on shower screens. Sometimes it's from a build-up of soap or shampoo which can be removed with bicarb and white vinegar. But in many cases, the cloudiness is from tiny air bubbles etched into the screen (often caused by caustic cleaning products) that Shannon calls 'glass cancer' and the damage is permanent. You can alleviate the problem by wiping with sweet almond oil on a cloth or pantyhose. To prevent it, don't use caustic cleaning products and clean with bicarb and white vinegar instead.

Q 'I find that my shower screen becomes streaky,' says Kaye. 'What do you suggest?'

PROBLEM: Streaky shower screen.
WHAT TO USE: Methylated spirits, white vinegar, water, cloth.

HOW TO APPLY: Mix 1 part methylated spirits with 1 part white vinegar and 2 parts water. The amount you need depends on how big the screen is. Rub the mixture over the screen with a cloth.

PROBLEM: Mould in silicone join.
WHAT TO USE: Bicarb, white vinegar, old toothbrush; or new silicone.
HOW TO APPLY: Mix the bicarb and white vinegar into a paste and apply with an old toothbrush. Try this a few times. If it doesn't shift, you'll need to replace the silicone.

SHOWER CURTAIN

Constant moisture and poor ventilation make the shower curtain a prime candidate for mould. Most shower curtains are made of fabric or plastic and can be washed once a fortnight on a cool cycle in a washing machine or in a laundry tub or bucket. To prevent further mildew, add a drop of oil of cloves to the rinse water.

Whatever you do, don't clean them with bleach. The curtains will look whiter but bleach breaks down the surface and makes them more susceptible to mould and you'll find them more difficult to clean later. Instead clean with 1 teaspoon of dishwashing liquid, ¼ teaspoon of oil of cloves and 1 litre of warm water. Fabric curtains look good but wear more quickly and need to be washed each week, more if you've got a home full of footballers. Wipe plastic shower curtains after each use and hook up over the rod so they don't collect water, condensation and mould.

SHOWER HEAD

Most people don't think to clean the shower head but it's vulnerable to staining. To clean, wipe with damp pantyhose. If the water in your shower head sprays in different directions, it's likely you've got hard-water fur. If you can see little black prickly things coming out of the nozzle, that's also hard-water fur. To get rid of it, use *CLR* or *Ranex*. Mix *CLR/Ranex* according to the directions on the packet in a bucket or old ice-cream container. Hold the container so that the shower head is completely immersed. Keep it there until the solution is absorbed. This should take a few minutes. Then turn on the shower: the black prickles will drop out and go down the drain. You can also unscrew the shower head and clean it inside the ice-cream container with *CLR/Ranex*.

Q 'We have green-coloured marks on our shower head,' reports Penny. 'What should we do?'

PROBLEM: Green marks on shower head.
WHAT TO USE: Disposable rubber gloves, *CLR/Ranex*, old plastic ice-cream container, water.

HOW TO APPLY: The marks are probably from mineral build-up or oxidisation. Put on rubber gloves, place *CLR* or *Ranex* and water (according to the directions on the pack) in an ice-cream container and immerse the shower head for 10 minutes. Rinse with water.

Taps

You always create a good impression if your taps are clean and shiny. Taps can be made of stainless steel, brass, copper, chrome, gold or powder coated. The best way to clean them is with bicarb and white vinegar, except powder-coated taps. Powder coating is a form of plastic that is heat sealed onto the surface of metal to colour it. It often comes in cream, white and black. Don't use abrasives, just wash with soap and water. An old pair of pantyhose is the easiest way to clean taps. Wrap them around the tap and move backwards and forwards in a sawing action. An old toothbrush also does the trick, particularly at getting into the area where the tap joins the basin or vanity top.

Tiles

Clean tiles once a week with bicarb and white vinegar. Have one sponge with bicarb on it and the other with white vinegar on it and put the vinegar-soaked sponge over the top of the bicarb-coated sponge, then wipe. The grout between the tiles is very porous and retains mildew.

To clean it, use bicarb and white vinegar and scrub with an old toothbrush. You should clean the grout every couple of months to avoid build-up.

One of the common complaints with tiles and grout in bathrooms is mould. The best way to deal with mould is to combine ¼ teaspoon of oil of cloves with 1 litre of water in a spray pack, lightly spray the solution over the affected area and leave for 24 hours. After that, clean the grout with bicarb and white vinegar using an old toothbrush. The visible mould should be gone. Lightly mist again with the oil of cloves mixture and repeat every 2 months. Oil of cloves is very strong and will burn plastic, so it must be diluted—once an item is burnt, it's very difficult to repair. If you have a burn stain from oil of cloves, mix equal parts glycerine and talcum powder and rub with pantyhose. It won't fix the burn but it will improve the appearance.

There is another way to keep mould under control but you may baulk at this suggestion. Keep a couple of slugs! Slugs will happily eat mould. They sleep during the day so if you create a little house for them, you won't step on them while showering!

Reapplying grout between your tiles is relatively easy and really gives your bathroom a great lift. To remove old grout, use a grout rake. Run this nifty tool backwards and forwards along the grout until it becomes powdery. Clean the area thoroughly and apply the new grout. Make sure you wipe off any excess grout before it dries.

Q 'I've got a black line over my white tiles,' says Bruce. 'What do you suggest?'

PROBLEM: Black line on white tiles.
WHAT TO USE: Pencil eraser or biro eraser, water.
HOW TO APPLY: It sounds as though someone has accidentally bumped an aerosol can over the tile and left a black line. Remove it with a pencil eraser or biro eraser dipped in water.

Q 'The builder left silicone on the tiles,' says Sarah. 'What can I do to remove it?'

PROBLEM: Silicone on tiles.
WHAT TO USE: Kerosene, single-sided razor blade.
HOW TO APPLY: Apply a little kerosene to a razor blade and use it to scrape under the silicone on the tiles. The silicone will slide off.

Q 'We've laid small dark tiles and a dark colour grout at the base of our shower,' reports Kellie. 'But it's really hard to keep the grout looking good, especially with soap. Any ideas?'

PROBLEM: Soap scum on dark-coloured grout.
WHAT TO USE: Broom, pantyhose, bicarb, white vinegar, sweet almond oil, cloth.
HOW TO APPLY: Force the head of a broom into the leg of a pair of pantyhose. Sprinkle the tiles with a light dusting of bicarb followed by a light spray of white vinegar and, while it's fizzing, scrub with the broom and rinse with water. If any white scum remains, polish with a couple of drops of sweet almond oil on a cloth.

Mirror

When Shannon learned that scuba divers keep their goggles clear by spitting into them, she tested this on the bathroom mirror and found that spit stops the mirror from fogging. Just spit onto a tissue and wipe it over the mirror. If this doesn't appeal to you, write on the mirror with pure soap then polish vigorously with a slightly damp paper towel. Shannon discovered this at the Easter Show where a man was selling 'Magic Mirror Demisting Sticks'. They turned out to be just soap.

Clean the mirror with methylated spirits and a paper towel.

Q 'My bathroom mirror has silicone smeared around one corner,' says Sandra. 'Can I remove it? It looks streaky.'

PROBLEM: Silicone on mirror.
WHAT TO USE: Single-sided razor blade, kerosene; or pantyhose, kerosene, white vinegar, paper towel.
HOW TO APPLY: If the silicone is quite thick, dip a razor blade in kerosene and slide it under the silicone and along the mirror to remove it. If it's only a very thin film of silicone, remove by dipping a rolled up pair of pantyhose in kerosene and rubbing over the silicone. Once the silicone has been removed, wipe with a little white vinegar on paper towel.

Hand Basin and Vanity

Clean the hand basin and vanity with bicarb and white vinegar. Sprinkle bicarb over the surface, then wipe with a vinegar-soaked sponge. Clean cupboards and shelving the same way. To prevent bottles breaking in your drawers, line them with a thin piece of foam rubber. This cushions any drops and makes cleaning the drawers easier.

Q 'What's the best way to clean the marble on my vanity?' asks Trish. 'Water seems to have penetrated the sealant.'

PROBLEM: Watermarks on sealed marble.
WHAT TO USE: *Brasso*, pantyhose.
HOW TO APPLY: In most cases, marble in a bathroom is sealed with polyurethane. If this is the case, apply a little

Brasso to rolled up pantyhose and rub in a circular motion. Be fast and don't apply too much pressure. This partially melts the polyurethane and removes bubbles that appear to be watermarks. You may need to reseal the surface—seek professional help.

PREVENTION: To provide a protective coating for marble, apply a good quality marble floor wax. Renew the wax regularly.

Q 'I've got a green copper mark on my plastic bathroom sink,' says Cheryl. 'How do I remove it?'

PROBLEM: Green copper mark on basin.
WHAT TO USE: Glycerine, talcum powder, pantyhose.
HOW TO APPLY: Clean with a mixture of equal parts glycerine and talcum powder. Polish on with a pair of pantyhose and leave for around half an hour then polish off.

Q 'I need help to remove yellow water marks on my white basin,' reports Johnny. 'It's where the water sits in the soap holders and around the plug hole.'

PROBLEM: Yellow water marks on basin.
WHAT TO USE: Talcum powder, disposable rubber gloves, *CLR/Ranex*.

HOW TO APPLY: It's likely to be from mineral deposit in the water. Sprinkle the affected area with talcum powder and allow to dry. Put on rubber gloves and apply *CLR* or *Ranex* to the talcum powder and allow to soak in. Rinse with water. Don't get *CLR* or *Ranex* on your skin because it can cause irritation.

Q 'How do you get *Tiger Balm* out of hair?' asks Monique.

PROBLEM: *Tiger Balm* in hair.
WHAT TO USE: Tea tree oil, dishwashing liquid, olive oil, warm water.
HOW TO APPLY: *Tiger Balm* has an oil and wax base. Mix 1 teaspoon of tea tree oil, 1 teaspoon of dishwashing liquid and 1 teaspoon of olive oil and massage into the scalp and hair. Rinse with warm water, massaging as you rinse. You may need to repeat.

PROBLEM: Mildew on vanity cupboard.
WHAT TO USE: Salt, bucket, hot water, oil of cloves, sponge.
HOW TO APPLY: Dissolve 1 cup of salt in a bucket of hot water. Add 2 drops of oil of cloves. Wipe this on the inside of the vanity with a sponge. This will also help to keep insects away.

Towels

If your towels are stiff and scratchy, see page 496.

Q 'I've got bath towels with tar-like marks on them,' says Diane. 'It's just a strange black mess.'

PROBLEM: Rubber on towels.
WHAT TO USE: Baby oil, white spirits, cotton ball; or *Aerogard*.
HOW TO APPLY: The black marks are probably decomposing rubber from the washing machine seals or plumbing. Soften the stain first with baby oil, then apply white spirits with a cotton ball. As an alternative, spray *Aerogard* directly onto the stain. Then wash normally.

Q 'I've got liquid foundation make-up on my towels,' reports Julie. 'And it won't come out in the wash. What do you suggest?'

PROBLEM: Liquid foundation on towels.
WHAT TO USE: Methylated spirits, dishwashing liquid.
HOW TO APPLY: Mix equal parts methylated spirits and dishwashing liquid and rub into the stain with your fingers. Wash normally.

Bathroom Walls

Moisture and poor ventilation are generally the reasons painted bathroom walls go mouldy. Leave the window open as much as possible and use ceiling vents.

For many, the smell of bleach equates to cleanliness— and while bleach does whiten surfaces, it doesn't necessarily remove dirt and isn't great for the environment or your health. (Bleach contains dioxins that can produce the environmental pollutants trihalomethanes, which are also believed to be carcinogenic.) For a less toxic cleaning option, sprinkle bicarb on a cloth, add some white vinegar and wipe over the walls. Each time you clean, add ¼ teaspoon of oil of cloves to a 1 litre spray pack of water and wipe over the walls. Oil of cloves will prevent mould growing and makes the walls easier to clean. It also has a nice fresh smell.

Q 'We're repainting our bathroom walls,' reports James. 'At the moment, there's quite a bit of mould on them. Is there anything we can use to stop the mould coming back once we've painted?'

PROBLEM: Mould on painted walls.
WHAT TO USE: Hospital-grade bleach, bicarb, white vinegar, sponge.

HOW TO APPLY: Because the mould is so severe, clean the surface twice with hospital-grade bleach. Then wipe bicarb and white vinegar over the walls with a sponge before you paint them to neutralise the bleach. Also use a mould inhibitor such as oil of cloves or a proprietary product before and during the painting.

Drains

Q 'I seem to have gunk down my bathroom drains,' reports Sue. 'How can I unclog them?'

PROBLEM: Clogged drains.
WHAT TO USE: Coat-hanger, pantyhose, bicarb, white vinegar, boiling water.
HOW TO APPLY: Some blockages occur when talcum powder or hair sticks to the inside edge of the drain. To prevent the problem, put gauze or a piece of pantyhose fabric underneath the drain grate. To clean, wrap a pair of pantyhose around the end of a straightened coat-hanger and knot it tightly. Use the coat-hanger just like a big bottle brush to scrub down inside the drain. Now put ½ cup bicarb down the drain and leave for 20 minutes, followed by ½ cup of white vinegar. Leave for half an hour and pour boiling water (from the kettle) down the drain.

Lounge, Dining and Family Rooms

Who doesn't love coming home after a long day, kicking off their shoes and lying back on a comfy couch? And if the remote is within reach, even better. These rooms are the social hub of the home—and in many houses they're combined in one big space. It's a great way to live, but it means that eating, drinking, playing and socialising are happening all through these spaces. Furniture tends to get a lot of use so there's more cleaning to do, particularly if you watch TV while eating and drinking. Someone is going to spill their latte on the couch, an adorable child is going to smear paint over the floor, battalions of muddy shoes are going to mark their path to the TV. Relax! Smile like they do in the cleaning commercials on TV, because we can fix everything! When working out how to fix a spill, think about the components of the stain and the surface it's on. Sort that out and you're on your way to a clean living area.

Unwanted water mark: *Ruth's story*

INCIDENT: *'I have a beautiful antique Chinese opium table that my friend's mother bought in China. But I very foolishly put a vase of flowers on it not knowing the vase was porous. It's left a horrible whitish stain on the table. I've tried to clean it with furniture polish but you can still see a pale circle.'*

SOLUTION: Warm some beeswax in the microwave or put the tin in a bowl of warm water to soften it. Once softened, add a little turpentine to the warmed wax and apply it to the table with a piece of lemon peel, using the outer, yellow side of the peel. Remove the interior of the lemon first so you don't get any juice on the table. Rub the outside of the lemon peel over the stain as though you were polishing with a cloth. Lemon peel contains a very fine oil which acts as a cleaner and is also a mild bleaching agent. Then rub the oil off with a cloth. You may need to do this a couple of times before the white ring is removed. If you need to reseal it, use a water-impermeable shellac.

Feta fall: *Sue's story*

INCIDENT: *'I've got a gorgeous Italian couch covered in microsuede. During a recent soiree, some marinated feta cheese dropped onto the couch. I dampened it with dishwashing liquid and water and there are now watermarks on the fabric. Can it be saved?'*

SOLUTION: To remove the watermark, make a bran ball (see below). Use the bran ball as though it is an eraser and rub over the upholstery in every direction. To remove the oily part of the stain (from the marinade), place a couple of drops of dishwashing liquid on your fingertips and massage into the stain until it feels like jelly. Remove the dishwashing liquid with a damp cloth and dry immediately and thoroughly by pressing with paper towel.

Couch Care

Shannon often sews while sitting on the couch but learned the hard way not to use the armrest as a pincushion!

In some homes, the couch is the most-used piece of furniture. Deal with stains as soon as possible because they become harder to remove when they set. If you're not sure what the stain is, first do a stain diagnosis (see page 577).

To clean upholstery, and other items that can't be put in the washing machine, use a bran ball.

To make a bran ball

Put 1 cup of unprocessed wheat bran in a bowl and add white vinegar, 1 drop at a time, until the mixture resembles brown sugar—it should be clumping but not wet. Place the mixture into the toe of a pair of pantyhose and tie tightly. Rub the pantyhose across the surface as though using an eraser. The bran ball is preferable to carpet cleaner when giving the couch a spruce up because it's gentler on fabrics.

After cleaning the couch, spray with *Scotchgard* (around once a year) to provide a layer of protection. And if you get lots of grubby marks, consider making or buying removable slipcovers that can be put in the washing machine. Much easier!

Vacuum the couch once a week, making sure to clean under and behind cushions. If you're lucky, you might even find some spare change. Every couple of months, remove all cushions and turn the couch upside down. Vacuum any bugs and discover lost items, as Shannon did with a ring once. If you find spider webs under the couch, wipe the corners with some lemon oil to deter future spiders. Insecticide spray works as well, though not everyone likes the fumes.

If yours is a house with four-legged friends, get rid of fur and hair by putting on disposable rubber gloves. Then wash your gloved hands with soap and water. This removes the powder from the gloves. Shake your gloved hands dry and drag them over the fur and hair on the couch. The water on the gloves makes them statically charged and the rubber draws the fur away. Shannon learned this trick after an old English sheepdog followed her home. It was the hairiest dog she'd ever come across and always seemed to drop white hair on dark colours and black hair on light colours. The poor thing had so much hair it used to cough up hairballs. She had the dog until she moved back to the city and found it a new home.

With food spills, always clean up as much as you can with paper towels, working from the outside to the inside of the spill. Remember to remove protein stains first with dishwashing liquid suds and a little cold water, and then deal with fat stains with dishwashing liquid suds and a little hot water. If you remove the fats first, you set the proteins and the task becomes so much harder. If in doubt, always treat the stain as though it has protein in it and use cold water first. If they're just grime stains, use unprocessed wheat bran and white vinegar.

Cushion covers generally need special care. If there's no care label attached, treat them as if they are made of silk. Wash in blood-heat water with a small amount of cheap shampoo and rinse in blood-heat water. Smooth the cover flat and place in the shade to dry. Put them back on when they're almost dry but just slightly damp. They'll be easier to put back on because the fibres are relaxed. No need to iron! If you want to iron cushion covers, always use a cool setting and place a clean cloth between the iron and the cover and, if possible, iron inside out. Don't use starch because they won't mould to the shape of the cushion insert.

To avoid vacuum-cleaner marks on fabric, put an old T-shirt or cloth over the end of the tube or head of the vacuum cleaner and secure with an elastic band. *Scotchgarding* furniture adds another layer of protection and prevents stains.

TIP

Keep paper towel or a Slurpex near your couch to mop up any spills as soon as they happen.

Q 'I have some lovely linen cushion covers with red silk appliqués and red silk cord around the edge,' says Megan. 'One cushion got a black (looked like grease) mark on it and so I hand washed it in cold water. The red silk wasn't colourfast and left orangey coloured splodges on the cushion. And the black mark still remains. Is there anything I can do?'

PROBLEM: Grease and dye on linen.
WHAT TO USE: Dishwashing liquid, cloth, cold water, *Colour Run Remover: Coloursafe*, cloth, salt, bucket.
HOW TO APPLY: To remove the grease mark, add a couple of drops of dishwashing liquid to your fingers and massage into the stain until it feels like jelly. Then wipe over with a cloth wrung out in cold water. To remove the dye run, mix 1 part *Colour Run Remover: Coloursafe* to 5 parts water, wring a cloth in the mixture and sponge over the affected area until the colour is removed. Then rinse in salt water (1 cup of salt per 9 litre bucket of cold water). Hang on the clothesline on a cool day or dry flat in the shade.

SPOTLESS CLASSIC
Pen marks on couch

Even if you don't have children, it's common to get pen marks on your couch. They can be tricky stains to tackle because different pens use different inks and each has a different solvent. As a general rule, biro pen marks are removed with rotten milk solids placed over the ink (see page 572). With permanent markers, write over the stain using the same pen and quickly follow with a cotton bud dipped in white spirits. Repeat until removed. With Artline *pens and whiteboard markers, wipe only over the mark with a cotton bud dipped in methylated spirits and repeat until removed. With fluorescent pens, write over the stain using the same marker quickly followed by a cotton bud dipped in white spirits. If you're not sure, do a test first using a cotton bud and the various solvents.*

COTTON/LINEN

Many people ask how to remove pen stains from fabric. The first thing you need to establish is what kind of ink is in the pen, which will be written on the pen. It's either water-based or spirit-based ink or permanent ink. The treatment is very different, as outlined below.

Q 'My 3-year-old got hold of a black permanent pen and wrote all over the cream furniture,' reports Melinda. 'It's a disaster!'

PROBLEM: Permanent pen on fabric.
WHAT TO USE: White spirits, cotton bud, cotton ball; or *Aerogard* or hairspray, cloth.
HOW TO APPLY: You'll need to do this very carefully and quickly. Apply some white spirits to a cotton bud and write over the permanent pen while also quickly wiping the white spirits off with a cotton ball, replacing it often. You could also spray *Aerogard* or hairspray, and wipe off with a cloth. Be careful with fabric and test a patch first.

PROBLEM: Ink stain on fabric.
WHAT TO USE: Milk, dishwashing liquid, water; or white spirits, cotton ball, talcum powder.
HOW TO APPLY: Rot the milk by leaving it in the sun until solids form. The time this takes varies according to the weather and the age of the milk. Place the solids on the stain, leave until you see the ink start to rise up in the solids, then wash the solids out using dishwashing liquid and water. You can also use white spirits applied with a cotton ball on either side of the stain. If you can't get underneath the stain, sprinkle talcum powder over the white spirits to absorb it.

PROBLEM: Rust stains on fabric.
WHAT TO USE: CLR, water, cotton ball, cotton bud; or salt, lemon juice; or salt, white vinegar, cloth, water.
HOW TO APPLY: Only use CLR if you can get to both sides of the fabric, as you must be able to rinse it off. Dilute 1 part CLR to 20 parts water. Hold a cotton ball on the non-stained side of the fabric and apply diluted CLR to the rust stain with a cotton bud. You will see the rust loosen from the fibres. Then rinse thoroughly with water. For a natural alternative, put salt on the rust then add lemon juice. Leave it to dry then repeat. It could take a few attempts before the rust shifts. Another option is a salt and white vinegar solution. Mix them together to form a thick paste and apply it to the rust mark. When the rust bleeds into the fabric, rinse with water.

Q 'I spilt coffee over the arm of my cotton couch,' reports Louise. 'The fabric can't be removed and I don't know what to do. Can you help?'

PROBLEM: Coffee on cotton.
WHAT TO USE: Glycerine, cotton ball, dishwashing liquid, damp cloth, paper towel.
HOW TO APPLY: Dab a cotton ball with a little glycerine and wipe over the stain. Leave for 20 minutes. Massage a couple of drops of dishwashing liquid into the stain using your

fingers. Wipe off with a damp cloth and dry by pressing with paper towel. Don't use too much moisture. Repeat if necessary.

Q 'My husband fell asleep while holding a glass of red wine and it spilled all over our pale loose linen sofa which had been *Scotchgard*ed,' reports Megan. 'At 3am, he got out my copy of *Spotless* and, in an attempt to undo the damage, proceeded to rub the red wine into the sofa. The care instructions state the linen can only be dry-cleaned. Help, please!'

PROBLEM: Red wine on upholstered linen.
WHAT TO USE: Paper towel or *Slurpex*, bicarb, cloth, white vinegar, vacuum cleaner.
HOW TO APPLY: Remove as much moisture as possible with paper towel or *Slurpex*. Then sprinkle a little bicarb over the area—it will turn a grey colour. Wring a cloth tightly in white vinegar and wipe over the mark. Repeat until the stain is removed. Pat dry with paper towel. If needed, vacuum using the brush attachment when it is dry.

Q 'My daughter has used crayons all over our light beige cotton couch,' reports Margie. 'What can I do?'

PROBLEM: Crayon on cotton.
WHAT TO USE: Pencil eraser, vacuum cleaner, tea tree oil, dishwashing liquid, damp cloth, paper towel.
HOW TO APPLY: Crayon contains wax, so rub over the marks with a pencil eraser then vacuum. Mix 2 drops of tea tree oil with 1 teaspoon of dishwashing liquid and massage over the crayon marks with your fingers until the crayon dissolves, then wipe with a damp cloth. Use as little moisture as possible on the stains. Dry by pressing with paper towel.

PROBLEM: Coloured pencil on cotton.
WHAT TO USE: Pencil eraser, methylated spirits, cotton bud, talcum powder, vacuum cleaner.
HOW TO APPLY: Rub over the pencil marks with a pencil eraser and vacuum. Wipe over the marks with methylated spirits on a cotton bud until the colour bleeds. Now cover with talcum powder. When the talcum powder dries, vacuum. Repeat if necessary.

PROBLEM: Oil on cotton.
WHAT TO USE: Dishwashing liquid, damp cloth, paper towel.
HOW TO APPLY: Put a couple of drops of dishwashing liquid on your fingertips and massage into the oil until it feels like jelly. Wipe repeatedly with a damp cloth and dry by pressing with paper towel.

PROBLEM: Steam cleaning didn't remove tea stains on cotton.
WHAT TO USE: Glycerine, cloth, white vinegar.
HOW TO APPLY: When you steam clean tea stains, it sets them into the fabric. To unset them, put a couple of drops of glycerine on a cloth and wipe over the stain. Leave for 20 minutes. Tightly wring out a cloth in white vinegar and wipe over the glycerine. Repeat until the stain is gone and wipe with a cold damp cloth before drying thoroughly.

Q 'I've got ear drop stains on my fabric chair,' reports Pat. 'What should I do?'

PROBLEM: Eardrops on cotton.
WHAT TO USE: Bran ball.
HOW TO APPLY: Wipe a bran ball (see page 138) over the ear drops.

Q 'I've got a lounge with a cotton valance around the bottom of it and it's got scuff marks from people's shoes on it. How do I get the marks off?' asks Lisa.

PROBLEM: Scuff marks on fabric.
WHAT TO USE: White spirits, cotton balls, methylated spirits or dishwashing liquid suds.

HOW TO APPLY: Apply white spirits to the scuff marks with a cotton ball. Use clean cotton balls on either side of the fabric and work the top cotton ball from the outside of the stain to the inside of the stain. If the white spirits leaves a smell, neutralise it with methylated spirits or dishwashing liquid suds.

Q 'My children were playing with lipstick and got some over the fabric ottoman,' reports Magda. 'Can I get it off?'

PROBLEM: Lipstick on fabric.
WHAT TO USE: Glycerine, cotton ball.
HOW TO APPLY: Put some glycerine on a cotton ball and wipe from the outside to the inside of the stain. Just make sure you don't get the fabric too wet.

Q 'My husband likes to read the newspaper in the lounge chair. But I've noticed that his chair has become really grubby on the arms from the newspaper ink. It's covered in a cream cotton fabric. Is there anything I can do?' asks June.

PROBLEM: Dirty marks on fabric.
WHAT TO USE: White vinegar, sponge, unprocessed wheat bran, handkerchief or muslin cloth; unprocessed wheat bran, white vinegar, bowl, soft brush.

Lounge, Dining and Family Rooms 149

HOW TO APPLY: For lighter marks, gently damp the dirty section of the chair with white vinegar on a sponge. Then wrap some bran in a handkerchief or muslin cloth and rub it over the damp section. For dirtier marks, dampen the bran with white vinegar in a bowl until it just starts to clump together (add white vinegar one drop at a time and mix thoroughly). The bran grains should be clumping, but not wet or sticky. If the fabric is really dirty, damp the whole area with white vinegar, then throw raw bran over the top and sweep backwards and forwards with a soft brush. Bran is a scourer and very absorbent.

PROBLEM: Oily stain on fabric.
WHAT TO USE: Dishwashing liquid, water, cloth or old toothbrush, paper towel.
HOW TO APPLY: The best way to remove oily stains from absorbent fabric is to put 2 drops of dishwashing liquid on your fingers and rub it into the stain until it feels like jelly. This emulsifies the stain and it rinses out in cold water.

PROBLEM: Cigarette smells in furniture.
WHAT TO USE: Bicarb, wooden spoon, vacuum cleaner.

HOW TO APPLY: Sprinkle the upholstery with bicarb then beat it with a wooden spoon. Once you've finished beating, vacuum the bicarb off.

BROCADE

Brocade is an intricately woven fabric made from any fibre. The weave is very fine so special care must be taken when cleaning it. Use white vinegar and unprocessed wheat bran as for 'Dirty marks on fabric' on page 148 to clean it, or go to a professional cleaner.

Q 'I was lucky enough to inherit my granny's antique chair, which is covered in brocade. But she must have had a leaking hot-water bottle because the chair is covered in water stains. What should I do?' asks Brenda.

PROBLEM: Water marks in fabric.
WHAT TO USE: Sponge, white vinegar, unprocessed wheat bran, muslin; or clean handkerchief, soft brush, vacuum cleaner.
HOW TO APPLY: Dampen the water marks with a sponge soaked in white vinegar, then wrap some bran in muslin or a clean handkerchief and wipe it over the vinegar. If the stains are really stubborn, you may need to apply the bran directly. Heap it over the vinegar, brush with a soft brush then vacuum off.

MICROSUEDE, MACROSUEDE, SUPERSUEDE AND NUBUCK

These popular coverings are usually treated to repel spills and stains. Whatever you do, don't use upholstery cleaner on these fabrics or it will leave a watermark and cause warping. Instead, clean with a bran ball (see page 138).

Q 'My budding artist left a mural on the microsuede lounge with a child's *Texta* pen,' says Jayne. 'The colour is mid-green. Can you help me?'

PROBLEM: *Texta* on microsuede.
WHAT TO USE: Cotton bud, methylated spirits, paper towel, cotton ball.
HOW TO APPLY: Dip a cotton bud in methylated spirits, wipe over the *Texta* mark and press with paper towel. The *Texta* will transfer to the paper towel. Repeat until removed. If you can, place a cotton ball behind the stain to stop it spreading through the fabric.

PROBLEM: Felt-tip pen on nubuck.
WHAT TO USE: White spirits, cotton bud, talcum powder, vacuum cleaner; or methylated spirits, cotton bud, paper towel.

HOW TO APPLY: What to use will depend on the type of ink. First, try white spirits on a cotton bud and wipe over the mark. Then apply talcum powder over the white spirits. Leave to dry and vacuum. If this doesn't work, use methylated spirits on a cotton bud and wipe over the mark. Press with paper towel until dry.

Q *'I was eating melted cheese on toast,' reports Larry. 'And some of the hot melted cheese landed on my microsuede lounge. What can I do?'*

PROBLEM: Melted cheese on microsuede.
WHAT TO USE: Ice-cubes, zip-lock bag, plastic knife, dishwashing liquid, damp cloth, paper towel.
HOW TO APPLY: Put an ice-cube in a zip-lock bag and place over the cheese. When the cheese is hard, remove the ice and scrape off the cheese with a plastic knife. To remove the oily smear, put a couple of drops of dishwashing liquid on your fingers and massage into the stain until it feels like jelly. Wipe over with a damp cloth and dry by pressing with paper towel.

Q *'How do you remove crayon from microsuede fabric?'*

PROBLEM: Crayon on microsuede.
WHAT TO USE: Brown bread, tea tree oil, pantyhose.

HOW TO APPLY: Crayon has wax in it so rub the mark with brown bread. If any crayon remains, wipe with a couple of drops of tea tree oil on pantyhose.

Q *'I've got 10 years' worth of sweat and body oil on a nubuck lounge,' says Mike. 'Is it time to recover it or can you save my beloved lounge/recliner?'*

PROBLEM: Sweat/body oil on nubuck.
WHAT TO USE: Bran ball, dishwashing liquid, damp cloth, paper towel.
HOW TO APPLY: Rub a bran ball (see page 138) over the affected area until it's clean. For any oily spots, massage in a little dishwashing liquid using your fingers until it feels like jelly, then wipe with a damp cloth. Dry by pressing with paper towel.

Q *'I spilt nail polish on a microsuede couch,' says Margaret. 'What can I do?'*

PROBLEM: Nail polish on microsuede.
WHAT TO USE: Acetone, cotton bud, methylated spirits or white vinegar, cloth.
HOW TO APPLY: Rub a little acetone (not nail polish remover) on a cotton bud over the nail polish. Once the polish has been removed, wipe over the spot with a little

methylated spirits or white vinegar on a cloth to remove the acetone. This must be done quickly or the acetone could damage the fibres in the fabric.

JACQUARD

Q 'A recent visitor was breastfeeding her baby on my jacquard chair and the baby regurgitated milk on it,' says Karen. 'It has a dark stain that I can't seem to get out. What do you suggest?'

PROBLEM: Baby milk vomit on jacquard.
WHAT TO USE: Cake of bathroom soap, cold water, damp cloth, bran ball.
HOW TO APPLY: If the stain has a dark edging, it's a protein stain. To remove, run a cake of bathroom soap under cold water and using it like a big crayon, scribble over the stain and wipe with a damp cloth. Press with paper towel to absorb moisture. If there's a watermark, rub a bran ball (see page 138) over the stain until removed.

TAPESTRY

Shannon used to do a lot of tapestries and petit point. Tapestry can be delicate so take care when cleaning it. The best way to clean tapestry is with dry unprocessed wheat bran, which will absorb the dirt. Rub a bran ball (see page 138) over upholstery. For smaller items, such as cushion covers, put 1 cup of unprocessed wheat bran inside a pillowcase. Place the tapestry in the pillowcase, close the top and shake vigorously—the bran acts as a scourer. Remove the tapestry (over a bin or outside) and shake away the bran.

Q 'I've got a piano stool that is covered in a wool tapestry,' says Shirley. 'It was a wedding gift from my aunt 50 years ago. And after years of use, you can hardly see the flowers any more. Can it be cleaned?'

PROBLEM: Dirty tapestry.

WHAT TO USE: Unprocessed wheat bran; or heavy cotton, woolwash, bucket.

HOW TO APPLY: Try cleaning it with bran as outlined above. If that doesn't work, test it for colourfastness by soaking a white cloth in white vinegar and applying to a small, less noticeable portion of the tapestry. If any colour comes off, it is not colourfast. If it is colourfast, remove the tapestry from the stool and stitch it to a piece of heavy cotton. Hand wash it in 1 teaspoon of woolwash or shampoo to a bucket of blood-heat water, then completely rinse the piece in blood-heat water before drying it in the shade. You can unstitch the cotton backing or leave it on. Either way, replace the tapestry on the stool while the cotton is still slightly damp because it will have more stretch. If it's not colourfast, take it to a restorer.

Make your own woolwash

You can make your own woolwash with 2 tablespoons of pure soap flakes, ½ cup of cheap hair conditioner and 2–3 drops of eucalyptus oil. Mix with a little warm water or put into a jar and shake. One teaspoon of this mixture is enough for a bucket of jumpers.

VELVET

In the 1960s, velvet was really fashionable. Shannon used to go to furniture upholsterers and use their offcuts to create clothes, particularly waistcoats. But velvet is one of the hardest fabrics to clean. Start by trying to remove as much fluff as possible. Wear disposable rubber gloves, wash your hands in soapy water, shake dry and rub the gloves over the velvet. The fluff should stick to the gloves. After you've removed as much as possible, give the velvet a light spray with a carpet cleaner. Leave it to dry then vacuum the carpet cleaner off.

PROBLEM: Grease stain on velvet.
WHAT TO USE: Bicarb, bristle brush, vacuum cleaner.
HOW TO APPLY: Sprinkle the stain with bicarb then brush it gently backwards and forwards with a bristle brush, not a nylon brush. Leave it for 10 minutes then vacuum or brush firmly.

Q 'I've got a water mark on my velvet couch which has made the velvet bits go all hard and bristly,' says Belinda. 'Can it be repaired?'

PROBLEM: Water mark on velvet.
WHAT TO USE: Bowl, unprocessed wheat bran, white vinegar, brush, vacuum cleaner.
HOW TO APPLY: In a bowl, mix bran with drops of white vinegar until it's just damp but not clumpy. Then apply the mixture to the water mark with your fingers and leave for a few minutes. Brush the area in circles and leave to dry. Then vacuum the bran.

PROBLEM: Bald patch in velvet.
WHAT TO USE: Matches, stranded cotton or silk, tufting tool.
HOW TO APPLY: First, you need to determine what the velvet is made of. Test a patch along a seam using the head of a hot match. If the fabric smells like burnt hair, it's cotton or silk. If it smells of plastic, it's polyester. Cotton has a matt finish. Silk has a high sheen. Find matching fabric, then use a tufting tool to stab and loop the fibres through the bald patch. (Tufting tools come with easy instructions but practise on a scrap piece of fabric first.) Then trim the cotton or silk threads to the same height as the velvet with sharp scissors. Embroidery or manicure scissors should do the job.

WOOL

The best way to clean a woollen lounge is with a bran ball (see page 138). If there's staining, put a small amount of cheap shampoo on your fingertips and massage into the stain. Wipe with a damp cloth and dry by pressing with paper towel. Don't use a hair dryer to dry wool because it will cause puckering.

LEATHER

If you think about it, leather is just toughened skin and like any skin it needs to be kept moist. To keep it looking good, clean leather couches once a week. Use a good quality leather conditioner but don't apply too much; 1 teaspoon impregnated in a cloth is enough for an entire couch. Keep a dedicated cloth in a plastic zip-lock bag for this purpose. Never use water to clean leather because it stiffens it. And always secure a cloth or T-shirt over the vacuum-cleaner head to prevent scratches in the leather.

Deal with any scratches first with shoe cream (not shoe polish) in a matching colour (available from shoe repair shops). After applying the shoe cream, rub the scratches with the back of a warmed stainless steel spoon to set the shoe cream and prevent it getting on your clothes. Now use a good quality leather conditioner and cleaner—it should feel like a moisturiser you'd be happy to put on your own skin. Place a small amount (again, don't overuse the product) onto a cloth and warm in the microwave in 10-second bursts so the conditioner melts into the cloth. When you've finished conditioning the couch, put the cloth into a zip-lock bag and seal it ready to use at the next cleaning session.

Most stains can be removed with white spirits. After applying the fluid with a cotton ball, sprinkle talcum powder to absorb it. Brush off the talcum powder when it's dry and treat with leather conditioner. Never use toothpaste as it can leave dry, rough or bleached spots.

Leather reacts differently if it's been waxed, plasticised or oiled so work this out before tackling any stains. To do this, place a single bead of water on an inconspicuous part of the leather. If the water rolls off, the leather coating is plasticised. If the water soaks into the leather, it's not sealed. If the water soaks in slowly, it's waxed.

Q 'I'm so cranky,' says Lynne. 'The kids sat on my dark brown leather lounge in their swimming costumes and the chlorine has faded the leather. Is there anything I can do?'

PROBLEM: Bleached brown leather.
WHAT TO USE: Walnuts, leather conditioner; or shoe cream, warm stainless steel spoon.
HOW TO APPLY: This only works with brown leather. Break a fresh walnut in half and rub the nut over the faded area.

Now apply a good quality leather conditioner to bring back the sheen of the leather. For lighter-coloured leather, use shoe cream in a matching colour and wipe over the stain. To set the colour, rub with the back of a warm stainless steel spoon.

Q 'What's the best way to remove nail polish from a leather lounge?' asks Claire.

PROBLEM: Nail polish on leather.
WHAT TO USE: Talcum powder, acetone, cotton bud, white vinegar, cloth, vacuum cleaner, leather conditioner.
HOW TO APPLY: Make a ring of talcum powder around the nail polish mark to protect the leather around the stain. Dip a cotton bud in acetone and wipe over the nail polish, then wipe straight away with a clean cotton bud. Repeat this process until the nail polish is removed. To neutralise the acetone, wipe with white vinegar on a cotton bud and sprinkle on talcum powder. When it dries, brush away with the back of your hand or vacuum. To finish, apply a small amount of quality leather conditioner.

Q 'I've got blue biro on a leather sofa,' reports Margaret. 'I did a test using methylated spirits and found some of the maroon colour came off on my white cloth. What should I do?'

PROBLEM: Biro on leather.

WHAT TO USE: Cotton bud, white spirits, talcum powder, leather conditioner.

HOW TO APPLY: It was a good idea to do a test first. It's best not to use methylated spirits on leather unless it's been plasticised. Instead, dip a cotton bud in white spirits and write over the biro. Sprinkle on talcum powder and brush away with the back of your hand when dry. Apply leather conditioner.

Q '**Can you tell me how to remove the dye from blue denim on my white leather couch and cream leather car seats please?**' asks Monica.

PROBLEM: Dye on leather.

WHAT TO USE: *Colour Run Remover: Whites*, water, cloth, talcum powder, leather conditioner.

HOW TO APPLY: To remove dye, use *Colour Run Remover: Whites*, which is available in the laundry aisle at the supermarket. Mix 1 part *Colour Run Remover* to 20 parts water and wipe over the stain with a cloth. Have a dry cloth in your other hand and wipe hand over hand. Sprinkle with talcum powder and brush away when dry. When finished, apply a little quality leather conditioner.

TIP

To prevent dye from running in fabric clothes (not leather or suede), wash in a heavy salt solution (1 kg of non-iodised salt per 9 litres of water).

Q 'I was making a correction really quickly,' says Jill, 'and accidentally spilled white-out on a leather lounge. Is it removable?'

PROBLEM: White-out on leather.
WHAT TO USE: White-out thinner, leather conditioner.
HOW TO APPLY: Apply the white-out thinner then resurface immediately with leather conditioner.

PROBLEM: Dog and cat scratches in dark-brown leather.
WHAT TO USE: Walnut; or shoe cream, cloth, leather dew; or camphor, mothballs and holder, lavender oil or lavender bags.
HOW TO APPLY: Remove the walnut from its shell, if it has one, and cut it in half. Then rub the cut walnut over the scratch so that its oils coat the scratch. Leave for 1 hour for the colour to cure. If the couch isn't brown leather, choose an appropriately coloured shoe cream but not shoe polish or wax. Apply the shoe cream with a cloth. It only feeds the areas that need it. After that, apply leather dew with a cloth to soften.

PREVENTION: Scatter camphor at the back of the couch, underneath the cushions, to deter a cat. You could also tuck a mothball holder between the cushions. Use lavender oil or lavender bags behind the seat cushions to deter a dog.

Q 'My daughter splashed some paint on our leather barstools,' reports Erin. 'I didn't notice for a couple of days and have tried to remove the stains with soap and water and then methylated spirits. But all I have done is make an ugly mark from the methylated spirits and the paint spots are still there. Can you help?'

PROBLEM: Paint on leather.
WHAT TO USE: Tea tree oil, white vinegar, pantyhose, white spirits, cotton ball, walnut or shoe cream, warm stainless steel spoon, leather conditioner.
HOW TO APPLY: The leather on barstools is high in wax so wipe with equal parts tea tree oil and white vinegar on pantyhose. Follow with a cotton ball dipped in white spirits. If the barstool is brown and colour comes away, break a walnut in half and rub the inside over the mark. For barstools in other colours, use shoe cream in a matching colour and apply with the back of a warmed spoon. When clean, rub on a small amount of quality leather conditioner.

THE UNEXPECTED

Q 'Our lounge room ceiling recently collapsed. Now fine plaster powder and insulating rockwool material have become ingrained in the black leather of the lounge chairs. I have vacuumed and cleaned three times with leather cream but the chairs still retain the powder and look a dirty grey in parts. Any ideas?'

A The leather cream has actually made the powder stick to the leather. To remove the dust, put an old sheet on the ground and turn your lounge upside down over it. Then shake the couch until all the plaster is removed. To remove the leather cream, use a good quality saddle soap. Each saddle soap uses a different technique, so follow the manufacturer's directions. Resurface the leather by rubbing with a matching tinted leather cream using the back of a warm stainless steel spoon.

VINYL

Q 'What's the best way to get rid of cigarette smoke smell in a vinyl-covered chair?' asks Samuel.

PROBLEM: Cigarette smoke smell in vinyl.
WHAT TO USE: Bicarb, disposable rubber gloves, white vinegar, cigarette ash, cloth.

HOW TO APPLY: Take the chair outside and turn it upside down. Sprinkle bicarb inside the chair and shake so the bicarb spreads throughout the chair. Leave for 20 minutes, turn the chair upright and shake out the bicarb. Put on rubber gloves and clean the vinyl surface with equal parts bicarb, white vinegar and cigarette ash on a cloth (be careful because the mixture can burn your skin). Follow by wiping thoroughly with a damp cloth.

Throws

Throws—or 'threws', as Trude and Prue call them—are a great way to change the look of a couch and keep you warm in winter. Mohair is a popular choice but it sheds and leaves hairs over your couch. The best way to minimise shedding is to wash the throw in a little cheap shampoo and blood-heat water. Then rinse in a little cheap hair conditioner and blood-heat water. The water temperature must be the same. Dry in the shade. When dry, place in a plastic bag and put into the freezer for half an hour. Cold fibres don't frizz or shed as easily.

Cane, Bamboo, Wicker and Water Hyacinth

Cane tends to be a very popular restoration item. Shannon's family has a set of early Victorian cane baby furniture that has been passed from family to family. The best way to clean cane, bamboo, wicker and water hyacinth is with a salt solution (1 cup of non-iodised salt per 9 litre bucket of water) on a cloth. Remove any residual water by wiping with a towel. Don't use soap or dishwashing liquid because they can swell the cane and dry it out, making it vulnerable to splitting.

How to fix a hole in cane furniture

Use some matching or similar cane that is longer than the hole you're repairing. Make it into single canes and soak in hot water. Then reweave the cane starting where the original cane is still solid. Don't cut the old pieces until it's been rewoven. Tuck the ends in and down at the end of each row. If you're replacing a seat, tack some outdoor canvas to the underside of the chair for reinforcement. Use spray paint rather than a brush to paint the cane. Revarnish with shellac in a spray bottle rather than enamel or polyurethane. One of the nicest things about cane furniture is its ability to flex and mould to the sitter. That's the squeaking sound you hear. Enamel and polyurethane weld the cane together as a solid block and you lose that comfort. They are also hard to remove if you decide you don't like the colour or if they get damaged. Shellac comes in a range of colours and is removable if you decide you don't like the colour.

Metal-framed Furniture

Chrome and stainless steel furniture can be cleaned with white vinegar and water on a cloth. If it's very dirty, use bicarb and white vinegar. Clean wrought iron with bicarb and white vinegar then wipe it either with baby oil or sewing machine oil. If it's painted, clean it with dishwashing liquid and water. To create a high sheen and to prevent rust and corrosion, clean metals with car polish. To clean aluminium, use cold black tea on a cloth. To remove rust from painted wrought iron, use steel wool and turpentine.

Timber Furniture

When cleaning timber, it is important to remember that you are cleaning the surface not the core. Timber can be sealed in polyurethane, varnish, shellac or beeswax. To identify the surface and use the appropriate solution, see page 572 for instructions. To remove scratches in polyurethane, use *Brasso* on a cloth and rub along the grain using speed, not pressure. It will look worse before it looks better.

One of the great things Shannon has found about being a restorer is learning what all the expensive cleaning products are made of. She discovered that furniture polishes are based either on lemon peel and beeswax, orange peel and beeswax, carnauba wax or silicone. Now you can make polish yourself! Be aware, though, that different timber finishes require different kinds of cleaning.

Lacquer is made with layers of rice paper, plant resin, mineral dyes and vegetable gum and is difficult to keep in good condition. It should never be kept at less than 30 per cent humidity or it will dry out and crack. If it's in a dry spot, put a large bowl of water under it or place potted plants around it to create your own mini tropical climate. Use a damp cloth, never wet, to clean it. Never use detergents and see a specialist restorer for any significant problems. Small chips in black items can be covered with black boot polish.

Laminate can be cleaned with bicarb and white vinegar.

Polyurethane can be cleaned with a damp cloth. For very dirty surfaces, use dishwashing liquid. Keep water away from scratched surfaces. To repair any bubbling, inject with a syringe under each bubble a small quantity of 1 part *Aquadhere* and 20 parts water. Put clingwrap over the bubble and weight it with a book or block. Leave for some time to allow it to dry.

Clean **shellac** with a good quality, silicone-free furniture polish or beeswax.

Varnish should be cleaned with a good quality, silicone-free furniture polish. If you have oily or grimy patches, scatter damp tea leaves over the stain and allow the tannins to break down and absorb the grime. Then polish with silicone-free furniture polish or beeswax.

Veneer should be cleaned with a good quality, silicone-free furniture polish applied with a soft cloth. Keep away from direct sunlight or the edges will lift.

If the wood on your new furniture is too shiny, wipe a mixture of talcum powder and cornflour over the surface with a piece of silk. If the wood is scratched and you would like to soften the mark, dampen the silk with white vinegar first. Damp silk is more abrasive.

PROBLEM: Scratches in timber.
WHAT TO USE: Baby oil; or coloured wax crayons, soft dry cloth.
HOW TO APPLY: Baby oil is great for taking out small scratches and stains in timberwork. For larger scratches, use coloured crayons that are made of wax. Mix colours to match your timber and draw over the scratch. Then lightly polish with a soft dry cloth.

PROBLEM: Scratches on polyurethane.
WHAT TO USE: Cornflour, silk bag, cloth; or *Brasso*.
HOW TO APPLY: Put cornflour into a silk bag and dampen it so that the cornflour works its way into the silk. This will act as a mild cutting agent. Rub the bag over the scratches then polish any residue off with a dry cloth. You can also polish with *Brasso*.

PROBLEM: Heat marks.

WHAT TO USE: Beeswax, lemon peel; or bicarb, olive oil, cloth.

HOW TO APPLY: If the damage isn't too bad, use some warmed beeswax applied with the yellow side of the lemon peel (remove the flesh first). If it's quite damaged, use a mixture of 1 part bicarb and 1 part olive oil, paint it onto the mark, leave for a few minutes, then polish it off with a cloth before polishing normally.

PROBLEM: Small amount of borer in furniture.

WHAT TO USE: *WD-40*; or old towels, kerosene, creosote, chemical resistant plastic, sawdust, fine sandpaper, *Aquadhere*.

HOW TO APPLY: Place the skinny nozzle of the *WD-40* can on each hole in the furniture and give a quick squirt. If there are more than ten holes, wrap the affected timber in old towels until the entire surface is covered, then pour a mixture of 10 parts kerosene and 1 part creosote over the towels. Wrap the area in chemical-resistant plastic and leave for 2–3 days. Be aware that this will remove any paint on the surface. Remove the plastic and towels, then finely sand back the timber. You may have to fill some of the holes created by the borer. The best way to do this is with sawdust. Finely sand a section of the timber on the underside or where it will not be seen. Then mix the sawdust with *Aquadhere* to the consistency of stiff peanut butter and fill the borer holes with it. Sand it smooth.

PROBLEM: White stain on dark timber.
WHAT TO USE: Beeswax, turpentine, lemon peel or orange peel; or walnut juice; or toothpaste.
HOW TO APPLY: The amount you need depends on how big the stain is. Warm 1 teaspoon of beeswax either in the microwave or by putting the tin in a small bowl of warm water. Mix it with 2–3 drops of turpentine. Then apply the mixture to the white stain with the outside or yellow part of a lemon peel. Take the inside of the lemon out first or the acid from the juice will bleach the timber. The oils and acids in the lemon are bleaching and moisturising agents. Orange peel works better with red cedar. Another technique involves cutting an unshelled walnut in half and rubbing the walnut over the white stain to darken it. One of the oldest ways to remove water rings from shellac is with toothpaste. Toothpaste is a mild abrasive and creates tiny holes over the water spot. When you wax it, the wax gets in behind where the stain was and fills up the air cavities.

Q 'I hosted a dinner party the other night which went really well except candle wax dropped onto the dining table,' says Jane. 'How can I get it off without damaging the timber?'

PROBLEM: Candle wax on timber.

WHAT TO USE: Ice, soft scraper, silk cloth, paper towel, hair dryer, rubber gloves.

HOW TO APPLY: Harden the wax with ice, then remove as much as possible with a soft scraper. Make sure you scrape along the grain of the timber. Rub the rest of the wax off with a damp silk cloth. Make sure it's real silk. If the wax has dripped onto unsealed timber, remove as much as possible with the silk cloth, then press a paper towel over the wax and heat with a hair dryer, keeping the paper towel over the wax as you dry. The wax will be absorbed by the paper towel. Keep changing the paper towel until the wax is completely removed. Wear rubber gloves so you don't get burnt fingers. Use a stop–start method so you don't overheat the timber and allow it to cool between each paper towel.

Q 'I've got some wax on a French-polished table,' says Carole. 'Can I get it off without ruining the polish?'

PROBLEM: Wax on polished timber.

WHAT TO USE: Warmed silk.

HOW TO APPLY: You must use pure silk. Warm the silk first by wetting it and then placing it in the microwave. Then rub it over the wax. You can use a dry piece of silk but it will take longer to remove the wax.

Lounge, Dining and Family Rooms 173

PROBLEM: Veneer lifting or bubbling.
WHAT TO USE: Syringe, *Aquadhere*, water, cloths.
HOW TO APPLY: Fill a syringe with 1 part *Aquadhere* to 20 parts water. The mixture should be the consistency of runny cream. Inject a small quantity into the centre of the bubble or underneath the edge of the piece that is lifting, then press down. Place a weight, such as a heavy book, on it while it dries. (Use a piece of clingwrap to protect the book.) To cover the injection hole mark, rub it with a hot damp cloth, leave it to dry and then polish with a dry cloth.

Q 'I've got an old sewing machine with a timber surface,' says Jan, 'but the veneer is cracking. Can it be fixed?'

PROBLEM: Cracks in timber veneer.
WHAT TO USE: Shellac, methylated spirits, cloth, 0000 steel wool; or *Aquadhere*, syringe, 0000 steel wool, methylated spirits, evenly bristled brush or sponge.
HOW TO APPLY: If only the varnish is cracked, apply a new coat of shellac. For pre-mixed shellac, use 1 part methylated spirits to 4 parts shellac. If the shellac is not pre-mixed, mix shellac flakes and methylated spirits to the consistency of milk and apply with a cloth. The shellac will seep into the cracks and create a seal. It may need two or three coats. Allow each coat to dry for 24 hours before applying the

next coat. Sand between coats with 0000 steel wool dipped in methylated spirits. If the surface is badly bubbled, use *Aquadhere* and a syringe as described in 'Veneer lifting or bubbling' on page 173. Once it's dry, dip 0000 steel wool in methylated spirits and rub it along the grain. Then apply shellac with an evenly bristled brush or sponge along the grain. Allow to dry between coats.

Q 'I have an unsealed timber coffee table,' says Sandy. 'And there are many water stains on it from glasses and cups. How can I remove the staining?'

PROBLEM: Water marks on timber.
WHAT TO USE: Pantyhose, cold strong black tea, beeswax or carnauba wax.
HOW TO APPLY: To replace the tannins in the bleached area and clean away fat and grime, scrub with a pair of pantyhose dipped in cold black tea. Polish with a fine coating of beeswax or carnauba wax.
PREVENTION: Protect timber surfaces with coasters.

Q 'My son ate greasy takeaway fish and chips at the coffee table,' explains Julie. 'And it's left a white cloudy stain on the timber. Can you suggest a solution?'

PROBLEM: Cloudy stain on timber.
WHAT TO USE: *Brasso*, cloth; or beeswax, lemon peel.
HOW TO APPLY: The heat has created tiny bubbles on the surface of the coffee table. To repair the timber, first work out what the table is sealed with (see page 572). If it's sealed with polyurethane, rub a small amount of *Brasso* on a cloth in the direction of the grain. It will look worse before it looks better. Just keep rubbing but don't add any more *Brasso*. If the surface is sealed in varnish, shellac or wax, apply warmed beeswax with the yellow side of a piece of lemon peel, rubbing in the direction of the grain. Work quickly.

Q 'I'm restoring a kauri pine chest of drawers,' says Martin. 'It's covered in shellac that is hard to get off. What do you suggest?'

PROBLEM: Removing shellac.
WHAT TO USE: Cotton or linen fabric, methylated spirits, clingwrap, 0000 steel wool.
HOW TO APPLY: Soak some cotton or linen fabric in methylated spirits so it's drenched. Lay it on the section of shellac you want to remove and leave for a while. The methylated spirits will break down the shellac and make it easier to remove. Methylated spirits evaporates very quickly so place clingwrap over the fabric to slow the evaporation.

Then scrub the shellac with 0000 steel wool dipped in methylated spirits. Alternatively, paint the drawers with methylated spirits and wrap them in clingwrap before scouring.

PROBLEM: Sticking drawers.
WHAT TO USE: Soap or candle wax; or spirit level, cardboard or block of wood, glue.
HOW TO APPLY: Rub the soap or candle wax along the runners. If this doesn't work, your chest of drawers may not be level. Check by using a spirit level, and if it's not even, put some cardboard or a block of wood under one of the legs. Also check that the joints of the drawer itself are secure. Re-glue them if they are loose.

Ornaments

Ornaments may be worth a lot of money, have sentimental value or simply be a decorating touch. They are lovely to look at but a challenge to clean with dust easily finding its way into every nook and cranny.

Brass should be cleaned using a proprietary cleaner. If you're coating it, use shellac because it can be removed more easily. Be aware that brass will tarnish even after being coated but the coating will help it last a little longer.

Bronze should be cleaned with a damp soapy cloth but never rub bronze or you'll remove the patina.

China ornaments require a little attention, particularly because dust can cause surfaces to craze. Whether they're clean or dirty, china pieces should be cleaned every six months. For an easy clean, add a tiny amount of sweet almond oil to a paintbrush and wipe over the dusty area. The dust will stick to the oil. If it's stubborn dust, aim a hair dryer on a low setting over the dust and use sweet almond oil on a small paintbrush for difficult-to-reach areas. Keep a small container of water in display cabinets so the pieces don't dry out and never put your cabinet against an exterior wall because heat or cold will come through. A constant temperature is best for china. Secure items vulnerable to bumping by putting *Blu-Tack* underneath them.

Clay ornaments should be vacuumed and dusted regularly. Never soak because clay absorbs moisture. If you wash, do so quickly and dry thoroughly so you don't lift the glaze.

Cloisonné is enamel fused into small wire pockets on the outside of a bronze, brass or copper vessel. Clean it with white vinegar and water. Never use soaps because it will tarnish.

Embroidery, where possible, should be kept out of direct sunlight. Keep it covered and inside cabinets. Hand wash gently if it's colourfast. If not, take it to a restorer or good dry-cleaner.

Ephemera should be kept as flat as possible under glass or in cabinets. Spray fabric with surface insecticide spray to keep bugs away.

Fabrics should be treated as you would your best table linen. Keep them well dusted and, where possible, vacuum.

Ivory can be cleaned with sweet almond oil applied with a cloth.

Lace should be hand washed in pure soap and rinsed very well. Glue medical gauze underneath a hole to hold it until you're ready to repair it properly. Embroider over the gauze in the same pattern as the lace and trim away any excess gauze.

Paper must be kept dust free and out of direct sunlight. Wash carefully with a slightly damp cloth. Just dab rather than wipe the paper. If in doubt, use a restorer or conservator.

Silver can be cleaned using a proprietary cleaner or bicarb and white vinegar. Polish with unprocessed wheat bran.

Timber can, if it's sealed, be cleaned using a good silicone-free furniture polish. If it's unsealed, clean with furniture oil.

Tinware can be wiped with warm soapy water and then dried thoroughly with a rag dampened with sewing machine oil. This will prevent rust. If tin does rust, apply *WD-40* with a cloth. To stop bugs eating paper labels on tinware, wipe the labels with a damp tea bag.

Q 'My daughter brought home some copper Buddha heads from Thailand,' says Katie.

'We sprayed them with a surface spray to get rid of any bugs, and black spots formed from the spray. Can we fix them?'

PROBLEM: Tarnished metal.
WHAT TO USE: Bicarb, white vinegar, cloths.
HOW TO APPLY: Make a paste with 1 part bicarb and 1 part white vinegar and apply it to the tarnish marks with a cloth. Don't get it on other surfaces or it will scratch. Allow the paste to dry then buff it off with a clean, dry cloth.

Glass Tabletops

Clean glass with methylated spirits and a cloth. Then wipe the glass with a paper towel until it squeaks. Never use furniture polish on glass and see a restorer for scratches.

Marble Tabletops

Q 'I've got water marks from leaving cups of tea on my marble-top table,' reveals Jocelyn. 'Can they be fixed?'

PROBLEM: Water marks in marble.
WHAT TO USE: Bicarb, white vinegar, water, soft brush.
HOW TO APPLY: Sprinkle bicarb over the stain, then mix 1 part white vinegar to 5 parts water and sprinkle it over the bicarb. When the mixture fizzes, rub with a soft brush.

Oriental Furniture

Oriental and Asian lacquered furniture can be difficult to clean. Never use heavy polishes because they can react with the lacquer and cause a bloom. If the surface is sticky, clean with pantyhose and a little skim milk and polish with a soft dry cloth. Use a little carnauba wax and beeswax on a cloth and polish over the whole surface. You can remove a build-up of wax with warmed pantyhose (put in the microwave for 10 seconds—no longer or they will melt). Polish in circles using speed, not pressure. Put potted plants near the furniture to provide humidity. If the plants start to die, the air is too dry and they need additional watering. You'll save the plant and be able to monitor the room's humidity.

TIP
Use skim milk to polish lacquered timber.

Fireplaces

If your fireplace is operational, clean it after each use. To clean the surrounds, simply dust the area. To clean grime from anything except timber surfaces, use white vinegar.

To work out when it's time to call the chimney sweep, scrape a fingernail on the inside of a cold chimney. If soot flakes off, rather than smears off, it's time for a clean. Other clues are excess smoke from the fire and soot falling down the chimney into the fireplace. Bronze, copper, brass, white metal, tin and iron are best cleaned with bicarb and white vinegar. Prevent further tarnishing by wiping with a little sweet almond oil on a cloth. This will also make future cleaning easier.

Q 'I've got smoke on the brickwork to the side of my fireplace,' says Jim. 'How can I get it off?'

PROBLEM: Soot stains around the fireplace.
WHAT TO USE: Water, ash, cloths, bicarb, white vinegar; or *Gumption*.
HOW TO APPLY: Add water to some powdered ash from the fireplace to create a slurry, or thin paste, and apply it to the stain with a cloth. Then wash with bicarb and white vinegar. For light stains, combine ash with *Gumption* and wipe over with a cloth.

PROBLEM: Candle soot stains on the wall.
WHAT TO USE: Vacuum cleaner, ash, sponges, soap, white vinegar, water.
HOW TO APPLY: Candle soot is very greasy, so vacuum any loose particles then rub the soot with a small amount of ash on a dry sponge. Then wipe a small amount of soap onto the soot with another sponge. The soap picks up the last

small pieces of soot. Finally, wipe down the surface with another sponge damped in white vinegar and water.

Q 'We've got a copper chimney above our slow combustion heater,' reports Matthew. 'The copper has gone black at the bottom. How do we fix it?'

PROBLEM: Blackened copper.
WHAT TO USE: Bicarb, cloth, white vinegar, pantyhose, bamboo skewer, copper coating, sweet almond oil.
HOW TO APPLY: Put bicarb on a cloth and wipe over the blackened areas. Now spray with white vinegar. While it's fizzing, scrub with a rolled up pair of pantyhose. Sometimes copper is coated in a clear varnish which can become pitted and look like small black spots. To determine if the copper has been coated, scratch an inconspicuous part using a bamboo skewer. If the copper is coated, prevent tarnish by respraying the surface with a copper coating. Or slow the corrosion by rubbing with a dab of sweet almond oil on a cloth.

Q 'How do I clean a bronze fire screen?' asks Robyn.

PROBLEM: Dirty bronze fire screen.
WHAT TO USE: Sweet almond oil, pantyhose.

HOW TO APPLY: Rub on sweet almond oil with a pair of rolled up pantyhose. It will give a great sheen without destroying the patina.

Mantlepieces

Clean mantlepieces according to what they're made of.

Marble—if stained, mix plaster of Paris and water to form a paste the consistency of peanut butter. Apply to the stain, allow to dry, then brush away. Seal with marble flooring wax. If you can't get marble flooring wax, use milk.

Granite—if stained, mix plaster of Paris and water to the consistency of runny cream. Apply the mixture and leave to dry. Rub off with pantyhose.

Sandstone, brick—if stained, mix equal parts cigarette ash, bicarb and white vinegar. Apply to the stain and scrub well with a brush. Rinse with a damp cloth. Don't use on limestone or marble because this mixture is too acidic.

Timber—can be easily damaged with smoke. If finished in plaster or paint, clean with a paste of bicarb and water. Polish on with a cloth, allow to dry and polish off with a cloth.

Heaters

Don't forget to clean heaters during the weekly clean because they are more efficient if they're dust free, clean and shiny. Of course, don't clean when they're on or still warm. Clean and polish reflector plates at the back of the heater with bicarb and white vinegar. This will also get rid of rust. Wipe the heating filaments with methylated spirits but don't turn the heater on until it's dried it out completely because methylated spirits is flammable.

If you have a gas or kerosene heater and are irritated by the fumes, place a saucepan of water beside the heater to absorb the fumes. Add a slice of onion to the water with kerosene heaters to help absorb the smells.

If finished in enamel, wipe the heater with pantyhose dipped in equal parts white vinegar and water. If made of chrome, sprinkle with bicarb, wipe with white vinegar on a cloth and wipe clean with a damp cloth.

Q 'I've got melted polyester on the glass of my gas heater,' says Natalia. 'Can it be removed?'

PROBLEM: Melted polyester on glass.
WHAT TO USE: Glycerine, talcum powder, pantyhose, damp cloth.
HOW TO APPLY: Make a paste of glycerine and talcum powder. When the glass is cold, apply the paste with pantyhose and scrub. Leave to dry and polish off with a damp cloth.

Q 'Our wood-burning fire has a glass door,' reports Gerry. 'And over the years, it's been badly stained brown-black which makes it difficult to see the flames and condition of the fire. Can you help?'

PROBLEM: Burnt/stained glass.
WHAT TO USE: Cigarette ash, bicarb, white vinegar, pantyhose, water.
HOW TO APPLY: Mix equal parts cigarette ash, bicarb and white vinegar. Apply to the glass with a pair of pantyhose and leave for about an hour. When dry, polish off with damp pantyhose.

Q 'My column oil heater blew up and oil spilt everywhere,' says Paul. 'I soaked the oil up with towels but the problem is getting the smell out of my towels. Can you help?'

PROBLEM: Heater oil on towels.
WHAT TO USE: Dishwashing liquid.
HOW TO APPLY: Because the oil has bonded to the towels, place a couple of drops of dishwashing liquid on your fingers and massage into the oil until it feels like jelly. After this treatment, wash normally. Don't forget to clean the area around the heater with dishwashing liquid on your fingers followed by a damp cloth.

Entertainment Systems

The main enemies of entertainment systems are dust, bugs and moisture.

Television screens, plasma screens and the exterior of most entertainment systems can be cleaned with 1 part methylated spirits to 4 parts water. Apply with a dust or lint-free cloth, such as a T-shirt. Don't use detergent because it will leave smear marks. Vacuum all the vents at the back of the system using the brush head of the vacuum cleaner. Wipe the back of all electrics with a cloth sprayed with surface insecticide spray to keep insects away. When they're not in use, close all the doors and compartments of entertainment systems to stop dust getting in. Remove dust from difficult-to-reach areas with a camera puffer brush.

VCR heads should be cleaned using a high-quality video head cleaner or take them to a repairer. Store VHS tapes vertically like a book so you don't stretch the tape.

DVDs should be stored flat or they buckle. Wipe them with a DVD cleaner regularly. CDs should be cleaned using a CD cleaner and cloth if they are sticking.

Cassette players should have their rubber rollers and heads cleaned with a cotton bud dipped in methylated spirits.

TVs

Having a massive plasma TV screen with multiple speakers means you can almost have the cinema experience at home—with much cheaper popcorn. To clean plasma TVs, consult the manufacturer's manual. Never use detergent or caustic cleaners because they could damage the screen. Most marks can be removed with a soft damp cloth.

During a Stain Clinic, Tom recommended *Plexus* plastic cleaner to clean LCD screens but said you must apply it with a cloth over the entire screen. We've since learned that *Plexus* is used to clean aircraft windshields and plastic in cars.

Q **'My girlfriend had a candle burning on top of the entertainment unit and wax dropped onto the fabric cover of the speaker on the TV. Can I get it out?' asks Mark.**

PROBLEM: Wax on fabric.
WHAT TO USE: Ice, plastic scraper, pins, tissues, hair dryer.
HOW TO APPLY: If possible, take the speaker cover off. Then put ice on the wax and remove as much as possible with a plastic scraper. Next pin tissues to the waxy side of the speaker, turn the cover over and use a hair dryer on the back of the cover. This warms the wax up and the tissues absorb it. If you can't remove the speaker cover, place a

tissue over the wax and use the hair dryer to melt the wax from the front side. The tissue will absorb most of it. Keep replacing the tissue until all the wax is absorbed. So you don't overheat the fabric, use a stop–start method.

STEREOS

Most stereos are made with aluminium-coated plastic or chrome-plated plastic. Expensive ones are made of metal. Use a non-abrasive cleaner, such as pantyhose, and be careful cleaning around electrics. You don't want to get any moisture or chemicals in them. Remove fingermarks with damp pantyhose. Clean inside a CD player regularly with a puffer brush (available from department and electronic stores) or the dust will clog the mechanism. Vacuum the cloth front of your speakers using the brush attachment. You'll know there's too much dust when there's a buzz in your speakers.

Q 'I've got black rubber foot marks on a wooden cabinet from my stereo speakers,' says Mick. 'How do you remove them?'

PROBLEM: Rubber marks on timber.
WHAT TO USE: Damp salt, cloth.
HOW TO APPLY: Rub the marks with a small quantity of damp salt on a cloth.

PREVENTION: To stop rubber from perishing, rub with talcum powder.

Q 'What's the best way to remove sticky tape residue from vinyl records?' asks Michelle. 'We've got some old *Golden Book* records we'd like to play to the kids.'

PROBLEM: Sticky tape residue on vinyl records.
WHAT TO USE: Tea tree oil, warm water, pantyhose.
HOW TO APPLY: Add ½ teaspoon of tea tree oil to 2 cups of warm water. Roll up a pair of pantyhose, dip into the solution and rub over the record in the direction of the grooves until the residue is removed. Allow to air dry.

Pianos

Most pianos are made of timber and are best cared for with a good furniture polish. Piano keys can be made of plastic, ivory or ivorite. You can tell which is which by the lines in the keys. Plastic keys have no lines. Ivory has slightly uneven lines. Ivorite keys have even lines. Clean plastic keys with glycerine. Ivory keys can be cleaned with sweet almond oil or, if very dirty, with methylated spirits then sweet almond oil. If the keys are really dirty, use a small quantity of toothpaste mixed with water and apply carefully with a cotton bud. Then apply the sweet almond oil, which will protect the ivory from cracking. Ivorite is cleaned with methylated spirits.

Q 'I own a piano that's French polished,' says Tim. 'But it's got white candle wax on it. How can I get it off?'

PROBLEM: Wax on timber.
WHAT TO USE: Ice-cubes, zip-lock bag, talcum powder, damp silk.
HOW TO APPLY: Put ice-cubes in a zip-lock bag and place over the wax. When the wax is cold, remove the ice and sprinkle talcum powder over the wax. Rub with a piece of damp silk in the direction of the grain. This cuts through the wax without damaging the surface.

Guitars

Q 'How can I clean my high tensile guitar strings to make them last longer?' asks Wayne.

PROBLEM: Cleaning guitar strings.
WHAT TO USE: Sweet almond oil, lint-free cloth.
HOW TO APPLY: Place a little sweet almond oil on a lint-free cloth (such as an old T-shirt) and wipe over the strings. Sweet almond oil prevents corrosion and helps keep metal in good condition.

Billiards

Q 'How do you repair discoloured billiard balls?' asks Lesley.

PROBLEM: Discoloured billiard balls.
WHAT TO USE: Glycerine, talcum powder, cloth (plastic); sweet almond oil, cloth (ivory); or toothpaste, water, cloth.
HOW TO APPLY: If they're made of plastic, mix equal parts glycerine and talcum powder to form a paste and polish with a cloth. If made of ivory, clean with sweet almond oil on a cloth. If plastic or ivory are very dirty, use equal parts toothpaste and water on a cloth before applying the methods described above.

Dining Tables

Shannon loves hosting big family gatherings around her dining table, which has special significance because it was her mother-in-law's. Jennifer's dining table is a converted shed door made by her father and it's been the location of many happy dinner parties.

The most common dining table problems raised at Stain Clinics involve heat and water. Both can be tricky to fix so always put some form of protection, such as mats, over a table if there are hot dishes, full glasses or vases. Before tackling any stain, you'll need to know the product used to seal the dining table. To find out, see page 572.

Q 'How do I clean heat/water marks from an antique French-polished table?' asks Lynn.

PROBLEM: Heat/water marks on French polish.
WHAT TO USE: Beeswax, microwave, lemon peel.
HOW TO APPLY: Warm beeswax in the microwave until it's just softened. Put it on the outer part (skin side) of a piece of lemon peel and rub quickly over the mark using speed rather than pressure. The wax and oil from the lemon will fill the heat and watermarks.

Q 'On remarriage, I gained a 14-seater French-polished timber veneer dining table,' reports Pamela. 'I was able to convince my husband we should enjoy the table and have had numerous dinner parties. Sadly, condensation from a jug ran under a large coaster and has left a slightly puckered semi-raised surface. Can it be fixed?'

PROBLEM: Water mark on French polish.
WHAT TO USE: Professional.
HOW TO APPLY: Because the surface has puckered it will need to be repaired by a professional. Some restorers make things look brand new which devalues the piece. Instead, choose a 'sympathetic' restorer to repair the table in keeping with its age and condition.

TIP

To clean French polish, make your own polishing cloth. Mix 1 tablespoon of beeswax, 2 drops of lavender oil and 2 drops of lemon oil in a microwave-safe bowl. Place a 100 per cent white cotton cloth over the top and put the bowl inside the microwave. Heat in 10-second bursts until the beeswax melts. Store the cloth in a zip-lock bag. To remove sticky fingerprints, polish the table with a pair of rolled up pantyhose. If the fingerprints are particularly greasy, sprinkle the table with a little cornflour before polishing with pantyhose.

WHAT NOT TO DO ...

Q 'I have accidentally spilt craft glue on our wooden dining table. I tried to remove the glue with a damp cloth and hot water which seems to have left a bleach mark. What can I do?'

A Moisture is bad news for timber because it makes it swell. Reduce bleaching by rubbing with a damp tea bag. Depending on the extent of the damage, the table may have to be sanded and resurfaced. In future, remove glue with damp pantyhose heated in the microwave for 10 seconds (no longer or the pantyhose will melt). Rub over the glue in the direction of the grain using speed, not pressure. Dry thoroughly with a cotton cloth.

Q 'I have a marble-covered dining table,' says Maria. 'And the marble is beginning to show fingerprints and other marks, such as glass rims. Any ideas?'

PROBLEM: Marking on marble.
WHAT TO USE: *Brasso*, cloth; or cake of bathroom soap, water, soft cloth, marble milk wax or skim milk.
HOW TO APPLY: If the marble is coated in polyurethane, rub with a little *Brasso* applied with a cloth using speed, not pressure. This partially melts the polyurethane. It will look worse before it looks better. If it's machine polished, rub with a soft cloth that's been rubbed with a cake of bathroom soap and water. Then apply a good quality marble milk wax or skim milk. To work out what the sealant is, see page 572.

Q 'When our son was a baby, he used to shove his peas under the table protector (unbeknown to us),' says Tyson. 'So now we have all these green stains over our polished wooden dining table. What can we do?'

PROBLEM: Peas on timber.

WHAT TO USE: Glycerine, talcum powder, cloth; or beeswax; sunlight or ultraviolet light.

HOW TO APPLY: Firstly, work out what the table is sealed with (see page 572). If the table has a polyurethane finish, polish with a paste of equal parts glycerine and talcum powder on a cloth. If the table has a shellac finish, use beeswax on a cloth. To remove any residual green, expose the stains to sunlight or an ultraviolet light.

Q'The green dye from my bamboo table mat has leached onto my varnished veneer dining table,' says Charmaine. 'What can I do?'

PROBLEM: Green dye on timber.

WHAT TO USE: *Brasso*, cloth, soft cloth; or *Colour Run Remover: Coloursafe*, cotton ball, silicone-free furniture polish.

HOW TO APPLY: Firstly, work out what the table has been sealed with (see page 572). If it's a polyurethane finish, use a little *Brasso* on a cloth, rub in the direction of the grain and polish with a soft cloth. It will look worse before it looks better. This removes a little of the finish and the dye. If finished in shellac, use a small amount of *Colour Run Remover: Coloursafe*. Apply with a cotton ball and rub in the direction of the grain until the colour is removed then wipe with a damp cloth. Use a silicone-free furniture polish.

Q 'I was given a table with a vinyl top that's been slightly water damaged,' reports June. 'The vinyl looks bumpy in some spots. Is there any way to flatten this out?'

PROBLEM: Buckled vinyl.
WHAT TO USE: PVA glue, water, syringe, plastic wrap, heavy object (such as a book).
HOW TO APPLY: Mix equal parts PVA glue and water and load into a syringe. Inject the glue under the buckled vinyl and rub with your fingers to flatten. Cover in plastic wrap and place a heavy object on top until it dries.

Tablecloths

Q 'I've got a damask tablecloth with mildew on it,' complains Lee. 'What can I do?'

PROBLEM: Mouldy cotton.
WHAT TO USE: Bucket, non-iodised salt, water, soft brush.
HOW TO APPLY: Soak the tablecloth in a bucket of salt water solution (1 kg of salt per 9 litres of water) overnight. Remove, gently squeeze but don't wring before hanging on the clothesline in the sun. Leave to dry and a salt crust will

form. Remove the crust with a brush and the mould/mildew will come away.

Q 'I had stains from a pot plant seep through to my white tablecloth cover,' reports Susie. 'How do I get rid of them?'

PROBLEM: Soil and mould on cotton.
WHAT TO USE: Oil of cloves, 1 litre spray pack, water, non-iodised salt, lemon juice, sunshine.
HOW TO APPLY: Mix ¼ teaspoon of oil of cloves in a spray pack of water. Lightly spray onto the tablecloth and leave for 24 hours. Place a little mountain of salt over the marks and squeeze on a little lemon juice to moisten the salt. Leave in the sunshine to dry, then wash and dry normally.

Q 'I've got a policy of using my lovely things,' says Maria. 'We had a barbecue the other day and I used my white damask tablecloth. Now it's got sausage grease and tomato sauce over it. Can the stains be removed?'

PROBLEM: Grease and tomato stains on tablecloth.
WHAT TO USE: *NapiSan*.
HOW TO APPLY: Tomato sauce fades in sunshine. You could also soak the stain in *NapiSan*. The sausage grease will also

come off with *NapiSan* or see 'Oily stain on fabric' on page 149. If you're using good linen in vulnerable situations, buy some heavy-grade plastic from the hardware store and use a hair dryer to mould the plastic over the tablecloth. Be careful not to keep the hair dryer in one spot for too long or the plastic will melt.

PROBLEM: Red wine stain on tablecloth.
WHAT TO USE: Bicarb, sponge, white vinegar, cloth; or glycerine.
HOW TO APPLY: For fresh stains, sprinkle some bicarb over the area then sponge with white vinegar. If the stain has set, rub bicarb in circles using a cloth dampened with white vinegar. For any hard-set stains, soak in glycerine before removing the stain normally.

Q **'One of my dinner guests misjudged the distance between the gravy boat and his plate,' says Carole. 'Now I've got a lovely brown stain on the tablecloth. What should I do?'**

PROBLEM: Gravy stain on tablecloth.
WHAT TO USE: Cake of soap, cold water, hot water.
HOW TO APPLY: Gravy contains proteins so you must remove them first with soap and cold water. Gravy also contains fat, which you remove with soap and hot water. Just make sure you clean with cold water first or you'll set the stain.

Silver

You can clean silver with a little bicarb followed by a little white vinegar. Rub it with a cloth while it's fizzing. Wear a pair of old cotton socks on your hands to prevent the acid from your skin transferring to the silver and causing it to tarnish. To prevent future tarnish, rub with a couple of drops of sweet almond oil on a cloth to seal.

WHAT NOT TO DO ...

Q **'My solid silver teapot set was heavily tarnished and blackened. So I washed it in warm dishwashing liquid. Then I wrapped it in aluminium foil and added a solution of bicarb and water to the inside of the pot and brought it to the boil for 3 minutes. The result is AWFUL. The silver appears to have undergone a chemical change. Please help!'**

A This technique not only removes tarnish but removes a layer of silver. If you want to restore the silver, you'll need to have it professionally replated. To clean silver, sprinkle with bicarb, add white vinegar and, while fizzing, rub with a soft cloth. To slow tarnishing, once it's clean, rub with a couple of drops of sweet almond oil on a cloth.

Office Equipment

This is another place where the enemies are dust, bugs and moisture. Vacuum often using the brush head attachment of the vacuum cleaner. Ventilate equipment well. If you have lots of cords around, tie them together with garbage bag ties so you don't get the spaghetti look.

Telephones are best cleaned with glycerine on a cloth. Never use alcohol-based chemicals because they'll affect the plastic. And never use eucalyptus oil on plastics.

COMPUTERS

If you share a computer with someone else, here's some alarming information. Research by the University of Arizona found the average office desktop harboured 400 times more bacteria than the average office toilet seat! To clean your computer, turn it off, turn the keyboard upside down and gently shake to remove any crumbs.

Computers can be cleaned in a couple of ways. For light cleans, use a warm-water damp cloth. Never use a wet cloth because the ports can corrode. For dirty surfaces, apply some antistatic CD spray to a cloth and wipe it over all the surfaces, including the venting hole. Never spray anything directly onto a computer or keyboard because moisture is bad for electrics. Instead, spray white vinegar or methylated spirits on a soft cloth and wipe the screen and keyboard. Jennifer thinks white vinegar is the best cleaner. To clean between the keys on your keyboard, use a little white vinegar or methylated spirits on a cotton bud. Other specialised cleaners are also available. It's fine to use your vacuum cleaner to remove dirt outside the computer but never use it inside the computer because it creates static electricity and could ruin it.

To deter bugs, spray surface insecticide spray (not any of the lure and kill varieties) on a cloth and wipe the back of the computer with it.

Keep computers ventilated by placing them at least 10 centimetres away from any wall.

MOUSE AND MOUSE MAT

You know it's time to clean the mouse when it becomes sticky and hard to manoeuvre. The latest ones are optical and can't be pulled apart but you can clean the case by wiping with a cloth dampened with white vinegar or methylated spirits. Make sure you clean the track wheel. To clean the underside of the mouse, dip a cotton bud in methylated spirits, wipe the slide points that make contact with the mat and dry upside down. Remove skin cells and sweat from the mouse mat and cord by wiping with methylated spirits on a pair of pantyhose.

Fax Machines

Clean the outside of the fax with a damp cloth. Clean rubber rollers with a little methylated spirits on a cotton bud. To remove cotton bud fibres, wipe again with a damp lint-free cloth.

Scanners/Photocopiers/Printers

Clean the outside as described for the fax. Clean the glass with a little methylated spirits on a lint-free cloth. Clean the buttons with methylated spirits on a cotton bud.

Desks

Q 'I wonder if you have tips on how to successfully remove ink stains from an old leather desk top?' asks Mark. 'I'd appreciate it!'

PROBLEM: Ink stain on leather.
WHAT TO USE: Rotten milk, white spirits, cloth, talcum powder, leather conditioner.
HOW TO APPLY: If it's ink from an inkwell, rot some milk in the sun until it becomes lumpy. Strain the solids and place over the stain until the ink bleeds into the milk solids. Remove the solids and wipe the remaining stain with white spirits on a cloth. Sprinkle with talcum powder, leave to dry and brush clean. Treat with leather conditioner.

Whiteboards

Q 'I want to remove permanent pen from my whiteboard,' says Eric. 'What's your advice?'

PROBLEM: Removing permanent pen from a whiteboard.
WHAT TO USE: Perfume, cotton ball; or methylated spirits.
HOW TO APPLY: Dab some perfume onto a cotton ball and wipe over the pen marks. If you don't have any perfume available, use methylated spirits applied with a cotton ball.

Books and Bookshelves

Shannon says she can't bear to part with books because they're like friends to her. Jennifer is also a keen reader but unless she wants to read a book again, she generally passes them on to family and friends.

Always store books away from direct sunlight and moisture. Clean bookshelves once a week with a duster, or vacuum with the brush head. To stop books becoming mildewy, sprinkle silicone crystals along the back of the bookshelf or wipe the back of the bookshelf with oil of cloves. To preserve old leather-bound books, rub the leather with a little sweet almond oil.

Q 'I've got cockroach droppings all over my books,' says George. 'How can I get rid of them?'

PROBLEM: Cockroach droppings on books.
WHAT TO USE: Vacuum cleaner, bicarb, old toothbrush; salt.
HOW TO APPLY: Vacuum first, then shut the book tight with the spine facing away from your hand. Sprinkle bicarb along the edges and rub with an old toothbrush. To prevent cockroaches returning, pile a bed of salt around the feet of the bookshelf.

Q 'How can you get rid of awful smells in old books?' asks Graeme.

PROBLEM: Smelly books.
WHAT TO USE: Talcum powder.
HOW TO APPLY: This is a very tedious process. Dust a page with talcum powder, then leave it in the sun for no more than three minutes or the UV rays will affect the paper. Clear the talcum powder, turn the page, apply more talcum powder, leave in the sun, remove the powder, and so on … for the whole book!

Q 'I've got brown marks in my books,' says Sue. 'What should I do?'

PROBLEM: Brown marks in books.
WHAT TO USE: This is called foxing or book worm and is a job for a professional conservator. Find one in the telephone book.

Q '*My document safe has a very musty smell and all the documents stink,*' says Jack. '*What can I do?*'

PROBLEM: Musty paper.
WHAT TO USE: White chalk, loose-leaf tea.
HOW TO APPLY: Put 6 sticks of white chalk inside the safe to absorb the moisture. Leave an opened packet of loose-leaf tea inside the safe to get rid of the smell. Close the door and leave for a week.

Decanters

Shannon used to make wine at home and will never forget the day she mistook some *Dettol* for homemade brew. Her throat had a menthol flavour for some time! It's best not to leave alcohol in your decanters for more than a day because it causes white cloudy smears or glass cancer. Spirits should be stored in screw-top bottles and decanted just for the evening. Decanters are best washed in warm water and oven dried. To oven dry, turn your oven on to a very low heat then place the decanter in the oven, turn the oven off and leave. Never put direct heat, such as from a hair dryer, on a decanter as you risk cracking the crystal.

Q 'I've got a red wine stain in my decanter,' says Judith. 'And it just won't budge. What do you suggest?'

PROBLEM: Red wine stain in decanter.
WHAT TO USE: Bicarb, white vinegar, uncooked rice, water, sweet almond oil, thin paintbrush.
HOW TO APPLY: Empty the decanter. Put 1 tablespoon of bicarb, 1 tablespoon of white vinegar and 1 tablespoon of uncooked rice inside and shake. This will remove the red pigment. Rinse with water and allow to dry. Put sweet almond oil on a thin paintbrush and run along the etched mark. Be aware the oil will affect the taste of the wine so use sparingly and rinse with water before reusing. Never leave wine in a decanter because it will etch into the glass.

Trays

Trays are a great invention. Use silver cleaner to clean silver trays and a damp cloth to clean other trays.

Q 'I've got a dull grey shadow on a silver tray,' reports Sue. 'Can I get rid of it?'

PROBLEM: Shadow on silver tray.
WHAT TO USE: White toothpaste, silver polish, cloths.
HOW TO APPLY: There are a couple of possible explanations

for this. Some trays have nickel silver on the inside and electroplated silver coating on the outside. The silver coating may be wearing thin and exposing the core. Another explanation is that the tray may have been repaired with a different quality silver which is ageing at a different rate. To remove the shadow, wipe white toothpaste over it then clean with a good quality silver polish. Make sure you wash all the silver polish off and then polish with a dry cloth.

Q 'What's the best way to clean a silver-plated tray?' asks Bill.

PROBLEM: Cleaning silver-plated tray.
WHAT TO USE: Bicarb, white vinegar, cloths; or unprocessed wheat bran, white vinegar, cloth.
HOW TO APPLY: Sprinkle bicarb over the tray like icing sugar, then splash vinegar over the top. Rub over the tray with a damp cloth before polishing it with a dry cloth. You can also mix bran and white vinegar to form a paste and rub it over the silver. Wipe off with a damp cloth then a dry cloth.

Ashtrays

The best way to clean ashtrays is with cigarette ash. With a damp cloth, rub ash over the ashtray and then wash in dishwashing liquid and water.

Create your own air freshener

Mix ½ teaspoon of vanilla essence, cinnamon oil or eucalyptus oil with a couple of drops of dishwashing liquid into a spray bottle filled with water. Or put some bicarb in a saucer with a couple of drops of your favourite essential oil and mix well. This will absorb odours and freshen the room. Never use eucalyptus oil if you're spraying painted surfaces or plastic because it will strip them!

Clocks

Heirloom and antique clocks should be cleaned by a professional. One of the best ways to maintain your mantle clock is to place an oily cloth inside the sounding box. Use baby oil or sewing machine oil. The dust and rust from the clock movements will fall to the cloth and stick rather than flying around and damaging the workings of the clock. The exterior should be cared for according to what it's made of. Glass should be cleaned with methylated spirits. Never clean keys with silver or brass cleaner. Just wipe them with an oily rag. No clock should ever sit against the wall as air needs to circulate around it. And always make sure clocks are level.

Flowers and Pot Plants

When Shannon was younger, her job was to arrange fresh flowers for every room in the house. Cut flowers will last longer if you trim their stems just before putting them in water. They will also last longer if you maintain the water level in the vase. Do this by adding ice cubes to the vase every morning and night.

With daisies and soft-leaf plants, trim excess foliage and add a pinch of salt and sugar to the water. This makes the flowers last longer and stops the water from smelling.

To keep English violets longer, immerse the whole violet in water for about two minutes and then place in a vase.

For roses, put a piece of copper in the water. Rescue wilting roses by trimming the stems and filling the vase with chilled water up to the bract or throat of the rose.

To prevent native flower stems going furry, put a small piece of charcoal in the water. Proprietary products are available as well.

Remove the stamens from lilies before putting them in the vase because they cause stains.

ARTIFICIAL FLOWERS

Plastic, fabric, silk and felt flowers can be dusted regularly with a hair dryer on the cool setting. To clean paper flowers, hold them upside down and lightly shake. Help retain their colour by keeping them away from sunlight and deter bugs by placing two cloves in a small green bag and attaching it to the stem. (Try to use a matching green so the bag is camouflaged.)

The art of drying flowers: *Merle's Story*

INCIDENT: *'My daughter just got married and I'd like to dry her wedding bouquet. It's made of coloured roses and tulips.'*

SOLUTION: Remove all florist wire, plastic and ribbons. Then place the bouquet upside down in a bowl slightly bigger than the bouquet. Slowly add sand to the bowl. As you do, vibrate the flowers so the sand gets inside all the petals. Try not to bend or damage the petals. When the bouquet is completely covered in sand, put the bowl in the microwave for one-minute bursts until the stems go woody. You can also use the oven on the lowest possible temperature for about three hours. A woody stem indicates that the bouquet is ready. Then let the sand cool before pouring it out. Don't touch the sand while it's hot. Replace the wires and ribbons. Dried flowers can be cleaned with a hair dryer on the cool setting. Keep bugs away with a couple of cloves.

VASES

Vases can be tricky to clean, particularly the big narrow ones. If you're having difficulty removing dirt, cover the stain in baby oil and leave it for a couple of hours. Then remove the oil with either a paintbrush or a bamboo skewer with chewed ends. Make sure the ferrule, or metal part, is covered on the paintbrush so you don't scratch the vase. To access those hard-to-reach areas, create a curl in the end of a bamboo skewer and work it into the area.

INDOOR PLANTS

It's best not to keep indoor plants near radios, TVs or other electrical equipment. Plants don't like electromagnetic fields, and electrical equipment doesn't like water. An economical way to clean indoor plants that like water on their leaves is to stand them in the shower with a fine mist. Have a shower yourself as a small amount of soap keeps plants healthy.

Q 'I've got ants making anthills in my pot plants,' says Cynthia. 'How can I get rid of them?'

PROBLEM: Ants in pot plants.
WHAT TO USE: Borax, icing sugar; or *Ant-rid*.
HOW TO APPLY: Mix 1 part borax to 1 part icing sugar and create a mountain near the ants. Be careful because borax is toxic. Wash the mixing spoon carefully after using it. Read the instructions before using *Ant-rid*. Wherever possible, find the source of the ants and pour boiling water on the nest rather than using poisons.

Floors, Walls and Windows

Shannon likes having carpet in bedrooms because it's a soft landing for your feet when you get out of bed but she prefers floorboards, cork or self-levelling vinyls elsewhere in the home (except in the bathroom where tiles are the best surface). Jennifer loves floorboards because they look good and are easy to clean. Choose what works for you, but don't stress about stains; thanks to gravity, a spill is almost inevitable.

If you're not spilling stuff on your floors, walls and windows, then you're not living. Kids running around, friends over for coffee or a Sunday barbecue, pets traipsing muck over the house … this is the stuff of life and, like life, it's messy. Wine will be spilled, greasy sausages will be dropped, wax will drip and grubby hands will leave an imprint. You can fix all these problems and never have to cry over spilt milk again.

Peanut butter panic: *Suzanne's story*

INCIDENT: *'We've got lovely new timber stairs. But sadly, before we sealed them, my son got peanut butter all over them. Can you help?'*

SOLUTION: Mix plaster of Paris and water to form a paste the consistency of peanut butter (sorry!). For every cup of mixture add 1 teaspoon of dishwashing liquid and 2 teaspoons of white vinegar. Place a 1 cm thick layer of paste over the stain. Leave to completely dry and brush off with a broom.

Jackson Pollock-style carpet: *Beverley's story*

INCIDENT: *'I was cooking some chips in the oven and thought I'd been very clever putting some baking paper down first to collect the fat. After we'd eaten, I bunched the baking paper up and transported it to the bin. But I obviously didn't close off all the corners because when I turned around, I discovered a trail of oil drips right across my carpet. I've tried to clean it with bicarb, commercial cleaners, a hot iron and dry-cleaning fluid. Nothing has worked!'*

SOLUTION: Fill a bucket with cold water and enough dishwashing liquid to generate a sudsy mix. Then apply the suds to the stain and scrub with an old toothbrush. Use as little water as possible. Then dry the spot with a paper towel or *Slurpex*, a chamois-like sponge block. Allow it to dry out and repeat the process until the stain has cleared. Dishwashing liquid helps break down fats and brings them to the surface.

Floors

Floors are probably the most susceptible part of the house to dirt, spills and stains. One of Shannon's tricks if someone's about to visit and her hard floors are looking a bit dirty is to damp an old T-shirt in water, wrap it around a broom head and run it over the floor. For regular cleaning, always vacuum or sweep before you mop. The next time you're about to sweep your floor, take an up-close look at the broom head. No doubt there's some dirt and grime on the bristles which will be added to the floors you're supposed to be cleaning. Before using, wash the broom head with a little dishwashing liquid and water, rinse under water and set aside in the sunshine, handle-end down, to dry.

TIMBER AND CORK

Sealed timber and cork floors are easy to clean and last longer than unsealed ones. Most are sealed in polyurethane, tung-oil, varnish or wax.

For timber and cork sealed in polyurethane, clean with 1 cup of white vinegar in a 9 litre bucket of warm (not hot) water. The warm water helps cut through grease. Apply with a broom head covered in pantyhose or an old T-shirt and dry and polish as you go by standing on a towel (shuffle forward). By doing this, you don't leave excess water on the polyurethane. If you leave excess water, you can get white bloom marks.

For timber and cork floors finished in tung-oil, varnish or wax, clean with cold black tea and warm water (1 cup of tea or 3 tea bags in a 9 litre bucket of water). Tea raises the tannin levels in timber and cork, helping retain the colour and quality.

Before you throw your old tea leaves out, lightly scatter them over your sealed timber floors! Yes, tea is a great way to clean them. Just make sure the tea leaves are damp, not wet. Then vacuum them up immediately. It's a tip Shannon learned from her grandmother who loved drinking tea as well. You can use tea bags instead by tying them behind your broom and then sweeping. After vacuuming, add a couple of drops of your favourite essential oil (Shannon uses lavender) to a bucket of water and wipe the floor with a mop.

If the timber is unsealed, sprinkle bicarb then splash white vinegar over the top. Scrub, then rinse with water.

To clean old urine stains on wood, use sugar soap. You may also need to repaint the wood or top up the varnish.

PROBLEM: Squeaky floorboards.
WHAT TO USE: Talcum powder, wax.

HOW TO APPLY: The squeakiness is usually caused by the boards rubbing together. Dust the floor with talcum powder, which will work its way between the boards and create a barrier. Then wax normally. Shannon discovered this living in a house where all the floorboards were squeaky except the ones in the bathroom where talcum powder was scattered. She scattered talcum powder in the other rooms and they stopped squeaking. Great discovery!

Q 'I've got double-sided carpet tape on my floorboards,' says Diana. 'When I try to remove it, it lifts the varnish as well. What can I do?'

PROBLEM: Adhesive on timber.
WHAT TO USE: Sticky tape, cloth, hot water, clingwrap, tea tree oil, tissues.
HOW TO APPLY: Remove as much of the adhesive gum as possible by putting sticky tape over the top and quickly lifting it. Do this several times. Then damp a cloth in hot water and lay it on top of the tape. Place clingwrap over the top of the cloth and leave for 5 minutes. Remove the clingwrap and the cloth and apply tea tree oil over the adhesive gum. Then roll the adhesive gum off with tissues.

TIP

To fix a dent in timber, place a hot, wet, used tea bag over the indentation and leave until the timber has expanded.

Blood/Meat juice

Q 'When I brought the shopping home, meat juice leaked through the plastic and left blood over the timber floor,' reports Anne. 'It's soaked through!'

PROBLEM: Blood/meat juice on timber.
WHAT TO USE: Plaster of Paris, water, white vinegar, broom.
HOW TO APPLY: Mix plaster of Paris and water to form a paste the consistency of peanut butter. For every cup of mixture, add 2 teaspoons of white vinegar. Apply a 1 cm thick layer of paste over the stain. Leave until completely dry and sweep away with a broom. Repeat if needed.

Cigarette burn

Q 'I have polished floorboards with a slight cigarette burn on the surface,' admits Brian. 'It looks like lightly burnt toast. How can I get it out?'

PROBLEM: Cigarette burn on timber.
WHAT TO USE: 3 per cent hydrogen peroxide, cloth, *Brasso*.

HOW TO APPLY: If the burn is on the surface and hasn't penetrated the polyurethane, immerse a cloth in 3 per cent hydrogen peroxide, tightly wring out, place over the stained area only and leave for 20 minutes. The burn will come away when you remove the cloth. If the burn has penetrated the surface, use the technique described above, then rub with a little *Brasso* on a cloth. For a burn the size of a 5 cent piece, use 1 drop of *Brasso* on a cloth and rub lightly and quickly in the direction of the grain. In the first couple of seconds, the mark will look worse before it looks better.

Dye

Q 'I have a blob of dark hair dye on a timber floor—found an hour later,' reports Sally. 'The floor is finished with wax and polyurethane. Help!'

PROBLEM: Hair dye on timber.
WHAT TO USE: Disposable rubber gloves, same brand and colour hair dye, cloth, anti-dandruff shampoo, warm water.
HOW TO APPLY: Put on rubber gloves to protect your skin. Apply the same hair dye to the stain with a cloth, rubbing in circles until the stain loosens. Follow immediately with a little anti-dandruff shampoo on a cloth and rub into the stain to loosen further. Continue rubbing until the entire stain has lifted, then wipe with a cloth dampened with warm water. This technique works on all surfaces.

Engine oil/grease

Q 'My new unsealed timber floor has a car oil stain on it,' reports Sam. 'The stain is greasy black and I need to remove it before sealing the floor. What do you suggest?'

PROBLEM: Engine oil on unsealed timber.
WHAT TO USE: Baby oil, cotton ball, disposable rubber gloves, dishwashing liquid, cloth, warm water.
HOW TO APPLY: Place a little baby oil on a cotton ball and rub on the stain until it looks muddy. Put on rubber gloves, place a couple of drops of dishwashing liquid on your fingertips and massage into the stain until it changes texture and feels like jelly. Wipe with a cloth dampened with warm water. If any oil remains, apply dishwashing liquid again. Leave the floor to dry for at least 2 days before sealing.

Fat/oil (cooking)

Q 'I have light-coloured floating floors,' says Richard. 'And the area around the stove has splatterings of fat from cooking. Would you be able to help me fix this? It looks like I have a dirty floor!'

PROBLEM: Fat/cooking oil on timber.
WHAT TO USE: Dishwashing liquid, pantyhose, *Brasso*, cloth.

HOW TO APPLY: The floor is likely to be coated in polyurethane. Place a couple of drops of dishwashing liquid on pantyhose and rub over the stain. Then wipe with another pair of damp pantyhose. You can even put the pantyhose on your feet so you don't have to bend over. For any remaining marks, apply a little *Brasso* with a cloth and rub in the direction of the grain, using speed not pressure.

PREVENTION: Constant exposure to oil can damage polyurethane so protect the area by placing a mat in front of the stove.

Nail polish

Q 'My daughter spilt nail polish on a wooden floor,' says Chris. 'What can I do?'

PROBLEM: Nail polish on timber.
WHAT TO USE: Acetone, cotton bud, pantyhose, white vinegar, cloth, *Brasso*; or beeswax.
HOW TO APPLY: For a polyurethane finish, use a little acetone applied with a cotton bud but work quickly using as little pressure and acetone as possible. Only rub over the nail polish, not the surrounding floor. When the colour is removed, neutralise with white vinegar on a cloth. If the surface is dulled, polish with a little *Brasso* on a cloth. For oil-based varnish, shellac or wax-based surfaces, use the

same technique as polyurethane but polish with a little beeswax rather than *Brasso*. Acetone can affect acrylic surfaces so you may need to reapply the acrylic after removing the nail polish.

Urine

Q 'How do I get rid of the smell of cat urine from floorboards in my house?' asks Elizabeth.

PROBLEM: Cat urine on timber.
WHAT TO USE: Ultraviolet light, white chalk, white vinegar, cloth, plaster of Paris, broom.
HOW TO APPLY: The first task is to find where the urine is. In a darkened room, turn on an ultraviolet light and the urine stains will show up yellow. Mark around the yellow stains with a piece of white chalk so you know where the offending areas are when the light is on. Wipe inside the chalk marks with a cloth wrung out in white vinegar. If the urine has soaked through the grooves of your floorboards, make a paste of plaster of Paris and water to the consistency of peanut butter. For every cup of paste, add 2 teaspoons of white vinegar. Paint a 1 cm thick layer of paste over the floorboards. When completely dry, brush off with a broom. You need to remove every bit of urine or the smell will remain.

Wax

Q 'I have a large red candle wax stain on our hardwood floor,' reports Ricky. 'The stain has probably been there for about a month. What's the best way to remove it without scratching the floor or removing the varnish? I normally clean the floors with warm water and a well-wrung mop.'

PROBLEM: Red wax on timber.
WHAT TO USE: Ice-cubes, zip-lock bag, plastic spatula, tea tree oil, cloth, ultraviolet light, cardboard.
HOW TO APPLY: Put a couple of ice-cubes in a zip-lock bag and place on top of the wax. Once the wax is chilled, flake it off with a plastic spatula. If a greasy stain remains, rub with a little tea tree oil on a cloth. In some cases, the red dye from the candle will penetrate the varnish and leave a stain. To remove it, aim ultraviolet light at the area (cover areas around the wax with cardboard or they'll lighten as well) checking every 2 hours until removed.

BAMBOO, CANE AND PALM

Newer types of flooring can be made from bamboo, cane and palm. Be aware that long-cut bamboo is sturdier than short-cut bamboo and both types need to be sealed to make it easier to clean. Only clean bamboo, cane and palm with 1 cup of white vinegar per 9 litre bucket of water. If the floor is exposed to sunshine, add 1 cup of black tea to the mixture. Don't use bicarb on it because it's too abrasive.

TILES

One house Shannon lived in had Spanish tiles with dark-coloured cement grout. Every time she cleaned, the edge of the tiles used to smear with dirt. That's because the previous owners never cleaned the grout and it had collected layers of dirt and grime. Shannon recommends using a plastic scourer (not a steel one) for this task. Simply stand on it and rub the scourer backwards and forwards over the grout.

To clean tiles, sprinkle a little bicarb over them, add a little white vinegar and when the mixture fizzes, sweep with a broom. To finish, wipe with a damp cloth. The vinegar may cause the room to smell a bit like a salad but this will dissipate and has the added benefit of making the floor non-slip. Most tiles are sealed with a glaze so that they're not porous. If tiles are not sealed, they'll stain easily (it's best to seal them). Don't clean glazed tiles with detergent because it makes them slippery and affects the surface.

To seal terracotta tiles or unglazed Spanish quarry tiles, mix 1 part *Aquadhere* to 20 parts water, mop it over the surface and leave it to dry completely. It should take between one and four hours to dry, depending on the weather. The seal will last for about 3 months.

TIP

If it looks as though someone has written on your tiles with a lead pencil, don't panic. These marks, called 'tile marks', are caused by metal touching the tiles. Remove by rubbing over the marks with a pencil eraser (for tiles with a smooth finish) or biro eraser (for tiles with a rougher finish) that's been dipped in water.

Q 'We have a tiled floor and our dog, on a few occasions, has not woken us up to go out to the bathroom,' says Jim. 'Consequently, the grout has become dark and discoloured from urine and poo. How can I get the stain out of the grout and stop him from returning to the same area?'

PROBLEM: Dog urine/poo on tile grout.
WHAT TO USE: White vinegar, cloth, lavender oil (urine); cake of bathroom soap, cold water, old toothbrush, white vinegar, lavender oil (poo).
HOW TO APPLY: The grout between tiles is very absorbent and stains easily. Remove the urine by rubbing with a cloth dampened with white vinegar. To remove the poo stains, rub a cake of bathroom soap over an old toothbrush, run it under cold water and scrub over the stain. Rinse clean by wiping with a cloth wrung out in white vinegar. Dogs don't

like the smell of lavender oil so add a couple of teaspoons to a 1 litre spray pack of water and lightly mist over the area. They'll stay away.

Q **'I've got a mop with a metal head and it's darkened my tiles,' reports Bill. 'Is there a solution?'**

PROBLEM: Metal residue on tiles.
WHAT TO USE: Bicarb, white vinegar, nylon brush, hot water, sticky tape.
HOW TO APPLY: Sprinkle bicarb over the tiles, then splash with white vinegar and rub with a nylon brush. Rinse with hot water.
PREVENTION: To prevent the problem, put sticky tape over the metal.

CONCRETE

Polished concrete has become popular in some modern homes but it needs to be cleaned regularly with bicarb and white vinegar because dirt and grit remove its sheen. For a comprehensive clean, sprinkle with bicarb, then spray on white vinegar and scrub with a broom. Rinse with water, allow to dry, then wax with carnauba wax using a polishing machine (available from hire companies or vacuum cleaner shops). Don't use beeswax because it's too soft and leaves a build-up.

Q Kerry's family had big plans to build their dream home. 'We bought a block of land in a valley and built a makeshift shed to live in while we constructed the main house. Time went by and we didn't end up building the house but decided to stay in the shed and do it up instead. But we've been living in it for eleven years and the concrete slab has become really dirty. How can we clean the slab before we put some tiles down?'

PROBLEM: Dirty concrete floor.
WHAT TO USE: Bicarb, white vinegar, stiff brush or stiff broom, warm water, mop.
HOW TO APPLY: Sprinkle bicarb over the surface, splash white vinegar over the bicarb, then scrub with a stiff brush or broom. Rinse with warm water and a mop. If it's really dirty you may need to do this a few times.

MARBLE/LIMESTONE

This flooring is porous and alkaline based, so don't use white vinegar to clean it because it can damage the surface. Instead, clean with pH neutral soap. Grate 1 teaspoon of soap into a 9 litre bucket of warm water, stir and wipe over the surface. To seal (do this when the surface has dulled), coat with a thin layer of good quality marble flooring wax.

RAMMED EARTH FLOORS

If you have rammed earth floors, maintain the polish by mixing 2 cups of powdered milk into a 9 litre bucket of water. Rub over the earth with a wet river stone (bought at nurseries). Drill a hole through your river stone and pull it around the floor. When drilling into stone, use a masonry bit, work on the slowest speed and fill the hole with a little water to keep the masonry bit cool.

CARPET

Buy the best quality carpet you can afford because the better the quality, the less wear and tear you'll get. One of Shannon's sisters bought cheap carpet and she had to replace it after five years. It's just not worth it.

You'll have to deal with stains on your carpet at some stage. To clean carpet, vacuum regularly. Scatter a light dusting of bicarb but don't create a ski field or you'll damage your vacuum cleaner. Your carpet will last longer if you steam-clean it at least once a year. Do it more often if you have heavy traffic—kids, pets, heavy boots. When removing stains, be very sparing with water and other types of moisture. If you use too much liquid, you'll get jute staining from the back of the carpet. More is not better. After removing the stain, remove as much moisture as possible with paper towels or a *Slurpex*.

Shannon suggests using a carpet cleaner every 3 months. After spraying the foam over the carpet, scrub it with a broom head wrapped in an old clean white T-shirt. Leave it to dry for about an hour, then vacuum. Doing this fairly regularly means your carpet never gets dirty enough to need a steam clean.

Shannon likes to clean woven carpet by scattering unprocessed wheat bran across the top of it and scrubbing with a dry broom. Then vacuum. If the carpet is particularly grimy, damp bran with white vinegar to form a clumpy, but not wet, mix and scatter it over the carpet. Then scrub with a broom before vacuuming.

To freshen up dingy carpets, make up a 1 litre spray bottle containing 1 part bicarb to 3 parts white vinegar and 5 parts water. Spray the carpet then sponge it, but don't go overboard and soak it. Sprinkling bicarb on the carpet before vacuuming is a good general carpet freshener, but won't necessarily clean stains. These will have to be spot cleaned.

Never put an iron on carpet. It will leave scorch marks on natural carpets and melt nylon or polyester ones. Shannon discovered this when her ironing board broke and she put some sheets on the carpet to iron. The iron penetrated all those layers and left a nasty singe mark.

How to use the vacuum cleaner

Shannon gets a great sense of satisfaction from vacuuming. She loves it. But to do it properly, you need to know about

Floors, Walls and Windows 231

your machine. Did you know there are other attachments for the vacuum cleaner? Find them inside the cover of the vacuum cleaner or in a separate bag. These other brushes and nozzles will change the way you vacuum. It'll be as though you had one hand tied behind your back all that time. These are the components of the vacuum cleaner and what they do.

- Barrel: This is the main part of the cleaner. It has an inlet and outlet connection. The inlet is where the hose goes. The outlet is where the air blows out of the machine and it's generally covered. You can attach the hose here to backflush. A leaf blower is simply a reverse vacuum cleaner.
- Bag: Located inside the barrel. Modern vacuum cleaners have a window that shows when the bag is full. If you don't have this, check the bag each time you use the cleaner. It's a good idea to change the bag regularly. The vacuum cleaner won't work efficiently if the bag is more than half full.
- Tube (hard part): Vary the length of the hard part to suit your height or according to what you're vacuuming. Make it shorter when vacuuming furnishings and longer when vacuuming floors. If you are tall, extra lengths are available from the vacuum cleaner shop.
- Tube (soft part): Is the hose connection.

- Main head: This can be set to have bristles up or down. Put the bristles down for shiny and hard floors. Put the bristles up for soft floors, unless you have pets. Clean any fur out of the bristles with a comb.
- Brush head: This small round attachment with long bristles is designed to clean cobwebs and the surface of furnishings, curtains and pelmets.
- Corner nozzle: Use this to access tiny spaces such as the sides of chairs, to clean around the buttons on padded furniture, or to get right into corners on skirting boards or into the grooves of sliding door tracks.

Work from the top of the room to the bottom of the room. Begin vacuuming with the brush head and remove cobwebs from the ceiling. Then clean the tops of things such as wardrobes, picture rails, dado rails, skirting boards, light fittings, window frames and sills, and so on. Then change to the corner nozzle. Go around the skirting boards and floors vacuuming corners and edges. Then attach the main head and clean under furniture first then the main areas. Start in one corner of the room and move diagonally across. Vacuuming diagonally puts less stress on the carpet fibres and leaves fewer marks. Just before you finish vacuuming, spray and suck up some insecticide into the cleaner to kill anything that might have landed in the bag. You could also apply no more than 2 drops of oil of pennyroyal to a tissue and suck it into the bag. Note that oil of pennyroyal should only be used as directed as it can be harmful to pregnant women and pets. Remember one drop means one drop.

If you're allergic to dust mites, suck a couple of damp tea bags into the vacuum cleaner bag before you start cleaning.

To find something small on the carpet, use your vacuum cleaner! Put a T-shirt between the head and the pole, vacuum the area and the item will stick to the T-shirt rather than going through to the bag. If you've dropped a packet of pins, needles or paper clips on the floor, attach a plastic magnetic strip across your broom or vacuum cleaner head with sticky tape. It'll pick them all up.

To clean the vacuum cleaner, vacuum inside the barrel and all the attachments, and clean the outside with a damp cloth. Wash the head in a mild dishwashing liquid solution but make sure to dry it well so it doesn't rust.

DIY STEAM-CLEANING

You've probably walked past a stand of carpet cleaners as you've left the supermarket. These can be hired and are easy to use. They come with a bottle of chemicals but only use half as much as the manufacturer recommends and top up with 2 tablespoons of bicarb, 2 tablespoons of white vinegar, 2 tablespoons of methylated spirits and 2 teaspoons of eucalyptus oil. If you have mystery stains on your carpet, add 2 teaspoons of glycerine. This recipe is also a great multi-purpose spot cleaner so leave it in a spray bottle and use when needed.

TIPS

- *Start early in the morning to allow time to dry.*
- *Make sure windows are open for ventilation. Fresh air will also speed the drying time.*
- *Work slowly, if you work too quickly, the water suction won't work.*
- *Use attachments to get right into corners.*
- *If the carpet is very dirty, you may need to steam twice.*
- *Put a note on the front and back door asking people to remove their shoes before stepping on your freshly steam-cleaned carpet. Always place a towel inside the front and back doors for people to wipe their feet.*
- *Spray* Scotchgard *over high traffic areas to add a layer of protection.*
- *Once cleaned and dried, keep a rug over the carpet in high traffic areas.*

WHAT TO DO:

Prepare the room by moving all the furniture to the centre. Clean the outside edges of the room first. Spot clean any stains, then vacuum. Then use the carpet steamer. Begin by working parallel to the wall (create stripes), then perpendicular to the wall (create checks) so you clean in all four directions. This means each side of the carpet fibre is cleaned. When you finish cleaning, run the steam-cleaner over the carpet without water in it (do not push the steam button). This will suck excess moisture out of the carpet and help it to dry faster. Allow the carpet to dry (about 3 hours), then vacuum. Always clean the head of your vacuum cleaner with a damp cloth so you don't transfer dirt to your clean carpet. Move the furniture back into place, placing clear plastic under any legs so they won't mark the carpet. Clean the middle of the room in the same way (stripes and checks). Allow to dry and vacuum.

If you use professional steam-cleaners ...

There are many chemicals used in steam-cleaning, including chlorine. If you've had your carpet professionally steam-cleaned and you get a fresh stain on it, before doing any spot cleaning, sponge the stain with a cloth that's been tightly wrung out in white vinegar. This will neutralise the chemicals. Don't worry, it's easy to do.

Many new carpet cleaning mixtures contain orange oil which can leave, surprise surprise, orange spots on your carpet. The residue is the problem. And while orange-based cleaning products can be good at removing stains, it must be rinsed and dried thoroughly. The thing is, some spots don't appear until about 6 months later. Yikes! This is what happened to Elsa.

Q 'Last year, I had our grey berber carpet professionally cleaned. The cleaner showed me some "new" orange-based solution which he sprayed on the walk areas. After cleaning, the carpet took about 4–5 hours to dry, whereupon I found slight orangey stains where he had sprayed the mixture. The other areas were fine. Just recently, another cleaner did our floors and this time it took about 12 hours to dry. The orange colour came to the surface and spread. I am now left with this orangey brown surface stain over a larger area. What can I do to remove it?'

A You can remove the stains but it takes a bit of work. Place a couple of drops of glycerine on an old toothbrush and comb through the bristles of the carpet. Hire a carpet cleaning machine and follow the technique described in DIY steam-cleaning, above. Use the cleaner again without water (and without pushing the steam button) so it sucks up excess moisture from the carpet. If there's good airflow, your carpet will dry quickly.

What to do when carpet gets wet

Water-soaked carpets smell awful. To dry the carpet out, hire an air blower (available from plant hire companies and councils). Follow the directions—each operates slightly differently. If the carpet is drenched, remove the batons from doorways and place a roll of paper towel under the edge of the carpet to lift it. This absorbs moisture near the doors and allows airflow under the carpet, helping it to dry faster. Once it has dried, sprinkle the carpet with bicarb and either stomp on the carpet or sweep with a stiff broom. Leave the bicarb for half an hour to an hour and then vacuum. Next, kill the mould spores by putting a ¼ teaspoon of oil of cloves into a 1 litre spray pack of water and lightly mist over the carpet. If you can't get hold of an air blower, use a combination of towels and pressure. Place the towels on the carpet and walk on them to absorb moisture. If there's brown staining once the carpet has dried, it means the jute backing has released tannin. Remove with ½ teaspoon of glycerine and ½ teaspoon of dishwashing liquid on an old toothbrush, working from the outside to the inside of the stain. Wipe with a damp cloth and apply paper towel (or towel for large areas) to remove moisture.

Q 'It's a rather sad story,' warns Bronwyn. 'My husband and I went away for the weekend and left the three teenage boys at home. The dog had an accident on the carpet and one of the boys cleaned it with the first thing he found in the cupboard, which was tile cleaner. He sprayed it on the carpet and now there's half an acre of brown on the carpet. What can I do?'

PROBLEM: Tile cleaner sprayed on carpet.
WHAT TO DO: Patch the carpet.

How to patch carpet

Cut around damaged part of the carpet into a manageable shape with a Stanley knife. Find a piece of the carpet (perhaps some leftover or cut from somewhere little seen, such as from inside a cupboard) a little larger than the stained area. Make sure the pattern is in the same direction. Then make a paper template of the stained area and transfer this to the piece of patch carpet. Cut the patch carpet around the template with a sharp knife. You'll need some carpet tape, which is available from carpet manufacturers, dealers and some supermarkets. Attach the tape under the edges of the damaged carpet so that the adhesive side is facing upwards. Make sure that half of the tape is under the old carpet and the other half is exposed in the hole. Then press the patch carpet into the hole, sticking it to the exposed half of the tape. Brush the carpet in both directions until the fibres line up on the edges. Stand on the area for five minutes to make sure it sticks well. Then place a book on top of the patch for 24 hours.

Barbecue sauce

Q 'I was eating dinner in front of the TV,' says Sam, 'and managed to get barbecue sauce on the carpet. What can I do?'

PROBLEM: Barbecue sauce on carpet.
WHAT TO USE: Damp cloth, white vinegar, paper towel, ultraviolet light, cardboard.
HOW TO APPLY: Remove the bulk of the stain with a damp cloth, then wipe with a cloth wrung out in white vinegar. Place paper towel over the top and stand on it to remove excess moisture. Aim ultraviolet light at the stain, protecting the surrounding carpet with cardboard. Check every 2 hours until the stain is removed.

Beer

Q 'I was enjoying a beer on a very hot day but spilled some on our white carpet,' says Ross. 'I did it yesterday and the added complication is it's dark beer. What should I do?'

PROBLEM: Dark beer stain on carpet.
WHAT TO USE: White vinegar, paper towel, dishwashing liquid, cold water, old toothbrush.
HOW TO APPLY: Because the stain is a day old, damp it with vinegar and blot it with paper towel. You'll absorb even more of the stain if you roll the paper towel into a ball and stand on it. Then add dishwashing liquid to cold water to generate a sudsy mix and spread the suds over the stain with an old toothbrush. Use as little water as possible. Let it dry and repeat the process until it's clean. For a new stain, remove as much of the beer as possible with a paper towel then mix dishwashing liquid with cold water and apply the suds to the stain.

Beetroot
PROBLEM: Beetroot on carpet.
WHAT TO USE: White vinegar, cloth, paper towel.
HOW TO APPLY: Immerse a cloth in white vinegar, tightly wring out and sponge over the stain until removed. Press with paper towel until dry.

Betadine

Q 'Some time ago, I managed to spill some *Betadine* on pink wool carpet,' reports Marjorie. 'Can I get it out?'

PROBLEM: Old *Betadine* spots on carpet.

WHAT TO USE: Lavender oil, cloth, white vinegar; or glycerine, old toothbrush, white vinegar, paper towel, dishwashing liquid, water, cloth.

HOW TO APPLY: Put a couple of drops of lavender oil on a cloth and wipe over the stain. Then wipe with a cloth wrung out in white vinegar. Alternatively, put a couple of drops of glycerine on an old toothbrush and apply to the stain working north–south and east–west across the carpet fibres. Leave overnight because it's an old stain. The next day, wipe over the stain with a little dishwashing liquid on a cloth, place paper towel over the top and stand on it to remove moisture. Wipe with a cloth wrung out in white vinegar, allow to dry and repeat until clean.

Bleach

Q 'How do I remove a bleach mark from a dark carpet?' asks Phil.

PROBLEM: Bleach mark on carpet.

WHAT TO USE: Folk art paint, toothbrush, hair dryer.

HOW TO APPLY: Replace the colour with folk art paint (available from art suppliers or craft stores) that matches the colour of your carpet. You may need to create your own mix from a couple of tubes. Test the paint on an inconspicuous corner of the carpet to make sure it's an exact match and allow each test section of paint to dry because many change colour. Don't use a hair dryer to speed up the drying process or you'll set the colour. Once you've got the right colour, use a toothbrush to brush the paint into the bleached spot on the carpet (use the toothbrush as though you were brushing your hair), feathering the edges so you don't get an obvious line. Then move a hair dryer backwards and forwards across the paint to set it.

Blood

Q 'What's the best way to remove blood from carpet?' asks Joan.

PROBLEM: Blood on carpet.
WHAT TO USE: Cake of bathroom soap, cold water, old toothbrush, damp cloth, paper towel, white vinegar, glycerine.
HOW TO APPLY: Blood is a protein stain. Dampen a cake of bathroom soap in cold water and scribble over the stain as though using a big crayon. Scrub with a toothbrush making sure you rub in every direction across the carpet fibre (north, south, east and west). Wipe with a damp cloth, place paper towel on top and stand on it to remove moisture. If you've applied any other product to the blood, neutralise it first by wiping with a cloth wrung out in white vinegar. Put a couple of drops of glycerine on a toothbrush,

scrub over the stain and leave for 20 minutes. Then use soap and cold water technique described above.

Blu-Tack

PROBLEM: *Blu-Tack* stain on carpet.
WHAT TO USE: Ice, plastic bag, scissors, sticky tape, talcum powder, white spirits or tea tree oil, cotton ball, tissue.
HOW TO APPLY: Removing *Blu-Tack* from carpet is quite difficult. Place ice on the *Blu-Tack* first, either directly or inside a plastic bag. The *Blu-Tack* should become stiff and you can cut most of it off with scissors. Don't cut the carpet fibres. Put sticky tape over the *Blu-Tack* and rip it up several times. Then sprinkle talcum powder over the remaining *Blu-Tack* and roll it between your fingers. The powder will draw the *Blu-Tack* out. For the remainder of the stain, use a little white spirits or tea tree oil on a cotton ball and rub it in a circle. Then rub a tissue over it and the *Blu-Tack* should stick to the tissue.

Boot polish

PROBLEM: Boot polish stains and scuff marks on carpet.
WHAT TO USE: Eucalyptus oil, cotton balls; or white spirits.
HOW TO APPLY: Rub eucalyptus oil over the spot with a cotton ball. An alternative is white spirits applied with a cotton ball.

Butter/margarine

PROBLEM: Butter/margarine on carpet.
WHAT TO USE: Dishwashing liquid, damp cloth, paper towel.
HOW TO APPLY: Put a couple of drops of dishwashing liquid on your fingertips and massage into the stain until it changes texture and feels like jelly. Wipe with a cold damp cloth. Place paper towel over the stain and press down to remove excess moisture.

Chewing gum

Q 'I've got some ingrained chewing gum in my carpet,' says Mary. 'I'd love to get rid of the awful stuff. What do you suggest?'

PROBLEM: Chewing gum on carpet.
WHAT TO USE: Ice, knife or scissors or ice-cream stick, cotton bud, white spirits, eucalyptus oil or tea tree oil, tissues, vacuum cleaner.
HOW TO APPLY: Put ice on the chewing gum to harden it. Then cut out the hardened gum with a knife, scissors or an ice-cream stick. Once you've removed as much chewing gum as you can, dip a cotton bud in white spirits and slowly work over the chewing gum. Then apply eucalyptus oil or tea tree oil to the gum and rub the area in circles with a tissue. Then vacuum.

Chocolate

Q 'I managed to get chocolate on my light-coloured pure wool carpet,' reports Karen. 'How do I get it out?'

PROBLEM: Chocolate on carpet.
WHAT TO USE: Cheap shampoo, cold water, paper towel.
HOW TO APPLY: Put a couple of drops of cheap shampoo on your fingers and massage gently into the carpet until the stain begins to loosen. If it starts to dry out, add a little cold water to your fingers and keep on massaging. Place paper towel over the stain and stand on it. Repeat until the stain is removed.

Coffee

PROBLEM: Coffee stain on carpet.
WHAT TO USE: Glycerine, old toothbrush, white vinegar, cloth, paper towel.
HOW TO APPLY: Put a couple of drops of glycerine on a toothbrush and work from the outside to the inside of the stain. Leave for 20 minutes. Wipe with a cloth wrung out in white vinegar. Place paper towel over the stain and press down to remove excess moisture.

PROBLEM: Old coffee and tea stains on carpet.
WHAT TO USE: Glycerine, cotton ball, sponge, white vinegar, bicarb, vacuum cleaner.

HOW TO APPLY: Apply glycerine to the stain with a cotton ball. Leave for 5 minutes then damp sponge the stain with white vinegar. Sprinkle with bicarb then vacuum when dry.

Cordial

PROBLEM: Red cordial on carpet.
WHAT TO USE: White vinegar, cloth, ultraviolet light, cardboard, paper towel; glycerine.
HOW TO APPLY: Wipe with a cloth wrung out in white vinegar. Aim ultraviolet light at the stain until it begins to fade (check every 2 hours). Cover around the stain with cardboard if the carpet is coloured. Again, wipe with a cloth wrung out in white vinegar. Place paper towel over the stain and press down to remove excess moisture. For old stains, wipe a couple of drops of glycerine over the stain first and leave for 20 minutes. Then use the above technique.

Cough medicine

Q 'I dropped a bottle of very sticky cough medicine on the berber carpet in our bedroom,' reports Sally. 'I've mopped and sponged it to no avail. Please don't tell me we will have to replace the carpet!'

PROBLEM: Cough mixture on carpet.
WHAT TO USE: White vinegar, warm water, pantyhose, paper towel.

HOW TO APPLY: Cough mixture is very high in sugar and requires extra persistence when removing it. Mix equal parts white vinegar and warm water. Dip a pair of rolled up pantyhose into the solution and wring out tightly. Scrub the stain in all directions (north, south, east and west) until removed. Place paper towel over the stain and stand on it. When the carpet appears to be almost dry, repeat the entire process. If a shadow returns in a couple of weeks, repeat. Sugar stains can be very stubborn because sugar crystallises in the carpet fibres and continues to resurface. Fortunately, you don't have to rub too vigorously—just repeatedly.

Crayon
PROBLEM: Crayon on carpet.
WHAT TO USE: Pantyhose, tea tree oil.
HOW TO APPLY: Place a couple of drops of tea tree oil on a pair of pantyhose and roll over the crayon mark in a circle. Don't forget to clean your pantyhose before using again or you'll transfer coloured crayon to the next job!

Cream

Q 'My 2-year-old wanted to help me bring the shopping in,' reports Megan. 'So I gave her a carton of cream which she dropped on a green rug. It's created a white shadow and really smells. What can I do?'

PROBLEM: Cream stain on rug/carpet.
WHAT TO USE: Dishwashing liquid, old toothbrush, paper towel; or white spirits, cotton ball, talcum powder, vacuum cleaner, carpet cleaner.
HOW TO APPLY: Attack the proteins first. Mix enough dishwashing liquid in cold water to generate a sudsy mix and apply just the suds to the stain with an old toothbrush. Then dry with paper towel. Remove the fats with dishwashing liquid suds mixed in hot water. Apply the suds only to the stain with an old toothbrush, then dry with a paper towel. An alternative is white spirits applied with a cotton ball. Sprinkle talcum powder over the white spirits to absorb it. Then vacuum. To get rid of the smell, use carpet cleaner.

Curry

Q 'Help!' exclaims Garry. 'I've got green chicken curry on my carpet. It looks awful.'

PROBLEM: Green chicken curry on carpet.
WHAT TO USE: Dishwashing liquid, white vinegar, cloth, paper towel, ultraviolet light, cardboard; or lavender oil, water, spray pack, pantyhose.
HOW TO APPLY: To remove the oils, place a little dishwashing liquid on your fingers and massage into the stain. Wipe with a cloth wrung out in white vinegar. Place

paper towel over the stain and press down to remove excess moisture. Aim ultraviolet light at the stain, protecting the carpet around the stain with cardboard, until it begins to fade (check every 2 hours). If the curry has any yellow colouring, combine 1 teaspoon of lavender oil and 1 litre of water in a spray pack, lightly spray over the area and scrub with pantyhose. Repeat until removed.

Dog poo

Q 'How do I remove dog diarrhoea from light bone-coloured carpet?' asks Joan. 'I've tried bicarb and white vinegar but a light yellow stain was left behind.'

PROBLEM: Dog poo on carpet.
WHAT TO USE: Comb, toilet paper, cake of bathroom soap, cold water, old toothbrush, paper towel, bicarb, white vinegar, cloth, vacuum cleaner.
HOW TO APPLY: The yellow stain could be from colouring used in some dog food or a tannin stain from using too much moisture on the carpet. To remove the diarrhoea, slide a comb underneath and lift as much as you can from the carpet. Place toilet paper on top to absorb it. Dip a cake of bathroom soap in cold water and scribble over the stain as though using a crayon. Don't use too much water. Then scrub the area with a toothbrush. Place several sheets of

paper towel on top and stand on them to remove moisture. Repeat until the stain is removed. For regular dog poo, remove as much as possible and apply the above technique. For any remaining stain, sprinkle with a little bicarb and wipe with a cloth wrung out in white vinegar. Leave to dry completely before vacuuming.

Q 'We have an elderly dog,' says Annie, 'and he's losing it a little bit. The other day he did a big poop in the hallway and walked it up and down the wool berber carpet. What can we do?'

PROBLEM: Pet mishaps on carpet.
WHAT TO USE: Paper towel, bicarb, white vinegar, sponge or nylon brush, vacuum cleaner; or bucket, cold water, dishwashing liquid, old toothbrush, white vinegar, water, bicarb, vacuum cleaner; or lavender oil, cotton ball, or camphor or mothballs; or bicarb, sponge, white vinegar, nylon brush, vacuum cleaner or stiff brush; or ultraviolet light, chalk.
HOW TO APPLY: Remove as much of the solids as possible then blot with a paper towel until the carpet is touch dry. Sprinkle bicarb over the spot then a little white vinegar. Scrub with a sponge or nylon brush and leave to dry. Then vacuum it out and, if there's any scent, do it again. Another way to fix the problem is to fill a bucket with cold water

Floors, Walls and Windows 251

and enough dishwashing liquid to generate a sudsy mix. Apply the detergent suds with an old toothbrush, using as little water as possible. Then fill a bucket with warm water and dishwashing liquid and apply the suds to the stain again with an old toothbrush. The reason you use both cold and warm water is because faeces contain proteins and fats. Leave to dry. Get rid of any pet urine smell by blotting with white vinegar and water. Then sprinkle with bicarb, allow it to dry and vacuum. Never soak urine stains on carpet because this will just push the stain further into the fibres.

Because animals like to return to the same spot, put a small amount of lavender oil on a cotton ball and lightly wipe it over the spot. This will deter dogs. Use a combination of camphor and water to deter cats unless you have coloured carpet, in which case put some mothballs near the spot. Camphor can bleach carpet.

For old pet stains, cover the spot with a large amount of bicarb then wipe with a sponge dipped in white vinegar and scrub with a nylon brush. Dry thoroughly. Then vacuum or sweep with a stiff brush.

In the rather infuriating situation of being able to smell but not locate an old stain, use an ultraviolet (UV) light, not a black light. UV lights can be hired from a chemist. Under the light, the stains will fluoresce and glow. (Don't look into the ultraviolet light because it could damage your eyes and, unless you want a tan, don't stand in front of it.) Mark the stains with chalk. Then you've got the task of cleaning the stain up and a lot of bicarb and a little white vinegar will come to your aid. Because the stains have been there for a while, you may have to repeat the treatment a few times.

Dye

Q 'I had a mishap with a hot water bottle,' admits Trish. 'It burst, spilled hot water onto a cushion and the dye from the cushion then soaked through to a pure wool cream-coloured rug. What can I do?'

PROBLEM: Dye on carpet.
WHAT TO USE: *Colour Run Remover: Whites*, cloth, blood-heat water, paper towel.
HOW TO APPLY: Mix 1 part *Colour Run Remover: Whites* to 5 parts water. Place a cloth into the mixture, wring it out tightly and wipe until the stain is removed. Then wipe with a cloth wrung out in blood-heat water. Apply paper towel to remove moisture. With white or pale cream carpet, use *Colour Run Remover: Whites*. With other carpet, use *Colour Run Remover: Coloursafe*.

Q 'I dye my own hair,' says Chrissie. 'Usually I do it in the bathroom, but this time I was in the bedroom and I dropped some on the carpet. How do you get it out?'

PROBLEM: Hair dye stain on carpet.
WHAT TO USE: Hairspray, carpet cleaner; or white spirits, cotton balls.
HOW TO APPLY: If you can get to the stain right away, use hairspray. Let it dry then treat with carpet cleaner. If you don't get to it immediately, put white spirits onto a cotton ball and wipe it over the stain. Then wipe with a clean cotton ball. Repeat until it's removed.

PROBLEM: Egg on carpet.
WHAT TO USE: Combs, tissue, cold water, cake of bathroom soap, damp cloth, cloth, cold water.
HOW TO APPLY: If it's raw egg, wrap two combs in a tissue so the teeth stick out. Slide the combs toward each other and lift the egg. Dip a cake of bathroom soap in cold water, scribble on the stain, then sponge with a damp cloth. If it's scrambled or cooked, scribble a cake of bathroom soap on the stain and sponge with a cloth wrung out in cold water.

Fanta

Q 'My child spilled some of her *Fanta* soft drink on our wool beige carpet,' reports Steve. 'The carpet has been professionally cleaned and they said the stain can't be removed. Can you help?'

PROBLEM: *Fanta* stain on carpet.

WHAT TO USE: White vinegar, cloth, ultraviolet light, cardboard, paper towel.

HOW TO APPLY: *Fanta* contains vegetable dye and sugar. Remove the vegetable dye by wiping over the stain with a cloth wrung out in white vinegar. Then aim ultraviolet light at the stain, protecting the carpet around the stain with cardboard. Check every 2 hours until the stain is gone. *Fanta* is high in sugar so you may get a shadow stain a couple of weeks later. If so, wipe with a cloth wrung out in white vinegar. Apply paper towel and stand on it to absorb moisture.

Fat

PROBLEM: Fat-based food stain on carpet.

WHAT TO USE: Paper towel, hair dryer, bucket, dishwashing liquid, old toothbrush; or white spirits, talcum powder, vacuum cleaner.

HOW TO APPLY: Roll some paper towel into a ball, warm the carpet with a hair dryer then place the ball of paper towel over the stain. Stand on the paper towel so that as much of the fat as possible is absorbed. Fill a bucket with warm water and enough detergent to generate a sudsy mix. Apply the suds to the stain with an old toothbrush and scrub using as little water as possible. Place clean paper towel over the stain and stand on it. Leave to dry.

Another option is to rub a small amount of white spirits into the fibres. Don't soak the carpet. Just damp it and lightly rub with paper towel. Cover with talcum powder to absorb the white spirits. Then vacuum the talcum powder.

Fluorescent pen

Q 'I've got pink fluorescent pen on my carpet,' reports Richard. 'What can I do?'

PROBLEM: Fluorescent pen on carpet.
WHAT TO USE: Ice-cubes, zip-lock bag, water, non-iodised salt, damp cloth, paper towel.
HOW TO APPLY: Place ice-cubes in a zip-lock bag. Slightly damp the stain with water and sprinkle a generous amount of non-iodised salt over the stain. Place the ice on top and leave until it melts. Remove the zip-lock bag and sponge the stain with a damp cloth. Apply paper towel to absorb all the moisture.

Fruit

Q 'I had some friends over the other evening,' reports Sally. 'And one of the strawberry daiquiris went spilling onto the carpet. Any suggestions?'

PROBLEM: Strawberry daiquiri stain on carpet.
WHAT TO USE: Cloth, white vinegar, ultraviolet light, cardboard.
HOW TO APPLY: Wring out a cloth in white vinegar and wipe over the stain. Aim ultraviolet light at the area, protecting the rest of the carpet with cardboard, and check every 2 hours until the stain fades.

PROBLEM: Fruit stain on carpet.
WHAT TO USE: White cloth, white vinegar, glycerine, cotton ball or old toothbrush, talcum powder, vacuum cleaner, carpet cleaner or *NapiSan Oxygen*, paper towel.
HOW TO APPLY: Make sure the carpet is colourfast*. For stains from fruits that go brown such as apricots, kiwifruit, apples, bananas and so on, put glycerine on the stain with a cotton ball or old toothbrush and sprinkle talcum powder over the top of it. Vacuum. Then use a carpet cleaner. Vacuum again. An alternative to carpet cleaner is a paste of water and *NapiSan Oxygen* on the stain for a few minutes. Wipe it off, rinse and dry with a paper towel, leave the carpet to dry, then vacuum.

* To test for colourfastness, soak a white cloth in white vinegar and apply to part of the carpet not on display. If any colour comes off, it's not colourfast and you may have to patch the carpet. How to do this is explained in 'How to patch carpet' on page 238.

Furniture indentations

PROBLEM: Furniture indentations on carpet.
WHAT TO USE: Damp cloth, hair dryer, hairbrush, hairspray.
HOW TO APPLY: Press a damp cloth over the spot. Then dry it with a hair dryer, fluffing the carpet with a hairbrush as you dry. If the carpet still lies flat, apply some hairspray and dry it again with a hair dryer making sure to backcomb.

Glycerine

Q 'I used glycerine to remove a coffee stain on my carpet,' reports Veronica. 'But now I'm left with what looks to be a wet mark. Can it be removed?'

PROBLEM: Glycerine on carpet.
WHAT TO USE: Cloth, white vinegar.
HOW TO APPLY: Wring out a cloth in white vinegar and wipe over the stain. Don't overuse glycerine. A couple of drops should be enough for an area 30 cm in diameter.

Glue

What to do will depend on the type of glue. To remove superglue, use superglue remover (available from hardware stores) or acetone. Craft and PVA glues (which go on white and dry clear) are removed with steam and rubbing with pantyhose. To generate steam, fill a watering can with boiling water and aim the steamy spout over the stain (don't get any water on the carpet). When the glue softens, rub with pantyhose. Two-part epoxy glues (*Araldite*) are removed with acetone (see 'Nail polish' on page 485 for instructions). Gums and paper glues are removed with a warm damp cloth. For contact adhesives (sticky tape, double-sided tape or shoe repair kits), use tea tree oil. A single drop will remove a large piece of tape. Put 1 drop on the top edge of the tape and allow to soak for 20 minutes. For sticky tape and masking tape residue, put 1 drop of tea tree oil on pantyhose and wipe over the glue.

Graphite powder

Q 'My husband was lubricating the baby's bedroom door hinges with graphite powder and spilt it over the sisal wool-blend carpet in that corner of the room,' says Simone. 'I have only tried vacuuming with no luck. Any suggestions?'

PROBLEM: Graphite powder on carpet.
WHAT TO USE: Cake of bathroom soap, cold water, 9 litre bucket, damp cloth, paper towel.
HOW TO APPLY: Graphite and other fine powders are often left behind when vacuuming. To pick up fine matter, dampen a cake of bathroom soap with a little cold water and dab it up and down over the graphite spots on the carpet. The graphite will stick to the soap. For a large

spill, keep a bucket of cold water next to you and dip as you go. Remove excess soap with a damp cloth. Apply paper towel to remove moisture. Alternatively, cut the soap into a sausage shape by cutting lengthways and trimming the corners with a warm knife. Roll backwards and forwards over the carpet. Use sewing machine oil or baby oil rather than graphite powder to lubricate hinges in a baby's room (graphite powder isn't great for a baby's lungs).

PREVENTION: Put a covering, such as newspaper, underneath the door when applying graphite powder or any other substances that may spill.

Grass

PROBLEM: Grass on carpet.
WHAT TO USE: White spirits, cloth, white vinegar, paper towel.
HOW TO APPLY: Dab white spirits on a cloth and wipe over the grass stain. Immerse another cloth in white vinegar, wring out tightly and wipe the area. Apply paper towel to absorb all the moisture.

Gravy

PROBLEM: Gravy on carpet.
WHAT TO USE: Cake of bathroom soap, cold water, old toothbrush, damp cloth, dishwashing liquid, paper towel.

HOW TO APPLY: This is a protein and oil stain. Dip a cake of bathroom soap in cold water and scribble over the stain as though you are using a crayon. Scrub over the stain with a toothbrush and wipe with a cold damp cloth. Put a couple of drops of dishwashing liquid on your fingers and massage into the stain until it feels like jelly. Then sponge with a damp cloth. Apply paper towel to absorb all the moisture.

Grease

There was confusion in *Spotless* about how to remove different types of grease. The treatment to use depends on whether the grease is dark or light coloured. As a general guide, dark-coloured grease is removed with baby oil followed by dishwashing liquid rubbed in with your fingers. Light-coloured grease is removed with dishwashing liquid rubbed in with your fingers. If you've used baby oil on a light-coloured grease stain, put dishwashing liquid on your fingers and rub into the baby oil until it feels like jelly and wipe with a damp cloth. Absorb moisture with paper towel.

> **Q** 'I've got car grease stains on wool-carpeted stairs,' says Trish. 'How do I get rid of them?'

PROBLEM: Car grease on carpet.
WHAT TO USE: Tissue, metal comb, disposable rubber gloves, dishwashing liquid, damp cloth, paper towel.

HOW TO APPLY: Wrap a tissue around a metal comb, wedge it under the grease and comb out as much as possible. If it's a large amount of grease, you may need to repeat this with clean tissues. Put on rubber gloves and rub dishwashing liquid into the stain with your fingers until it changes texture and feels like jelly. Remove the dishwashing liquid by wiping with a clean damp cloth. Apply paper towel to dry.

Hair gel

Q 'I've got hair gel on my carpet,' reports Sue. 'What can I do?'

PROBLEM: Hair gel on carpet.
WHAT TO USE: Dishwashing liquid, damp cloth, tea tree oil, paper towel.
HOW TO APPLY: Rub a couple of drops of dishwashing liquid into the gel with your fingers until it feels like jelly and wipe with a warm damp cloth. If the gel contains wax, mix ½ teaspoon of tea tree oil with ½ teaspoon of dishwashing liquid and rub into the carpet using your fingers. Wipe with a damp cloth. Apply paper towel to absorb moisture.

Hair serum

Q 'My daughter emptied my anti-frizz hair serum onto our bedroom carpet,' reports Susie. 'It's a rental home and I'm pretty sure the carpet is wool.'

PROBLEM: Anti-frizz hair serum on carpet.
WHAT TO USE: Glycerine, cloth, dishwashing liquid, old toothbrush, damp cloth, paper towel.
HOW TO APPLY: If the stain is brown in colour, wipe with a couple of drops of glycerine on a toothbrush. Then put a couple of drops of dishwashing liquid onto the toothbrush and scrub over the stain. Two drops of each is enough for a 30 cm circle. Wipe over with a damp cloth. Apply paper towel with pressure to absorb moisture. If it is grey in colour, use dishwashing liquid as described above.

Ice-cream

problem: Ice-cream on carpet.
WHAT TO USE: Cake of bathroom soap, cold water, cloth, dishwashing liquid, damp cloth, white vinegar, dry cloth, paper towel.
HOW TO APPLY: Ice-cream is high in protein, fat and sugar and each element will have to be removed separately but in this order. First, remove protein by dipping a cake of bathroom soap in cold water and scribble over the stain as though using a crayon. Scrub with a toothbrush and sponge with a damp cloth. Second, remove fats by putting a couple of drops of dishwashing liquid onto your fingers and massaging into the stain until it feels like jelly. Wipe with a damp cloth. Third, remove sugar by wringing out a cloth in white vinegar. Place the white

vinegar cloth in one hand and a dry cloth in the other and wipe over the stain, hand over hand as though you're stroking a cat. Apply paper towel with pressure to absorb all the moisture.

Ink

There are many different types of ink and to complicate matters each requires a different solution. If you don't know what's been used, test with methylated spirits on a cotton bud. If this doesn't work, use white spirits.

Biros—place rotten milk solids over the stain. You will see the ink absorbing into the milk solids. When the ink has visibly soaked into the milk solids, slide a comb under the solids to lift without squashing. Remove any residue by washing with a little soap on a damp cloth.

Gel pens—place methylated spirits on a cotton bud and wipe over the stain until removed. Rub off with paper towel.

Fine-point liners—dip a cotton bud in methylated spirits and wipe over the liner. For stronger grade liners, use white spirits in the same way.

Permanent markers—contain their own solvent so use the same permanent marker and draw over the mark. Then dip a cotton bud in white spirits and wipe over the mark. Sprinkle with talcum powder and vacuum. Repeat the white spirits step if necessary.

Q 'Our house was broken into,' says Robyn. 'The police came and collected fingerprints, but they left all this black powder on the carpet and I don't know how to get it off. I rang the police and they didn't know either!'

PROBLEM: Black ink stain on carpet.
WHAT TO USE: Milk, cloth, dishwashing liquid, lemon juice; or white spirits, cotton balls, talcum powder, vacuum cleaner.
HOW TO APPLY: The black powder is ink-based. Rot some milk in the sun (the time it takes will vary) and rub the solids into the stain with a cloth. Leave for a few minutes then wash with a little dishwashing liquid, lemon juice and water. An alternative is white spirits applied with a cotton ball. Then sprinkle some talcum powder to absorb the dry-cleaning fluid. Vacuum.

Q 'Our puppy chewed a red biro pen and got ink all over our white carpet,' says Bob. 'What should we do?'

PROBLEM: Red ink stain on carpet.
WHAT TO USE: White spirits, cotton balls, white vinegar.
HOW TO APPLY: Red ink is particularly hard to remove. Apply white spirits to a cotton ball and rub it over the stain. Then apply white vinegar to a cotton ball and rub it

over the stain. Keep on doing this until the stain is removed.

Insects

Q 'I think I have an insect stain on our beige wool carpet,' queries Jill. 'And it's been there for some time. What should I do?'

PROBLEM: Insect stain on wool carpet.
WHAT TO USE: Glycerine, cloth, dishwashing liquid, old toothbrush, damp cloth, paper towel.
HOW TO APPLY: Wipe over the stain with a couple of drops of glycerine on an old toothbrush. Then dip a cake of bathroom soap in cold water and scrub over the stain. Rub a toothbrush in all four directions—north, south, east, west—over the top. Wipe with a cold damp cloth, apply paper towel and stand on it to dry it thoroughly. If it's insect faeces (looks like an orange splash), dip a cake of bathroom soap in cold water and scribble over the stain. Wipe with a cold damp cloth, apply paper towel and stand on it to dry thoroughly.

Jam

PROBLEM: Plum jam spilt on wool carpet.
WHAT TO USE: Cloth, white vinegar, water, glycerine, old toothbrush, paper towel.

HOW TO APPLY: Wring a cloth out in white vinegar and wipe over the stain. Wipe straight away with a dry cloth. Repeat hand over hand, as though you're stroking a cat. If there's a light brown stain, use a couple of drops of glycerine on a toothbrush and brush over the top of the carpet fibres. Leave for 20 minutes and use the vinegar solution. Apply paper towel with pressure to absorb moisture.

Jelly beans

Q 'I've got jelly beans on my white carpet,' says Margaret. 'They've been mashed into it.'

PROBLEM: Jelly beans on carpet.
WHAT TO USE: Comb, dishwashing liquid, old toothbrush, damp cloth, paper towel.
HOW TO APPLY: Wedge a comb beneath the mashed jelly bean and remove as much as possible. Put a couple of drops of dishwashing liquid on a toothbrush and brush over the carpet fibres in each direction. Remove the dishwashing liquid with a warm damp cloth. Repeat until the stain is removed. Apply paper towel with pressure to absorb moisture.

Lemonade

Q 'One of the kids spilled lemonade on our dark-pink carpet some time ago and we can't shift it,' complains Michael. 'Do you have a suggestion?'

PROBLEM: Old lemonade/sugar stain on carpet.
WHAT TO USE: Glycerine, cotton ball, sponge or cloth, bicarb, nylon brush, clean white cloth, white vinegar; or dishwashing liquid, water, nylon brush, paper towel.
HOW TO APPLY: A sugar stain is very difficult to remove because it seeps right into the back of the carpet. For old stains, apply some glycerine to the stain with a cotton ball, and leave for a few minutes. Then wipe it off with a sponge or cloth. Sprinkle bicarb over the stain and scrub it in with a nylon brush. Then soak a clean white cloth in white vinegar, wring it out and place it over the bicarb. Stand on the cloth so it absorbs the bicarb and stain. You may need to repeat this a few times. If the stain still doesn't shift, mix dishwashing liquid and water to create a sudsy mix and scrub the suds into it with a nylon brush. Then place a paper towel over the spot to absorb the stain. You may need to repeat this a few times as well.

Lipstick

Q 'The other day, my son decided to help with the vacuuming,' says Rick, 'and he managed to suck up some lipstick which got stuck in the bristle of the cleaner head. Now there's lipstick all over the carpet. What can we do?'

PROBLEM: Lipstick stain on carpet.

WHAT TO USE: White spirits, cotton ball, bicarb, vacuum cleaner.
HOW TO APPLY: Use white spirits applied with a cotton ball to soften the colour of the lipstick stain. Then sprinkle bicarb over the stain. Then vacuum.

Lubricant (personal)

PROBLEM: Lube on carpet.
WHAT TO USE: Cake of bathroom soap, cold water, paper towel; or dishwashing liquid, damp cloth, paper towel.
HOW TO APPLY: There are two varieties of personal lubricant. One is gelatine-based and is high in protein. The other is oil-based. It is quite easy to work out which type of lube it is. Gelatine-based lube has a stain with a dark outer edge and oil-based is even in colour. For gelatine-based stains, use a cake of bathroom soap, dip it in cold water and scribble over the mark. Scrub with an old toothbrush before applying paper towel to absorb moisture. For oil-based stains, put a couple of drops of dishwashing liquid on your fingers and massage into the area until it's jelly-like. Wipe with a damp cloth. Apply paper towel to absorb moisture.

Make-up

Q 'My wife opened a tube of foundation make-up and dropped it all over our white wool carpet,' reports Brian. 'Is there a way to get it out?'

Floors, Walls and Windows   269

PROBLEM: Make-up on carpet.

WHAT TO USE: Dishwashing liquid, old toothbrush, paper towel, carpet cleaner; or lemon juice or ultraviolet light, cardboard.

HOW TO APPLY: Work out if the make-up has oil in it first. If it contains oil, clean that out by mixing dishwashing liquid in cold water and applying just the suds to the stain with an old toothbrush. Dry with a paper towel. Then clean the area with carpet cleaner. Sunlight will bleach the stain. If you can't get the carpet into the sun, apply some lemon juice to the stain or hire an ultraviolet light. Protect the unstained part of the carpet by covering it with cardboard or it will bleach as well. Leave the ultraviolet light on the stain for up to 24 hours, checking it every two hours. Don't look into the ultraviolet light because it could damage your eyes.

Mayonnaise

PROBLEM: Mayonnaise on carpet.

WHAT TO USE: Dishwashing liquid, damp cloth, paper towel; or cake of bathroom soap, cold water.

HOW TO APPLY: Mayonnaise contains a lot of oil. Put dishwashing liquid on your fingertips and massage into the stain until it feels like jelly. Remove the residue with a damp cloth and apply paper towel to absorb moisture. If it's whole egg mayonnaise, use a cake of bathroom soap and cold water first. Then massage in dishwashing liquid with your fingers. Wipe with a damp cloth and apply paper towel to remove moisture.

Mould

PROBLEM: Mould on carpet.
WHAT TO USE: Oil of cloves, water, 1 litre spray pack, vacuum cleaner, non-iodised salt, stiff broom.
HOW TO APPLY: If the mould is from condensation, combine ¼ teaspoon of oil of cloves with 1 litre of water in a spray pack, lightly mist over the carpet and leave for 24 hours. Vacuum the next day. If the mould remains, repeat. If the mould is from chronic damp over a large area, use the oil of cloves and water mixture first and leave for 24 hours. Scatter non-iodised coarse salt over the affected area and sweep with a broom before vacuuming. If you can still smell the mould, it's best to remove the carpet and install floorboards. WARNING: Don't use more oil of cloves than suggested. Oil of cloves is a volatile oil and can cause damage if used in large quantities or incorrectly.

People often complain about mouldy smelling homes at Stain Clinics. Mould can be harmful to your health, so it's best to deal with it promptly! The first step is to determine the areas of highest mould concentration. If it's in the walls, you might need to have a damp course put under the house (you'll need professional help with this). To alleviate the problem, mix ¼ teaspoon of oil of cloves with 1 litre of water in a spray pack and lightly mist over the mouldy surfaces. If you have floorboards, spray over them or under them if you possibly can. Regularly spray through vents under the house.

Milk

PROBLEM: Milk on carpet.
WHAT TO USE: Bathroom soap, cold water, old toothbrush, paper towel.
HOW TO APPLY: Dampen a cake of bathroom soap in cold water and scribble over the stain as though using a big crayon. Use an old toothbrush and rub in every direction over the carpet fibres. Rub with a damp cloth and place paper towel over the stain and stand on it to absorb all the moisture. Yes, the smell is awful but once you remove the stain, the smell will go too!

Mud

Q 'Fresh mud has been tramped through the house,' complains Vicky. 'What do you suggest?'

PROBLEM: Black mud on carpet.
WHAT TO USE: Stiff brush, vacuum cleaner, cake of bathroom soap, cold water, paper towel.
HOW TO APPLY: Allow the mud to dry or it will smear. Once it is dry, rub with a brush and vacuum. If it was rubbed

when wet, dampen a cake of bathroom soap in cold water and scribble over the area. Rub with a damp cloth and apply paper towel to remove moisture. Allow to dry and brush vigorously before vacuuming.

Nail polish

Q 'Our 5-year-old was playing with nail polish and got a massive blob on the carpet,' reports Craig. 'Of course, it's right in the middle of the room. Is there a solution?'

PROBLEM: Glue or nail polish stain on carpet.
WHAT TO USE: Fine-toothed metal nit comb, tissue, cotton balls, acetone, hair dryer, cloth, methylated spirits; or superglue-removing liquids.
HOW TO APPLY: This is a time-consuming and difficult task. Wrap a fine-toothed metal nit comb in a tissue so the teeth come through the tissue. Don't use a plastic comb because the acetone will melt it. Place the comb at an angle to the base of the carpet and wedge it underneath the stain. Dip a cotton ball in acetone and rub it over the top of the stain with the comb underneath. Work the stain row by row, using a clean cotton ball for each row. Acetone can affect carpet so make sure it doesn't penetrate the base. Replace the tissue if it's wet. This process is slow and may need to be repeated a few times. If it's an epoxy

resin stain, warm it first with a hair dryer. Then dip a cloth in boiling water, wring it and lay it over the stain until the cloth starts to cool. Then pinch and pull the cloth to remove as much of the resin as possible. Repeat this a few times before using the acetone. To get rid of the smell of acetone, use methylated spirits and water. You can use acetone to remove superglue from carpet but it takes a long time. Try superglue-removing liquids for a quicker result.

Nappy rash cream

Q 'How can I get lanolin-based nappy rash cream out of our new carpet?' asks Donna.

PROBLEM: Nappy rash cream on carpet.
WHAT TO USE: Dishwashing liquid, tea tree oil, cold water, damp cloth, paper towel, talcum powder, pantyhose.
HOW TO APPLY: Massage a couple of drops of dishwashing liquid into the stain with your fingers. Mix 1 teaspoon of tea tree oil with 1 cup of cold water and wipe the mixture over the area with a well-wrung cloth. Apply paper towel to absorb the moisture. For zinc-based nappy rash creams, remove as much as possible by sprinkling with talcum powder and scrubbing with pantyhose. Then use the above technique.

Orange juice

PROBLEM: Orange juice on carpet.
WHAT TO USE: Paper towel, white vinegar, cloth, ultraviolet light, cardboard, glycerine, old toothbrush.
HOW TO APPLY: Remove as much orange juice as possible with paper towel. Wipe with a little white vinegar on a cloth. Apply more paper towel. Aim an ultraviolet light at the stain, protecting the carpet around the stain with cardboard, until it fades. Check the UV light every 2 hours. For an old stain, wipe over the area with a couple of drops of glycerine on a toothbrush before using the above technique.

> **Q** 'I tried to get an orange juice spill out of the carpet with washing detergent and warm water,' reports Lynn, 'and now the stain has set and gone rusty. I need help!'

PROBLEM: Orange juice stain set on carpet.
WHAT TO USE: *NapiSan Oxygen*, cloths, paper towels.
HOW TO APPLY: Lynn's effort had the effect of setting the stain. Test in an unobtrusive spot to make sure this remedy won't leach the colour*. Unset the stain with a paste of water and *NapiSan Oxygen*, leaving it for a few minutes. Then remove the paste with a cloth and blot any

moisture with a paper towel. You may have to repeat this process a couple of times. Be careful not to get water on the carpet base or it will stain. Have lots of paper towels at hand to absorb any moisture immediately. Repeat if necessary.

* If the carpet isn't colourfast (check by soaking a white cloth in white vinegar and applying to a part of the carpet not on display; if any colour comes off, it's not colourfast), you may have to patch the carpet. How to do this is explained in 'How to patch carpet' on page 238.

Pollen

Q 'We've got some lilies sitting on a table in the lounge room,' says Mike, 'and the stamens have fallen off onto our white berber carpet leaving a yellow stain. Can we get it out?'

PROBLEM: Pollen stain on carpet.
WHAT TO USE: Lavender oil, cotton balls; plastic bag.
HOW TO APPLY: Apply a little lavender oil to a cotton ball and wipe over the effected area. Some pollens will be easy to remove, others will need several attempts. To avoid the problem, Shannon suggests you remove the stamens before putting your flowers on display. The best way to do this is by putting a plastic bag over your hand and pulling the

stamens off into the plastic bag. Then wrap the bag over itself and throw it in the bin. That way your hands won't come into contact with the stamens.

Pot plant mark

Q 'My pot plant has marked the carpet with a big brown mark,' says Linley. 'How can I fix it?'

PROBLEM: Pot plant mark on carpet.
WHAT TO USE: Glycerine, old toothbrush, cloth, white vinegar, paper towel.
HOW TO APPLY: This is a tannin stain. Put a couple of drops of glycerine on a toothbrush and scrub over the stain. Leave for 20 minutes. Wring a cloth in white vinegar, rub over the area, then apply paper towel to absorb moisture. Repeat until the stain is removed.

Red wine

Q 'I had some friends over to watch a DVD and one of them dropped red wine on the carpet,' says Steven. 'What's the best way to get it out?'

PROBLEM: New red wine stain on carpet.
WHAT TO USE: Bicarb, vacuum cleaner, white vinegar, nylon brush.
HOW TO APPLY: Cover the stain with a good amount of

bicarb and let dry for a few minutes. Then vacuum and re-apply a smaller amount of bicarb, add a little white vinegar and scrub with a nylon brush. Leave it to dry, then vacuum.

SPOTLESS CLASSIC
Red wine stain

This is one of the most common carpet stains. Don't throw salt or soda water over the red puddle. Instead, use bicarb and white vinegar, ensuring you don't use too much moisture or you'll get staining from the jute backing of the carpet, which releases a brown tannin stain if it gets wet. Remove jute stains with ½ teaspoon of glycerine and ½ teaspoon of dishwashing liquid on an old toothbrush, working from the outside to the inside of the stain. Wipe with a damp cloth and apply paper towel to remove moisture.

Absorb as much of the red wine spill as possible with paper towel. Sprinkle with a little bicarb and the stain will change from red to pale grey. Don't use too much bicarb or it will whiten the carpet around the stain. Wring a cloth out in white vinegar, wipe and leave to dry completely, then vacuum. Repeat if needed.

For old stains, apply a little glycerine with an old toothbrush. Then use the above technique.

PROBLEM: Old red wine stain on carpet.
WHAT TO USE: Cloth, white vinegar; or methylated spirits, cloth.
HOW TO APPLY: Damp the stain with a cloth dipped in white vinegar. If the stain doesn't come out, lightly damp it with methylated spirits on a cloth.

Rubber

PROBLEM: Rubber mark on carpet.
WHAT TO USE: Damp cloth, non-iodised salt, pantyhose, vacuum.
HOW TO APPLY: Wipe the mark with a damp cloth, sprinkle it with non-iodised salt and scrub with pantyhose. Wipe again with a damp cloth and vacuum.

TIP

If you've pulled up old carpet and there are rubber marks on the concrete underneath, dampen the area with a little water. Sprinkle with coarse salt and sweep with a stiff broom. Allow to dry and vacuum. Repeat if necessary.

Rust

Q 'My office chair didn't have stoppers,' says Mark. 'And has left rust stains on the carpet. Can they be removed?'

PROBLEM: Rust stains on carpet.

WHAT TO USE: Talcum powder, disposable rubber gloves, CLR/*Ranex*, water, cloth, damp cloth, white vinegar.

HOW TO APPLY: Make a circle of talcum powder around the stain to prevent the solution spreading into other parts of the carpet. Put on rubber gloves, mix 1 part *CLR* or *Ranex* to 20 parts water and wipe the stain with a cloth.

Immediately wipe with a damp cloth. Then wring a cloth in white vinegar and wipe. Rust removal products are quite harsh and can damage the glue at the back of the carpet so you need to work quickly. Repeat in this order: wipe with the mixture, wipe with a damp cloth, wipe with white vinegar then absorb excess moisture with paper towel.

Did you know?

Carpet beetles eat woollen carpets, leaving a black mark near the wall or doorframes. To remove the black marks, brush with non-iodised salt and vacuum. To deter them, stab 1 whole clove into a bay leaf and place at 1.5 m intervals along the walls.

WHAT NOT TO DO ...

Q 'About 6 months ago, I spilt a cup of black tea on my cream carpet. I mopped it up and everything seemed okay. Shortly afterwards I had the carpet professionally cleaned. Since then I've noticed a darker patch where the tea spilt. I applied a large amount of glycerine, white vinegar and bicarb. It is now worse than ever. It's like the stain has grabbed the glycerine and turned it oily brown. I've just used a commercial carpet spot cleaner on it but there's only a slight improvement. Help!'

A Before tackling a stain, think about what's been used on it already. In this case, the stain was affected by chemicals used by the commercial cleaner combined with the tea residue. Neutralise the chemicals by wiping with a cloth wrung in white vinegar, then apply paper towel to remove moisture. When using glycerine, or any moisture on carpet, use only a small amount. Don't wet the carpet because you'll cause stains from the jute underlay. If you do get a jute stain from the back of the carpet, mix ½ teaspoon of glycerine and ½ teaspoon of dishwashing liquid on an old toothbrush and brush onto the surface of the stain, working from the outside to the inside. Wipe with a damp cloth and apply paper towel to remove moisture. Repeat if necessary.

Silicone

Q 'My husband is a plumber and tracked blue silicone on the carpet,' complains Judy. 'Can it be removed?'

PROBLEM: Blue plumber's silicone on carpet.
WHAT TO USE: Metal comb, kerosene, pantyhose, dishwashing liquid, disposable rubber gloves, paper towel.
HOW TO APPLY: Dip a metal comb in a little kerosene and comb the silicone out of the carpet, removing as much as possible. Dip pantyhose in a little kerosene and scrub vigorously to remove the stains. This will require quite a bit of elbow grease—kerosene doesn't dissolve silicone but makes it easier to remove and you'll have to rub hard. To remove the kerosene, put on rubber gloves and massage dishwashing liquid into the spots. Wipe with a damp cloth before applying paper towel and stand on it to absorb moisture. Tell your husband to leave his dirty shoes outside!

Singe marks

PROBLEM: Singe/burn on carpet.
WHAT TO USE: White cloth, white vinegar, 3 per cent hydrogen peroxide, damp cloth, scissors.
HOW TO APPLY: Test the carpet for colourfastness first. Do this by soaking a white cloth in white vinegar and applying it to a part of the carpet not on display. If any colour comes off,

it's not colourfast. If it is colourfast, cut a cloth to the size of the burn and dip it in 3 per cent hydrogen peroxide. Then lay it over the mark for two minutes. Rinse with a damp cloth. If the burn is very bad or the carpet isn't colourfast, clip the surface of the wool with scissors or patch it. How to do this is explained in 'How to patch carpet' on page 238.

Sugar

Sugar stains are tricky to remove because sugar crystallises and sticks to carpet fibres. If you don't remove all the sugar, the stain goes darker. For details, see *'Fanta'* on page 253.

Shoe polish/scuff marks

If you get shoe polish on carpet, wipe with a little methylated spirits. If the stain is from liquid shoe polish, which contains wax, use methylated spirits followed by a little tea tree oil.

Soot

Q 'How can I remove black soot from carpet?' asks Tom. 'We have a gas fireplace and fake coals and often get sooty bits on the carpet.'

PROBLEM: Soot on carpet.
WHAT TO USE: Vacuum cleaner, cake of bathroom soap, water, pantyhose, paper towel.

HOW TO APPLY: Vacuum as much of the soot as possible. Dampen a cake of bathroom soap in water and roll it over the sooty carpet—the soot marks will stick to the soap. Repeat until removed. Wipe with damp pantyhose to remove excess soap. Apply paper towel to remove moisture. WARNING: If a gas heater places soot in the room, the jets could be blocked or there may be something wrong with your heater. Consult a professional.

Sorbolene cream

Q 'I dropped some sorbolene cream on the carpet,' says Wayne. 'What do you suggest?'

PROBLEM: Sorbolene cream on carpet.
WHAT TO USE: Dishwashing liquid, damp cloth, paper towel.
HOW TO APPLY: Put a couple of drops of dishwashing liquid on your fingers and massage into the stain until it feels like jelly. Wipe with a damp cloth. Apply paper towel to remove moisture.

Soup

Q 'I've spilt a cup of thick pea soup on my carpet,' reports Christina. 'How can I get it out?'

PROBLEM: Soup on carpet.

WHAT TO USE: White vinegar, cloth, pantyhose; cake of bathroom soap, cold water (removes protein); white vinegar, cloth, ultraviolet light, cardboard (removes vegetable dye); dishwashing liquid, damp cloth (removes fats and oils); white vinegar, cloth, ultraviolet light, cardboard (red colourant).

HOW TO APPLY: Remove as much of the soup as possible. Wipe with a dab of white vinegar on a cloth and rub with pantyhose. For soup that's high in protein, damp a cake of bathroom soap with cold water and scribble over the stain, then wipe with a damp cloth. If high in vegetable dye (tomato, pumpkin), wipe with a dab of white vinegar on a cloth, then apply ultraviolet light to the stain, checking every 2 hours until the dye fades. Protect the carpet around the stain with cardboard or it will lighten as well. If high in fats and oil, massage dishwashing liquid into the stain with your fingers and wipe with a damp cloth. If there's any chilli or red colourant, sponge with white vinegar on a cloth before applying ultraviolet light (protect surrounding carpet with cardboard).

Spaghetti bolognese

Q 'I'm in big trouble,' admits John. 'I dropped a full plate of spaghetti bolognese on beige carpet and a white cotton sofa. It's a part of the house where eating usually isn't permitted. Can I be redeemed?'

PROBLEM: Spaghetti bolognese stain on carpet.
WHAT TO USE: Cold water, soap, sponge, ultraviolet light, cardboard.
HOW TO APPLY: Because spaghetti bolognese contains protein, use cold water and soap with a sponge to remove the proteins first. Then use an ultraviolet light. Cover the non-stained area with cardboard to protect it and leave the light on the stain for up to 24 hours, checking it every two hours. (Don't look into the ultraviolet light because it could damage your eyes and, unless you want a tan, don't stand in front of it.) You can do this with the couch too, but putting it in the sun is better.

Suntan lotion

Q 'I have a couple of stains on my daughter's bedroom carpet,' reports Tracey. 'The stain that's most difficult to shift is tanning moisturiser. There are now two blotches of yellow in the middle of the beige carpet.'

PROBLEM: Suntan lotion on carpet.
WHAT TO USE: Dishwashing liquid, damp cloth (oil); glycerine, old toothbrush, white vinegar, cloth, paper towel (tannin).
HOW TO APPLY: This is an oil and tannin stain. To remove the oil, put a couple of drops of dishwashing liquid on

your fingertips and massage into the stain until it's viscous and jelly-like. Wipe with a damp cloth. To remove the tannin stain, apply a couple of drops of glycerine to a toothbrush and rub over the stain. Leave for around 20 minutes. Wipe with a dab of white vinegar on a cloth. Apply paper towel to remove moisture. Repeat if necessary.

Timber stain

Q 'There was a leak on the floor in our dining area and the carpet got very wet,' reports Sally. 'The dining table legs have leached colour into the carpet, which is now badly stained where the legs stood. What can I do?'

PROBLEM: Timber stains on carpet.
WHAT TO USE: Glycerine, old toothbrush, cloth, white vinegar, paper towel.
HOW TO APPLY: This is a tannin stain. Put a couple of drops of glycerine on a toothbrush and comb over the fibres. Leave for 20 minutes. Wipe with a cloth wrung out in white vinegar. Apply paper towel to remove moisture. Don't place the table on the carpet until completely dry.
PREVENTION: Put stoppers or clear plastic under the table legs.

Tomato sauce

PROBLEM: Tomato sauce on carpet.

WHAT TO USE: Cloth, white vinegar, ultraviolet light, cardboard.

HOW TO APPLY: Tomato sauce contains a vegetable dye. Remove as much as possible before wiping with a cloth wrung out in white vinegar. Then aim ultraviolet light over the area, protecting the surrounding carpet with cardboard. Check every 2 hours until the dye is removed.

Toner

Q 'I've spilled bubble-jet ink on the carpet,' reports Jean. 'Help!'

PROBLEM: Toner on carpet.

WHAT TO USE: Rotten milk, comb, cold water, cloth, paper towel.

HOW TO APPLY: To remove the ink, rot some milk in the sun until it forms lumps. Strain the lumps and place them over the stain to absorb the ink. When the ink has been absorbed, lift the rotten milk lumps off the carpet with a comb. Clean the remainder by scribbling with a cake of bathroom soap and cold water. Apply paper towel to remove moisture.

Tree sap

Q 'I've got tree sap on my carpet,' says Joanne.

PROBLEM: Tree sap on carpet.
WHAT TO USE: Tea tree oil, old toothbrush, damp cloth, paper towel.
HOW TO APPLY: Apply a couple of drops of tea tree oil to a toothbrush and scrub. Wipe with a damp cloth. Apply paper towel to absorb moisture.

Urine

PROBLEM: Urine on carpet.
WHAT TO USE: Ultraviolet light, white chalk, cloth, white vinegar, paper towel.
HOW TO APPLY: If you don't know where the stain is, use ultraviolet light in a darkened room and the urine will glow yellow. Mark around the stains with white chalk so you know where they are when the light is turned back on. Wipe with a cloth dampened with white vinegar. Apply paper towel to remove moisture. Repeat if necessary.

Vegemite

Q 'How can I get *Vegemite* and butter out of my wool-blend carpet?' asks Ben. 'It's been trodden in.'

PROBLEM: *Vegemite* and butter on carpet.
WHAT TO USE: Dishwashing liquid, damp cloth, paper towel.
HOW TO APPLY: *Vegemite* and butter toast always lands buttered side down! Put a little dishwashing liquid on your fingertips and massage into the carpet. Wipe with a damp cloth. Apply paper towel to remove moisture. Repeat until the mark is removed.

Vomit

PROBLEM: Vomit on carpet.
WHAT TO USE: Stain Diagnosis.
HOW TO APPLY: It depends what's been vomited up. Consult the 'Stain Diagnosis' on page 577. If the vomit contains bile, wipe with a cloth wrung out in white vinegar.

Q 'What can you do about old vomit stains in the carpet?' asks Maryann.

PROBLEM: Old vomit stains on carpet.
WHAT TO USE: Glycerine, cotton ball, milk, cloth, vacuum cleaner, cloth, carpet cleaner.
HOW TO APPLY: How to clean vomit will depend on what's in it. Because the stain has been there for some time, apply glycerine with a cotton ball to the stain. Then rot some milk in the sun (the time it takes will vary) and apply the solids to the stain with a cloth. Leave until almost dry,

vacuum and then wash the solids out with a damp cloth. Then clean the area with carpet cleaner.

Water

Q 'I spilled a bottle of water on the carpet,' says Christine. 'It's left a water mark. What can I do?'

PROBLEM: Water mark on carpet.
WHAT TO USE: Talcum powder, vacuum cleaner, glycerine, toothbrush, white vinegar, cloth, paper towel.
HOW TO APPLY: If the carpet is still wet, cover with a sprinkling of talcum powder and leave for around 20 minutes, or until dry. Then vacuum. When the mark has dried, wipe the top of the carpet fibres with a couple of drops of glycerine on an old toothbrush. Leave for 20 minutes. Then wipe with a cloth wrung out in white vinegar. Apply paper towel to remove moisture.

Wax

PROBLEM: Candle wax stain on carpet.
WHAT TO USE: Ice, blunt knife, metal comb, paper towel, hair dryer.
HOW TO APPLY: Put ice on the wax to harden it then scrape as much away as possible with a blunt knife. Wedge a metal comb underneath the wax and put a paper towel on top of the wax. Then use a hair dryer over it. The paper towel will

absorb the wax. Repeat until all the wax is removed. Never use an iron on carpet as it can char natural fibres or melt synthetic fibres.

Zinc cream

Q *'How do you get zinc out of carpet?' asks Tom.*

PROBLEM: Zinc cream on carpet.
WHAT TO USE: Talcum powder, pantyhose, baby oil, dishwashing liquid, damp cloth, paper towel.
HOW TO APPLY: Sprinkle a little talcum powder on the stain and scrub with pantyhose. Place a couple of drops of baby oil on a cloth and rub into the stain. For any remaining stains, massage in a little dishwashing liquid using your fingertips until it feels like jelly. Wipe with a damp cloth. Apply paper towel to remove moisture.

RUGS AND MATS

Rugs are handy for high-traffic areas and if you have children. The less dirt a rug or mat accumulates, the longer it will last. And, unlike carpet, you can take it outside and give it a good whack.

To take care of an Oriental rug, give it a vacuum, then wrap a hair brush in an old T-shirt that's been soaked in a small amount of hair conditioner and warm water. Brush the rug with this until it's damp but not wet. This will keep the fibres soft. Once you've finished, use the hairbrush again, without the T-shirt, to fluff the fibres up. Then vacuum again. The number of times you'll need to do this will depend on how much traffic the rug gets. If it has a lot of feet tramping over it, do this every two months. Your rugs are less likely to absorb stains if you *Scotchgard* them after cleaning.

PROBLEM: Rug/mat edge is lifting.
WHAT TO USE: Rubber mesh or wire claw.
HOW TO APPLY: One option is to place a rubber mesh on the back of the rug or mat. Another option is to attach a wire claw to the edge of the rug to help keep it flat. Both are available from carpet manufacturers.

Q 'I have a large dirty flokati rug to wash,' says Bonnie. 'What do you suggest?'

PROBLEM: Dirty flokati rug.
WHAT TO USE: Unprocessed wheat bran, white vinegar, broom, vacuum cleaner; or bath, blood-heat water, cheap shampoo and conditioner.
HOW TO APPLY: For regular cleaning, mix 1 kg unprocessed wheat bran with drops of white vinegar (one at a time) and stir until it forms clumps that resemble brown sugar. Sprinkle over the rug, sweep with a stiff broom and

vacuum. If very dirty, wash in the bath using blood-heat water and a little shampoo and conditioner. Walk up and down the rug in the bath and remove as much dirt as possible. Then rinse in blood-heat water and dry in the shade. Shake the rug occasionally to fluff up the fibres. You don't want a flat flokati!

Q 'I've got a Turkish wool rug,' reports Pip. 'But the cotton fringing is no longer white. What can I do?'

PROBLEM: Dirty cotton fringing.
WHAT TO USE: Paper towel, cheap shampoo, old toothbrush, damp cloth; or dry shampoo for blonde hair, hairbrush.
HOW TO APPLY: Roll up paper towel and place it under the fringe. Then apply 1 teaspoon of shampoo to every 30 cm of fringe with a toothbrush, being careful not to get it on the rug itself. Remove the shampoo with a damp cloth. Dry with paper towel. Alternatively, spray with dry shampoo and brush with a hairbrush.

SISAL

Sisal is a type of weave and can be made of plant fibres or horse hair. Many people love the look of sisal but it can be a bit tough on bare feet and it soils easily. Sisal is best cleaned by sweeping. Never use wet cleaners on it. Shannon finds the best cleaning method is mixing unprocessed wheat bran and white vinegar until clumpy but not wet. Scatter it over the sisal and sweep backwards and forwards, then vacuum. Bran acts as a scourer and absorbent.

Q 'My daughter's cat drank green food colouring and peed on my oatmeal-coloured sisal carpet,' says Maggie. 'I've already used white vinegar but now have two orange-coloured stains that get darker in rainy weather. What can I do?'

PROBLEM: Green food colouring and white vinegar on sisal.
WHAT TO USE: Glycerine, old toothbrush, white vinegar, cloth, ultraviolet light, cardboard.
HOW TO APPLY: The orange-coloured spots are likely to be a tannin stain from using too much white vinegar. Put a couple of drops of glycerine on a toothbrush and scrub over the marks. Leave for 20 minutes. Then sponge with a cloth wrung out in white vinegar. To remove the green food colouring dye, wipe with a cloth wrung out in white vinegar. Aim ultraviolet light at the stain, protecting the carpet around the stain with cardboard, until the green is gone.

Q 'I have a sisal carpet and managed to stain it with (I think) water from a *Damp Rid* container,' says Tony. 'What do you suggest?

PROBLEM: *Damp Rid* on sisal.

WHAT TO USE: Unprocessed wheat bran, white vinegar, vacuum cleaner, dishwashing liquid, old toothbrush, oil of cloves, 1 litre spray pack, coarse non-iodised salt, pantyhose.

HOW TO APPLY: This is difficult to remove because *Damp Rid* contains silicone. Mix 1 kg of unprocessed wheat bran with drops of white vinegar (one at a time) and stir until it becomes clumpy and resembles brown sugar. Sprinkle over the area and brush it back and forward. Leave for half an hour and vacuum. Place dishwashing liquid on a toothbrush and scrub over the stain. Put ¼ teaspoon of oil of cloves into a 1 litre spray pack of water and mist over the stain. Then lightly sprinkle a little salt (2 teaspoons of salt per 30-cm diameter) and rub with pantyhose. Allow to dry and vacuum. If this doesn't work, you'll need to patch the sisal. For details, see page 238. The good thing about patching sisal is the ribs hide the joins so you won't notice the patch job.

COIR

This is made of coconut fibre and attracts insects so vacuum regularly. To deter bugs, apply no more than 2 drops of oil of pennyroyal to a tissue and suck it into the vacuum cleaner before cleaning. Note that oil of pennyroyal should only be used as directed as it can be harmful to pregnant women and pets. Remember one drop means one drop. You can also leave mint bags in the corner of the room to deter bugs. Use a mixture of unprocessed wheat bran and white vinegar to clean as described with sisal.

Q 'I warmed a tub of *Vicks VapoRub* and managed to spill it onto my coir carpet,' says Kate. 'What can I do?'

PROBLEM: *Vicks VapoRub* on coir.
WHAT TO USE: Unprocessed wheat bran, stiff broom, dishwashing liquid, old toothbrush, damp cloth, paper towel.
HOW TO APPLY: This is a tricky one. Sprinkle lots of unprocessed wheat bran and sweep it back and forth over the stain with a stiff broom. Keep replacing the bran until it stops sticking to the coir. Place a couple of drops of dishwashing liquid on a toothbrush and scrub with the grain over the coir. Once it feels like jelly, wipe with a damp cloth. Put some paper towel over the top and stand on it to absorb moisture.

LINOLEUM, VINYL AND SELF-LEVELLING PLASTICS

Linoleum, or lino, is formed by coating hessian or canvas with linseed oil. Developments with plastics mean there are now numerous variations on the lino theme. Clean by sprinkling bicarb over the surface, then splashing white vinegar on top and mopping. Then rinse with hot water and leave to dry.

Q 'I've got large marks from a ballpoint pen on my lino floor,' reports Julie. 'How do I get it off?'

PROBLEM: Ink/ballpoint pen stain on linoleum.
WHAT TO USE: Cotton bud, white spirits; or milk, old toothbrush; or kerosene, cotton ball.
HOW TO APPLY: Dip a cotton bud in white spirits and wipe it over the biro marks. You could also rot some milk in the sun. Scrub the solids into the stain with an old toothbrush, then wash out. If the ink is red, and the flooring is lino, apply kerosene with a cotton ball. Those with vinyl or self-levelling plastics will have to live with the red. It's impossible to move!

Q 'I have cushion vinyl on my kitchen floor,' reports Pat. 'And there are a number of stiletto heel indentations. Can I remove these marks?'

PROBLEM: Indentations on vinyl.
WHAT TO USE: Commercial steamer, glycerine, water.
HOW TO APPLY: Hire a commercial steamer (from plant and equipment hire) and add 2 teaspoons of glycerine to the

water reservoir (around 9 litres). Clean the floor on the highest temperature.

PREVENTION: Stiletto heels place a huge amount of pressure on vinyl (and other) floors, so ask visitors to remove them. Have some slippers or thongs available for the guest to wear.

Q 'How do you get purple crepe paper stain off cream vinyl?' asks Frank.

PROBLEM: Purple crepe paper on vinyl.
WHAT TO USE: Lavender oil, glycerine, pantyhose.
HOW TO APPLY: This is tricky because the chemical formula to make dye can be similar to the chemical formula to colour lino, so removing one will remove the other. Make a paste of equal parts lavender oil and glycerine and apply to the stain with pantyhose. Polish it out with clean pantyhose.

Q 'We've got scuff marks on our vinyl floors from shoes,' reports Robyn. 'How can we get them off?'

PROBLEM: Rubber scuff marks on vinyl.
WHAT TO USE: Biro eraser, coarse salt, broom or vacuum cleaner.

HOW TO APPLY: The marks are likely to be from rubber on shoes. Rub over with a biro eraser or coarse salt and sweep or vacuum.

Q 'What's the best way to remove rust from lino?' asks Betty.

PROBLEM: Rust on lino.
WHAT TO USE: Lemon, non-iodised salt, damp cloth.
HOW TO APPLY: Cut a lemon in half, sprinkle with salt and scrub over the rust stains. Wipe with a damp cloth. Repeat if necessary

Q 'The blue wording from a plastic bag has sweated itself onto the lino of our new caravan,' reports Rachael. 'We live in the Top End where temperatures get rather high and humid. What can you suggest?'

PROBLEM: Ink on lino.
WHAT TO USE: Rotten milk, coarse salt, glycerine, pantyhose.
HOW TO APPLY: Rot some milk in the sun (the time taken will vary). Mix 2 tablespoons of rotten milk solids, 1 tablespoon of salt and 1 teaspoon of glycerine and place the smelly mixture over the stain. Leave for around 20 minutes. Polish off with pantyhose.

Q 'How do I clean a sticky vinyl floor in the kitchen?' asks Jim.

PROBLEM: Sticky vinyl floor.
WHAT TO USE: Coarse salt, 9 litre bucket, cloth, water, stiff broom.
HOW TO APPLY: To remove the stickiness, put 1 kg of salt into a bucket of water, stir until it dissolves, wipe the solution over the floor with a cloth and leave to dry and form a salt crust. Sweep off with a broom.

Q 'How can I remove a build-up of hairspray from my embossed lino floor?' asks Raine.

PROBLEM: Hairspray on lino.
WHAT TO USE: Hairspray, pantyhose, anti-dandruff shampoo, cloth, water.
HOW TO APPLY: Spray the floor with hairspray (it contains its own solvent). While the hairspray is still wet, wipe with pantyhose. Alternatively, spray a rolled up ball of pantyhose with hairspray and wipe over the floor. Another option is to wipe the area with a little anti-dandruff shampoo on a cloth, then rinse with water.
PREVENTION: Apply your hairspray outside.

General cleaning guide for floors

Surface	What to use	How to clean	How often
Wool, nylon and blend carpet	Bicarb	Lightly sprinkle the bicarb over the floor and leave for half an hour before vacuuming	Once a week. More if there's lots of traffic
Sisal, seagrass, plant fibre or copra	Mix 1 cup unprocessed wheat bran and ½ teaspoon white vinegar	Sprinkle the mixture over the floor and firmly sweep with a stiff broom, leave for half an hour before vacuuming	Once a week. This flooring soils easily
Sealed timber floorboards, parquetry, floating floors, particle board, bamboo, cork	Mix ½ cup black tea, 1 cup white vinegar and 9 litres tepid water in a bucket	Sweep/mop the solution over the floor with a clean broom covered with a pair of pantyhose. Dry with an old towel under your feet as you go	At least once a week depending on the amount of traffic

Surface	What to use	How to clean	How often
Glazed tiles (terracotta, ceramic or porcelain), terrazzo	Bicarb. Combine 1 cup white vinegar with 9 litres tepid water in a bucket	If dirty, sprinkle first with a light scattering of bicarb. Sweep/mop the solution over the floor with a clean broom covered with a pair of pantyhose. Dry with an old towel under your feet as you go	At least once a week depending on the amount of traffic
Unglazed tiles (terracotta, ceramic or porcelain), cement brick, slate	Bicarb. Combine 1 cup white vinegar with 9 litres tepid water in a bucket	If dirty, sprinkle first with a light scattering of bicarb. Sweep/mop the solution over the floor with a clean broom covered with a pair of pantyhose. Dry thoroughly with an old towel under your feet as you go	At least once a week depending on the amount of traffic

Surface	What to use	How to clean	How often
Marble/limestone	Grate 1 teaspoon of pH neutral soap into a 9 litre bucket of warm water. To seal (when the surface is dull), coat with a thin layer of marble flooring wax or limestone milk	Sweep/mop the solution with a clean broom covered in pantyhose. Dry with an old towel under your feet as you clean. When dry, apply a small quantity of quality marble flooring wax or limestone milk	At least once a week depending on the amount of traffic
Linoleum	Combine 2 teaspoons kerosene, 2 teaspoons dishwashing liquid and ½ cup white vinegar with 9 litres tepid water in a bucket	Sweep/mop the solution over the floor with a clean broom covered with a pair of pantyhose. Dry with an old towel under your feet as you go	At least once a week depending on the amount of traffic

Surface	What to use	How to clean	How often
Vinyl	Bicarb. Add 1 cup white vinegar, 2 teaspoons glycerine with 9 litres tepid water in a bucket	If dirty, sprinkle first with a light scattering of bicarb. Sweep/mop with a clean broom covered with a pair of pantyhose. Dry with an old towel under your feet as you go	At least once a week depending on the amount of traffic

Doors

Doors are often neglected during a cleaning routine but it's easy to wipe over them with a damp cloth. Clean doorknobs with a bran ball (see page 138). Grab some lavender oil—which strips through grease without damaging paint and leaves a fresh, clean smell—sprinkle a few drops on a cloth and wipe over doors and doorjambs. To remove dirty fingerprints, put 1 teaspoon of lavender oil in a 1 litre spray pack of water, spray onto pantyhose and wipe over the fingermarks.

One of Shannon's tricks if the house is a bit untidy and visitors are about to arrive is to wipe the doorjambs with lavender oil. The smell creates an impression of cleanliness and also keeps insects away! Clean doors every couple of months or when they become grubby. If the door has a high polish or laminate finish, clean with dishwashing liquid and water. If it has a French polish finish, use a good quality, non-silicone furniture polish. Wipe greasy hand marks with a damp cloth. Door handles made of chrome, brass or glass should be cleaned with bicarb and white vinegar on one sponge.

If the door lock is jammed or stiff, use a graphite puffer either in the hole of the lock or in the slots around the edge of the lock tongue. To prevent further cleaning, put newspaper or other covering over the floor when puffing graphite powder into the lock.

TIP
Hinges feel cold and damp when you touch them because metal attracts condensation, which makes them more susceptible to rust.

If the door is sticking and you can't work out where to sand it, rub chalk down the doorframe, shut the door and the chalk will transfer to the part of the jamb that needs sanding.

Hinges operate more smoothly and are protected from rust if wiped with a smear of petroleum jelly (*Vaseline*) or sewing machine oil. Wipe across the horizontal lines of the hinge.

TIP
Remove rust from screws by sprinkling salt over a cut lemon and wipe over the screws. To prevent screws from further rusting, paint the heads with clear nail polish. If you need to remove the screws, wipe over the nail polish with acetone.

EASY SOUNDPROOFING
- Use a brush strip seal on your front door; it reduces noise and keeps dust and dirt out of your home.
- Pin a cloth panel on the back of the door to baffle sound.
- Add another layer of curtains.

- To reduce noise from stereos, televisions, pianos, etc, place soft rubber stoppers underneath to minimise vibrations.
- To stop doors from rattling, put a felt strip on the doorjamb.

HOW TO FIX A KEY BROKEN IN A LOCK

Have you ever broken a key in a lock? To repair it yourself, you need some superglue—which is hopefully on the same side of the locked door as you are! Put a very small amount of superglue on the broken edge of the key in your hand and line it up very carefully with the broken edge in the lock. Do not get glue on the lock itself. Connect the head and shaft of the key and hold it carefully for 3 minutes. Then gradually ease the broken piece out. Avoid twisting the key when pulling it out. Make sure you have a replacement key cut!

Lamps and Light Shades

Lamps illuminate a room and are generally responsible for creating the mood as well. At the flick of a switch, you can get light but electricity contains positive ions that attract dust. Clean soft and hard lampshades every week with a bran ball (see page 138). Glass light shades should be cleaned in warm water. Clean brass and metal arms with a good quality brass polish. And make sure you don't get cleaning product in the electrical fittings.

To cut down on bugs, spray the tops of light shades with surface insecticide spray.

Every time you change a light bulb, clean the other light bulbs with a cloth and they'll shine brighter. To prevent halogen lights corroding, wipe the connection on the bulb with a cloth once a week.

To clean metal lamp bases, use bicarb and white vinegar on a cloth. For glass lamp bases, use white vinegar on a cloth. For timber lamp bases, use black tea on a cloth. For plastic lamp bases, use a paste of equal parts glycerine and talcum powder on a cloth. For ceramic lamp bases, use white vinegar on a cloth.

Each week, wipe a damp cloth over cold light bulbs and, if there are bugs, remove the light bulb and vacuum the light socket (make sure it's switched off at the powerpoint). The combination of heat and dead insects can make the fitting brittle. If, like Shannon, you have lights positioned at the top of a high stairwell, put a sponge over the hook of an extendable plastic broom handle to reach. Dip the sponge in a bucket of 1 teaspoon of lavender oil per litre of water.

To remove fly speck, mix equal parts tea tree oil and water, dip in a cotton bud and spin the cotton bud over each bit of speck to remove it.

Q 'Some pieces of our glass chandelier have rust stains from the internal metal rod,' says Dan. 'Do you have any suggestions on how to remove them?'

PROBLEM: Rust on metal.
WHAT TO USE: Methylated spirits, pantyhose.
HOW TO APPLY: It's likely the rust was caused by a chlorine-based cleaner. To remove, rub the metal with methylated spirits and pantyhose. See below for details on how to clean a chandelier.

PROBLEM: Broken light bulb in the light socket.
WHAT TO USE: Rubber gloves, carrot.
HOW TO APPLY: Make sure the light is off and that you're wearing some rubber gloves. Get a carrot, cut the top off and jam the carrot base into the light bulb socket. Then twist or turn and remove. Make sure you remove any small pieces of broken glass before putting in a new light bulb.

HOW TO CLEAN CHANDELIERS

They're beautiful and decadent and difficult to clean. However, the task of cleaning is made a little easier with the product *Crystal Clear*. Turn the light off at the switch and put a sheet or towel underneath the chandelier of a size suitable to cover the entire drip line. Using a ladder so you can reach the chandelier comfortably, remove the light bulbs and put a small plastic bag over each of the fittings so you don't get moisture in the electrics. Dust the tops of the chandelier with a soft brush then spray a generous amount of *Crystal Clear* until the chandelier is damp and starting to drip. The dirt and dust will run off. If it's been a while since you last cleaned it, you may need to apply *Crystal Clear* again. When the chandelier is completely dry, clean and return the light bulbs.

Walls

It's inevitable that you'll get marks on the walls, especially in high-traffic areas or if you have little people with grubby hands who use the wall as a convenient support. Be careful using commercial products to clean marks because most have an alcohol base that can break down the paint surface and leave a bleached shiny spot. Clean your walls every couple of weeks either with a broom or vacuum cleaner. Put an old T-shirt over the top of the broom or vacuum to prevent bristle marks. Some dirty marks will come off with a light spray of lavender oil and water on a cloth. You could also try using a good pencil eraser or rolling brown bread into a ball and rubbing it against the wall. If these don't work or the walls are very dirty, mix bicarb and white vinegar on a cloth and rinse with a clean, damp cloth. Wring the cloth tightly before applying. For build-up around switches, apply white vinegar and water sparingly

Floors, Walls and Windows   311

with a sponge. To avoid drip lines, start cleaning from the bottom and work your way up, drying as you go. To prevent spider webs on the ceiling and wall edges, put a small drop of lemon oil on your cobweb brush. Spiders don't like lemons.

If you have wallpaper, clean it with a slice of brown bread. For large areas, cut a loaf of brown bread lengthways and leave overnight so it goes a little stale on the cut edge, then wipe directly on the wallpaper. Don't forget to vacuum the crumbs!

PROBLEM: Crayon marks on walls.
WHAT TO USE: Cotton ball, white spirits, soft brush, clean cloth.
HOW TO APPLY: Damp a cotton ball in white spirits and wipe over the mark. Then brush the mark gently with a soft brush. Blot the rest with a clean cloth. Always work from the outside to the inside of the mark.

PROBLEM: Mould on walls.
WHAT TO USE: Oil of cloves, bucket, soft cloth or sponge.
HOW TO APPLY: Put 4–5 drops of oil of cloves in a bucket half filled with water. Wipe this over the mouldy wall with a soft cloth or sponge. The mould may not come off all at once but the oil of cloves will continue to kill it. Dust the mould off later.

PROBLEM: Double-sided tape on the wall.
WHAT TO USE: Dishwashing liquid, clean fabric, clingwrap; or hair dryer, cloth, white spirits, cotton bud.
HOW TO APPLY: Add a little dishwashing liquid to boiling water, wet some clean fabric in it, wring it out and place it over the tape. Then put clingwrap over the top of the fabric and leave until the heat penetrates the glue. You should be able to lift the edge of the tape with your fingers when it's ready. Never use a knife because you can tear the paint on the wall. Alternatively, heat the adhesive with a hair dryer, then rub a piece of cloth over it and peel away. The remaining adhesive can be removed with white spirits on a cotton bud.

> **Q** 'I have lots of stick-on plastic hooks on the wall left from the previous owners,' reports Eloise. 'I've pulled the hook bits off but can't remove the thick, tacky glue behind. What do you suggest?'

PROBLEM: Glue on walls.
WHAT TO USE: Tea tree oil, plastic wrap, plastic knife.
HOW TO APPLY: Place a drop of tea tree oil on the top edge of the glue patch and cover with plastic wrap. Leave for 20 minutes. Remove the plastic wrap and slide a plastic knife behind the glue. If it doesn't come away, replace the plastic wrap and leave for another 20 minutes, then try again.

SPOTLESS CLASSIC
How to deter spiders

Many people hate spiders and spider webs. The kind way to keep spiders away from your home is with lemon oil. You can buy lemon oil (lemon essence doesn't work) or use the oil from lemon skin. Rub some lemon skin or sprinkle 1–2 drops of lemon oil along the bristles of your broom (clean, of course) and wipe the broom over the areas where spiders are likely to set up home—you'll collect the old webs as you go. If you're not able to use a broom, mix 5 drops of lemon oil with 1 drop of dishwashing liquid in a 1 litre spray pack of water and lightly spray over the area. This mixture doesn't kill spiders or remove cobwebs, it simply deters them. You'll need to reapply every 3 months.

Q 'I have an oil-based fly spray unit that dispenses on a timed basis,' reports Brian. 'It's left a mark on the wall. What can I do?'

PROBLEM: Fly spray unit mark on wall.
WHAT TO USE: Dishwashing liquid, pantyhose, damp cloth (painted walls); or brown bread (wallpaper).

HOW TO APPLY: If the wall is painted, place a little dishwashing liquid on pantyhose and rub over the area, then wipe with a damp cloth. For wallpaper, use a slice of brown bread and rub gently over the stain.
PREVENTION: Put flyscreens on your windows. All commercial fly sprays are toxic.

WALLPAPER

You may be a sandwich short at lunch because of this. A slice of fresh bread rubbed over wallpaper is a great way to clean it. The kind of bread you use will depend on the colour of the wallpaper. Brown bread is more abrasive but may transfer colour to light walls.

Q 'I've got mouldy wallpaper,' complains Lesley. 'What should I do?'

PROBLEM: Mouldy wallpaper.
WHAT TO USE: 9 litre bucket, warm water, non-iodised salt, cloth, soft broom.
HOW TO APPLY: Fill a bucket with warm water, add 1 kg of salt and mix. Wring a cloth in the mixture and wipe over the walls. Leave to dry and form a salt crust. Brush the crust away with a clean, soft broom and the mould will come away with it.

Q 'I've got three boys under the age of 10 and, one day, they decided to plaster the wallpaper with peanut butter, jam and margarine,' says Jane. 'It's a disaster!'

PROBLEM: Peanut butter, jam, margarine on wallpaper.
WHAT TO USE: Dishwashing liquid, paper towel, damp cloth.
HOW TO APPLY: Do not use water. Put dishwashing liquid onto a paper towel and wipe it over the wallpaper. The dishwashing liquid will break down the fats in the food. You'll need to do this several times. Then wipe with a damp cloth.

LIGHT SWITCHES

Remove greasy fingermarks around light switches with 1 teaspoon of lavender oil in a 1 litre spray pack of water. Spray a small amount onto a cloth and wipe away the greasy fingermarks (do not spray the mixture directly onto the light switch or you could short the electrics).

WALL HANGINGS

Q 'I've had a macramé wall hanging for many years,' reports Jenny. 'I have vacuumed it regularly but I'm concerned that if I hand wash it, not only will the colour from the beads run, it would lose its shape. Can you help?'

PROBLEM: Dirty macramé wall hanging.
WHAT TO USE: Unprocessed wheat bran, bowl, white vinegar, pillowcase, bowl, vacuum cleaner.
HOW TO APPLY: The macramé wall hanging is likely to be raw cotton twine and is easy to clean. Place 2 cups of unprocessed wheat bran in a bowl and gradually stir in drops of white vinegar until the bran clumps together and resembles brown sugar. It shouldn't be wet. Place the mixture in a pillowcase, add the wall hanging, secure the top and shake thoroughly. Gently remove the wall hanging (outside or over a bin) and shake out the excess bran. If needed, lightly vacuum to remove any remaining bits of bran.

COLUMNS

Q 'We have columns inside and outside our home that have rust stains on them,' says Bill. 'I tried to remove the rust with diluted hydrochloric acid but used an orange-coloured sponge which dissolved from the acid. So now I have rust that is stained orange. What should I do?'

PROBLEM: Rust and orange dye on sandstone composite.
WHAT TO USE: Cake of bathroom soap, water, scrubbing brush, glycerine.
HOW TO APPLY: To remove the acid and rust, run a cake of bathroom soap under water and scribble over the stain.

Then scrub with a scrubbing brush. Rinse with water. If the orange colour doesn't come away, add 1 teaspoon of glycerine to the rinse water.

TIP

When painting a room, open the windows for ventilation. Leave a saucer of milk in the room or cut an onion and place it in a saucepan of water. The water is absorbent and attracts the fumes.

Pictures, Paintings and Mirrors

Look after your paintings just in case the one you inherited from Uncle Harry is worth a fortune. Even if you don't have a hidden treasure, care should still be taken looking after them.

Acrylic paintings can be cleaned with a damp cloth.

To remove residue and dust from **oil** paintings, clean with stale urine, salt and potato. Yes, you did read stale urine! Collect 1 litre of female urine and leave it in the sun for a week. It will reduce to ½ litre. Then add 1 tablespoon of salt and 2 tablespoons of raw grated potato to it. Allow the mixture to sit for half an hour. Damp a cloth in the mixture, wring it and then wipe over the painting. Then damp a clean cloth in water and wipe the painting gently. Pat it dry. You can also rub brown bread over the painting to clean it. For any serious cleaning problems, see a restorer.

Water colours should be cleaned by a professional.

Never use alcohol-based cleaners such as methylated spirits or turpentine on **gilded** frames. Most gilding is covered with a layer of shellac and alcohol-based cleaners will compromise it. Instead, dust the frame with a hair dryer on the cool setting. This should be enough to clean it, but if dirt remains, wipe a damp cloth over the frame and then dry it with a soft cloth.

Clean **glass** with methylated spirits and a cloth. But be careful not to get methylated spirits around the edges or it could seep into the print. **Polycarbonate** should only be cleaned with a damp cloth. Clean **metal** and **timber** as you would furniture. Clean **plastic** with glycerine.

Protect paintings by spraying a cloth with surface insecticide spray and wiping it over the back of picture frames. Don't touch the painting, just the frames.

Mirrors can be cleaned with methylated spirits but be careful of edges, particularly with gilded frames. Rather than buying a new mirror, which can be very expensive, find a lovely old second-hand frame and see a glazier who will supply, cut and fit a mirror to size very cheaply.

PROBLEM: Flaked or chipped gilding.
WHAT TO USE: Soft cloth, *Gilder's Size* and *Gilder's Gold Dust*.

HOW TO APPLY: Clear any dust with a soft cloth then paint the bare section with a thin coat of *Gilder's Size*. Allow it to dry until it's tacky then dust with *Gilder's Gold Dust*, which is very fine gold dust. Brush off any excess.

Windows

The best way to clean glass windows is with methylated spirits and water in a spray pack. Spray the solution on the window then polish the glass with a paper towel. When cleaning windows, always use vertical stripes on the outside and horizontal stripes on the inside. That way you can tell which side a smudge is on. The vertical stripes should be on the outside because that's the way rain falls, and any horizontal lines catch moisture and dust and leave grimy lines. Vertical lines allow the dirt to run away, leaving windows looking cleaner for longer. Don't use newspaper to clean windows. They used to be good when the ink contained lamp black, but today's newspapers use rubber-based ink, which leaves a smear. Use paper towels instead.

In addition to methylated spirits and water, you can also clean windows with equal parts white vinegar and water in a 1 litre spray pack. If your windows are exposed to bore water or fertiliser, clean them as often as possible or you could get glass cancer. Have a squeegee dedicated for the task.

If you have painted window frames and sills, clean them regularly because exposure to the sun breaks down the surface of the paint and allows dust to stick. To clean, mix 1 teaspoon of tea tree oil, 1 teaspoon of lavender oil and ½ teaspoon of dishwashing liquid in a 1 litre spray pack of water. Wipe over the windowsills with pantyhose. If you do this task every week, you'll only need to do a wipe over each time.

WINDOW FRAMES AND SILLS

Every time you vacuum the floor, vacuum the windowsills as well. Then wipe them with a mixture of 1 cup of white vinegar to 1 bucket of water. Keep putty in good condition by wiping a small amount of linseed oil over it twice a year if the putty is unpainted. If the putty is painted, make sure it's painted all the way to the glass otherwise the putty will allow oil to smear out over the glass. To help prevent rubber seals perishing, wipe them with white vinegar and water. Never poke at silicone because if you break the seal it becomes exposed and mildew can grow. Clean it with water.

Clean marble windowsills with bicarb and 1 part white vinegar to 5 parts water. Then polish with *Cera Wax*. To inhibit mildew, add 1 drop of oil of cloves to ½ cup of *Cera Wax*.

For sandstone windowsills, clean with bicarb and white vinegar. Inhibit mildew by adding oil of cloves to hot rinse water.

Floors, Walls and Windows 321

Clean painted timber windowsills with white vinegar and water. If they're varnished, clean with a good quality, non-silicone furniture polish. Wipe unsealed cedar with a good quality furniture oil which will continue to feed the timber. If it's gone grey, wipe it with a wet tea bag, then allow it to dry before oiling it.

Rubbing a cake of soap along the window frame and sashes will allow the window to move more smoothly.

Q 'When cleaning around the painted wooden frames of my glass doors, the sugar soap dribbled onto a number of window panes,' says Ben. 'How can I get this off?'

PROBLEM: Sugar soap on glass.
WHAT TO USE: White vinegar, cloth; or sweet almond oil, cloth.
HOW TO APPLY: Sugar soap is caustic and has eaten into the glass. Wipe with white vinegar on a cloth. If this doesn't work, wipe with sweet almond oil on a cloth. Reapply as needed, usually every 3 months.
PREVENTION: If using sugar soap, neutralise immediately with white vinegar and water.

Q 'My husband has been making leadlight windows for our house,' says Charmaine. 'It involves using leadlight cement to glue the glass in place, whiting to remove the excess cement and stove black to make the lead black. But the stove black has become stuck to the cement remnants and is difficult to clean. Any suggestions?'

PROBLEM: Leadlight cement on glass.
WHAT TO USE: Flat-bladed scalpel.
HOW TO APPLY: Use a flat-bladed scalpel (or leadlight knife) to cut the cement off. Tell your husband to use blacking rather than stove black when leadlighting. Blacking is a tar-like substance and can be removed with whiting (both are available from leadlighting and some hardware stores).

Q 'Can you advise how to clean anodised aluminium window frames?' asks Simon. 'It's more than just dirt. There are spots of corrosion.'

PROBLEM: Corrosion on aluminium.
WHAT TO USE: Damp black tea bag, pantyhose, cloth.
HOW TO APPLY: Place a damp black tea bag into the toe of a pair of pantyhose and rub directly over the corrosion. Alternatively, dip pantyhose into a cup of black tea and wipe over the corrosion. The tannins in tea react with aluminium oxide and dissolve it.

Q 'How can I get old tint film off windows?' asks Brett.

PROBLEM: Old tint film on windows.
WHAT TO USE: Dishwashing liquid, water, 1 litre spray pack, plastic wrap, credit card.
HOW TO APPLY: Put 2 teaspoons of dishwashing liquid in a spray pack of water and spray over the tint-side of the window. Place plastic wrap the same size as the windows over the glass. Leave for around 20 minutes, then run a credit card along the edge of the tint and peel tint and the plastic wrap away. The tint should come away easily. If it doesn't, lay the plastic wrap back over the tint and leave for longer. Don't do this in direct sunlight.

Q 'How can I remove scratches on window glass?' asks Sam.

PROBLEM: Scratches on glass.
WHAT TO USE: Sweet almond oil, cloth, whiting, glycerine, cloth.
HOW TO APPLY: For light scratches, dab sweet almond oil on a cloth and wipe over the scratched area. For deep scratches, apply equal parts whiting (available from leadlighting and some hardware stores) and glycerine with a cloth and polish the scratches out.

Q 'There's gloss paint on my aluminium window frames,' reports Brenda. 'How can I get it off?'

PROBLEM: Gloss paint on aluminium.
WHAT TO USE: A helper, cardboard, paint scraper, pantyhose, heat gun.
HOW TO APPLY: You'll need assistance with this job so enlist a helper. Cover the glass in cardboard to protect it. Put some pantyhose over a paint scraper and have one person apply the heat gun to the area in quick, even strokes. Be careful not to get heat near the silicone or glass. While the paint is still warm, the other person removes the paint with the scraper.

Q 'How can I remove obstinate masking tape from my windows and aluminium frames?' asks Virginia.

PROBLEM: Old masking tape on glass.
WHAT TO USE: Tea tree oil, pantyhose.
HOW TO APPLY: When masking tape adhesive ages or warms, it becomes very hard to remove. Apply a few drops of tea tree oil to a rolled up pair of pantyhose and scrub over the adhesive. If it doesn't come off straight away, let the tea tree oil sit on it for around 20 minutes. Scrub again. Don't do this when the sun is shining on the window or the adhesive will smear.

Q 'The previous tenants of my rental property had a dog that sat with its nose pressed to the window looking in,' says Don. 'There's a mark on the window that I can't shift. I've tried methylated spirits, a scraper and steel wool without success. Can you help please?'

PROBLEM: Saliva on glass.
WHAT TO USE: Sweet almond oil, cloth.
HOW TO APPLY: Saliva contains acid and other chemicals that have etched the glass and caused glass cancer. Polish with a couple of drops of sweet almond oil on a cloth.

CARING FOR LEADLIGHT WINDOWS

If you don't look after leadlights they could become brittle and your window will rattle. Clean windows first with whiting and a bristle brush. Then pack blacking, which is a kind of linseed putty, underneath the edges of the leads or cames like glue. Use an old boot brush to rub the blacking in until there is an excess of blacking oozing out of the cames. Leave it to dry for two hours. Then clean by sprinkling whiting over each pane of glass and over the cames. Scrub with a brush until it's all cleaned. Never use excessive force or you'll stretch the leads. Shannon recommends you have leadlights cleaned by a professional leadlighter every 5 years.

Don't use this technique with Tiffany lamps because they are made of copper and are very fragile. These must be cleaned by a professional.

BLINDS

PROBLEM: Dirty fabric/upholstered blinds.
WHAT TO USE: Unprocessed wheat bran, white vinegar, pantyhose
HOW TO APPLY: Make a bran ball (see page 138) and rub along the blinds.

Q '**My very creative 2-year-old son used my good friend's white polyester Roman blinds as a canvas,**' says Jacqui. '**They're now covered in blue biro. And although my friend isn't too bothered by the biro, I am! Can you help?**'

PROBLEM: Blue biro on blinds.
WHAT TO USE: Methylated spirits, cotton bud; or white spirits, cotton bud.
HOW TO APPLY: What to use will depend on the type of biro. To find out, wipe over the mark with methylated spirits on a cotton bud. If the colour comes away, continue to wipe with methylated spirits on the cotton bud. If not, use white spirits on a cotton bud.

Q 'I've just moved into a house and the kitchen plastic blind has food and fat stains all over it,' says Natalie. 'How do I clean it?'

PROBLEM: Food stains on plastic blind.
WHAT TO USE: Dishwashing liquid, damp pantyhose.
HOW TO APPLY: Put a couple of drops of dishwashing liquid onto damp pantyhose and scrub. Wipe with damp pantyhose.

Q 'I've got mildew on my blinds,' says Rose. 'Any solutions?'

PROBLEM: Mildew on blinds.
WHAT TO USE: Oil of cloves, 1 litre spray pack, stiff brush.
HOW TO APPLY: Put ¼ teaspoon of oil of cloves into a spray pack of water and lightly spray over the blinds. Leave to dry. After 24 hours, brush the dead mildew spores away with a stiff brush.

PROBLEM: Insect droppings on blinds.
WHAT TO USE: Bucket, dishwashing liquid, cloth.
HOW TO APPLY: Fill a bucket with water and enough dishwashing liquid to generate a sudsy mix. Apply the suds to the stains with a damp cloth.

PROBLEM: Food splattered on blinds.
WHAT TO USE: Bucket, dishwashing liquid, cloth.
HOW TO APPLY: Fill a bucket with water and enough dishwashing liquid to generate a sudsy mix. Apply the suds to the stains with a damp cloth.

VENETIAN BLINDS

Don't throw your old kitchen tongs out. They can be recycled and reinvented as venetian blind cleaners. Glue some sponge to both inside edges of the tongs and leave to set. Then place the tongs over the top and bottom of each blind, pinch the tongs together and run them along. The sponge can be wet or dry. To clean the cords, use a mixture of white vinegar and water and apply with a sponge. Start from the top and wipe down so the liquid soaks into the cord. The second time you do this, squeeze the moisture from the cord. You may have to do this a few times to remove all the dirt.

To thoroughly clean venetian blinds, take them down and lie them outside. Fill a bucket with a mild dishwashing liquid solution and then, with a broom, wash the venetians backwards and forwards, shutting one side and then the other. Hang them on the clothesline and wash them down with a hose. Leave to dry.

WOODEN BLINDS AND PLANTATION SHUTTERS

Wooden blinds and shutters can be dusted in the same way as venetian blinds—with those old tongs! You can also clean them by putting on some white gloves and running your fingers along the top and bottom of the slats. The only problem is your fingers may become sore if there are a lot of blinds to clean.

ROMAN BLINDS

The hoisting mechanism of Roman blinds is complicated and delicate so have them cleaned professionally. You may spot clean them with a bran ball (see page 138).

Q 'I had a bee swarm in my house,' reports Sally. 'The bees dumped their nectar load all over the Roman blinds. Can I clean them?'

PROBLEM: Bee nectar on blinds.
WHAT TO USE: *NapiSan Oxygen*, plate, cloth.
HOW TO APPLY: Mix *NapiSan Oxygen* with water on a plate, damp a cloth in it, wring it out and spot clean the nectar spots. Leave to dry.

CURTAINS

Someone living on a busy road will have to clean their curtains more often than someone living in a sleepy hollow. Hand wash or dry-clean curtains according to the instructions. Wash your curtains in a bath (if you have one). Fill the tub with blood-heat water and add a little cheap shampoo. Immerse the curtains and give them a good swish around. Then rinse in blood-heat water. To deter cockroaches and inhibit mould, add 1 cup of non-iodised salt to the rinse water. Dry upside down in the shade so the colour doesn't run and the fabric doesn't wrinkle and buckle but before they dry completely, hang them back in position so you don't need to iron them. Just make sure the windows are clean or you'll have dirty curtains again. You can spot-clean curtains with a bran ball (see page 138).

To clean **chintz** and **cretonne** curtains, place a cup of unprocessed wheat bran in a saucepan with 1 litre of water and slowly bring it to the boil. Let it simmer for a few minutes and then strain it. Combine the strained liquid with an equal amount of lukewarm water. Dip the curtains and then hang them straight. This will clean and stiffen the fabric. If you need to replace the sheen on chintz or cretonne, use a combination of 1 part glycerine, 1 part egg white and 20 parts water in a spray pack. Spray it on the front surface of the fabric then use a warm iron. Don't use this on muslin, net or fine lace.

Velvet curtains should be cleaned with unprocessed wheat bran in either a muslin or silk bag. Rub the bag over the tufts. When ironing velvet curtains, fold them so the naps (hairy sides) face each other and iron the back. If you get an iron mark, wring a cloth in white vinegar and place it over the nap. Fold the velvet over the cloth to create a white vinegar sandwich and press with a cool iron.

When ironing curtains, always iron top to bottom. This will keep the top edges straight and the curtains will hang better.

PROBLEM: Yellowed nylon curtains.
WHAT TO USE: Washing powder, methylated spirits.
HOW TO APPLY: Wash the curtains with washing powder in the washing machine and add ½ cup of methylated spirits to the rinse cycle. Then hang them on the washing line until they're almost dry before hanging them back on the rod to fully dry. Never put nylon in the dryer.

Q 'My cat sprayed on my new curtains,' says Chris. 'The smell is awful and there's a slight stain.'

PROBLEM: Cat spray on curtains.
WHAT TO USE: *NapiSan*, lavender oil, 1 litre spray pack, camphor flakes.
HOW TO APPLY: To remove the stain, wash the curtains in a bucket with *NapiSan* (for quantity, follow directions) and water. Add a few drops of lavender oil to the water to get rid of the smell. Rinse and hang on the line. If the smell

remains, add a couple of drops of lavender oil to water in a spray pack and spray over the area. Leave some camphor flakes nearby to deter the cat.

Q 'I have silk curtains with light brown stains on them,' reports Sally. 'I put one curtain in the washing machine and added a colourfast bleach. I put the other curtain in a strong bleach mixture. It's a disaster! They went a murky yellow/light brown colour! Are they ruined forever?'

PROBLEM: Stained silk.
WHAT TO USE: 3 per cent hydrogen peroxide, washing soda, 9 litre bucket, warm water, white vinegar, plate.
HOW TO APPLY: The bleach has burnt the silk fibres but try this option. Mix 2 cups of 3 per cent hydrogen peroxide and 8 tablespoons of washing soda in a bucket of warm water. Immerse the curtains and put a plate on top, to keep them fully in the solution. Leave for 6 hours. Remove the curtains from the bucket and place in a tub of warm water with 1 cup of white vinegar. Rinse thoroughly and hang in the sunshine to dry. If the fabric is too fragile to attempt this, you could dye the curtains with a quality silk dye. Next time, bleach silk in 2 tablespoons of washing soda and 4 tablespoons of 3 per cent hydrogen peroxide in 9 litres of water.

Floors, Walls and Windows 333

Q '**I have rubber-lined curtains that have been stained very badly by cockroaches,**' reports Jane. '**They have obviously been hiding in the folds. What can I do?**'

PROBLEM: Cockroach poo on rubber-lined curtains.
WHAT TO USE: Damp cloth, non-iodised salt, glycerine, cloth, soapy water.
HOW TO APPLY: Wipe over the rubber backing with a damp cloth. Sprinkle salt on a damp cloth and scrub over the rubber. Remove the stain from the fabric side of the curtain by wiping with a dab of glycerine on a cloth. Leave for 20 minutes, then wash in soapy water. Dry in the shade so the backing doesn't buckle. Add 1 cup of salt to the rinse water to deter cockroaches.

Q '**How can we remove the smell of dry-cleaning fluid from our curtains?**' asks Bobbie.

PROBLEM: Dry-cleaning fluid smell in curtains.
WHAT TO USE: Bathtub, blood-heat water, white vinegar, sunshine.
HOW TO APPLY: Fill a bath (or large tub) with blood-heat water and add 1 cup of white vinegar. Place the curtains in the bath and swish about. Rinse in blood-heat water and hang the curtains on the clothesline to dry. When they are

almost dry, hang them back in position and you won't need to iron them.

TIP

If there are bushfires or lots of smoke, dampen some sheets and hang them over the top of your curtains against the glass. The sheets will protect your curtains from smoke damage and are easier to clean.

Ceiling

Shannon moved into a house where the ceiling was drooping so much it looked like clouds. It had got that way because a couple of the tiles were loose and water had penetrated. But it was such a beautiful ceiling that she decided to salvage it. After asking around, Shannon learned that hessian bags could do the trick. First, use a ceiling jack to lift and flatten the ceiling. Then soak the bags in resin. Climb into the ceiling cavity and place the bags over the wooden beams so that half the bag is resting on one side of the plaster and the other half on the other side. The resin in the hessian sticks to the ceiling plaster and, when it dries, draws up the plaster and stays hard. This is much cheaper than putting in a new ceiling!

To protect the wiring in your ceiling, paint it with creosote. Rats like to eat wiring and this will keep them away.

If there's fly speck on the ceiling, put a pair of pantyhose over the head of a broom and dampen with a little water. Sprinkle a little bicarb on the broom and sweep across the ceiling—the speck will attach to the pantyhose. If there are smoke stains, apply the same technique but dampen the broom with white vinegar, then sprinkle with bicarb and sweep while the mixture is fizzing. Leave to dry, then sweep with a clean dry broom. Remove mould by covering the broom head with pantyhose and spraying with ¼ teaspoon oil of cloves in a 1 litre spray pack of water. Sweep in parallel stripes over the area. Repeat after 24 hours. The second clean removes the staining. If the mould continues to appear, you could have a problem with drainage, poor flashing in the gutter or a broken tile. Find the source of the problem and have it repaired.

Q 'We got rid of some rats,' reports Richard, 'but they left urine stains in the ceiling. What should we do?'

PROBLEM: Rat urine in the ceiling.
WHAT TO USE: Oil of cloves, oil of pennyroyal, 1 litre spray pack, bicarb.

HOW TO APPLY: Mix 1 teaspoon of oil of cloves and 2 teaspoons of oil of pennyroyal with 2 litres of warm water in a spray pack. Go into the roof of the house and spray the mixture on the stains. Then sprinkle bicarb over the stain to absorb the urine. You may need to repaint the ceiling if the stain has penetrated. Note that oil of pennyroyal should only be used as directed as it can be harmful to pregnant women and pets. Remember one drop means one drop.

Q 'I can't stand the smell of naphthalene flakes,' reports Rebecca. 'I've put the flakes around to deter a rat at my place. Is there any way to get rid of the smell?'

PROBLEM: Smell of naphthalene flakes.
WHAT TO USE: Lemon thyme.
HOW TO APPLY: Sprinkle some lemon thyme wherever the naphthalene was placed. The better way to deter rats is with snake poo, as explained below!

GETTING RID OF MICE

When Shannon lived in the bush, some mice took up residence in her house. After a while, she noticed they'd disappeared. A few months later, she saw a massive snake sliding from the ceiling, thankfully outside the house. Its length was the height of the building. Then the mice came back. Shannon mentioned this to a neighbour who told her snakes deter mice. So the solution for mice is either to have a snake in the house or, more pleasantly, scatter some snake poo inside the ceiling or under the house. The poo is a small pellet, doesn't smell and should last for about twelve months. Ask your local reptile park for some.

The Bedroom

We spend a third of our lives in the bedroom. Sure, most of it is spent sleeping, but when you're awake, it's your room. It's a sanctuary. There's no good reason why you should trip over a pile of dirty clothes in the middle of the night or breathe in musty fumes from a damp bath towel. So how can you make your bedroom a joy to slumber in? And what can you do if breakfast in bed becomes breakfast all over the bed, or your morning cup of tea ends up on the doona, or you mark your sheets with biro after writing a report in bed? Read on and all will be revealed. A clean and stain-free bedroom isn't hard to achieve and you'll sleep so much more sweetly.

Never paint your toenails in bed: *Sue's story*

INCIDENT: *'It was so stupid! I was painting my toenails in bed and dropped some polish on the sheets. And of course it's the brightest red nail polish you can imagine. And they're my favourite sheets—lovely Egyptian cotton. Is there anything I can do?'*

SOLUTION: Put a cotton ball behind the stain then soak another cotton ball in acetone (not nail polish remover) and rub it in a circular motion on the front of the stain. Use the dry cotton ball as backing. Work from the outside to the inside of the stain. Keep on doing this until all the colour is removed, replacing the cotton balls as you go. With some nail polish, this process will need to be repeated up to five times.

Perish panic: *Jill's story*

INCIDENT: *'My granddaughter is devastated. I didn't notice a small hole in a hot-water bottle and during the night, it slowly leaked. The problem wasn't so much the watermark but the rubber which transferred to her brand new white quilt cover. What can I do?'*

SOLUTION: Stretch the stained part of the quilt cover over the edge of a table or ironing board until it's taut. Sprinkle a little non-iodised salt over the rubber, roll a pair of damp pantyhose into a ball and vigorously rub over the salt. The salt will stick to the rubber and remove it without damaging the quilt. As for the hot-water bottle, you could patch the hole but it's only worth it if the rest of the bottle isn't perishing.

Bed

A bed has many functions. In addition to sleep, it's somewhere to recuperate when you're ill, a snuggly place to read a good book or, when the kids pile into it, an adventure land of mountains and valleys. The importance of a clean and comfortable mattress becomes really evident when you don't have one. Just ask any backpacker, especially one scratching bed bug bites! Shannon likes to air, turn and vacuum mattresses often. If you can, let yours air for about 15 minutes every day before making the bed. And get into the habit of turning the mattress over and backwards, each week if possible. This may sound excessive but it keeps the coils even and stops the mattress from sagging. To help you remember where you are in the rotation cycle, attach a different coloured safety pin to each corner. Shannon also recommends a monthly sprinkle of bicarb over the mattress; leave it for a couple of hours and then vacuum it off.

An indispensable part of any bedding is a mattress protector. It's a great washable barrier between you and the mattress and allows air to circulate. Wash it according to the instructions every third time you change your sheets. If you have a bed head, vacuum it once a week.

If you spill something on the mattress, use as little moisture as possible to clear it off. It's better to apply a little bit of solvent a few times than use too much at one time. Use a hair dryer to speed up the drying time.

HOW TO KILL DUST MITES

Shannon suffers from asthma and uses this remedy to kill dust mites. Put a tea bag into a spray bottle filled with cold water; let it sit for 3 minutes and then lightly spray the liquid over the mattress. The tannins in the tea kill mites. And no matter how clean you are, you can get bed bugs, which live wherever people do. Keep them contained with tea tree oil. Rub some onto your fingers and then wipe around the edge of the mattress. Use surface insecticide spray over the edges and ends of the bed, but not over the top of the mattress and not just before you're about to sleep in the bed.

Q 'On weekends, I love having a cup of tea in bed,' confesses Leanne. 'But one morning, I lost control of the cup and now the mattress is covered in tea. What can I do?'

PROBLEM: Tea stain on the mattress.
WHAT TO USE: Glycerine, cotton ball, dishwashing liquid, cloth, hair dryer.

HOW TO APPLY: Apply glycerine with a cotton ball. Use enough to make the surface of the mattress damp but not soaked. Leave for 10–15 minutes then wash it off with a little dishwashing liquid on a damp cloth. Leave to dry or speed dry with a hair dryer. Never hand a sleepy person a cup of tea in bed because it's likely to end up all over the mattress. It's happened to Shannon!

PROBLEM: Coffee stain on the mattress.
WHAT TO USE: Glycerine, cotton ball, dishwashing liquid, cloth, hair dryer.
HOW TO APPLY: Apply glycerine with a cotton ball. Use enough to make the surface of the mattress damp but not soaked. Leave for 10–15 minutes then wash it off with a little dishwashing liquid on a damp cloth. Leave to dry or speed dry with a hair dryer.

PROBLEM: Fresh bloodstain on the mattress.
WHAT TO USE: Cake of soap, cloth.
HOW TO APPLY: Moisten the cake of soap with cold water and rub it on the stain, working from the outside to the inside of the stain. Rinse several times with a cloth wrung out in cold water. Leave it to dry and repeat if needed.

PROBLEM: Old bloodstain on the mattress.
WHAT TO USE: Cornflour, cloth, stiff brush.

HOW TO APPLY: Make a paste of cornflour and water to the consistency of thickened cream. Paint it on the stain with a cloth and leave to dry. Brush the dried mixture off with a stiff brush. You may need to do this a few times.

> **Q** 'I write a lot in bed,' says David. 'But I had a disaster when my ballpoint pen broke and ink went everywhere, including into the mattress. What should I do?

PROBLEM: Ink/ballpoint pen stain on the mattress.
WHAT TO USE: Milk, dishwashing liquid, cloth; or white spirits, cotton ball, dishwashing liquid, sponge, paper towel, hair dryer, talcum powder, vacuum cleaner.
HOW TO APPLY: Rot some milk in the sun (the time it takes will vary). Then place the milk solids on the stain, and with your hand, gently rub the solids in a circle over the stain. As the area dries, you will see the ink start to rise up through the milk solids. Remove the solids with some dishwashing liquid suds on a cloth, using as little water as possible. An alternative to rotten milk is white spirits applied with a cotton ball. To remove the white spirits, apply a damp soapy sponge repeatedly until no odour remains. Use paper towels to dry as much as you can, then dry the mattress in the sun. If you can't get the mattress in the sun, dry it with a hair dryer. If any odour remains,

damp the area with a cloth, cover with talcum powder and allow the powder to absorb the last of the odour. Vacuum.

PROBLEM: Semen stain on the mattress.
WHAT TO USE: Cake of soap, cloth, ice.
HOW TO APPLY: Damp a cake of soap with cold water and rub it over the stain. Leave it for 2 minutes then rub the soap off with a damp cloth. Allow to dry. For old semen stains, ice the stain before applying soap.

Q 'My child is a bed-wetter,' reports Jane. 'Urine has soaked into his mattress. What do you suggest?'

PROBLEM: Urine stain on the mattress.
WHAT TO USE: Dishwashing liquid, cloth, hair dryer, lemon juice or white vinegar, cloth.
HOW TO APPLY: Add a little dishwashing liquid to water to generate a sudsy mix. Scrub the suds into the stain with a cloth and, if you can, put the mattress in the sun. If you can't, use paper towels to dry as much as you can. Then dry with a hair dryer. Neutralise the smell with lemon juice or white vinegar applied sparingly with a damp cloth.

PROBLEM: New red wine stain on the mattress.
WHAT TO USE: Old toothbrush, white vinegar, paper towel.

HOW TO APPLY: Dip an old toothbrush in white vinegar and rub it over the stain. Blot the stain with paper towels. Repeat until clean. Then dry thoroughly.

PROBLEM: Old red wine stain on the mattress.
WHAT TO USE: Glycerine, cotton ball, bicarb, white vinegar, soft brush, dishwashing liquid, soapy sponge, paper towel, hair dryer, vacuum cleaner.
HOW TO APPLY: Loosen the stain with glycerine applied with a cotton ball until the edge of the stain begins to lighten. Make a paste with 1 dessertspoon of bicarb and 2 dessertspoons of white vinegar and scrub into the stain. Wait until it stops fizzing then rub it off with a soft brush. Leave until the stain begins to disappear. Then wipe it off with a damp soapy sponge. Blot with paper towels and dry with a hair dryer. Then vacuum.

Q 'We've stored an inner-spring mattress in a caravan for six months,' reports Jenny. 'It really smells. What do you suggest?'

PROBLEM: Smelly mattress.
WHAT TO USE: Household steamer, lavender oil, bicarb, vacuum cleaner.
HOW TO APPLY: Hire a household steamer, put a couple of drops of lavender oil in the water and apply the steam to

the entire mattress. A steamer works a bit like a reverse vacuum cleaner. Then put the mattress in the sunshine. If you can, lie it on top of the clothesline so air can circulate around the mattress. If you can't get it into the sun, dust bicarb over the mattress and leave it until it's completely dry, then vacuum. Turn and repeat on the other side. Push up and down on the mattress while sniffing the air vents on the side of the mattress. If smell is released, you need to steam again!

Q 'My cream valance has a rust stain from an old wire bed base,' says Ian. 'How can I get it off?'

PROBLEM: Rust on cotton valance.
WHAT TO USE: Disposable rubber gloves, *CLR/Ranex*, cloth, cold water; or non-iodised salt, lemon juice, sunshine or ultraviolet light.
HOW TO APPLY: Put on rubber gloves, place a little *CLR* or *Ranex* on a cloth and wipe over the rust. As soon as the rust starts to bleed into the rest of the fabric, rinse in cold water. If needed, repeat. If you don't want to use harsh chemicals, put a little mountain of salt over each rust spot and squeeze drops of lemon juice on top—enough to moisten the salt but not collapse it. Leave in the sunshine or under ultraviolet light. Repeat if needed. Dense rust stains can take quite a while to fade.

Q 'I've got a 30-year-old cherry-stained bed head,' reports Joan. 'Is there an easy way to remove scratches from it?'

PROBLEM: Scratches in timber bed head.
WHAT TO USE: Tinted beeswax, cloth; or crayon, hair dryer, pantyhose.
HOW TO APPLY: Wipe the scratches with tinted beeswax (available at hardware stores) on a cloth. Another option is to scribble over the scratch with a crayon in a matching colour. Aim a hair dryer over the top to gently melt the crayon into the scratch and buff with a rolled up pair of pantyhose.

Q 'My parents are about to visit and I wanted to freshen up a mattress used by my teenage son,' says Helen. 'Any ideas?'

PROBLEM: Freshening up a mattress.
WHAT TO USE: Damp cake of bathroom soap, stiff scrubbing brush, damp cloth, bicarb, tennis racquet/cricket bat, vacuum cleaner.
HOW TO APPLY: You'll need to start preparing at least 2 days before you want to use the mattress. Most mattress stains can be removed by rubbing with a damp cake of bathroom soap and scrubbing with a brush. Once the stains are removed, wipe with a damp cloth and then the fun part begins!

Sprinkle the mattress with a light dusting of bicarb and use a tennis racquet or cricket bat to whack the mattress—Shannon points out this is a good way for you to release any pent-up anger you may be feeling. Leave the bicarb on the mattress overnight and vacuum using the brush attachment. Flip the mattress and repeat on the other side.

Q 'I've got mould in a futon mattress,' reports Bronwyn. 'How can I get it out?'

PROBLEM: Mould in the mattress.
WHAT TO USE: Salt, water, 9 litre bucket, water, old sheet, sunshine, stiff broom.
HOW TO APPLY: Add 1 kg of salt to a 9 litre bucket of water and stir until the salt dissolves. On a sunny day, take the mattress outside and rest it on an old sheet. Dip a clean broom in the salt solution and scrub into both sides of the mattress. Allow to dry and a salt crust to form. Brush away the salt crust with a broom and the mould will come away as well.

TIP

If there's lots of clutter in your bedroom, get a 'clutter bucket'. Place anything that doesn't belong in the room in the bucket and sort through it when you have finished cleaning.

CARING FOR WATERBEDS

I know all about waterbeds because I have one. They're particularly helpful for people with arthritis because you don't get pressure points on your joints. I clean them using the '333' technique. Every 3 months add the proprietary chemical to the water. Every 3 months pull the cover off and wash it as you would a doona. And every 3 months wipe in and around the bag and underneath the plastic reservoir. Make sure you dry the area thoroughly with a towel before returning the bedding.

The water level is crucial. To work out the right level, lie on the bed with your sleeping partner. If you both roll towards the middle, you need to add more water. If you both roll towards the sides, you need to remove some water. And when you are replacing the water, use warm rather than cold water.

If you get a hole in the bladder, call a professional. I've found that the cost of repairing or replacing the bladder is fairly reasonable and attempting to do it yourself is tricky. Failing to repair properly will give you a rude shock in the middle of the night and a disaster the next day when you try to dry everything out. Water beds hold a lot of water!

SHEETS

There's nothing better than getting into bed with clean, fresh sheets. When selecting sheets, choose natural fibres such as cotton, silk or linen. I hate polyester satin sheets. They may look good but they're cold in winter and like lying on a plastic bag in summer! Wash your sheets once a week in a good detergent. If you can, dry them in the sun because it's a great antibacterial and leaves them smelling fresh.

Shannon loves sheets to have that starchy feel. You can make your own starch from rice. Strain the water after you cook rice and add it to the rinse water in the washing machine. The sheets will be really white and firm against your skin and the rice powder helps prevent sweat.

SPOTLESS CLASSIC
Tea stains on sheets

It's easy to spill a cuppa in bed. Fortunately, it's also easy to whip off the sheets and remove the stain. If you get to the spill right away, wipe with a little glycerine on a cotton ball and wash the sheets on a cold setting in the washing machine. For an old stain, wipe with a little glycerine on a cotton ball followed by a little white spirits on a cotton ball and leave for 10–15 minutes. Wash on a cold setting in the washing machine and dry in sunshine.

With accidental spills, work out what the stain is made of (see 'Stain diagnosis' page 577) and then work out its solvent, remembering that protein stains need to be removed first with cold water before fat stains are removed with hot water. If you do it the other way around, you'll set the protein stain.

Q 'Most of the time I can't be bothered removing my make-up before I go to bed,' admits Kristie. 'I then often transfer the make-up to my sheets during the night. What's the best way to get it off?'

PROBLEM: Lipstick/greasy make-up stain on the sheets.
WHAT TO USE: Cotton balls, methylated spirits; or white spirits, cotton balls.
HOW TO APPLY: Hold a cotton ball on the back of the stain, then dip another cotton ball in methylated spirits and rub it in a circular motion over the stain, working from the outside to the inside of the stain. Replace the dirty cotton balls as needed until the stain is removed. If the lipstick is dark, use white spirits in the same way. Then wash in the washing machine. See also 'Oily stain on fabric' on page 149.

PROBLEM: Fruit juice stains on the sheets.
WHAT TO USE: *NapiSan.*
HOW TO APPLY: Wash the sheets in the washing machine and hang them in sunshine. If you can't dry the sheets in the sun, soak them in *Napisan* before washing then tumble dry. If the sheets are white, use *NapiSan Whitening*. If the sheets are coloured, use *NapiSan Oxygen* or *NapiSan Plus*.

PROBLEM: Candle wax stain on the sheets.
WHAT TO USE: Ice, blunt knife or scissors, white spirits, cotton balls, paper towel, iron.
HOW TO APPLY: Put ice on the wax and remove as much of the wax as possible, either with a blunt knife or scissors. Don't damage the fabric! Then apply white spirits with a cotton ball on either side of the wax, working in a circular motion. For any remaining marks, put several layers of paper towel on the ironing board, put the sheet on top, then place more paper towels over the wax and iron over the paper towels. Replace the paper towel regularly until all the wax is removed.

Q 'I had a cut on my knee which bled through the bandage and onto my sheets,' reveals Jessica. 'I washed the sheets in hot water, which has set the stain. Can it be fixed?'

PROBLEM: Bloodstain on the sheets.
WHAT TO USE: Cake of soap; *NapiSan*; or glycerine, cotton balls.
HOW TO APPLY: Damp the soap in cold water and rub over the stain. Then rub the stain against itself vigorously until it's removed. You may need to do this a few times. Put the sheets through the washing machine on the cold cycle. An alternative is to soak the stain in *Napisan*. If the stain has

set, apply glycerine with a cotton ball to either side of the stain. Rub in circles from the outside to the inside of the stain until it starts to shift at the edge, then wash in *NapiSan* and cold water.

PROBLEM: Semen stain on the sheets.
WHAT TO USE: Cake of soap.
HOW TO APPLY: Damp the soap in cold water and rub over the stain. Then rub the stain against itself until it's removed. Put the sheets in the washing machine on the cold cycle.

PROBLEM: Egg yolk stain on the sheets.
WHAT TO USE: Cake of soap, cold water, warm wash.
HOW TO APPLY: Damp the soap in cold water and rub over the stain. Then put the sheets through the washing machine on a warm setting to remove the fats.

PROBLEM: Chocolate stain on the sheets.
WHAT TO USE: Cake of soap; or white spirits, cotton balls.
HOW TO APPLY: Damp the soap in cold water, then rub over the stain before soaking in cold water. Wash the sheets in the washing machine on a warm or hot cycle. If the fabric is polyester satin, use white spirits applied with a cotton ball to the stain with another cotton ball held at the back of the stain. Rub in a circular motion, working from the outside to the inside of the stain. Then wash normally.

PROBLEM: Ink/ballpoint pen stain on the sheets.
WHAT TO USE: Milk; or white spirits, cotton balls.
HOW TO APPLY: Rot a carton of milk in the sun (the time this takes will vary). Then heap the solids over the stain with your hand. Leave until the ink starts to soak into the solids. Then wash the rotten milk out in the washing machine on the warm cycle. Alternatively, apply white spirits with a cotton ball, working in a circular motion from the outside to the inside of the stain. Remove all the colour before placing the sheets in the washing machine on the warm cycle.

PROBLEM: Vomit stain on the sheets.
WHAT TO USE: *NapiSan*.
HOW TO APPLY: Rinse out the solids first with water, then put the sheets through the washing machine and dry them in the sun. If you can't dry them in the sun, soak them in *NapiSan* before putting them through the washing machine. Then put them in the dryer. Always wash vomit as soon as possible because mould can grow on it overnight and will stain.

Q 'How can I whiten sheets that have yellowed?' asks Dave.

PROBLEM: Yellowed sheets (poly-cotton and cotton).
WHAT TO USE: Methylated spirits; or *NapiSan Plus*, water.

HOW TO APPLY: If the sheets are poly-cotton, dip in methylated spirits and wring out tightly. Wash normally in the washing machine. For 100 per cent cotton sheets, soak overnight in *NapiSan Plus* and warm to hot water. Wash normally and dry in sunshine.

Q 'What's the best way to remove bore water stains on sheets?' asks Jean.

PROBLEM: Bore water stains on sheets.
WHAT TO USE: White vinegar, warm to hot water.
HOW TO APPLY: Soak the stained areas in white vinegar overnight. Wash normally and dry in sunshine.

Q 'Help me!' pleads Sheree. 'I've got ointment stains on my sheets. How do I get them out?'

PROBLEM: Ointment on sheets.
WHAT TO USE: Dishwashing liquid, warm water; or tea tree oil, cloth.
HOW TO APPLY: Most ointments are made with 80 per cent oil and 20 per cent water. To remove oil, put a couple of drops of dishwashing liquid onto your fingers and rub into the stain until it feels like jelly. Rinse in warm water. If this doesn't work, rub the stain with tea tree oil on a cloth. Wash normally and dry in sunshine.

Soundproof your bedroom

Shannon has lived in some really noisy places. She's lived next to train lines, under flight paths, on main roads—even above a massage parlour! You can reduce noise by restricting the sound vibrations. Place objects, such as wardrobes, against the wall to muffle sound. Use heavy curtains, several lightweight curtains or ruffled curtains to minimise noise. Fluffy items help. If noise is coming from underneath, don't lean your bed against the wall and put high-density foam rubber squares under the four corners of your bed. Layering carpets and rugs also helps to reduce noise levels. If the noise is coming from above, hang mosquito nets or parachutes from the ceiling or put up some wall hangings. Put felt spots behind picture frames and mirrors on walls to prevent vibration. You could also put pelmets over windows.

DOONAS/BEDCOVERS

Doonas and bedcovers play a big role in a bedroom's decoration and there are many varieties and styles to choose from. Doonas can be made of goose feathers, wool or synthetics. Wash them twice a year or even more if you sweat a lot. You can tell it's time for a wash when the fibres are packed down and lumpy, or the doona smells. Some doonas can be put through the washing machine. Just check the manufacturer's instructions first. Others, regardless of the filling, can be washed in a bath or large washing sink. If you don't have one, try to borrow a friend's.

Fill the bath with water warmed to blood temperature and half a cap of woolwash for a double-sized doona. Lay the doona in the bath then get in yourself and stomp up and down on the doona until you get rid of all the dirt and grime. Empty the bath, fill it again with clean, blood-heat water and stomp over it again. Let the water out, fill the bath again with clean, blood-heat water and allow it to soak through the doona.

After you've rinsed the doona, drain the water from the bath and tread on the doona to squeeze out as much moisture as possible. Place the doona in a large garbage bag rather than a basket so you don't leave a drip trail. Then take the doona outside and put it on an old sheet. If you don't have a lawn, place it flat over the top of the clothesline. Leave it to dry for quite some time, then shake it and turn it. You need to do this about three times until it's almost dry. Then hang it on the clothesline using lots of pegs so you don't put stress on any one spot. Unless you already have a stitched ridge, don't fold the doona over the line. Instead, peg it by the two outside edges on separate lines so that it forms a U-shape. This allows air to circulate. When it's almost completely dry, whack it with your hand or an old tennis racquet. This fluffs up the fibres or loosens the feathers. Then put it back inside the doona cover to protect it against spills and grime.

If you can't be bothered washing your doona, at least hang it on the clothesline in the sun to allow the UV rays to kill bacteria.

WHAT NOT TO DO ...

Q 'My 2-year-old has put a large amount of liquid foundation on my 100 per cent cotton quilt,' says Erica. 'I've washed it in *NapiSan* and that didn't work. What can I do?'

PROBLEM: Liquid foundation and *NapiSan* on cotton.
WHAT TO USE: Water, white spirits, cloth, dishwashing liquid.
HOW TO APPLY: *NapiSan* isn't the correct solvent and you'll need to remove that first by rinsing the entire quilt in water before tackling the stain. To remove the colour, wipe over the stained areas with a little white spirits on a cloth until the colour is removed. To remove the oil, put a couple of drops of dishwashing liquid on your fingers and massage into the stain until it feels like jelly. Wash normally and dry in sunshine.

Q 'Our silk doona cover was accidentally washed in the washing machine and has lost its nice feel and softness,' reports Julie. 'Can we do anything about it?'

PROBLEM: Silk in washing machine.

WHAT TO USE: Blood-heat water, cheap shampoo, cheap hair conditioner.

HOW TO APPLY: Hand wash in blood-heat water and 1 teaspoon of shampoo (for a single-size cover). Rinse in blood-heat water and 1 teaspoon of hair conditioner. Rinse again in blood-heat water and dry flat in the shade.

PREVENTION: Always hand wash delicate items. To put the least amount of stress on fibres and dyes, ensure the rinse water is the same temperature as the wash water.

Q 'I've managed to get red *Tiger Balm* on my new cotton bedspread,' says Sue. 'Help!'

PROBLEM: Red *Tiger Balm* on cotton.

WHAT TO USE: Cake of bathroom soap, warm water, tea tree oil, cotton ball.

HOW TO APPLY: Red *Tiger Balm* contains beeswax and chilli oil. Dip a cake of bathroom soap in warm water and scrub over the stain. Rinse in water. Wipe with a little tea tree oil on a cotton ball and wash normally.

Q 'My husband has sleep apnoea and uses a special machine to help him sleep,' reports Lucy. 'What's the best way to clean the respirator mask and the straps?'

PROBLEM: Dirty respirator mask and straps.
WHAT TO USE: White vinegar, cold water, solution for contact lenses.
HOW TO APPLY: Respirator masks are made of a polycarbonate/silicon compound. Clean with 2 teaspoons of white vinegar and 1 litre of cold water. Soak for 20 minutes and rinse with contact lense solution (used to clean contact lenses and available at the chemist). The straps are made of wetsuit material. Clean with 2 teaspoons of white vinegar per 1 litre of cold water and leave for 1 hour. Massage the straps with your hands in cold water. Dry in the shade.

PILLOWS

Shannon likes her pillows in all shapes, sizes and densities. Pillows can be made of foam, feather, blow fibre or kapok. Use a pillow protector as well as a pillowcase and wash them weekly. The reason why you should use a protector is to stop the pillow compacting or needing as much washing.

To hand wash pillows, wash them in woolwash the same way that you would wash your doona as described on page 359. Allow them to dry in an elevated area so the water can drip away. The top of the clothesline is ideal. Turn the pillows regularly while they're drying but never compress them while they're wet. When you think they're dry, leave them for another hour to make sure the centre has dried completely.

To machine wash pillows in a top loading washing machine, place two pillows in the washing machine so they sit flat around the drum and meet end to end. Allow water to fill the washing machine and rinse right away. Add 1 tablespoon of cheap shampoo and repeat. Rinse again with clean water. Dry pillows flat on a drying rack or on top of the clothesline. If using the clothesline, spread a towel over the top of the clothesline, peg in place and put the pillows on top. To prevent pillow fibres matting, turn every 2 hours until the centre of the pillow is completely dry.

Q '**What's the easiest way to remove mascara from pillowcases?' asks Thelma.**

PROBLEM: Mascara on cotton.
WHAT TO USE: Methylated spirits, cotton ball; or white spirits, cotton ball.
HOW TO APPLY: It depends on the type of chemicals in the mascara. First try treating the stain by wiping with methylated spirits on a cotton ball. If that doesn't work, apply white spirits to a cotton ball and wipe over and into the stain. Wash normally and dry in sunshine.

BLANKETS/THROWS

Blankets and throws are handy because they're light, portable and cosy. It's a good idea to have a variety on hand to choose from, including woollens for the cooler months and cottons the warmer. Blankets should be aired regularly, preferably once a week, and outside if possible.

Woollen blankets should be washed once every 4–6 months in shampoo and conditioner, the cheaper the better because they contain less perfume. For single-sized blankets, use 3 dessertspoons of shampoo with water warmed to blood temperature, rinse, then use 3 dessertspoons of conditioner with water warmed to blood temperature. Use double the amount for double-sized blankets. After rinsing, dry them in the morning sun or dappled shade, not the afternoon sun, or the blankets will stiffen. To prevent wear marks and to help them dry faster, hang them in a U shape across two lines on the clothesline. To prevent water dripping on the floor when going to the clothesline, line a clothes basket with a big plastic garbage bag before adding your just-washed blankets. Once they're dry, your blankets will be lovely, clean and soft.

Machine wash blankets only if the manufacturer's instructions indicate that you can. If you use the washing machine, add 1–1½ caps of woolwash for a double blanket. If you wash the blanket in the bath, use 2 caps of woolwash or shampoo. Don't leave blankets to soak. Just wash them in blood-heat water, rinse in blood-heat water and hang to dry. If you agitate woollen blankets too much, the blanket will shrink, leaving you with a felt wad instead of a soft blanket.

Cotton blankets can be machine washed the same way as sheets. **Faux mink** blankets can either be hand washed with woolwash or shampoo in blood-heat water or dry-cleaned. Make sure you brush with a hairbrush as it dries.

Never put **sheepskin** in the washing machine or agitate it. Instead, wash sheepskin underblankets with woolwash or shampoo in a bath, sink or bucket. Dry them lying flat. Just before the sheepskin is completely dry, brush it with a hairbrush in all directions.

Read the washing instructions before cleaning an **electric** blanket. If it doesn't have any instructions, take it to a reputable dry-cleaner.

If you have space, store blankets in a blanket box or, better still, a camphor wood box because this will keep insects away. Otherwise, keep blankets in the cupboard but protect them with some camphor inside a handkerchief and plastic bag. Prick little holes in the plastic and put it inside your blankets. This will keep insects and other nasties away but won't mark your blankets. Store doonas the same way.

Q **'Do you have any advice on how to remove cat hair from woollen blankets?' asks Joan. 'Mine are covered.'**

PROBLEM: Cat hair on blankets.
WHAT TO USE: Disposable rubber gloves, cake of bathroom soap, water.
HOW TO APPLY: Put on disposable rubber gloves and wash your gloved hands with a cake of bathroom soap and water. Shake dry (don't use a towel). Stroke the blanket with your gloved hands and the cat hair will attach to the rubber gloves.
PREVENTION: To deter cats, put some camphorated oil, naphthalene or *Vicks VapoRub* near the bedroom door and the cat won't enter the room. Reapply every 6 months or so.

SHEEPSKIN UNDERLAY

Q 'In winter, I have sheepskin under my sheets,' reports Andy. 'How should I wash it?'

PROBLEM: Washing sheepskin underlay.
WHAT TO USE: Cheap shampoo, blood-heat water, hairbrush.
HOW TO APPLY: Place 1 teaspoon of shampoo in a tub of blood-heat water and immerse the sheepskin. Gently massage the sheepskin with your hands as though you were washing your hair. Rinse in blood-heat water. To prevent stiffening, dry slowly in the shade and brush regularly with a hairbrush.

Chests of Drawers, Bedside Tables and Wardrobes

Chests of drawers, bedside tables and wardrobes come in a range of finishes including French polish, beeswax, polyurethane, laminate, veneer and varnish and take many forms. They can be built-in or stand alone, old or new. Those with a shellac, French polish or varnish finish should be cleaned once a month with a good quality, silicone-free furniture polish. Just put a small amount of polish on a cloth, wipe it over the piece, then wipe it off with the other side of the cloth. A good furniture polish should remove most small scratches.

Those with a laminate or polyurethane finish can be cleaned with a damp cloth. If they're very dirty, use bicarb and white vinegar. Keep polyurethane pieces away from windows because the sun's UV rays will yellow them.

To clean the inside of drawers, take your clothes out and vacuum. If the area is very dirty, use white vinegar and water on a sponge. To deter nasties, put some lavender oil or tea tree oil on a cloth and wipe over the drawer or cupboard interior. A cake of soap left in the drawer will also deter bugs and scent your clothes. You can also buy scented and anti-bug drawer liners to fit into your drawers. These will also protect your clothes from the tannins in the wood.

If you apply make-up at a dressing table with a timber surface, protect it with a glass tile or mirror tile. A mirror tile is preferable because it gives backlighting and your make-up will be applied perfectly. I also like to put foam in my bedside table drawers so that if I drop make-up bottles or jewellery, they won't break!

To keep moths, silverfish and other nasties away, make a wardrobe sachet (see page 575).

PROBLEM: Sticking drawers in furniture.
WHAT TO USE: Soap or candle wax; or *Gumption*, sponge.
HOW TO APPLY: Take the drawer out. If it has wooden runners, rub them with soap. You can also use rub candle wax along the runners. For plastic runners, polish with *Gumption* on a sponge. If this doesn't work, your chest of drawers may be uneven. You can check this with a spirit level horizontally and vertically. If it is not level, put some cardboard or a small block of wood under one of the legs to steady it. You could also have a problem with the backing sheet of the drawer, which may need to be refastened or replaced if it's buckled. A lot of modern furniture is built with cheap backing sheets and if they buckle it takes the drawers out of alignment. It's easy to check this by looking at the back of the cupboard and making sure the sheets are flush to the edge. You can replace them yourself or get professional help. Also check that the joints of the drawer are secure. If you're re-painting your drawers, don't paint the sides of each drawer or they will stick!

Q 'I've just bought a second-hand chest of drawers made of oak,' says Susan. 'But there's a really strong smell of incense. Can I get rid of it?

PROBLEM: Incense smell in drawers.
WHAT TO USE: Bicarb, tea leaves.
HOW TO APPLY: Leave 1 opened packet of bicarb and 1 opened packet of regular black tea leaves in each closed drawer for 1 week (you can reuse the same packets for each drawer). The bicarb absorbs smells and the tea releases smells. The smell should take about 1 week to clear. If it doesn't, repeat.

TIP

If there's damp in your wardrobe, tie 6 sticks of white chalk together with string or ribbon and leave inside the wardrobe to absorb moisture. When the chalk sticks are wet, place them in the sun until they dry out. You can use them over and over again. For serious continuous damp, seek professional advice.

Q 'How do you remove beeswax from a wardrobe?' asks Bill.

PROBLEM: Beeswax on wardrobe.
WHAT TO USE: Mineral turpentine, water, cloth.

HOW TO APPLY: Mix 1 part mineral turpentine with 1 part water and wipe the mixture over the beeswax with a cloth.

How to hang clothes in the wardrobe

Most people have a system for sorting out where their clothes go in the wardrobe. But if you don't, and you're tired of wasting time searching for that shirt you know is in there somewhere, this is what I do.

Clothes last longer if they're hung rather than folded, so hang as much as you can. The exception is woollens and knits, which should be stored flat.

Use good coat-hangers. Wooden hangers are the best, plastic are okay and wire coat-hangers need to be wrapped with foam strips or old shoulder pads pinned on the shoulders of the hanger.

Divide your wardrobe into sections, putting similar types of clothes together. All your shirts should be together, for example. Then order the sections by size, putting the longest garments at one end and the shortest at the other end. You can further sort your clothes by colour. One suggestion is by the colours of the rainbow. Then order by sleeve length and seasonal weight.

The beauty of this system is that if your skirt is not in the wardrobe, then it's in the wash or at the dry-cleaners. You won't spend hours searching.

PROBLEM: Moths in the wardrobe.
WHAT TO USE: Camphor ball, cloves, lavender, eucalyptus oil, small muslin bag.
HOW TO APPLY: Place 1 camphor ball, 4 cloves, a sprig of lavender and a couple of drops of eucalyptus oil into a small muslin bag. Tie it, then hang it on the rod in your wardrobe. You'll deter silverfish, moths, dust mites and other insects and keep your clothes smelling fresh. Replace eucalyptus and lavender every two months. Replace the others yearly.

Q 'When you've had your clothes sitting on a coat-hanger for a while, the hanger can leave a mark,' reports Terzine. 'If you don't have time to iron it out, is there anything you can do?'

PROBLEM: Hanger marks on clothes.
WHAT TO USE: Spray pack, body heat.
HOW TO APPLY: Before you put the garment on, damp spray the spot with water where the hanger has left its indentation. When you put the garment on, your body heat will interact with the water and smooth the marks out. To prevent the problem, wrap the shoulder line of your coat-hanger with foam strips or old shoulder pads.

Q 'A glass of water spilled on my bedside table,' reports Veronica. 'The water dripped down to the felt pads under the feet of the table and stained the carpet. What do you suggest?'

PROBLEM: Felt pad staining on carpet.
WHAT TO USE: *Colour Run Remover: Coloursafe*, water, cloth, damp cloth, white vinegar, steamer.
HOW TO APPLY: This is a dye stain. Mix 1 part *Colour Run Remover: Coloursafe* with 5 parts water. Wring out a cloth in the mixture and wipe this cloth and a damp cloth hand over hand until the stain is removed. To remove the *Colour Run Remover*, wipe with a cloth wrung out in white vinegar. Repeat until removed. Remove felt pads from the bedside table with a steamer and replace with new neutral-coloured felt pads.

TIP

Clean the vents on your clock radio with the vacuum cleaner using the brush attachment. Dust regularly with damp pantyhose. Improve the reception by wiping the end of your aerial with a little white vinegar.

Hampers/Clothes Baskets

If there's space in your bedroom, keep a hamper to store dirty clothes. If clothes are really smelly, take them to the laundry right away because a nasty odour in the corner of your bedroom is not conducive to a good night's sleep. If you don't have space in your bedroom, nominate a place in the laundry for dirty clothes. Although tempting for some, never leave them in a pile on the floor.

Q *'My cast-iron chest has gone rusty,' reports David. 'Can it be fixed?'*

PROBLEM: Rust on cast-iron chest.
WHAT TO USE: Rubber gloves, rust converter, roller, methylated spirits, cloth.
HOW TO APPLY: Don't scrub the rust first because there'll be nothing left to convert! Put on rubber gloves, then apply the rust converter with a brush, rag, sponge or roller. Apply sparingly. You'll know if you've used too much if you get a white powdery coating. If this happens, wash it off with methylated spirits on a cloth.

Mirrors

Q *'My cedar mirror frame has this white stuff on it,' says Hayden. 'How do I remove it?'*

PROBLEM: White markings on timber.
WHAT TO USE: Damp pantyhose, fine grade sandpaper.
HOW TO APPLY: This is a bloom caused by salt and timber oil mixing together. If the mirror frame is sealed, remove the marks by scrubbing with a pair of damp pantyhose. Reseal if needed. If it's not sealed, rub fine grade sandpaper for timber along the grain until the bloom is removed.

Jewellery

Jewellery that has become dull can be brightened by adding ½ teaspoon of dishwashing liquid to a bucket of warm water. Gently scrub with an old toothbrush and dry each piece with a clean tea towel or cotton cloth. Don't wash items in a sink in case the plug comes loose: you don't want your precious jewellery going down the drain!

Use nothing more than a little water to clean absorbent precious stones such as jade, opal, some agates, cloudy quartz and emerald.

Pearls should only be cleaned in a mild salt solution—1 teaspoon of salt for 600 millilitres of water.

Ivory can be cleaned with sweet almond oil on a cotton bud. Other jewellery should be cleaned with a proprietary product.

Always wipe earring hooks with methylated spirits and a cotton ball to remove bacteria.

Never use heat or chemicals on jewellery. If in doubt, take it to a jeweller.

JEWELLERY BOXES

Clean jewellery boxes as you would other furniture. The easiest way to clean the inside is to vacuum it. Just make sure you cover the vacuum cleaner tube with an old T-shirt just in case you suck up a stone! I came up with this solution after dropping a small box with about 30 small gemstones in it that had all been collected from old pieces of jewellery. I dropped the box on a multicoloured, long-pile carpet. The stones are now a gorgeous necklace!

Q 'I'd like some advice on a safe home-cleaning solution for my platinum, gold and diamond engagement ring,' says Michelle. 'What do you suggest?'

PROBLEM: Dirty platinum, gold and diamond jewellery.
WHAT TO USE: Bowl, warm water, white vinegar, sable paintbrush.
HOW TO APPLY: Platinum, gold and diamond jewellery is easy to clean. Fill a bowl with 1 cup of warm water and 1 teaspoon of white vinegar. Dip a sable paintbrush in the solution and gently wipe over the jewellery.

Q 'My wife has a cameo brooch made of ivory,' reports Roy. 'It's gone a deep yellow colour. Can it be restored to the original white?'

PROBLEM: Yellowed ivory.
WHAT TO USE: Sweet almond oil, talcum powder, cotton bud, damp cotton bud.
HOW TO APPLY: Ivory yellows with age and you can't make it white again. Clean by mixing sweet almond oil and talcum powder to form a paste the consistency of runny cream and apply with a cotton bud. Polish off immediately with a damp cotton bud.

Q 'My antique silver chain is tarnished,' says Pat. 'What can I do?'

PROBLEM: Tarnished silver.
WHAT TO USE: Bicarb, white vinegar, cloth.
HOW TO APPLY: Sprinkle a little bicarb over the tarnished area followed by a little white vinegar over the top. As it fizzes, rub with a cloth and the tarnish will come away. Buff with a cloth.

Clothing and Shoes

If you look after your clothes and shoes, they'll last longer—a smart move if you spend a small fortune on both. Most garments have care labels with information about the type of fabric and how to best clean it, which is worth checking and following. What the labels don't include, however, is what to do when accidents happen. Of course you're going to get spills and stains on your clothes, they're a barrier between you and the world. Whether it's finding melted choc-top on your jeans after the movies, spilling soy sauce on your jacket when eating sushi or dropping a blob of tomato sauce from your meat pie on your footy shirt, it's best to tackle stains as soon as you can. The longer you leave them, the harder they are to remove. Start by working out what's in the stain. If it has several components, remove proteins first, then fats, then chemicals.

Damaged delicates: *Brad's story*

INCIDENT: *'My girlfriend went away and left me to do the washing. But I didn't get to it for a few days and when I did, there were mould spots on her lightly coloured lingerie. Please help me!'*

SOLUTION: Wipe the mouldy areas with a cloth dampened with methylated spirits. Add 1 cup of non-iodised salt to a 9 litre bucket of warm water, immerse the garments and soak overnight (salt water won't damage delicates). Gently wring but don't rinse the items, hang on the clothesline to dry and a salty crust will form. Brush the crust off with a soft brush and the mould will come away with it. Wash the lingerie in cheap shampoo and blood-heat water, rinse and dry on the clothesline.

Clothing

To help you find your solution as quickly as possible, we've listed problems alphabetically. If you don't know what's caused a stain, do a stain diagnosis first (see page 577). Also, when removing stains from synthetic material, such as rayon, *Lycra*, nylon, elastane, spandex, etc, wipe with methylated spirits on a cloth before washing. Stains often become trapped in synthetic fibres and methylated spirits opens them up and allows them to be released.

Q 'I spilt a jar of anchovies and olive oil on my blue denim jeans which are 98 per cent cotton and 2 per cent elastane,' says Marike. 'How do I get the oily marks off?'

PROBLEM: Anchovy on denim.
WHAT TO USE: Cloth, methylated spirits, cake of bathroom soap, cold water, dishwashing liquid, bicarb.
HOW TO APPLY: The jeans contain elastane, so wipe the stain with a little methylated spirits on a cloth first. Remove the anchovy by scribbling with a cake of bathroom soap that's been run under cold water. Then remove the oil by massaging a couple of drops of dishwashing liquid into the stain with your fingers until it feels like jelly. Rinse the jeans in cold water. Wash and dry normally.

Q 'My daughter loves drinking apple juice,' reports Uriah. 'And I've got several marks on my shirt. What can I do?'

PROBLEM: Apple juice on cotton.
WHAT TO USE: Glycerine, cloth.
HOW TO APPLY: Rub the stain with a little glycerine on a cloth, leave for 20 minutes and wash and dry normally.

Q *'I've got baby oil splashes over my T-shirt,'* reports Sandra. *'How do you get it out?'*

PROBLEM: Baby oil on cotton.
WHAT TO USE: Dishwashing liquid, warm water.
HOW TO APPLY: Put a couple of drops of dishwashing liquid on your fingers and massage into the oil stains until it feels like jelly. Rinse under warm water then wash and dry normally.

PROBLEM: Baked beans on cotton.
WHAT TO USE: Cold water, cloth, white vinegar, sunshine.
HOW TO APPLY: The staining is from tomato sauce, which is a vegetable dye. To remove the stain, rinse in cold water, wipe with a cloth wrung out in white vinegar and wash normally. Dry in sunshine.

PROBLEM: Banana on cotton.
WHAT TO USE: Tea tree oil, cloth (peel); or glycerine, cloth (flesh).
HOW TO APPLY: Banana peel contains a resinous sap that is removed by wiping with a little tea tree oil on a cloth. The banana flesh causes a tannin stain and needs to be wiped with a little glycerine on a cloth before washing normally.

Q '**I'm a banana cutter,' reveals Kevin, 'and I've got banana sap all over my clothes. Can I get it out?'**

PROBLEM: Banana sap on fabric.
WHAT TO USE: Glycerine, cotton balls, white spirits.
HOW TO APPLY: Apply glycerine to the stain with a cotton ball to remove the latex in the sap, then apply white spirits with a cotton ball to remove oxides. Then wash normally.

PROBLEM: Beetroot on cotton.
WHAT TO USE: Cloth, white vinegar, 9 litre bucket, water.
HOW TO APPLY: For a small stain, wipe with a cloth wrung out in white vinegar. For a large stain, fill a bucket with cold water, add 1 cup of white vinegar and soak the garment for 20 minutes. Wash and dry normally. If you've got kids, this is a great stain removal trick to show them because they can see the beetroot colour disappearing like magic from the fabric.

Q '**I've got berry stains on my clothes,' says June. 'How can I get them out?'**

PROBLEM: Berry stains on cotton.
WHAT TO USE: Cloth, white vinegar, glycerine, sunshine.
HOW TO APPLY: For berry stains that change colour (blueberry, blackberry), wipe with a cloth wrung out in

white vinegar, then wipe with a dab of glycerine on a cloth. Wash normally and dry in sunshine. For other berries (strawberry, raspberry), wipe with a cloth wrung out in white vinegar, then wash normally and dry in the sun. Don't use soap or heat because they set berry stains.

Q 'My six-year-old daughter wore her brand new white ladybird T-shirt under a pecan tree,' says Megan, 'and bird dropping landed on her. What can I do?'

PROBLEM: Bird poo on cotton.
WHAT TO USE: Cold water, cake of bathroom soap (protein); or warm water, cake of bathroom soap (seed); or white vinegar, cloth, glycerine (fruit).
HOW TO APPLY: The treatment depends on what the bird has eaten—protein, seed or fruit. For protein (generally brown or black poo), scribble over the stain with a cake of bathroom soap that's been run under cold water. Rinse under cold water and wash and dry normally. For seed (generally white poo), scribble over the stain with a cake of bathroom soap that's been run under warm water. Rinse under warm water and wash and dry normally. For fruit (generally purple or orange poo), wipe with a cloth wrung out in white vinegar, then wipe with a little glycerine on a cloth and leave for 20 minutes. Wash and dry normally.

Q 'Is there a way to get bitumen (tar) out of denim jeans?' asks Robyn. 'They have been washed in ordinary laundry powder but most of the tar didn't budge. Is it possible to salvage them?'

PROBLEM: Bitumen/tar on denim.
WHAT TO USE: Disposable rubber gloves, kerosene, baby oil, dishwashing liquid, warm water.
HOW TO APPLY: Put on rubber gloves and rub equal parts kerosene and baby oil (around 1 tablespoon of each for a stain 10 cm in diameter) into the mark with your fingers. You'll see the tar beginning to spread and look worse. Add a couple of drops of dishwashing liquid and continue to massage with your fingers until it resembles jelly. Rinse in warm water. If any bitumen remains, repeat until removed. Wash and dry normally.

Q 'I'm having a problem removing a stain caused by splashes of black bean sauce on a pale pink T-shirt,' says Pip. 'I'd appreciate your help.'

PROBLEM: Black bean sauce on cotton.
WHAT TO USE: White vinegar.
HOW TO APPLY: Flush the stain with white vinegar. If it proves stubborn, rub in with your fingers. Wash and dry normally.

Q '**I was at the movies and got chewing gum on my trousers,**' says Kevin. '**How do I get it off?**'

PROBLEM: Chewing gum on cotton.
WHAT TO USE: Knife/scraper, tea tree oil, tissue.
HOW TO APPLY: Remove as much chewing gum as you can with a knife or scraper. Apply a few drops of tea tree oil to a tissue and rub over the chewing gum in a circular motion. Little gum balls will form that can be plucked from the cotton. Continue until the gum is removed.

Q '**I was enjoying some potato wedges dipped in chilli sauce,**' says Matthew. '**But, tragically, not all of the sauce made it into my mouth and went on my T-shirt instead. What can I do?**'

PROBLEM: Chilli sauce on cotton.
WHAT TO USE: White vinegar or lemon juice, cloth, dishwashing liquid, warm water.
HOW TO APPLY: Chilli sauce is high in alkaline and oil. Wipe with a cloth wrung out in white vinegar or lemon juice until most of the red colouring transfers to the cloth. To remove the oil, add a couple of drops of dishwashing liquid to your fingers and massage into the stain. Rinse in warm water.

Q 'How do you remove chocolate ice-cream from a T-shirt?' asks Maureen.

PROBLEM: Chocolate ice cream on T-shirt.
WHAT TO USE: Cake of soap.
HOW TO APPLY: As the chocolate contains protein, you must use cold water. Vigorously rub the stain with soap and cold water. Then wash normally.

PROBLEM: Chocolate on cotton.
WHAT TO USE: Dishwashing liquid, cold water or damp cloth.
HOW TO APPLY: Put a couple of drops of dishwashing liquid on your fingers and massage into the stain. Rinse in cold water or with a damp cloth.

PROBLEM: Chocolate on wool.
WHAT TO USE: Cheap shampoo, cold water or damp cloth.
HOW TO APPLY: Massage shampoo into the stain with your fingers and rinse in cold water or with a damp cloth.

PROBLEM: Coffee on cotton.
WHAT TO USE: Glycerine, cotton ball.
HOW TO APPLY: Wipe with a dab of glycerine on a cotton ball and leave for 20 minutes before washing normally.

Q 'I wore my favourite purple silk organza dress to my engagement party,' reports Diana. 'But I managed to get cream from the cake in a couple of spots. Can you offer any assistance?'

PROBLEM: Cream on silk.
WHAT TO USE: Dishwashing liquid, blood-heat water, white vinegar, cloth.
HOW TO APPLY: The staining is caused by fat in the cream. Remove by massaging the fatty spots with a little dishwashing liquid on your fingers. When it feels like jelly, rinse in blood-heat water. Silk can develop watermarks from spot removal, so dry slowly in the shade. If you do get watermarks, immerse a cloth in equal parts white vinegar and water and wring out so it's just damp. Wipe over the stain, pressing heavily in the centre and easing the pressure as you move towards the outside. Dry flat in the shade.

Q 'How do I remove yellow curry stains from cotton fabric?' asks Sunil.

PROBLEM: Curry stain (yellow) on cotton.
WHAT TO USE: Lavender oil, cloth.
HOW TO APPLY: Place a couple of drops of lavender oil on a cloth and wipe over the stain until removed. Wash and dry normally.

Q 'I've got custard stains on my pants,' admits Ainslee. 'How can I get them off?'

PROBLEM: Custard on cotton.
WHAT TO USE: *NapiSan Plus*, water.
HOW TO APPLY: Make a paste of *NapiSan Plus* and water and place over the stains. Leave for 20 minutes, then wash and dry normally. If the custard is flavoured, remove that stain first (consult the relevant advice elsewhere in the book eg: chocolate) and then remove the custard stain.

Q 'My deodorant has left white stains on my shirts,' says Susie. 'It's like it's permanently caked on now. Can I remove this?'

PROBLEM: Deodorant stains on fabric.
WHAT TO USE: *NapiSan Oxygen*.
HOW TO APPLY: Make a paste with *NapiSan Oxygen* and water to the consistency of peanut butter. Apply it to the deodorant stains and leave for 15 minutes, then wash the shirts as usual in the washing machine.

Q 'How do you remove diesel from polyester and cotton clothes?' asks Jim.

PROBLEM: Diesel on polyester and cotton.

WHAT TO USE: Disposable rubber gloves, baby oil, cloth, dishwashing liquid, warm water (cotton); or methylated spirits, cloth (polyester).

HOW TO APPLY: You don't want diesel all over your hands so put on rubber gloves and wipe with a little baby oil on a cloth. Put a couple of drops of dishwashing liquid on your fingers and massage over the baby oil. When it feels like jelly, rinse in warm water. With synthetic fibres, first wipe with a dab of methylated spirits on a cloth.

Q **'I practise judo three times a week,' reports Tony. 'And I've got brown marks on my collar from dirt and sweat. What can I do?'**

PROBLEM: Dirt and sweat on cotton.
WHAT TO USE: *NapiSan OxyAction MAX*, warm to hot water.
HOW TO APPLY: Mix *NapiSan OxyAction MAX* and warm to hot water to form a paste the consistency of peanut butter. Apply to the stain and leave for 20 minutes before washing and drying normally.

Q **'What's the best way to get dirt stains out of a cotton sports shirt that has velvety numbers?' asks Brian. 'I don't want to damage the print by soaking it.'**

PROBLEM: Dirt on cotton.
WHAT TO USE: *NapiSan Plus*, cold water.
HOW TO APPLY: Mix *NapiSan Plus* and cold water to form a paste the consistency of peanut butter and place over the dirty marks (avoiding the velvet). Leave for 20 minutes and wash and dry normally.

PROBLEM: Egg on cotton.
WHAT TO USE: Cold water, cake of bathroom soap.
HOW TO APPLY: Rinse in cold water and rub with a cake of bathroom soap. If needed, rub with your fingers to remove the stain. Wash and dry normally.

PROBLEM: Fish sauce on cotton.
WHAT TO USE: Cake of bathroom soap, cold water, old toothbrush (protein); dishwashing liquid, cold water (oil).
HOW TO APPLY: Fish sauce is high in protein and oil. To remove the protein, run a cake of bathroom soap under cold water, apply to an old toothbrush and scrub over the stain. To remove the oil, massage a couple of drops of dishwashing liquid into the stain using your fingers until it feels like jelly. Rinse in cold water.

WHAT NOT TO DO ...

Q 'I have a white T-shirt that I think is either cotton or a poly-cotton mix. I'm not sure exactly what stains are on it (I presume they're food stains). But I applied white spirits to the stains before washing. To my horror, grey patches appeared in the places where I had dabbed the white spirits and my T-shirt smelled terrible. After this, I put the T-shirt in a bucket of water containing *NapiSan OxyAction MAX* and left it to soak for a week, after which I washed it again. The smell has gone but the grey stains are still there (that said, the stains have faded slightly). What can I do now?'

A The reason the T-shirt turned grey is because the stain was a combination of oxide and protein. Before attempting any stain removal, do a stain diagnosis (see page 577). If in doubt, try a dab of glycerine or a dab of white vinegar on a cloth first. They're great cleaners and don't set stains. In this case, massage a little glycerine into the stains using your fingers. Leave for 20 minutes and scrub with a cake of bathroom soap that's been run under cold water. Repeat until the stains are removed.

Q 'I've got fluorescent highlighter pen on my cotton trousers,' says Mark. 'Can I get it off?'

PROBLEM: Fluorescent highlighter pen on cotton.
WHAT TO USE: Fluorescent highlighter pen, cotton ball, white spirits; or 9 litre bucket, non-iodised salt, plastic bag, freezer.
HOW TO APPLY: Fluorescent pen contains its own solvent—so, strange as it may seem, you will need to draw on the trousers again using the same pen. While the ink is wet, rub with a little white spirits on a cotton ball. Wash and dry normally. If this doesn't work, fill a bucket with water and add 1 cup of salt. Dip the stain in the salt solution, remove and place the garment in a plastic bag. Put it in the freezer and leave overnight. Remove from the plastic bag and wash and dry normally.

Q 'My son purchased a leather jacket in Melbourne last week which was discounted because there's pink highlighter on both sleeves,' reports Jayne. 'Can you help?'

PROBLEM: Fluorescent pen on leather.
WHAT TO USE: White spirits, cotton bud, talcum powder, leather conditioner.
HOW TO APPLY: Obviously the discount was so good he didn't think about how to remove the stain. Dip a cotton bud in white spirits and rub over the pen mark, then sprinkle with talcum powder. Leave to dry and brush the

talcum powder away with your hand. Repeat if necessary. If the surface of the leather becomes dry, use a good quality leather conditioner.

Q 'I dropped make-up on the front of my favourite white shirt,' says Theresa. 'It's synthetic. What can I do?'

PROBLEM: Foundation make-up on synthetics.
WHAT TO USE: Methylated spirits, dishwashing liquid; white spirits, cloth, *NapiSan Plus*, water.
HOW TO APPLY: The shirt is synthetic, so wipe with methylated spirits first. Massage a little dishwashing liquid into the stain using your fingers and rinse in just-warm water. Repeat if needed. If there's a faint shadow, wipe with a little white spirits on a cloth. Wash and dry normally. If the make-up contains colourstay, use the above technique and apply a paste of *NapiSan Plus* and water to the stain. Leave for 20 minutes and wash and dry normally.

Q 'How can I remove grass and other greasy stains from the knees of my trousers?' asks Phil.

PROBLEM: Grass and grease on cotton.
WHAT TO USE: White spirits, cloth, dishwashing liquid.

HOW TO APPLY: To remove grass, wipe with a dab of white spirits on a cloth. To remove grease, put a couple of drops of dishwashing liquid on your fingers and massage into the stain until it feels like jelly. Rinse and wash and dry normally.

Grease

If you get grease on fabric, there are two methods of cleaning them, described below. If the problem is recurring, use the first method.

Q 'I work in the transport industry,' says Tom, 'and I'm always getting grease on my clothes. What should I do?'

PROBLEM: Grease on fabric.
WHAT TO USE: Baby oil, cotton ball, *NapiSan*.
HOW TO APPLY: Baby oil is a mineral oil that breaks down grease. Put baby oil on a cotton ball and apply it to the grease. Rub it in circles. Then soak the garment in *NapiSan* and hot water before washing.

Q 'My daughter was given a new nightie by her nanna,' says Patrick, 'but I'd been washing grease off my truck and it ended up on the nightie. Needless to say, I'm not too popular. Can the nightie be fixed?'

PROBLEM: Grease on fabric.
WHAT TO USE: White spirits, cotton balls, oxygen-based bleach.
HOW TO APPLY: This is a difficult job. Rub the spots first with white spirits applied with a cotton ball. Then soak the nightie in oxygen-based bleach. It may be easier to buy a new pair of pyjamas.

Q 'My son regularly gets mechanical grease on his woollen work jacket,' reports Debbie. 'It has a cotton lining and reflector stripes on the outside over the wool. What can I do?'

PROBLEM: Grease on wool.
WHAT TO USE: Dishwashing liquid, blood-heat water, cheap shampoo, blood-heat water, cheap hair conditioner, towel.
HOW TO APPLY: Put a couple of drops of dishwashing liquid on your fingers and massage into the stain. Rinse in blood-heat water, then wash in a little shampoo and blood-heat water. Rinse in a little hair conditioner and blood-heat water. Then rinse again in blood-heat water, gently wring out and dry flat on a towel in the shade.

Q 'While at the hairdressers, I got hair dye on my shirt,' reports Sherry. 'How do you get it out?'

PROBLEM: Hair dye on cotton.
WHAT TO USE: Same hair dye, disposable rubber gloves, cheap shampoo, cold water; or hairspray.
HOW TO APPLY: This sounds odd but it works. Hair dye contains its own solvent, so go back to the hairdresser and get the same brand and colour hair dye. Put on rubber gloves and rub a small amount of hair dye into the stain. When the stain starts to loosen, rub with a little shampoo on your fingers. Rinse in cold water and wash and dry normally. If the stain has just happened, spray with hairspray, allow to dry and brush off with the back of your hand.

Q 'How do you remove hairspray from a woollen jumper?' asks Deidre.

PROBLEM: Hair spray on wool.
WHAT TO USE: Cheap shampoo, blood-heat water, cheap hair conditioner, towel.
HOW TO APPLY: Wash the garment in a little shampoo and blood-heat water. Rinse in a little hair conditioner and blood-heat water. Then rinse again in blood-heat water, gently wring out and dry flat on a towel in the shade. To minimise stress on wool fibres, always use blood-heat water.

Q 'When I was travelling, the blue from my asthma pack rubbed onto my yellow polyester viscose slacks,' says Jocelynne. 'Can I get it off?'

PROBLEM: Ink stain on fabric.
WHAT TO USE: Milk; or white spirits, cotton ball.
HOW TO APPLY: Rot a carton of milk in the sun and spread the solids over the stain. Leave until the ink begins to rise into the milk solids. Then wash the rotten milk out in the washing machine. Alternatively, apply white spirits with a cotton ball, working in a circular motion from the outside to the inside of the stain until it's removed. Then wash normally.

Q 'I got lip balm on my cotton knit dress,' reports Patricia. 'How can I get it out?'

PROBLEM: Lip balm on cotton.
WHAT TO USE: Dishwashing liquid, white spirits, cotton ball, blood-heat water.
HOW TO APPLY: Place a little dishwashing liquid on your fingers and rub into the stains. If the lip balm is coloured, wipe with a little white spirits on a cotton ball. Rinse in blood-heat water and wash and dry normally.

Q 'I'm a celebrant,' says Janice. 'And there's always stray lipstick at weddings. Is there something I can carry in my handbag to fix any stains before the photos?'

PROBLEM: Lipstick on cotton.
WHAT TO USE: Small cloth, white spirits, pantyhose, zip-lock bag, damp cloth.
HOW TO APPLY: Saturate a cloth with white spirits and place in the toe of a pair of pantyhose. Cut the pantyhose, secure the cloth inside and tie off so it fits neatly into a zip-lock bag and store in your handbag ready to use. When needed, remove the cloth from the bag, wipe over the offending lipstick and then wipe with a damp cloth.

Q 'I know this is unusual,' says Julie. 'But how do you remove lipstick from a resuscitation dummy?'

PROBLEM: Lipstick on plastic.
WHAT TO USE: White spirits, cotton ball, damp cloth.
HOW TO APPLY: While it's a good idea to learn resuscitation, consider hygiene as well. Each person should use their own mouthguard on the dummy. To remove the lipstick, wipe with a dab of white spirits on a cotton ball, then wipe with a damp cloth.

Q 'How do I get *Liquid Paper* correction fluid out of black trousers?' asks Damien.

PROBLEM: *Liquid Paper* on cotton.
WHAT TO USE: *Liquid Paper Thinner*.
HOW TO APPLY: There's a product called *Liquid Paper Thinner* which is often available from most shops that sell *Liquid Paper*. It comes with a sponge brush, which is ideal to remove the mark. Follow the manufacturer's instructions.

Q 'I had an ink stain on my shirt that I removed with rotten milk,' reports Jo. 'It's left a faint grease-like stain. What can I do?'

PROBLEM: Mark from rotten milk.
WHAT TO USE: Methylated spirits, cloth.
HOW TO APPLY: The greasy mark indicates the garment has synthetic fibres in it and the milk has become trapped. Wipe with a little methylated spirits on a cloth and wash and dry normally.

Q 'I pulled out an old cream satin evening gown which was covered in mildew,' says Barbara. 'Is it fixable?'

PROBLEM: Mildew on satin.
WHAT TO USE: Hair dryer, clothes brush, salt.
HOW TO APPLY: Blow a hair dryer over the satin until it is warm. This causes the mildew to blow up and fluff up. Then rub a clothes brush in the direction of the watery-looking part of the satin. If any black marks remain, cover them with dry salt and brush backwards and forwards with a clothes brush. Then brush off.

Mould

Sally brought her mother's silk wedding dress from the 1960s to a Stain Clinic. The dress had become part of the kids' dress-up box and the silk had mould and dirt all over it. Shannon advised her to use kitty litter to absorb the stains because the fabric was delicate and the staining extensive. Sally was stunned. The technique involves half filling a large lidded box with clean kitty litter. Cover the kitty litter with a piece of plastic wrap, punch small holes in the plastic, then place the dress on top. Put the lid on the box and leave for 3 days. The kitty litter absorbs the moisture that's causing the mould. To remove mould from silk, put coarse non-iodised salt in the toe of a pair of pantyhose and wipe over the stains. Leave to air in the sun. This technique works for any delicate or antique fabric.

Q 'How do I remove mould from leather jackets?' asks Barbara. 'They've been hanging in a wardrobe and there are white and mouldy looking spots on them.'

PROBLEM: Mould on leather.
WHAT TO USE: Baby oil or leather conditioner, oil of cloves, microwave-safe bowl, cloth, microwave, cloth, zip-lock bag.
HOW TO APPLY: If the leather doesn't darken when a drop of water is placed on it, use baby oil rather than leather conditioner, it's much cheaper. Place 2 tablespoons of good quality leather conditioner or baby oil and ¼ teaspoon of oil of cloves in a microwave-safe bowl. Stir thoroughly and place a cloth on top. Place the bowl in the microwave and warm in 10-second bursts until the mixture melts into the cloth. Allow to cool, wipe the cloth over the leather and leave for 24 hours. Use another cloth to remove the mixture. Store the cleaning cloth in a zip-lock bag to use again (simply warm it again in the microwave).

Q 'There's a big blob of mustard on my work shirt,' reports Tim. 'What should I do?'

PROBLEM: Mustard on cotton.
WHAT TO USE: Dishwashing liquid, cold water, lavender oil, cloth.

HOW TO APPLY: Put a couple of drops of dishwashing liquid on your fingers and massage into the stain until it feels like jelly. Rinse in cold water. If any yellow mark remains, wipe with a little lavender oil on a cloth and wash and dry normally.

Q 'I buy a lot of second-hand clothes,' says Joyce. 'But they often have a musty smell about them. What do you suggest?'

PROBLEM: Musty smell on clothes.
WHAT TO USE: Tea bag.
HOW TO APPLY: The musty smell is caused by dust mites and mildew. To get rid of it, put a tea bag into the washing machine after the water has filled, but before it starts agitating. Hold the bag in the water for 2 minutes then remove. The tannins in the tea kill dust mites. If you suffer dust mite allergy, keep a damp tea bag in a plastic bag in your handbag to sniff when you're in second-hand stores. It'll stop you from sneezing.

Q 'I've got old car grease stains on my overalls,' says Paul. 'Can I get it out?'

PROBLEM: Old car grease/engine oil on fabric.
WHAT TO USE: Baby oil, dishwashing liquid, water.

HOW TO APPLY: Car grease has a high carbon content, so rub the stain with a little baby oil. As soon as the stain starts to loosen and spread, massage in dishwashing liquid with your fingers. When it feels like jelly, rinse in water.

Oil stains

Oils ain't oils! The higher the carbon content, the more difficult the oil stain is to remove. As a general rule, remove dark oils such as car grease with a dab of baby oil on a cloth followed by dishwashing liquid massaged in with your fingers. To remove light oils, such as olive oil, massage dishwashing liquid into the stain with your fingers. If you accidentally used baby oil on a light oil stain, fix by massaging dishwashing liquid into the stain with your fingers until it feels like jelly, then rinse in blood-heat water.

Q 'During a blackout, I managed to back into a freshly painted wall,' reports Rodney. 'Now I've got paint marks on the seat of my trousers. Can I fix it?'

PROBLEM: Paint on fabric.
WHAT TO USE: Turpentine, methylated spirits, acetone, cotton bud, cotton balls.

HOW TO APPLY: To work out what kind of paint it is, get three small containers—one each for turpentine, methylated spirits and acetone. Dip a separate cotton bud in each and apply it to the stains, then rub the stain between your thumb and your forefinger. Whichever takes colour is the solvent.

The paint is most likely water-based. Because it has dried, soak the stained area with methylated spirits. Then soak two cotton balls in methylated spirits and place them on either side of the fabric. Rub the top cotton ball in a circular motion, working from the outside to the inside of the stain. Then wash the trousers as you would normally. If the paint is oil-based, use mineral turpentine or acetone in the same way.

PROBLEM: Peanut butter on cotton.
WHAT TO USE: Dishwashing liquid, cold water.
HOW TO APPLY: Remove as much peanut butter as possible. To remove the oil, put a couple of drops of dishwashing liquid on your fingers and massage into the stain until it feels like jelly. Rinse with cold water and wash and dry normally.

PROBLEM: Pear on cotton.
WHAT TO USE: Glycerine, cloth.
HOW TO APPLY: Pear is high in tannins. Wipe with a little glycerine on a cloth and leave for 20 minutes. Wash and dry normally.

Pen marks

There are different stain removal techniques for the type of pen used. We've mentioned how to remove ballpoint pen ink (see page 356); here's how to remove those other pen marks.

Permanent markers—*write over the mark using the same pen. Then wipe with white spirits on a cotton bud. Wash and dry normally.*

Artline—*wipe with methylated spirits on a cotton bud. Wash and dry normally.*

Whiteboard marker—*wipe with methylated spirits on a cotton bud. Wash and dry normally.*

Fluorescent pen—*write over the mark using the same pen, then wipe the mark with white spirits on a cotton bud. Alternatively, fill a 9 litre bucket with water and add 1 cup of non-iodised salt, dip the stain in the salt solution, gently wring and place in a plastic bag before putting in the freezer. Wash and dry normally.*

Gel pens—*soak in methylated spirits for 10 minutes and rub over the pen mark with your fingers. If the mark doesn't come out, soak again in methylated spirits for a further 10 minutes. You don't need to rub too vigorously. Repeat until removed. Wash and dry normally.*

Q 'I spilt some pumpkin soup over my favourite shawl,' says Raquel. 'What should I do?'

PROBLEM: Pumpkin on wool.
WHAT TO USE: White vinegar, cold water, cloth; or lavender oil, cloth, cheap shampoo, blood-heat water.
HOW TO APPLY: Pumpkin is high in vegetable dye. Remove as soon as possible with equal parts white vinegar and cold water on a cloth. If the pumpkin has set, wipe with a dab of lavender oil on a cloth and leave for 20 minutes. The shawl is made of wool, so wash in shampoo and blood-heat water.

Q 'I got red wine on my linen suit,' says Max. 'What can I do?'

PROBLEM: Red wine on cotton.
WHAT TO USE: Cloth, white vinegar, blood-heat water.
HOW TO APPLY: Wipe with a cloth wrung out in white vinegar until the red colour is removed. Rinse in blood-heat water and wash and dry normally.

Q 'I used to get rust off my sailing clothes with a product called *Rustyban*,' reports David. 'It was taken off the market and I'm wondering what I can use now.'

PROBLEM: Rust on fabric.
WHAT TO USE: Cotton ball, cotton bud, CLR; or lemon juice and salt.
HOW TO APPLY: Rustyban was withdrawn from the market because it was toxic. Try CLR instead. Put a cotton ball behind the stain and dip a cotton bud in CLR. Rub it over the rust until it starts to lift. Then hand wash the garment straight away—the rust should come off. CLR is a very strong product so be careful. If you'd rather use something natural, try lemon juice and salt. Damp the rust spot with lemon juice and then rub salt over it until the rust starts to move from the fibres. Hand wash and begin the process again until all the rust comes out. This could take some time.

> **Q** 'I was drying my clothes in front of the heater,' reports Rebecca. 'And a cotton shirt was scorched. Can I fix it?'

PROBLEM: Scorch mark on cotton.
WHAT TO USE: 3 per cent hydrogen peroxide, cloth, iron.
HOW TO APPLY: Wring out a cloth in 3 per cent hydrogen peroxide. Place the cloth over the scorch mark and run a cool iron over the top. The burn mark will transfer to the cloth. If it doesn't, the cotton has been charred and can't be fixed. If you love the shirt, sew or appliqué a patch over the top or dye the shirt a darker colour.

Q 'I've got seafood stains on my shirt,' says Graham. 'What can I do?'

PROBLEM: Seafood on cotton.
WHAT TO USE: Cold water, dishwashing liquid.
HOW TO APPLY: Seafood contains protein and oil. Rinse in cold water first. Put a couple of drops of dishwashing liquid on your fingers and massage into the stain. Rinse in cold water and wash and dry normally.

PROBLEM: Soy sauce on cotton.
WHAT TO USE: White vinegar, cloth.
HOW TO APPLY: Wipe the stain with a cloth wrung out in white vinegar, then wash and dry normally.

Q 'I was out for dinner the other night,' says Lisa. 'And I managed to get squid ink over my pale blue jumper. What can I do?'

PROBLEM: Squid ink on wool.
WHAT TO USE: Rotten milk, spatula, cheap shampoo, blood-heat water.
HOW TO APPLY: Rot some milk in the sun until it forms lumps. Place the lumps on the ink stain. When the ink has been absorbed by the milk solids, remove the solids with a

spatula. Because it's made of wool, wash in a little shampoo dissolved in blood-heat water.

Q 'How can you make clothes anti-static?' asks Bill.

PROBLEM: Static in clothes.
WHAT TO USE: Cheap hair conditioner, water, 1 litre spray pack.
HOW TO APPLY: Add 2 teaspoons of hair conditioner to the rinse cycle when washing your clothes. If you get static when wearing clothes, add ½ teaspoon of hair conditioner to a 1 litre spray pack of water and lightly mist over the clothes.

Q 'I have a gorgeous red pashmina,' says Sally. 'But the label has fallen off, leaving a sticky residue. How can I fix this?'

PROBLEM: Sticky label on wool.
WHAT TO USE: Tea tree oil, pantyhose, damp cloth, cheap shampoo, blood-heat water.
HOW TO APPLY: Rub the area with a little tea tree oil on a pair of pantyhose, then wipe with a damp cloth. Because it's made of wool, wash in a small amount of shampoo dissolved in blood-heat water.

Q *'I hate the dressing on new shirts,' says Stephen. 'Is there a way you can soften them so they're like your old favourite shirts?'*

PROBLEM: Stiff brand new shirts.
WHAT TO USE: Bicarb, laundry detergent, white vinegar.
HOW TO APPLY: Put the shirts through the washing machine, adding ½ cup of bicarb to your laundry detergent and ½ cup of white vinegar to the rinse water.

Q *'I have a relatively new denim jacket and the fabric is quite stiff,' reports Rhonda. 'Is there a way to soften it?'*

PROBLEM: Stiff denim jacket.
WHAT TO USE: Bicarb, laundry detergent, white vinegar, warm water.
HOW TO APPLY: The denim jacket is stiff because it's covered in a dressing to make it look good on the hanger in the shop. To strip away this dressing and soften the jacket, add ½ cup of bicarb to the laundry detergent, place ½ cup of white vinegar in the fabric conditioner slot and wash on a warm setting.

PROBLEM: Stretched cotton-knit jumper.
WHAT TO USE: Wide-toothed comb, Fuller's Earth.

HOW TO APPLY: Use a wide-toothed comb to evenly stretch the jumper. Then put it in the washing machine on the hot water setting. Before it reaches the spin cycle, remove the jumper and put it in the dryer. The water superheats and shrinks the fibres. You can also add 1 tablespoon of Fuller's Earth to the wash cycle to help shrink it.

Q 'My husband was wearing sunscreen and it's marked the neckline of his shirt,' says Sandra. 'Can I get it off?'

PROBLEM: Sunscreen on cotton.
WHAT TO USE: Dishwashing liquid; or *NapiSan OxyAction MAX*, water.
HOW TO APPLY: Place a couple of drops of dishwashing liquid on your fingers and rub into the stain until it changes texture and feels like jelly. Leave for 15 minutes and wash and dry normally. Alternatively, soak in *NapiSan OxyAction MAX* and water for 15 minutes, then wash and dry normally. The latter works better with self-tanning creams.

Q 'My cotton business shirts have sweat stains that just won't wash out,' says Steve. 'Do you have a suggestion on what to do because the shirts aren't cheap!'

PROBLEM: Sweat marks on cotton.
WHAT TO USE: *NapiSan Oxygen*.
HOW TO APPLY: Make a paste with *NapiSan Oxygen* and water to the consistency of peanut butter and apply this to the stain. Leave for 15 minutes before washing. You must use *NapiSan Oxygen* rather than just *NapiSan*.

PROBLEM: Sweat stains on poly-cotton shirt.
WHAT TO USE: Methylated spirits, cloth, *NapiSan Plus*, water.
HOW TO APPLY: In our climate, perspiration is a common problem and you might need to try a few different brands of deodorant before finding one that suits your body chemistry. Be aware that sweat clings more to synthetic fibres than natural ones. This shirt contains synthetic fibres, so wipe the armpits with a little methylated spirits on a cloth. Make a paste of *NapiSan Plus* and water, paint over the stained area and leave for 20 minutes. Wash and dry normally.

Q 'My car broke down the other day and, as I was looking under it, I got tar and gravel over my shorts,' says Frank. 'Can I get it off?'

PROBLEM: Tar on fabric.
WHAT TO USE: Scissors or blade, baby oil, cotton balls, kerosene or white spirits .

HOW TO APPLY: If you can, place the fabric in the freezer. Then cut off as much tar as possible with scissors or a blade. Then damp the back of the stain with baby oil on a cotton ball. Let it soak for a little while and then rub the front of the stain with a cotton ball dipped in either kerosene or white spirits. Make sure you work from the outside to the inside of the stain. Use clean cotton balls, one after the other, until the tar is removed. Do not heat tar or it will spread.

PROBLEM: Tomato sauce on cotton.
WHAT TO USE: Cloth, white vinegar; or *NapiSan Plus*, water, sunshine.
HOW TO APPLY: Tomato sauce is a vegetable dye. Wipe the stain with a cloth wrung out in white vinegar. Wash normally and dry in sunshine. If the stain is stubborn, make a paste of *NapiSan Plus* and water and leave on the stain for 10 minutes. Wash normally and hang in sunshine.

Q 'I got toothpaste on my suit,' reports Hussain. 'What should I do?'

PROBLEM: Toothpaste on wool.
WHAT TO USE: White vinegar, water, cloth.
HOW TO APPLY: Mix equal parts white vinegar and water. Wring out a cloth in the mixture and wipe over the stain.

Toothpaste contains peroxide and could bleach the wool so don't leave it for long.

Q 'My clothesline is under a gum tree and I have brown stains on my washing,' complains Craig. 'The items are mostly made of cotton.'

PROBLEM: Tree sap (gum) on cotton.
WHAT TO USE: Tea tree oil, cloth, glycerine.
HOW TO APPLY: This is both a resin and tannin stain. Wipe with a dab of tea tree oil on a cloth. Then wipe with a dab of glycerine on a cloth and leave for 5 minutes. Wash the clothes in the washing machine again.
PREVENTION: If your clothesline is under a tree and you can't move either, place an old sheet over your washing while it's drying. Ultraviolet light will still penetrate through the sheet and dry your clothes.

PROBLEM: Tree sap on fabric.
WHAT TO USE: Cotton balls, white spirits.
HOW TO APPLY: Put a dry cotton ball behind the stain and dip another cotton ball in white spirits. Wipe it over the stain in a circular motion, going from the outside to the inside of the stain. Then wash normally.

Q 'I was eating a tuna salad for lunch and dropped some tuna on my skirt,' reports Deanna. 'It's left an oily mark. Can I get it off?'

PROBLEM: Tuna (in oil) on cotton.
WHAT TO USE: Cold water, dishwashing liquid.
HOW TO APPLY: This is a protein and oil stain. To remove, rinse in cold water, then put a couple of drops of dishwashing liquid on your fingers and massage into the stain until it feels like jelly. Rinse in cold water and wash and dry normally.

Q 'I've got *Vaseline* on my trousers,' complains Carol. 'How do you get it out?'

PROBLEM: *Vaseline* on cotton.
WHAT TO USE: Dishwashing liquid, warm water.
HOW TO APPLY: Place a couple of drops of dishwashing liquid on your fingers and massage over the spots until it feels like jelly. Rinse in warm water and wash and dry normally.

Q 'We were at Carols by Candlelight and wax dripped onto my husband's corduroy trousers,' says Kay. 'We tried putting ice onto it and it didn't work!'

PROBLEM: Wax on corduroy fabric.
WHAT TO USE: Paper towel, white spirits, cotton balls.
HOW TO APPLY: On an ironing board, place a few layers of paper towel on top of one another and then place the trousers on top of them rib side down. Then put more layers of paper towel on top of the stained trousers and run a hot iron over them. The wax will be absorbed by the paper towel. For the final bit of wax, put white spirits onto a cotton ball and wipe over the area.

Q 'I spilled hot wax on a cotton shirt,' says Bill. 'The wax came off but left a white mark which I can't remove. What do you suggest?'

PROBLEM: Wax on cotton.
WHAT TO USE: Paper towel, ironing board, iron, tea tree oil, cloth.
HOW TO APPLY: Place several sheets of paper towel on top of your ironing board and lay the wax-stained garment on top. Put several more sheets of paper towel on top of the stain and apply a warm iron. The wax will melt into the paper towel. Keep changing the paper towel until all the wax is removed. If there's a greasy mark, wipe with a little tea tree oil on a cloth before washing normally.

Q 'My daughter works as a beauty therapist,' says Sandra, 'and she waxes a lot of legs. As a consequence, her black synthetic slacks have wax on them. How should I get it off?'

PROBLEM: Wax on synthetic fabric.
WHAT TO USE: Paper towel, hair dryer.
HOW TO APPLY: Put a paper towel on either side of the wax and blow a hair dryer over the area. The paper towel will absorb the wax. Keep on replacing the paper towel until the wax is removed.

Q 'I stored my clothes during winter,' says Amber. 'They've now got yellow marks on them. What can I do?'

PROBLEM: Yellow marks on cotton.
WHAT TO USE: Non-iodised salt, lemon juice, sunshine; or bicarb, cold water; or *CLR/Ranex*, cloth, cold water, white vinegar; or methylated spirits, cold water; or glycerine, cloth.
HOW TO APPLY: If the clothing is old or antique, the yellow will be from mineral salts used to stiffen the fabric when it was made. Place a little mountain of salt over each mark, add enough drops of lemon juice to moisten the salt and leave in the sun to dry. If the yellow marks are from milk

residue (common with baby clothes), see page 461. If the yellow has been caused by contact with plastic, mix bicarb and cold water to form a paste the consistency of peanut butter, apply to the stain, allow to dry and brush off. If the fabric is sturdy, treat as though it's rust and wipe with a dab of *CLR* or *Ranex* on a cloth. Rinse with cold water as soon as the yellow mark bleeds into the rest of the fabric, then neutralise by wiping with a cloth wrung out in white vinegar. If the fabric is synthetic, wipe with a dab of methylated spirits on a cloth and rinse in cold water. If the stain is from timber shelving, wipe with a couple of drops of glycerine on a cloth, leave for 20 minutes then wash and dry normally. Don't store clothes unless they've been laundered and completely dried. Always store in acid-free paper.

PROBLEM: Yoghurt on cotton.
WHAT TO USE: Cold water, cake of bathroom soap.
HOW TO APPLY: Rinse in cold water and rub with a cake of bathroom soap. Rinse in cold water and wash and dry normally.

FUR

Q 'My mum gave me her old mink jacket,' says Jo. 'I have no idea how to clean it.'

PROBLEM: Cleaning fur or faux fur coats.
WHAT TO USE: Pillowcase, unprocessed wheat bran.
HOW TO APPLY: Place the coat in a large pillowcase and add 1 kg of unprocessed wheat bran. Secure the top of the pillowcase and shake vigorously for about 3 minutes. Open the pillowcase and lightly shake the item as you remove it, so the bran stays in the pillowcase. This technique is also good for wool, mohair or camel coats and is a quick way to clean suits.

LEATHER AND SUEDE

PROBLEM: Oily stains on suede.
WHAT TO USE: White spirits, cotton bud or cotton ball, talcum powder, soft bristle brush; or unprocessed wheat bran, white vinegar.
HOW TO APPLY: Damp the stain with white spirits applied with a cotton bud or cotton ball, then cover the white spirits with talcum powder and allow to dry. Brush the talcum powder out with a soft bristle brush. Repeat if necessary. You can clean suede by rubbing unprocessed wheat bran over it. Remove sweat marks by damping some white vinegar on the marks, then rub with bran.

How to repair a small hole in a leather jacket

Most people have a leather jacket for life unless it was one of those bat-wing 1980s numbers. Getting a hole is usually devastating, but here's how you can keep the jacket alive.

Find a matching piece of leather. This could be taken from the inside of the hemline or seam or under an armpit seam. Cut a paper template 1 mm larger than the shape of the hole, place it on top of the leather piece and cut around it to make the patch. Sand the back of the leather patch with sandpaper so that you thin the edges. On a piece of linen or cotton that is 1 cm larger all round than the leather patch apply malleable contact adhesive or specialist leather adhesive and glue on the patch.

The patch will now be sitting in the middle of the sticky, adhesive-covered piece of linen or cotton. Line the patch up with the back of the hole and attach. You'll find it's a little thick where the two layers overlap. Lay the face of the leather on a smooth surface such as a breadboard and tap the back of it with a flat-headed hammer. The leather will smooth out and appear to be one piece of leather again.

Turn it over again so you're looking at the front. Warm a spoon, dip the back of it in a little *Vaseline* and lightly rub the patched area. For hard leather surfaces, use paraffin wax.

Q Angela loves her old red leather jacket, 'I've had it for years. But it's got deodorant smeared on it. Is there any way I can get this off?'

PROBLEM: Deodorant on leather.
WHAT TO USE: White spirits, cotton bud, talcum powder, leather dew.
HOW TO APPLY: Apply white spirits to the smears with a cotton bud, then sprinkle with talcum powder. Allow it to absorb, then clean the jacket with leather dew (following the directions on the packet).

Q 'How do you get chewing gum off a leather jacket?' asks Victor.

PROBLEM: Chewing gum on leather.
WHAT TO USE: Ice, scissors or a blade, white spirits, cotton bud, sticky tape, leather dew.
HOW TO APPLY: Put ice on the gum. Once it has hardened, cut as much off as possible with scissors or a blade, but be careful not to cut the surface of the leather. Then apply white spirits with a cotton bud. Remove the last of the gum with sticky tape. Keep on ripping the sticky tape away as though you're waxing a leg. Do this until all the gum has been removed. Then treat the spot with leather dew.

SILK

The best way to wash silk is with shampoo and with conditioner in the rinse water. Use the same amount as you would with your hair. Never dry silk on a windy day because all the fibres go stiff and cause white dusty marks, white lines and water marks.

PROBLEM: Water marks on silk.
WHAT TO USE: Clean white silk square.
HOW TO APPLY: As taught to Shannon by her grandmother, rub the clean white silk square gently across and down the grain of the silk. Don't rub diagonally.

PROBLEM: White lines on silk.
WHAT TO USE: White vinegar, salt.
HOW TO APPLY: When hand washing silk, put white vinegar into the rinse water and the white lines won't appear. To keep silk soft, put a teaspoon of salt in the washing water.

> **Q** 'I'm not sure if it's coffee or red wine,' admits Les, 'but it's stained the elbow of my white raw-silk jacket. I took it to the dry-cleaners and the stain is still there. Can it be fixed?'

PROBLEM: Coffee or red wine stain on silk.
WHAT TO USE: Glycerine, cotton balls, white spirits.
HOW TO APPLY: If it's an old red wine or old coffee stain, use glycerine first. Apply it with cotton balls on both sides of the fabric and leave for a few minutes. Then use white spirits applied with cotton balls, working in a circular

motion from the outside to the inside of the stain. If you spill red wine or coffee on clothing, treat it straight away with white vinegar then take it to the dry-cleaner.

Q **'I splashed black coffee over my favourite silk tie,' says Geoff. 'It just won't shift!'**

PROBLEM: Coffee stain on silk.
WHAT TO USE: Glycerine, cotton ball, washing power, white vinegar, towel.
HOW TO APPLY: Apply glycerine to the stain with a cotton ball. Then wash the tie with washing powder in blood-heat water. Rinse in blood-heat water and, to prevent the tie stiffening, add a little white vinegar. Then dry it flat on a towel in the shade.

VELVET

To clean velvet, put 1 cup of unprocessed wheat bran in a pillowcase, add the item and seal the top of the pillowcase. Sit on it for an hour a day over the course of a week. Remove and shake away the bran.

TIP

If clothing has sequins, protect them by placing the clothes in a pair of pantyhose or a pillowcase when washing.

WOOLLENS

PROBLEM: Dirty woollen coats, dresses or skirts.

WHAT TO USE: Salt, clean handkerchief or piece of linen, bristle brush.

HOW TO APPLY: This is an alternative to dry-cleaning and much cheaper. Sprinkle the item with salt about as thickly as poppy seeds on bread. Then rub with a clean handkerchief or piece of linen. Don't go in circles but up and down with the grain of the fabric. Once the item is clean, give it a really good shake and brush with a bristle brush.

Q 'I've had to throw away four jumpers this year because of moth holes,' complains Marian. 'And that's despite hanging mothballs around my woollens. Do you have any suggestions to stop moths in their tracks? I don't like using chemicals and would prefer natural remedies.'

PROBLEM: Moths in woollens.

WHAT TO USE: Cedar chips, bay leaves, camphor flakes, whole cloves.

HOW TO APPLY: There are two types of jumper-chewing moths and both are repelled by a mixture of 2 large cedar chips, 2 bay leaves and 1 teaspoon of camphor flakes (store in the toe of a pair of pantyhose). The holes may also be

from silverfish that are deterred with whole cloves (add
2 whole cloves to the above mixture). To repair the hole in
your jumper, see *How To Be Comfy* for instructions on how
to darn or apply an appliqué.

PREVENTION: For an all-round bug deterrent, combine 2 bay
leaves (moth deterrent), 5 whole cloves (kill mould spores
and deter silverfish), 1 tea bag (kills dust mites), 2 heads of
lavender (add fragrance and deter flying insects), 2 cedar
chips (deter moths) and 1 tablespoon of bicarb (absorbs
moisture and helps prevent mould) and place in a piece of
muslin or the toe of a pair of pantyhose. Leave where
nasties lurk.

Q 'How can you stop jumpers from pilling?' asks Bill.

PROBLEM: Pilling on woollens.
WHAT TO USE: Fuller's Earth, 15 litre bucket, blood-heat
water, soft brush; or ironing board, disposable razor.
HOW TO APPLY: Woollens pill if they're not washed properly
or if the fibres are stressed. Stir 2 tablespoons of Fuller's
Earth into a 15 litre bucket of blood-heat water. Immerse
the garments and leave for 5–10 minutes. Rinse in blood-
heat water, gently wring and dry flat in the shade. As they
dry, stretch them into shape and brush away the pilling
with a soft brush. If any pills remain, shave with a razor.

To fix pilling in synthetic jumpers, stretch over the end of an ironing board and shave with a razor.

Q 'I'm a bachelor,' says Geoffrey. 'And I accidentally put my jumper into the washing machine and it's shrunk. Can it be fixed?'

PROBLEM: Shrunken jumper.
WHAT TO USE: Bucket, Fuller's Earth, towel, two wide-toothed combs; or Epsom salts.
HOW TO APPLY: For dark-coloured jumpers, fill a nappy-sized bucket with blood-heat water and add 2 tablespoons of Fuller's Earth. For light-coloured jumpers, add 4 tablespoons. Put the jumper in and gently agitate it with your hands until it's thoroughly wetted. Let it sit for 10–15 minutes and then rinse thoroughly in blood-heat water. Don't leave it for longer than this or it will bleach. Lie the jumper flat on a towel in a shady spot and leave it to dry. Gently stretch it back into shape as it's drying. To make it stretch more evenly, use 2 wide-toothed combs on either side of the jumper and stretch the jumper with the combs as it's drying. It's not as effective, but you could also use 2 tablespoons of Epsom salts, instead of Fuller's Earth, to a bucket of blood-heat water.

TIP

To stop angora jumpers from shedding, place them in a plastic bag, remove as much air as possible and put in the freezer for 20 minutes to an hour. Remove from the freezer (brrrr!) and hang them for 10–20 minutes, to come to room temperature, before wearing.

Caring for woollens

No one likes wearing a scratchy jumper. To restore woollens and blended woollens to their fluffy glory, wash in cheap shampoo and blood-heat water, then rinse in cheap hair conditioner and blood-heat water. Gently wring and dry flat on a towel in the shade. The reason for using cheap shampoo and hair conditioner is they have fewer oils and perfumes and are gentler on the wool fibres. It's also important to have the wash and rinse water at the same temperature to reduce stress on the wool fibres. And to prevent shrinkage or sagging, dry flat in the shade.

It's a little trickier cleaning structured woollens such as suits, coats and jackets. To clean them, fill a pillowcase with 1 kg of unprocessed wheat bran and place the garment inside. Close the top of the pillowcase and give a vigorous shake. A more passive approach involves sitting on the closed pillowcase for an hour a day over the course of a week. Just make sure you get all the bran out when you remove the garment or it might look as though you've got bad dandruff.

WHAT NOT TO DO ...

Q 'I have a white wool (55 per cent wool and 45 per cent polyester) coat that I soaked in *NapiSan*. This turned it a shade of blotchy yellow/tan. I then soaked it in hydrogen peroxide (6 per cent and 18 per cent) and used a colour run remover but it does not seem to have helped in any way. What do I do?'

A Chlorine-based bleaches burn wool, which is why the coat turned a yellowy brown colour. In this case, the fibres have been damaged. It may be beyond repair but try this solution. Mix 2 cups of 3 per cent hydrogen peroxide, 8 tablespoons of washing soda and 9 litres of blood-heat water in a bucket. Place the coat in the mixture and put a plate over the top so it stays immersed. Leave for 6 hours. Add 1 cup of white vinegar to a tub of blood-heat water and rinse the coat thoroughly. Dry flat in the shade. If the fabric is too fragile for this, dye it with a quality cold water wool dye. For an even dye, make sure the tub is large enough for the coat to move around easily.

> **TIP**
>
> *Use the same dye water to colour other items, such as pillowcases and sheets or tired-looking bras.*

ZIPPERS

PROBLEM: Sticky zippers.

WHAT TO USE: White vinegar, lead pencil, graphite powder or glycerine, talcum powder.

HOW TO APPLY: For metal zippers, apply some white vinegar to the zipper then rub the metal with a lead pencil or apply graphite powder. Work it up and down. Graphite isn't as effective as a lead pencil, because it doesn't contain clay, but it will work with a little persistence. For nylon zippers, apply some glycerine, working it up and down. Then sprinkle with talcum powder.

PROBLEM: Loose zippers.

WHAT TO USE: Salt.

HOW TO APPLY: To make zippers stick, add a little salt to them. This works with metal or nylon zippers.

Q 'The zipper on my sailing jacket has salt build-up on it,' says William. 'Can it be fixed?'

PROBLEM: Salt on metal zippers.

WHAT TO USE: Cloth, white vinegar, lead pencil.
HOW TO APPLY: Wipe the zipper with a cloth dipped in white vinegar first, then rub it with a lead pencil.

SUITS

To make your suits look snappy, keep dry-cleaning to a minimum. The chemicals used in dry-cleaning weaken the fibres and shorten the life of the suit. Instead, after wearing, give a good brush before hanging on wooden hangers (wire ones don't offer enough support). And don't cram your suits into the wardrobe or they'll become wrinkled. If you're very particular, remove creases with a steamer rather than an iron because it's gentler on the fibres.

PROBLEM: Shine on a suit.
WHAT TO USE: Cloth, white vinegar, unprocessed wheat bran, brown paper, iron.
HOW TO APPLY: For a dark-coloured suit, damp a cloth in white vinegar and wipe it over the suit. Then place brown paper over the suit and iron. For light-coloured suits, damp a cloth in 1 part white vinegar to 4 parts water, wring it out and lay it over the shiny section of the suit. Steam-iron the suit.

JACKETS

Q 'I've got a funky suede jacket,' boasts Brad. 'But it's got general dirt markings over it. What do you suggest?

Clothing and Shoes   431

PROBLEM: Dirty suede.
WHAT TO USE: Unprocessed wheat bran, white spirits, pillowcase, cotton ball, talcum powder, brush.
HOW TO APPLY: Mix 1 cup of unprocessed wheat bran with drops of white spirits until the mixture forms clumps that resemble brown sugar. Place the mixture in a pillowcase, add the suede jacket and then, as the Fonz used to say, sit on it! Do this for an hour a day (while watching TV or eating dinner) over the course of a week. The bran will scour the dirty marks away. Remove the jacket (somewhere outside is best) and shake until it's free of bran. If there are grubby marks on the collar, wipe with a little white spirits on a cotton ball, then sprinkle with talcum powder and when dry, wipe off with a brush.

Q 'I have one of those puffy jackets with a down filling which I keep in a zipped garment cover,' reports Sue. 'Recently, I took it out and noticed the white jacket looks slightly yellow in certain parts. What can I do? The fabric is *HyVent*.'

PROBLEM: Stained *HyVent* fabric (waterproof).
WHAT TO USE: Lemon juice, cloth, cake of bathroom soap, blood-heat water, damp cloth.
HOW TO APPLY: Wipe the stains with a little lemon juice on a cloth, then rub with a cake of bathroom soap that's been

dipped in blood-heat water. Wipe with a damp cloth and dry in the shade.

Q 'My husband's favourite leather jacket has stains on the collar from his neck,' says Carol-Ann. 'Any ideas?'

PROBLEM: Sweat marks on leather.
WHAT TO USE: White spirits, cloth, talcum powder, brush, saddle soap.
HOW TO APPLY: Wipe with a little white spirits on a cloth, sprinkle with talcum powder and brush away when dry. If the staining is extensive and has soaked into the leather, clean with saddle soap, following the manufacturer's instructions.

Q 'I have a *Driza-Bone* coat which needs to be cleaned,' reports Joanne. 'It's about 20 years old and in good condition.'

PROBLEM: Dirty *Driza-Bone*.
WHAT TO USE: Cake of bathroom soap, cold water, pantyhose, damp cloth, white spirits, cotton ball, cloth, baby oil.
HOW TO APPLY: Run a cake of bathroom soap under cold water and place in the toe of a pair of pantyhose. Rub over

the coat then wipe with a damp cloth. For bad staining, apply a little white spirits to a cotton ball and wipe over any marks. To keep it waterproof, dab baby oil onto a cloth and wipe over the coat in even strokes.

TIES

Q 'I've spilt oily noodles on an expensive silk tie my wife bought me for Christmas,' says Omar. 'Any ideas to help save the marriage would be greatly appreciated.'

PROBLEM: Oily noodles on silk.
WHAT TO USE: Cheap shampoo, blood-heat water, towel, iron.
HOW TO APPLY: We may not be able to save your marriage but fixing the tie is easy. Wash in a little shampoo and blood-heat water. Rinse with blood-heat water, gently wring excess moisture and lay flat on a towel in the shade to dry. Iron on a cool setting.

Bags and Handbags

The great thing about a handbag is you don't have go on a diet to wear one. They really are 'one size fits all'! I love handbags that can store as much as possible, the bigger the better and the more the merrier. Store bags in a cool dry place covered in a calico bag or old pillowcase.

PROBLEM: Smelly leather handbag/suitcase.
WHAT TO USE: Tea leaves, leather dew.
HOW TO APPLY: The bag may smell because it wasn't tanned properly or is made of goat or kangaroo hide. To get rid of the smell, wipe the leather with damp tea leaves. This will cure the leather. Then treat it with leather dew. If the interior of the bag is made of leather and also smells, empty a packet of dry tea leaves into it and leave for a couple of weeks.

PROBLEM: Mouldy handbag.
WHAT TO USE: White vinegar, cloths, oil of cloves, leather dew; or white spirits, cotton ball, talcum powder, brush.
HOW TO APPLY: Mix a small quantity of white vinegar and water and wipe it over the mould with a cloth. Then wipe with a clean cloth. Add 1 drop of oil of cloves to leather dew on a cloth and wipe over the bag. The oil of cloves will inhibit further mould growth. For black or old mould stains, apply white spirits with a cotton ball and sprinkle talcum powder over the top. Once it's dried, brush the talcum powder off.

PROBLEM: Dirty handbag lining.
WHAT TO USE: Washing powder; or white spirits, cotton ball.
HOW TO APPLY: Some bag linings can be removed. Others are attached but can still be pulled outside the bag. If the lining is cotton, clean it with washing powder and water. If

there's lipstick, make-up or ballpoint pen marks apply white spirits with a cotton ball. Then clean in washing powder and water. To dry, put the leather part of the bag in the shade and the lining in the sun. If you can't do this, dry the whole bag in the shade. The lining must be completely dry before you put it back inside the bag.

Q 'I've got grease stains on a light tan leather bag,' says Amy. 'The grease has left dark stains on the leather.'

PROBLEM: Grease stains on leather bag.
WHAT TO USE: White spirits, cloth, talcum powder, brush; or leather conditioner.
HOW TO APPLY: What to do will depend on the type of leather. For hard-tanned leather (shiny, waxy finish), wipe with a little white spirits on a cloth. Then sprinkle with talcum powder and brush off when dry. If it's soft-tanned leather (low sheen finish/kid or kangaroo hide), oil the bag with leather conditioner and leave for 2 weeks (it takes that long to dry). The stains will lighten as the bag dries.

Q 'I pulled out my old white *Glomesh* bag from the cupboard,' reports Evelyn. 'And it's covered in brown stains. I have no idea what they are. Can they be removed?'

PROBLEM: Brown marks on white *Glomesh* bag.
WHAT TO USE: *CLR/Ranex*, cotton bud (rust); or *Colour Run Remover: Whites*, cotton bud (dye); or glycerine, cloth (dirt).
HOW TO APPLY: The brown marks could be from several sources. Do a test first to see which solvent works. For rust, use *CLR* or *Ranex* on a cotton bud. For dye, use 1 part *Colour Run Remover: Whites* to 5 parts water on a cotton bud. For dirt, wipe with a little glycerine on a cloth. If none of these solutions work, see a restorer.

Q 'I've got mould on a suede handbag,' says Mary. 'Any ideas?'

PROBLEM: Mould on suede handbag.
WHAT TO USE: White spirits, cotton ball, non-iodised salt, talcum powder, brush.
HOW TO APPLY: Wipe the mouldy area with white spirits on a cotton ball. Then sprinkle on a mixture of 1 part salt to 3 parts talcum powder. Leave until completely dry and brush off.

Shoes

If you're feeling lazy about looking after your shoes, just think about how much it will cost to replace them.

Store very good shoes in a shoe bag or calico bag to stop them from going mouldy. After wearing **leather** and **vinyl** shoes, dust the insides with a little bicarb. Wipe the outside with a cloth that's been smeared with *Vaseline*. Bicarb reduces the amount of sweat your feet produces and the *Vaseline* makes shoes waterproof. Just don't forget to dust out the bicarb before you wear the shoes again.

Dust bicarb into **cloth** and **running shoes** and vacuum it out before wearing them. Most cloth shoes can be hand or machine washed.

Sprinkle talcum powder on **rubber** soles and the outside of rubber boots to stop them perishing.

Clean **suede** shoes with a brass wire brush (not aluminium or steel wire) and white spirits. Spray suede and cloth shoes with *Scotchgard* to keep them clean for longer and waterproof. For **nubuck** or **super suede** shoes, purchase a small proprietary brand sandblock for cleaning.

Keep the ankles of boots unwrinkled and firm by putting an old paper towel roll inside them so they don't flop over.

Make sure you use the correct shoelaces on shoes. If they're too thin, you place strain on the holes. If they're too thick, you place strain on the front of the shoe. The lace should move through the hole with a light resistance, not a drag nor a run.

If you get a hole in the sole of your shoe, put newspaper on the inside of the sole and use a product called *Spread-a-sole*. Apply it in several thin coats and it will form a new sole.

If nail heads are coming through your shoes it means your heels may need to be replaced or boosted. Hammer the nails back in, making sure you cover the head of the nail with a small piece of wood.

Serious scuff marks can be removed with leather dew or boot polish rubbed on with the back of a hot spoon. For suede shoes, use white spirits applied with a cotton bud. Sprinkle with talcum powder and brush off.

It's annoying when you buy a new pair of shoes and they're too tight when you put them on at home. If you can't return them, try to stretch them. But we warn you—there's a lot of variation in shoes and many are delicate so we can't guarantee you won't damage them using this technique. With that disclaimer in mind, here's what you can do. If the shoes are made of hardy leather, heat the inside of the shoe with steam and rub the outside with petroleum jelly (*Vaseline*). Wear thick socks, put on the shoes and walk around until the shoes cool.

Q '**My husband has a pair of suede boots with rubber soles,**' **reports Elsa.** '**Every time he takes a step, they squeak. Is there any way I can quieten them?**'

PROBLEM: Squeaky shoes.
WHAT TO USE: Glycerine, cotton bud; or talcum powder.

HOW TO APPLY: Wipe along the seams with glycerine on a cotton bud. Alternatively, sprinkle talcum powder inside the shoes and that will gradually remove the squeak.

Q 'I've got food stains on my suede shoes,' says Elizabeth. 'What do you suggest?'

PROBLEM: Food stains on suede.
WHAT TO USE: White spirits, cloth, talcum powder, brush.
HOW TO APPLY: Put a little white spirits on a cloth and wipe over in even strokes. Then sprinkle with talcum powder, leave to dry and brush off.

Q 'I've got chamois shoes,' reports Hazel. 'And have no idea how to clean them.'

PROBLEM: Dirty chamois shoes.
WHAT TO USE: Cake of bathroom soap, pantyhose, damp cloth.
HOW TO APPLY: Put a cake of bathroom soap into the toe of some pantyhose and rub over the shoes. Wipe with a damp cloth. Dry the shoes in the shade.

Q 'I was in a busy pub and someone's drink landed on my expensive new leather shoes. What can I do?' asks Sam.

PROBLEM: Beer on leather shoes.
WHAT TO USE: Glycerine, cotton ball, white spirits, cotton bud, talcum powder, brush.
HOW TO APPLY: Apply glycerine to the stain with a cotton ball. Then apply white spirits with a cotton bud. Sprinkle over with talcum powder to absorb the white spirits. When completely dry, brush off.

PROBLEM: Rubber soles are perishing.
WHAT TO USE: Salt, stiff brush; or cloudy ammonia, water, salt, stiff brush.
HOW TO APPLY: Scour the rubber with salt and a stiff brush. This will rejuvenate them. Alternatively, use a combination of 1 part cloudy ammonia, 5 parts water and 1 part salt and scrub with a stiff brush.

Q 'My wife was filling up the car with petrol and she got splashback all over her leather shoes,' reports Brian. 'She loves those shoes.'

PROBLEM: Petrol on leather shoes.
WHAT TO USE: White spirits, cotton ball, talcum powder.
HOW TO APPLY: Apply white spirits with a cotton ball to the affected area. Then sprinkle talcum powder over the white spirits to absorb it. Leave the shoes until they're dry then brush off the talcum powder.

PROBLEM: Velcro not working.
WHAT TO USE: Fine-toothed comb.
HOW TO APPLY: Damp the velcro with water and comb it on both sides with a fine-toothed comb. This gets the fluff and dust out.

Q 'I was at the supermarket and a woman dropped a jar of cucumbers on the ground and the oil splattered onto my shoes,' reports David. 'Can I fix them?'

PROBLEM: Oil on leather shoes.
WHAT TO USE: White spirits, cotton ball, talcum powder.
HOW TO APPLY: Put white spirits onto a cotton ball and wipe it over the stain on the shoes. Then cover this area with talcum powder, which will absorb the oil. When it's dry, brush the powder off.

How to care for stockings

You wouldn't bother doing this with cheap stockings, but it's worth it with expensive ones. Put soap in one toe and your hand in the other toe and then rub them together as though you're washing your hands. This stretches the fibres and removes more dirt. To prevent ladders and catches in stockings, spray them with hairspray and leave them on a hanger to dry. You'll need to reapply the hairspray each time you wash them.

UGG BOOTS/SHEEPSKIN

The best way to clean ugg boots or sheepskin shoes is in the washing machine. Put 1 teaspoon of cheap shampoo in each boot and place them into a pillowcase. Wash in cold water on the gentle cycle. When drying, stuff newspaper or old towels inside each boot and leave in the shade, so they don't go stiff.

Q 'I've spilt fat or oil on my new sheepskin slippers,' says Morag. 'How can I clean them?'

PROBLEM: Fat/oil on sheepskin.
WHAT TO USE: Cheap shampoo, damp cloth.
HOW TO APPLY: Massage a little shampoo into the stains with your fingers and rinse with a damp cloth. Dry the slippers in the shade or they'll go stiff. If using the washing machine, wash in cold water on the gentle cycle, then dry in the shade.

Gloves

Q 'How can I clean my red leather gloves?' asks Sammy.

PROBLEM: Dirty leather gloves.
WHAT TO USE: Saddle soap.
HOW TO APPLY: Put the gloves on and massage your hands with saddle soap, making sure you get the saddle soap over every part of the glove. They're ready to wear. For kid gloves, use a bran ball (see page 138).

Q'I am desperate to know how to remove mould from my suede gloves,' states Maxine. 'What do you suggest?'

PROBLEM: Mould on suede.
WHAT TO USE: Oil of cloves, water, 1 litre spray pack, stiff brush.
HOW TO APPLY: Mix ¼ teaspoon of oil of cloves in a spray pack of water. Lightly mist over the gloves (don't saturate them) and leave in the shade to dry. Brush the mould off with a stiff brush. If any mould remains, repeat.

Hats

Shannon collects hats in many different styles, from Georgian to contemporary. She even has a pop-up silk top hat! Special hats should be stored in a hatbox or on a hat block and kept on a flat surface. If the hat has a high crown and you don't have a hat block, pack it with acid-free tissue paper. Shannon's great-aunt Letitia loved wearing berets and taught her how to clean them through her amazing notes. Hand wash woollen berets in woolwash and dry them over a dinner plate so they retain their shape. To bleach a straw hat, rub it with white spirits and a little salt then rub the mixture off well.

PROBLEM: Sweat marks on felt hats.
WHAT TO USE: Fuller's Earth or potter's plaster, paintbrush, brush.
HOW TO APPLY: Sweat on light-coloured hats can be removed with Fuller's Earth. Mix Fuller's Earth and water to the consistency of soft butter. Then paint it over the sweat marks with a paintbrush, leave to dry and then brush out. For dark-coloured felt hats use potter's plaster made to the consistency of soft butter. Put the mixture over the sweat stain with a paintbrush and allow it to dry completely before brushing it off.

PROBLEM: Straw hat has gone floppy.
WHAT TO USE: Pastry brush, egg white, towels, clingwrap.
HOW TO APPLY: Dip a pastry brush in egg white and wipe both sides of the hat with it. Put towels in the crown of the hat, cover a flat surface with clingwrap, sit the hat on top and allow it to dry hard.

Q 'I'm a fan of felt hats,' says Simon, 'but mine seems to have shrunk. Can it be stretched?'

PROBLEM: Felt hat has shrunk.
WHAT TO USE: Fuller's Earth, hat block or damp newspaper.
HOW TO APPLY: Mix Fuller's Earth and water to the consistency of peanut butter. Spread it over the areas that need to be stretched and leave for about 5 minutes. Then force the hat over a suitably sized hat block or pack the inside of the crown with damp newspaper until it's the right size. Leave to dry in the shade, not the sun. The drying time will depend on the thickness of the hat.

Q 'My husband owns a dark-coloured *Akubra* hat,' reports Geraldine. 'What's the best way to clean the band on the inside of the hat?'

PROBLEM: Dirty *Akubra* hat.
WHAT TO USE: White spirits, cotton ball, talcum powder, brush; or Fuller's Earth, water, damp cloth.
HOW TO APPLY: Wipe the stains with a dab of white spirits on a cotton ball, then sprinkle with talcum powder to absorb the white spirits. Leave to dry and brush off. For light-coloured *Akubra*s, make a paste of Fuller's Earth and water, leave over the dirt marks for a few minutes, then remove with a damp cloth.

Q 'I've got a genuine Panama hat,' reports Wally. 'But it's got sweat marks on it. What do you suggest?'

PROBLEM: Sweat marks on hat.

WHAT TO USE: Fuller's Earth, water, damp cloth; or bran ball.

HOW TO APPLY: Mix Fuller's Earth and water to form a paste the consistency of thick cream and place on the marks. Leave for a few minutes and remove with a damp cloth. Alternatively, clean with a bran ball (see page 138).

Kids' Stuff

Children are a great source of joy, but also a great source of mess. Even the most vigilant parents can find themselves removing *Vegemite* smears from the couch or crayon marks from a wall. And let's not forget projectile vomit or muddy footprints tracked through the house on a rainy day; it's all part of the rich tapestry of family life. It doesn't matter if the stains are accidental or from a rush of creativity from your child, you can find the solutions here!

Just a little accident: *Matthew's story*

INCIDENT: *'My toddler has just moved on from nappies. He's going pretty well but sometimes he gets really excited, forgets there's no nappy and pees. The problem is that the urine runs into his shoes and smells awful. Is there anything I can do?'*

SOLUTION: Dab the stain with some white spirits applied with a cotton ball. Then sprinkle talcum powder over the white spirits both inside and outside the shoe. Allow to dry and then brush. To neutralise the smell, put lemon juice on a cloth and wipe it over the shoes. Cloth and vinyl shoes can be washed in the washing machine or hand washed and dried in the sunshine.

Smelly teddy: *Jane's story*

INCIDENT: *'We have a much-loved old teddy bear which is starting to smell. Is there a way to make him less stinky?'*

SOLUTION: Mix 1 cup of unprocessed wheat bran with drops of white vinegar until the mixture forms clumps that resemble brown sugar. If the teddy smells mouldy, add 2 drops of oil of cloves. Put the mixture into a pillowcase and place the smelly teddy inside. Secure the top of the pillowcase and shake well. Remove the ted (preferably outside or over a bin) and shake away the bran. If the teddy bear is still smelly, find a dry-cleaner that works with conservation pieces.

Routine Clean

Babies and young children are extremely vulnerable to bacteria so a clean home is very important. Use tea tree oil—a non-toxic antibacterial and antiseptic—instead of harsh chemical cleaners. Dilute 1 teaspoon of tea tree oil in 1 litre of water and store in a spray pack. Lightly spray over hard surfaces and wipe with a clean cloth. Regular vacuuming is important as children are susceptible to dust and dust mites. Wipe over suckable surfaces each day because bacteria breed in saliva. Used nappies should be removed and dealt with as soon as possible.

TIP

You may not know that the most common cause of oral thrush in babies (white cloudy marks on gums and cheek linings) is from people sticking their fingers in the baby's mouth. Don't allow it!

Clean toddlers' rooms twice a week. Vacuum and spray with the tea tree oil and water solution and wipe with a cloth. Don't use bleaches or other heavy chemical cleaners which can be harsh on little lungs. Help toddlers learn where clothes and toys go by placing labels on drawers with the name and picture of what's in each drawer. They could even draw the pictures themselves.

From when your children reach the age of 4, keep

this word in mind: 'washable'. If you're searching for inspiration, look around your local kindergarten, where floors, walls and toys are washable. From this age, encourage your children to put their own toys and clothes away. Show them how to sweep the floor in their room and make a game of removing marks on walls. To get them excited about cleaning, mix bicarb and white vinegar together, they'll love to watch the fizzing.

Children often drop small items like doll accessories or building blocks on the floor. An easy way to find them is to place either a T-shirt or flywire between the head and tube of the vacuum cleaner. When you vacuum, the item will become trapped and won't go into the bag. Flywire is preferable because you can hear when the item hits it.

If you need to remove felt pen marks from the carpet, use white spirits applied with a cotton ball or cotton bud, depending on how big the stain is. Make sure you rub from the outside to the inside of the stain. Have a dry cloth or *Slurpex* to soak up the white spirits as you go to stop the carpet getting too wet.

Protect carpet in children's rooms by laying down plastic carpet protectors on the floor. You can buy them by the metre at department stores. There are some specially designed for children, with colourful designs and without those nasty spikes.

Another common problem with children is the accidental, or deliberate, placement of stickers on furniture or the wall. These can be removed with a small quantity of dishwashing liquid and hot water in a spray bottle. Spray the solution over the sticker then place a clingwrap square over the top and leave for a few minutes. The sticker will come off with the clingwrap and can be re-stuck where it was supposed to go.

Crayon is very difficult to remove from walls. Use a pencil eraser dampened in a bowl of soapy water and rub it over the crayon. The wax in the crayon will roll off in balls. If the mark is really bad put some bicarb on a damp cotton bud and wipe the mark. Try not to rub outside the crayon mark because it could make the walls go shiny. If it's a large area, use an old toothbrush.

Q **'How do I remove playdough from a beautiful silk and wool woven rug?' asks Sarah. 'It's been there for a few months.'**

PROBLEM: Playdough on rug.
WHAT TO USE: Vacuum cleaner, non-iodised salt, pantyhose.
HOW TO APPLY: When playdough dries out, it becomes powdery and easy to vacuum. If necessary you can scrub it with a little salt on pantyhose and vacuum thoroughly. Repeat until the playdough is removed.

TIP

Before removing a Band-Aid, wipe across the outside with tea tree oil and leave for 5 minutes. The Band-Aid will come off easily with no tears.

Baby Bottles

Wash baby bottles with cold water first to get rid of any remaining milk. Give them a good scrub with a bottlebrush then put them in sterilising solution. The steriliser can give teats a cloudy look. Always rinse sterilising solution with boiled water, particularly with bottles and eating utensils. No baby likes the taste of swimming pool water! The easiest way to fix the awful taste is to rub salt over the cloudy bits and then rinse in boiled water. They're still sterile and the teats stay in better condition. Preserve rubber nipples by wiping with non-iodised salt before rinsing in boiled water.

Bed-wetting

If your child wets the bed, protect the mattress with a breathable waterproof mattress cover. To remove urine, wipe both sides of the mattress with white vinegar on a cloth and sprinkle with talcum powder. Leave in the sunshine until dry then vacuum. To clean a mattress made of tea tree bark, sprinkle with bicarb, leave in the sunshine and then vacuum.

Clothes

Use pure soap flakes or laundry detergent for sensitive skin (to make your own, see page 571) when washing babies' clothes. To soften baby clothes and remove the soap residue, put ½ cup of white vinegar in the rinse cycle of the washing machine. Another issue with baby clothes is scratchy seams. Run the back of your hand along the inside of clothing to feel for any scratchy bits. If there's any irritation, use iron-on cotton binding to cover the seams.

STORING CLOTHES

Put labels on children's drawers to help them learn how to put clothes away. Include a picture and the name of the clothes to help them.

Q 'I've been storing baby clothes in the cupboard for the past 4 years,' says Petra. 'I need to use them again but they've gone yellow. Can I get the yellow out?'

PROBLEM: Yellow marks on clothes.
WHAT TO USE: *NapiSan*, bucket, water, acid-free paper.
HOW TO APPLY: The yellow marks are age stains. Add ¾ of a capful of *Napisan* to a 7 litre bucket of warm water and soak overnight. And next time you're packing the clothes away, put a piece of acid-free paper in between each layer of

clothing. Age stains come from acid fumes in plastic bags, cardboard boxes or shelving.

Q 'I had some woollen baby clothes in storage,' reports Rebecca. 'And they've got rusty marks on them. What can I do?'

PROBLEM: Rust on wool.
WHAT TO USE: Blood-heat water, cheap shampoo, towel; or non-iodised salt, lemon juice, sunshine.
HOW TO APPLY: Place the garments in blood-heat water and massage 1 teaspoon of shampoo over the stain. Rinse in blood-heat water, gently wring out and dry flat on a towel in the shade. For stubborn stains, cover with a little mountain of salt and add drops of lemon juice until the salt is moistened. Dry in the sun. Hand wash in shampoo and blood-heat water, rinse well, wring out and dry flat in the shade.

Q 'Disaster!' exclaims Judy. 'My son has orange *Texta* on a 100 per cent cotton light grey track suit. What can I do?'

PROBLEM: *Texta* on cotton.
WHAT TO USE: Methylated spirits, cotton ball.
HOW TO APPLY: Wipe the marks with methylated spirits on a cotton ball. Wash normally.

Q 'My son's baby shawl has been packed away for 30 years,' reports Sue. 'I recently unwrapped it to find a dark yellow stain on it. What can I do?'

PROBLEM: Yellow stain on wool.
WHAT TO USE: Cheap shampoo, blood-heat water, towel.
HOW TO APPLY: The stain is likely to be old milk. To remove, wash with 1 teaspoon of shampoo in 9 litres of blood-heat water. Rinse in blood-heat water, gently wring out and dry on a flat towel in the shade.
PREVENTION: To avoid yellowing marks, store clothes in acid-free paper which is available at newsagents.

Q 'My son had a cold,' reports Lisa. 'And I rubbed *Vicks VapoRub* onto his chest. But it also got onto his T-shirt. How can I get it out?'

PROBLEM: *Vicks VapoRub* on cotton.
WHAT TO USE: Dishwashing liquid.
HOW TO APPLY: Put a couple of drops of dishwashing liquid on your fingers and massage into the stain until it feels like jelly. Wash and dry normally.

Q 'My 6-year-old dripped vivid blue icy pole down the front of his T-shirt,' reports Anne. 'How can I get it out?'

Kids' Stuff   457

PROBLEM: Blue icy pole on cotton.
WHAT TO USE: Sunshine, white vinegar, cloth.
HOW TO APPLY: These stains are usually removed by the washing machine as long as they're dried in sunshine which fades the stain. If the stain remains, wipe with white vinegar on a cloth, wash normally and hang it on the clothesline in the sun to dry.

Q 'My daughter got chocolate ice-cream on her favourite cotton T-shirt,' says Alice. 'She is heartbroken. Is there a way to get the stain out?'

PROBLEM: Chocolate ice-cream on cotton.
WHAT TO USE: Cake of bathroom soap, cold water.
HOW TO APPLY: Dip a cake of bathroom soap in cold water and scribble on the stain as though you're using a big crayon. Wash and dry normally.

Q 'When I washed my daughter's school windcheater, the burgundy dye ran into the white collar and it's now pink,' says Christine. 'Can I fix it?'

PROBLEM: Dye run in cotton.
WHAT TO USE: 9 litre bucket, water, *Colour Run Remover: Coloursafe*.

HOW TO APPLY: Soak overnight in a bucket of water and *Colour Run Remover*. Use twice as much *Colour Run Remover* as suggested by the manufacturer. Wash and dry normally.

PREVENTION: To make clothes colourfast, mix 4 cups of non-iodised salt in a 9 litre bucket of water, place clothes in the bucket and leave for 5 minutes. Wash normally. Salt removes excess surface dye and acts as a setting agent.

Q '**My son plays cricket,' reports Tania. 'And I'm finding it difficult to remove the red markings from the cricket ball. Do you have a suggestion?'**

PROBLEM: Cricket ball marks on cotton.
WHAT TO USE: White spirits, cotton ball.
HOW TO APPLY: Cricket balls are made of dyed red leather and the ball is often polished with the bowler's sweat or saliva. Rub the marks with a little white spirits on a cotton ball then wash and dry normally. White spirits also removes grass stains.

TIP

To stop white Lycra *becoming see-through when you get sweaty, spray it with a light mist of hair spray. Allow to dry before wearing.*

Q 'My daughter's white socks are really dirty,' says Anne. 'Is there a way to get the whiteness back?'

PROBLEM: Dirty white socks.
WHAT TO USE: Cake of bathroom soap, water.
HOW TO APPLY: Put a cake of bathroom soap in the toe of one sock and run under water. Put your hand in the other sock and rub the two together for about 15 seconds. Remove the cake of soap then wash and dry normally.
PREVENTION: Socks often become dirty around the toes because dye from school shoes leaches into the socks when little toes get sweaty. To prevent this, lightly spray inside each shoe with hair spray and allow to dry before wearing.

Q 'I have a white tulle dress (to be used as a flower girl's dress) that had several artificial flowers attached to it with what appears to be a heat glue gun,' says Margaret. 'I've managed to remove the flowers using hot water but cannot remove the glue. Do you have any suggestions?'

PROBLEM: Glue on tulle.
WHAT TO USE: Heatproof jug, boiling water, pantyhose.
HOW TO APPLY: Fill a heatproof jug with boiling water and stretch the gluey tulle over the mouth of the jug. Allow the steam to loosen the glue then remove the tulle and rub the

glue with a pair of pantyhose. The glue will roll off the pantyhose.

Cots

Every parent, including Shannon, has a story about messy cots. Ideally, mattresses should be aired every day. This just involves removing the sheets, which you can hang over the side of the cot. It's a good idea to stand the mattress on its end once a week and, if you can, place it in the sun. Sunshine is a fantastic killer of bacteria. Turn the mattress over when you return it to the cot. If you have any spills or stains, sponge them as quickly as possible and stand the mattress up to dry. Use a child-safe mattress protector that has a zipper rather than elastic to hold it.

Wash sheets and bedding in washing detergent for sensitive skin and dry in the sun rather than in the dryer because UV light kills bacteria. If you can't dry things in the sun and have to use the dryer, iron items afterwards so that the steam heat can help kill any remaining bacteria. If there's a problem with dust mites, put 2 tea bags in a 1 litre spray pack of water, allow to steep for 5 minutes, remove the tea bags and lightly mist over mattresses and pillows.

Make sure the cot is sturdy and safe. Stiff hinges can lead to accidents, so keep them well oiled with baby oil by adding a drop and allowing it to work through the hinges and slides.

SPOTLESS CLASSIC
Baby vomit on sheets

What to do will depend on the type of vomit. If the vomit is just milk, a normal wash on a cold cycle should do the job. For bad staining, rub with a cake of bathroom soap, add some cold water and scrub. Wipe with white vinegar on a cloth. If there's other food in the vomit, do a stain diagnosis (see page 577).

Q 'My baby vomited in her cot. It went all over the sheets and all through the mattress,' reports Kate. 'She only drinks milk and eats vegetables but it's incredible how much mess a small baby can produce. I've already scrubbed the surface of the mattress and it still smells. What can I do?'

PROBLEM: Vomit on sheets.
WHAT TO USE: Lemon juice, water, spray pack.
HOW TO APPLY: If you can, put the mattress in the sun—this will dry it out and kill bacteria. Wash the sheets in the washing machine and dry them in the sun. To get rid of the smell, mix 1 tablespoon of lemon juice with 1 litre of water in a spray pack and spray it over the mattress. Leave in the sun to dry.

Nappies

Most Australian babies wear disposable nappies. If your baby wears cloth nappies, clean them with two separate buckets.

Fill Bucket 1 with a nappy soaker. Fill Bucket 2 with hot water and 1 teaspoon of tea tree oil. Shake the solids from the nappy into the toilet, rinse, then put the nappy in Bucket 1. Leave it for 12 hours then swap the nappy to Bucket 2. Leave it for 20 minutes then put it in the washing machine. Use hot water in the washing machine and, depending on the size of the load, add 1 teaspoon to ½ cup of white vinegar to the rinse water. Dry in the sun if possible.

Nappies are unlikely to have greasy stains on them so use less nappy soaker and opt for an enzyme-free detergent to avoid residue build-up and nappy rash. If you like to wash with bicarb, white vinegar or essential oils but have a new-style nappy, check that these won't affect its elasticity. Don't be seduced by antibacterial products: they aren't necessary when cleaning nappies.

It's best to dry nappies on the clothesline where the sun sterilises and removes stains. It's also gentler on the nappy fibres, so they'll last longer. If you have to use the dryer, iron the nappies afterwards to kill any bacteria. Bucket 2 and the vinegar clear the soap residue that often causes nappy rash. If your baby has a rash, rub it with paw paw cream. It's a good idea to use nappy liners as well. Nappy rash in newborns is often caused by plastic pilchers. Invest in old-fashioned woollen flannel pilchers or fluffies for the first 3 months.

TIP

To disguise the smell of a nappy bucket, mix 2 tablespoons of bicarb, ½ teaspoon of dried sage, ½ teaspoon of dried thyme and 2 drops of lavender oil on a saucer and place near the bucket.

Hard Furnishings

Clean hard furnishings and hard toys with 1 teaspoon of tea tree oil added to 1 litre of water in a spray bottle. Wipe it off with a cloth. Tea tree oil is a great disinfectant and is non-toxic.

HIGHCHAIRS

Highchairs tend to be sealed in material that can be cleaned easily. Wipe highchairs straight after using them and before the food sets. Mix a couple of drops of tea tree oil with warm water and sponge clean. If you haven't been able to clean before the *Weetbix*, rusks or arrowroot biscuits have become as hard as cement, place a sponge in hot water, wring it and then let it sit over the hardened food for 10 minutes. This will soften the food. Then clean it with tea tree oil and water. If your child makes a huge mess when eating, place a flattened garbage bag underneath the highchair to catch the rejected food.

OLD WICKER FURNITURE

Wicker furniture should be cleaned with a mixture of 1 teaspoon of tea tree oil to 1 litre of water. Apply with a soft brush. If the furniture is heavily painted, add ½ teaspoon of glycerine to the mix.

PLAYPENS/SECURITY GATES

Most playpens and security gates are made with powder-coated aluminium and are easy to clean with a damp cloth.

Prams/Strollers/Baby Packs

Prams, strollers and baby packs have removable parts that can be washed with water and kept clean. Aluminium strollers need special care because they can become smell traps. Hose or scrub them with 1 teaspoon of dishwashing liquid or tea tree oil to 1 litre of water. Do this once a fortnight and then dry the pram in the sun. To clean canvas, mix 1 cup of salt in a bucket of water. Apply the solution and scrub with a nylon brush. Leave the pram in the sun until it's dry, then brush the salt off. In case the stroller runs over some dog poo, run the wheels over a mat or use a damp cloth to wipe them before you go inside. If there's mould on a pram, wipe with a strong salt solution (1 kg of non-iodised salt per 9 litres of water) with a couple of drops of oil of cloves added to prevent mould. Allow to dry. Brush the salt crust off with a stiff brush and the mould will come away with it.

Q 'We use a sheepskin in our daughter's pram,' says Tessa. 'Is there a way to wash it so it doesn't go hard?'

PROBLEM: Washing sheepskin.
WHAT TO USE: Blood-heat water, cheap shampoo, soft hairbrush.
HOW TO APPLY: Hand wash in blood-heat water with 1 teaspoon of cheap shampoo added, then rinse in blood-heat water and gently wring. The rinse water temperature must be the same as the wash water. To dry, lie it flat in the shade and brush regularly with a hairbrush. If the sheepskin dries too quickly, it will go stiff.

Toys

You can clean chewable toys by wiping them with pantyhose dipped in 1 teaspoon of tea tree oil per litre of water. Many new toys contain oils and plastics that stain. One of Jennifer's friends was horrified when her daughter brought playdough home from a birthday party filled with a green liquid. The liquid found its sticky way under the bed, went hard and stuck to the carpet. How could she remove it? If you don't know what a stain is made of, feel it with your fingers. If it feels oily, massage dishwashing liquid into the stain with your fingers until it feels like jelly, then wipe with a damp cloth. If it still sticks, wipe with white spirits on a cloth. If there's fluorescent colouring, place ice-cubes in a zip-lock bag and leave over the area until the ice almost melts. Remove the zip-lock bag and wipe with a strong salt solution (1 cup of non-iodised salt in 1 litre of water) on a cloth. Dry with paper towel.

Shannon stores children's toys in clear plastic stackable boxes with lids to keep dust at bay. Because the container is clear, your kids can see what's inside. These boxes can even be stored under the bed.

TIP

When visiting a doctor's surgery, take your own toys to reduce the risk of contact with germs from other children.

Q 'How do you prevent sling shot rubbers from drying out?' asks Rob.

PROBLEM: Preserving rubber.
WHAT TO USE: Salt, talcum powder.
HOW TO APPLY: Wipe the rubber with equal parts salt and talcum powder. Store in the shade.

Q 'My children's favourite plastic bath toys have mould on the inside,' says Maria. 'What can I do?'

PROBLEM: Mouldy bath toys.
WHAT TO USE: Oil of cloves, 9 litre bucket, warm water.
HOW TO APPLY: Add 2¼ teaspoons of oil of cloves to a bucket of warm water. Place the toys inside, squeeze so water gets inside and leave for 2 hours. Remove, squeeze out the water and set aside to dry.

TIP

If electronic games get wet, unscrew the back cover and leave on a tray in the sun. Turn the parts regularly so they don't corrode and wipe across the electric board with a dry paintbrush. When you put it back together, it should work again. You may need to replace the batteries. Clean the outside of electronic games with a drop of glycerine on paper towel.

STORING TOYS

Shannon's a big fan of the 'clutter bucket'. Each child (or adult) has their own bucket in a different colour. All their things that become scattered around the house can be collected with the bucket. Shannon also suggests creating your own toy storage out of old cardboard boxes. Spray the boxes with insecticide first, because insects are attracted to cardboard, then paint them. Label them with the name and a picture of what goes into the box so your kids learn to associate the words with the item. It also makes putting toys away a fun activity.

Hang stuffed toys along a line. Get a piece of clothesline twine or cotton sash twine and put plastic pegs along it. Hang the line from shelving units and peg the toys on one after another. Kids love doing this themselves.

Plastic sewing boxes or fishing boxes are great for storing little things like dolly's accessories or nuts and bolts from building sets.

CLEANING TOYS

Wash wooden toys in mild dishwashing liquid and water but never soak them or the timber will swell. Remove pen marks from wood with white spirits and from plastic with glycerine, both applied with a cotton ball.

Read the label to find out how to clean stuffed toys. If you're unsure, vacuum regularly and sponge the surface with tea tree oil and water to get rid of dust mites.

Plastic toys can be cleaned and sterilised with a mixture of tea tree oil, glycerine and water.

Fix dolly's hair by combing glycerine through it.

Repair torn pages from books with micropore, which is a fine cotton tape used in bandaging. Micropore is thin enough to read through and doesn't leave yellow lines like sticky tape.

Use a professional cleaner for special or antique toys.

The Laundry

For modern convenience, today's laundry is up there with TV remote controls and *Google*. It's retreated into a cupboard, the washing line retracts into a wall and both the washing machine and dryer can be operated without interrupting a mobile phone conversation with your sister in Helsinki. But which washing powder is the best? What's the best way to hang your washing? And how do you remove an ink stain?

Shannon still remembers the first time she saw her grandmother remove an ink stain using rotten milk solids. She thought it looked like magic as the black ink was drawn into the white milk. And today, all those years later, rotten milk is still an effective way to remove ballpoint pen ink (other inks have different solvents) from fabric. Jennifer's friend got dye from a new suede handbag over her expensive cream skirt and her dry-cleaner said it couldn't be cleaned without damaging the fabric. She used the rotten milk technique and it worked a treat. With other stains, don't rush in and make a bigger mess. Instead, work out what the stain is made of and then apply the correct solution.

Repairing a manky mink: *Karen's story*

INCIDENT: *'My 11-year-old son got a synthetic mink blanket for his birthday last year and he loves it. But I put it through the washing machine and it's gone all dull and scratchy. I couldn't bear to tell him and was going to buy a new one and substitute it. But before I could, he found the blanket and is really upset. He even pointed out to me that the washing instructions indicate hand wash only. Is there a solution?'*

SOLUTION: Put 150 ml of cheap hair conditioner into a bath filled with blood-heat water. Put the blanket in and leave it for 1 hour. Don't rinse the blanket, just hang it in the shade or cover it with a sheet if it's in the sun. When it's almost dry, brush it backwards and forwards on both sides with a nylon or bristle hairbrush. Then leave it to dry completely.

Tissue issue: *Jake's story*

INCIDENT: *'I know it's stupid. But I didn't bother to check the pockets before putting some clothes in the washing machine. Of course, there was a random tissue that has spread everywhere. How do I remove all that fluff from the wash?'*

SOLUTION: There are two things to clean here: the interior of the washing machine and the contents of the wash. To remove the fluff from the washing machine, put your hand inside the toe of a pair of pantyhose and wipe over the drum. To remove the fluff from your clothes, put on a pair of disposable rubber gloves, wash your gloved hands with a cake of bathroom soap and water and shake dry. Stroke over the linty fabric and the lint will attach to the rubber gloves.

Washing

Shannon thinks the washing machine is one of the best inventions. She loves throwing dirty things in and, like magic, getting clean things out. Here are Shannon's general principles for washing clothes:

- Remove stains before washing clothes. If very dirty, soak before washing but only soak wool and silk for 20 minutes. If the item contains synthetic fibres, wipe with a dab of methylated spirits, then treat the stain before washing.
- Less dirt will be removed from clothes if the washing machine is overloaded.
- Sort clothes into different fabric types, then separate whites from colours. After sorting, check pockets (you don't want a stray tissue in the wash), close zippers and do up buttons.
- Wash whites and colours separately. You're less likely to get that grey look if you further separate colours into pale blues and greens, put darker blues and greys together, and wash blacks, browns and reds together. I make a pile of clothes in each of these colour ranges and wait until there's a full load.

- Use the least amount of chemical and heat to clean. Cooler temperatures are gentler on fabrics and help clothes to last longer. To work out the appropriate temperature, consult the garment labels on the items you are washing. Only cotton and linen can handle very hot temperatures.
- Always make sure the lint filters in the dryer and washing machine are clean. You'll get a better result and it's safer.
- Don't overpack the washing machine or dryer. With top-loading machines, pack clothes loosely so that you can still access the agitator. Never fill more than ⅓ of the dryer space with damp clothes.
- The best fabric softener is ½ cup of bicarb added to the washing powder, then add ½ cup of white vinegar to the rinse cycle.
- Buy products according to quality rather than cost. A suggested range includes:
    - Good quality washing powder or liquid
    - Oxygen bleach that doesn't bleach colour
    - High whites bleach soaker
    - Antibacterial
    - Woolwash with eucalyptus or cheap shampoo
    - Box of pure soap flakes
    - Bottle of cheap hair conditioner.

- Choose soap powder based on its oxygenated properties and enzyme content. When soap powder comes into contact with water, it creates a chemical reaction and effervesces, allowing bubbles of oxygen to attack stains. Enzymes attack proteins and fats. Cheaper powders tend to have bleaching agents and are not as good for your clothes.
- Liquid soap is usually better than powder because fewer particles are left on your clothes. This does vary according to the washing machine with some front-end loaders performing better with powder.
- If you suffer from skin allergies, test the washing powder on your skin before using it on your clothes.
- If someone in the house has a cold, add ¼ cup of lemon juice or ¼ cup of white vinegar to the rinse water to remove bacteria.
- Add ¼ cup of white vinegar to the rinse water if anyone in your family has sensitive skin.

HOT VERSUS COLD WATER

Only use hot water if you have really soiled clothes, otherwise it's not necessary. If the item has normal soiling, use the warm setting. I tend to use the warm setting with a cold rinse. Never use hot water on delicates. Nylons should only be washed in cold water.

TIP

Have a separate basket for stained items that need to be spot-cleaned before washing.

SPOT CLEANING

Damp the stain with water first. Mix *NapiSan Oxygen* and water to form a paste to the consistency of peanut butter. Leave the paste on the stain for 5–15 minutes and, unless it's hand wash only, put the item through the washing machine.

STARCHES

The best starch is rice water. Next time you're cooking rice, keep the water after it's boiled. There are two ways of using it. You can either dilute it 1 to 1 with water and put it in a spray bottle ready to apply when you're ironing or you can add it to the rinse water in the washing machine.

SOAKING

You may think the longer you soak your clothes, the more dirt is removed but this is not the case. The more delicate the fabric, the less time it should sit soaking (the exception is in salt water). Twenty minutes is generally enough time for an item to soak. Never soak woollens for more than 20 minutes because the fibres will shrink, even in cool water. And be aware that proprietary products such as *NapiSan* contain chlorine and can leave yellow marks on wool and silk. It's better to clean them with cheap shampoo in blood-heat water. To remove the yellow marks, see 'Clothing and Shoes', page 377.

COLOURFAST

If you have new clothes and you're not sure if they're colourfast, try this test. Wring out a white cloth in white vinegar and place the cloth over an inconspicuous part of the garment and iron. Colour will transfer to the cloth if it's not colourfast. Alternatively, wring out a white cloth in white vinegar and pinch it over an inconspicuous part of the garment. The colour will transfer to the cloth if it's not colourfast. To make an item colourfast, place in a 9 litre bucket of water with 2 cups of non-iodised salt. Soak for 1 hour and wash normally.

COLOUR RUN

Jennifer was really annoyed when her shirt became pink after a rogue red item found its way into the washing machine. If you have a similar disaster, use the proprietary product, *Colour Run Remover* (which used to be called *Runaway*). There are two varieties: *Colour Run Remover: Whites* and *Colour Run Remover: Coloursafe*. Rather than add *Colour Run Remover* to the washing machine as suggested by the manufacturer, soak items in a tub or bucket with twice the amount of product recommended. If the item is made of wool or silk, soak for 20 minutes in blood-heat water. For other fabrics, soak overnight.

At our Stain Clinics many people complain about the 'lamington look' of lint on their clothes. To prevent this, clean the lint filter on your washing machine before each wash and remove lint from the drum by wiping with damp pantyhose. Use one-third less washing powder than is recommended by the manufacturer and dissolve the powder particles in water before adding to the wash. Another tip is to use a gentle wash cycle. If clothes are washed too vigorously with too much washing detergent, they become statically charged and collect lint. To remove the static charge in clothes, place 1 teaspoon of cheap hair conditioner in a 1 litre spray pack of water and lightly mist over the clothes as they dry. To remove really tough lint, put on disposable rubber gloves, wash your gloved hands with a cake of bathroom soap and water, shake dry and wipe your hands across the fabric. The lint will stick to the rubber gloves.

QUICK STAIN REMOVAL GUIDE FOR FABRICS

This is only a brief guide to stain removal. For more detailed instructions, consult the relevant advice in the book.

Banana
Wipe with a little glycerine and leave for 15 minutes, then wash normally.

Barbecue sauce
Wipe with a little white vinegar, wash normally and hang in sunshine to dry.

Beer (including dark beer)
Paint a paste of *NapiSan OxyAction MAX* and water on the stain and leave for 15 minutes, then wash normally.

Beetroot
Soak in white vinegar until the stain is removed, then wash normally.

Bird droppings
It depends on what the bird has eaten—either protein, seed or fruit. With protein (generally black or brown poo), scribble over the stain with a cake of bathroom soap and cold water. With seed (generally white poo), scribble over the stain with a cake of bathroom soap and warm water. With fruit (generally purple or orange poo), wipe with a cloth dampened with white vinegar, then wipe with a dab of glycerine on a cloth and leave for 20 minutes before washing normally.

Blood
Rub the stain out with cold water and a cake of bathroom soap then wash normally on the cold setting. If you can't put it through the wash, use a thin paste of cornflour and cold water to draw out the stain. Allow to dry and brush away. For old blood stains, use cold water and a cake of bathroom soap and vigorously rub the stain against itself.

Carrot
Wipe with a little white vinegar and hang in the sun. Carrot stains respond to UV rays.

Chewing gum
Harden the gum with an ice-cube and cut as much off as possible with scissors or a blade. Then apply a little tea tree oil with a rolled up pair of pantyhose and work the remaining gum out by rubbing it in circles. White spirits also works.

Chilli sauce
Wipe with white vinegar or lemon juice until most of the red colouring transfers to the cloth. To remove the oil, add a couple of drops of dishwashing liquid to your fingers and massage into the stain until it feels like jelly before washing normally.

Chocolate
Scrub with a cake of bathroom soap and cold water, then scrub with a cake of bathroom soap and hot water before washing normally.

Chocolate ice-cream
Scrub with a cake of bathroom soap and cold water before washing normally.

Collar grime
Mix *NapiSan OxyAction MAX* and water to form a paste the consistency of peanut butter. Apply to the stain and leave for 20 minutes. Wash and dry normally.

Cooking oil
Soak up as much oil as possible with paper towel. Apply a little dishwashing liquid and massage into the stain with your fingers until it feels like jelly. Rinse with a little warm water. Wash normally.

Coffee/tea
For fresh stains, use a little glycerine applied with a cotton ball, then wash normally. For old stains, use a little glycerine, followed by a little white spirits and a little dishwashing liquid, then wash normally.

Crayon
Mix 2 drops of tea tree oil with 1 teaspoon of dishwashing liquid and massage over the crayon marks with your fingers, then rinse with water and wash normally.

Deodorant
Apply a little white spirits with a cotton ball before washing. For stiffened armpits, apply a paste of *NapiSan Plus* and water, leave for 15 minutes before washing normally.

Dog poo
Dip a cake of bathroom soap in cold water and scribble over the stain as though using a crayon, then rub before washing normally.

Egg yolk
Use a cake of bathroom soap and cold water first, then a couple of drops of dishwashing liquid and warm water.

Fruit juice
Wash in white vinegar and hang in the sunshine to dry. UV light breaks down fruit colouring. For stone fruits and fruits with high tannin levels, treat the stain with a little glycerine first.

Grass
Sponge with a little white spirits before washing normally.

Gravy
Dip a cake of bathroom soap in cold water and scribble over the stain. Put a couple of drops of dishwashing liquid on your fingers and massage into the stain until it feels like jelly. Then wash normally.

Grease
For dark-coloured grease use baby oil and for light-coloured grease apply dishwashing liquid to the stain and rub with your fingers to emulsify. Rinse under cold water.

Hair dye
Use the same brand and colour hair dye (hair dye contains its own solvent). When the stain starts to loosen, rub with a little anti-dandruff shampoo on your fingers. If the stain has just happened, spray with hair spray before washing normally.

Ink/ballpoint pen
Apply rotten milk solids or a little white spirits to the stain. Use a little glycerine first on red ink.

Lipstick/make-up
Apply a little white spirits with a cotton ball.

Mascara
Sponge the stain with methylated spirits, then blot with paper towel.

Mayonnaise
Massage a little dishwashing liquid into the stain with your fingers and wash in cold water. The massaging makes the mayonnaise water-soluble.

Milk
Wash normally on the cold cycle.

Mud
For red clay mud, apply a dab of white spirits then wash. For black mud, wash in the washing machine.

Nail polish
Use pure acetone on a cotton bud or ball, not nail polish remover.

Paint
For water-based paint, use a dab of methylated spirits. For oil-based paints, use a dab of turpentine.

Pen marks

Solutions vary according to the type of pen. **Permanent markers**—write over the mark using the same pen. Then wipe with white spirits on a cotton bud. Wash and dry normally. *Artline*—wipe with methylated spirits on a cotton bud. Wash and dry normally. **Whiteboard marker**—wipe with methylated spirits on a cotton bud. Wash and dry normally. **Fluorescent pen**—write over the mark using the same pen, then wipe the mark with white spirits on a cotton bud. Alternatively, fill a 9 litre bucket with water and add 1 cup of non-iodised salt, dip the stain in the salt solution, gently wring and place in a plastic bag before freezing in the freezer. Wash and dry normally. **Gel pens**—soak in methylated spirits for 10 minutes and rub with a cotton bud dipped in methylated spirits. Repeat until removed. Wash and dry normally.

Rubber

Dampen and rub with coarse non-iodised salt.

Rust

Use *CLR* or *Ranex* or lemon juice and non-iodised salt.

Sap

Sponge with a little tea tree oil.

Shoe polish
Use a little methylated spirits applied with a cotton ball. Alternatively, use a little tea tree oil applied with a cotton ball.

Soft drink
Treat as though it's a fruit stain because soft drinks are coloured with vegetable dyes.

Soy sauce
Wipe with white vinegar before washing normally.

Sunscreen
Massage a little dishwashing liquid into the stain with your fingers, then wash with warm water.

Sweat
Make a paste of *NapiSan Plus* and water, leave on the stain for 15 minutes, then wash in the washing machine. To prevent sweat marks, experiment until you find a deodorant that works for you. Everyone's body chemistry is different which means some people will need a deodorant and others will need an antiperspirant. Make sure your deodorant has dried before putting on your clothes.

Tar
Massage in a little baby oil followed by a little kerosene on a cloth.

Tomato sauce
Wipe with white vinegar and wash normally. Dry in sunshine.

Turmeric
Wipe with a little lavender oil before washing normally.

Urine
Wash normally and dry in sunshine.

Vegemite
Will generally come out in the wash. If stubborn, put a couple of drops of dishwashing liquid on your fingers and massage into the stain. Then wash normally.

Vomit
Wash normally and dry in sunshine or use *NapiSan Plus* if the stains are stubborn.

Watermelon
Quickly deteriorates and ferments causing a smell. Sponge with white vinegar and sprinkle with bicarb to remove the stain and the smell.

Wax
Place ice-cubes on the wax until the ice starts to melt. Scrape away as much wax as possible with a blunt knife, then lay sheets of paper towel over your ironing

board. Place the stained material over the ironing board and cover with more paper towel before ironing with a cool iron. If a greasy mark remains rub it with a little tea tree oil.

Wine

For new red wine spills, absorb moisture with paper towel, then wipe with a little white vinegar on a cloth. For old red wine spills, wipe with a dab of glycerine on a cloth and sprinkle with bicarb. It will turn grey. Allow to dry, wipe with a little white vinegar and vacuum. For white wine stains, both old and new, sponge with white vinegar on a cloth.

CLEANING THE WASHING MACHINE

If you think about all the dirt and grime that passes through your washing machine, it's no surprise it needs to be cleaned. Each month, add ½ cup of bicarb to the wash slot and ½ cup of white vinegar to the rinse slot and wash on a quick cycle. If you get a random tissue or disposable nappy washed through the machine, allow the drum to fill with water, add 2 tablespoons of cheap hair conditioner, 2 tablespoons of bicarb and leave filled for 1 hour before rinsing and wiping with pantyhose. Don't forget to clean the exterior, seals and hinges of the machine. To clean the seals, wrap an old tea towel around a plastic knife, dip in white vinegar and work under and around the seals. Wipe hinges with 2 drops of machine oil and clear away any fluff and dirt. If you keep your washing machine clean, you won't need to call the repairer as often.

Q 'My washing machine is 20 years old,' reports Wendy. 'It's still working remarkably well, but has a mildewy smell. Is there a solution?'

PROBLEM: Mildew smell in washing machine.
WHAT TO USE: New hose; or bicarb, white vinegar.
HOW TO APPLY: The smell could be from a variety of sources. Check the netting sections in the lint catchers first. The smell could also come from the hose, which is very easy to change. Another source could be the joints in the plumbing. If it's from the machine bowl, when it's dry, wipe it with bicarb and white vinegar. If the smell persists, run the washing machine on empty with 1 cup of bicarb and add 2 cups of white vinegar during the rinse cycle.

Q 'I've got black stuff in my washing machine,' says Ngaire. 'What should I do?'

PROBLEM: Black stuff in washing machine.
WHAT TO USE: Bicarb, white vinegar; or replace seals.
HOW TO APPLY: Add ½ cup of bicarb to hot washing water. Then add ½ cup of white vinegar to the rinse water. If this doesn't work, replace the seals on your washing machine.

The Laundry 491

Q 'I've got mould in the rubber seal of my front loading washing machine,' says Sue. 'What should I do?'

PROBLEM: Mould on rubber seal of washing machine.
WHAT TO USE: Oil of cloves, water, 1 litre spray pack, pantyhose, damp salt.
HOW TO APPLY: Mix ¼ teaspoon of oil of cloves with water in a spray pack and lightly spray over the area. Leave for 24 hours. Rub with a pair of pantyhose dipped in damp salt. Respray with oil of cloves solution and leave to dry.

Q 'We have a rather old washing machine and one of the last loads stained all our clothes,' says Meg. 'We believe it's from a build-up of all the fabric softeners which have collected grease and dirt during various washes. What can we do to remove these stains?'

PROBLEM: Washing machine staining clothes.
WHAT TO USE: Damp pantyhose, bicarb, white vinegar.
HOW TO APPLY: To remove the current grime, wipe the inside of the drum with damp pantyhose. Make sure you get behind the seals. Run an empty load with ½ cup of bicarb in the washing slot and ½ cup of white vinegar in the fabric conditioner slot using a quick cycle. Instead of using fabric softener, try this washing formula. Use one-third the

quantity of your regular detergent and for a large top loader, add ½ cup of bicarb and ½ cup of white vinegar; for a large front loader, add 2 tablespoons of bicarb and 2 tablespoons of white vinegar.

TIP

New flannelette sheets can leave a load of fluff in your washing machine. To avoid this, wash them on a heavy duty cycle with ½ cup of bicarb added to the laundry detergent and ½ cup of white vinegar in the fabric softener slot. Dry on the clothesline, not in the dryer. Many flannelette sheets contain polyester and if placed in the dryer they wear more quickly and pill.

Q 'We live in the mining town of Newman,' says Penny. 'And our washing machine is caked in red dirt from iron ore. Is there anything we can flush through the machine to remove the dirt?'

PROBLEM: Red dirt in washing machine.
WHAT TO USE: Bicarb, white vinegar, bucket, water.
HOW TO APPLY: Place 1 cup of bicarb in the washing water and 1 cup of white vinegar in the fabric conditioner slot of the machine. Remove heavy dirt by soaking the clothes in a bucket of water saved from the bath or shower before

placing them in the washing machine. It means your machine won't have to work as hard. Reuse the bucket water over your garden.

FABRIC CARE SYMBOLS
Be aware that these vary from country to country.

Washing
- 95°C cotton wash—maximum and most effective temperature
- 60°C
- 40°C
- 40°C with bar—synthetics wash
- 40°C with broken bar—wool wash
- hand wash only symbol
- chlorine may be used
- do not use chlorine

Ironing
- hot iron
- warm iron
- cool iron

Dry cleaning
- must be professionally cleaned
- do not dry-clean

Dryer

- may be tumble dried
- dry on high heat setting
- dry on low heat setting
- do not tumble dry

Q 'I washed a spandex/viscose top in warm water,' says Rhonda. 'But I accidentally used the fast spin on the washing machine. It's now stretched about two sizes bigger. Can I possibly shrink it back to the right size?'

PROBLEM: Stretched synthetic fabric.
WHAT TO USE: Methylated spirits.
HOW TO APPLY: Soak the garment in methylated spirits for 20 minutes, remove and squeeze but don't wring out. Dry flat in the shade. Most synthetic fibres have a memory and return to their original shape. When dry, wash normally using a gentle spin.

TIP

When trying to get a whiter than white look, many people reach for bleach. But most bleaches and mould-removal products simply whiten the mould rather than kill the spores that allow mould to grow. A better option is to use oil of cloves, which kills mould spores.

Q '**I get a sudsy residue on dark clothes when washed in my washing machine,**' reports Annabelle. '**What's wrong?**'

PROBLEM: Soap residue on clothes.
WHAT TO USE: Less washing detergent; or repairer.
HOW TO APPLY: A sudsy residue on clothes could mean you're using too much washing detergent, the lint filter hasn't been cleared or something is wrong with your washing machine. Try using one-third less washing detergent and clean the lint filter. If the problem persists, water may not be entering the washing machine at the right rate and you'll need to consult a repairer.

Q '**I've got black tar in my washing machine,**' complains Jenny. '**It came from my son's work clothes. What can I do?**'

PROBLEM: Tar in washing machine.
WHAT TO USE: Baby oil, pantyhose, talcum powder.
HOW TO APPLY: Wipe the tar with a dab of baby oil on pantyhose. When it softens, puff some talcum powder over the top. Rub with clean pantyhose and the tar will come away in little balls.

Q 'I didn't hang my washing out right away,' reports Mandy. 'Apart from being a bit smelly, my daughter's cream-coloured shirt has mouldy spots on it. Can it be fixed?'

PROBLEM: Mouldy spots on cotton.
WHAT TO USE: Warm water, *NapiSan Plus*; or non-iodised salt, water, 9 litre bucket, brush.
HOW TO APPLY: Soak in warm water and *NapiSan Plus* for 20 minutes. If any mould remains, combine 1 kg of non-iodised salt with a bucket of water and soak the shirt in the solution overnight. Remove, gently wring (but don't rinse) and hang in the sun to dry. A salt crust will form as it dries. Brush the salt off and the mould will come with it. Wash and dry normally.

Towels

We're constantly asked at Stain Clinics how to make towels less scratchy. One of the main reasons they become scratchy is washing detergent residue. To fix, add ½ cup of bicarb to the washing detergent and ½ cup of white vinegar to the fabric conditioner slot. If towels have become yellow with age, add ¼ cup of lemon juice to your normal wash and hang in the sun to dry.

Q 'I perform massages and use white towels,' says Ngaire. 'What's the best way to remove massage oils from them?'

PROBLEM: Massage oil on towels.
WHAT TO USE: Dishwashing liquid; or bucket, warm water, dishwashing liquid, tea tree oil.
HOW TO APPLY: Place a couple of drops of dishwashing liquid on the oil stain and rub with your fingers until it feels like jelly. Wash normally. If the stain is substantial, get a large bucket (big enough for you to get your feet in) and fill with warm water and 2 teaspoons of dishwashing liquid. If the oils are dense, add 1 teaspoon of tea tree oil to the mixture. Place the towels in the bucket, put your feet inside and stomp up and down. Tip the entire contents of the bucket into the washing machine and wash normally. The stains will be removed and your feet will be nice and clean as well!

TIP

It's best not to use orange oil to remove oil stains because over time, the orange oil can leave a residue and stain if not completely rinsed out. Instead, place a couple of drops of dishwashing liquid on your fingers and massage into the oil. Wash and dry normally.

Sink

Q 'I have a plastic laundry tub,' says Bob. 'And it's got a blue-green stain on it. Can it be removed?'

PROBLEM: Stained plastic.
WHAT TO USE: Glycerine, talcum powder, pantyhose, damp cloth.
HOW TO APPLY: Mix glycerine and talcum powder to form a paste the consistency of runny cream. Polish the stain with a pair of pantyhose and repeat until removed. Wipe with a damp cloth.

Hand Washing

It doesn't take much more effort to hand wash your more delicate clothes and they'll thank you for it. First, spot clean any stains. Then fill a laundry tub or bucket with blood-heat water. Only ever wash delicates or wool in blood-heat water. To test for blood heat, sprinkle a few drops of water on the inside of your wrist. If you can't feel the water—that is, if it's the same temperature as your wrist—it's blood heat. Next add a small quantity of cheap shampoo to the water. Gently wash the garment by hand and leave for around 10–20 minutes to soak; any longer and the fibres will reabsorb the dirt and the cold water will strain delicate fibres. Then rinse in clean blood-heat water. The temperature of the rinse water must be the same as the temperature of the wash water. Remove the rinse water by placing the garments in the washing machine and using the spin cycle. Either hang the garments on the clothesline or lay them flat on a towel in the shade to dry. Avoid using the dryer if you can. If it's raining, use a clothes drying rack or hang the items from a coat-hanger in the bathroom.

TIP

If you hand wash after gardening, you'll clean your hands and clear your pores as well.

Dry-Cleaning

It's common for clothing manufacturers to include a 'dry-clean only' label so they're not liable for any damage but some of the garments sent to the dry-cleaner can be hand washed. The exception is structured or tailored clothing which should go to a dry-cleaner because of the shape of the garment. With fabrics such as rayon, silk or viscose, test first by rubbing a wet cotton bud into a seam and leaving it to dry. If the fabric crinkles, it can't be hand washed because the fabric will shrink. Be careful with darker coloured rayon, silk and viscose garments which may lose colour if hand washed. You can hand wash wool, linen, cashmere and cotton.

Hanging Out the Washing

These days, we're more likely to put clothes in the dryer but it means missing out on one of the best antibacterial cleaners around—the sun. The sun also adds fragrance to your clothes so I suggest making the effort to hang your clothes on the line. Keep this in mind when hanging out the washing: if you hang your clothes as flat as possible, you'll have less ironing to do because there'll be fewer creases. Have the clothes basket at waist height and store pegs beside the basket. Don't leave pegs on the clothesline because UV light and rain cause them to deteriorate.

Hang each item by the strongest section of the garment and always place pegs in unobtrusive spots. Trousers and skirts should be hung from the waistband. Shirts should be hung from the tails and pegged on the side seams. Shirts can also be hung on a coat-hanger with a plastic shopping bag over the wire to prevent rusting.

Woollens are best dried lying flat on a white towel. If you have to hang something woollen, put an old stocking through the sleeves and peg the stocking to the line.

Use plastic bags to hang delicates on the clothesline. Place the plastic bag over the line and drape the delicates over the bag, then wrap the bag back over the delicates and peg.

Never hang silk on a windy day because the fibres tangle and are difficult to smooth out.

You're less like to get holes if you hang socks by the tops rather than the toes. Hang anything with a nap or fluff with the fluff surfaces facing each other. This works particularly well with towels that have a velvety finish on one side and a normal finish on the other. Drape the towel in half over the line with the 'velvet' side on the inside. They'll take longer to dry but it's worth it when one side is fluffy and soft.

Old netted bags from the fruit shop make great peg bags because water drains through them. Wrap the netted bag around a coat-hanger that has been opened into a circle. The hook makes it easy to hang.

To stop birds hovering over your clothesline and potentially soiling your clothes, tie some coloured ribbons to the line and allow them to flutter. You could also hang some old CDs on the line. Birds don't like sharp movements.

Tumble Drying

Drying in the sun is preferable but that's not always an option. Before using your dryer make sure you clean the lint catcher. To cut back on ironing, fold your clothes as soon as they come out of the dryer. If you're in a hurry and need to speed up the drying process, put a dry tea towel in with your clothes. It will absorb moisture.

To get rid of static, wash and dry synthetics separately from clothes made of natural fibres. Never overdry synthetic fibres. Remove them from the dryer slightly damp and hang to dry naturally either on a clothesline or on hangers. Drying racks are cheap to buy and easy to put up and down. If you do use the dryer, make sure you remove any lint and don't allow clothes to become bone dry or they'll be stiff.

If you get a dry powdery build-up in the lint catcher or around the seals on the dryer or across dried clothes, this is excess soap, which indicates that the rinse cycle on the washing machine isn't working properly. Reduce the amount of washing detergent you use by one-third and add ½ cup of white vinegar in the fabric conditioner slot.

Ironing

It's hard to imagine a time when irons had to be heated on the stove before being used; now, they're *Teflon* coated and super steaming with multiple functions. Some are even smart enough to turn themselves off if you forget. We can't wait for the day when they can do the ironing by themselves.

Many years ago when Shannon's eldest daughter was a baby, she used to iron professionally. One of the main rules of good ironing is to go with the grain. Find out which way the grain runs by holding the fabric and pulling it. If it's taut, you're on the grain. If you have stretch, you're not on the grain.

Before you begin ironing, consult the care label on the

garment and set the iron to the correct temperature. Begin ironing clothes that require the least amount of heat and work your way up—that way you avoid scorching your clothes.

As a general rule, iron the least important part of the garment first because you're more likely to crease that part as you move the garment around. Iron the most important part last—the part that people see the most. If you're in a hurry, fill a spray pack with 1 litre of water and 1 teaspoon of lavender oil and mist over your clothes before you put them on. Shannon loves using this technique: it removes creases—and it keeps mozzies and flies away.

Shannon likes to iron clothes while they're slightly damp because it speeds up the process. Have some water in a spray pack and squirt a mist over the clothes before running the iron over them. She also likes to set the iron on low temperatures and use lots of steam.

When you're ironing wool, use a damp white linen tea towel over the top. Rest and press the iron but don't leave it in the one spot for too long.

Use spray starches sparingly because they can damage your clothes and make your floors slippery.

Shannon likes to protect buttons on shirts by making a cardboard cutout like a thick letter 'c' and placing this under the button. Slide the iron between the shirt and the cardboard. Shannon has her 'c' tied to the iron with a piece of elastic.

To sharpen pleats when ironing, lay the garment over the end of the ironing board and, using glass-headed or steel-headed pins, pin the pleats into position on the ironing board. Hold the pleat taut at both ends. Put a damp cloth over the pleat and run the iron gently up and down. For sharp, long-lasting creases, rub soap down the inside of the crease before you iron the garment. This will stop your pants getting baggy knees!

If clothes become shiny from ironing, immerse a clean white cloth in white vinegar, wring out well and place over the shiny area. Run a cool iron over the top. This also gives clothes a quick spruce up if they've been in the cupboard for too long.

If you scorch white clothes while ironing, immerse a clean cloth in 3 per cent hydrogen peroxide, wring out tightly, place over the mark and iron on a cool setting.

The legs of old pyjamas make great ironing-board covers. Secure them with safety pins underneath the board.

Speed up the ironing process by putting a sheet of aluminium foil under the ironing board cover.

Clean an iron when it's cold with bicarb and white vinegar. Just make sure you clean it all off properly with water before using it again. To clean the sticky build-up on the bottom of the iron, get a piece of rough blotting paper, preferably white, and rub the hot iron backwards and forwards over it until no more marks come off.

If there are white flecks coming out of your iron, that's aluminium oxide. To fix, pour a weak tea solution—1 tea bag in 1 cup of warm water left to steep for 30 seconds—or equal parts white vinegar and water into the iron. Turn the iron on and press the steam button until the liquid has worked through the iron. Add clean water and continue to press the steam function until the iron sprays clean water. To prevent this problem, remove water from your iron after using it. If the holes are blocked, add 2 drops of *CLR* or *Ranex* to the water, turn the iron on, hold it horizontally and push the steam button down. Rinse with clean water.

Q 'Is there any way to unpleat permanent pleating?' asks Alison.

PROBLEM: Unpleating permanent pleating.
WHAT TO USE: Steam from the iron.
HOW TO APPLY: The effectiveness of this technique will depend on whether the fabric is natural or synthetic. For natural fabrics, remove the pleat using lots of steam from the iron. It's very difficult to get pleats out of synthetic fabrics because they have a memory and return to their original pleats.

Q 'What's the best way to iron a damask table cloth?' asks Sue.

PROBLEM: Ironing damask.
WHAT TO USE: Old blanket, iron.
HOW TO APPLY: Make sure the ironing board has thick padding. An old folded blanket will do. Slightly damp the tablecloth then iron with the warp of the fabric. The warp goes down the fabric, the weft goes across the fabric.

Q 'I've got an iron mark that's stiff and shiny on my polyamide/elastane trousers,' says Leonie. 'What can I do?'

PROBLEM: Iron melt.
WHAT TO USE: Cotton cloth, white vinegar, iron.
HOW TO APPLY: Hopefully the fibres are melted rather than burnt. Immerse a cloth in white vinegar, wring out and place over the area. Use a cool iron over the top. If the mark won't come out, it's permanently damaged. To save the garment, soak a piece of cotton corduroy in white vinegar, place over the garment, cord side down, and apply a hot iron. This creates a ridging pattern over the fabric which covers the scorch mark.

Q 'I've got a burn stain on my iron,' says Josie. 'It looks like black muck. How can I get it off?'

PROBLEM: Burn on iron.

WHAT TO USE: Old towel, pantyhose, bicarb, white vinegar.
HOW TO APPLY: Turn the iron off and allow to cool. Put an old towel over your ironing board and pull a pair of pantyhose over the end of the ironing board until taut. Sprinkle bicarb on the pantyhose and spray the surface of the iron with white vinegar. Wipe the cold iron over the pantyhose. Repeat if necessary.

Ironing without an iron

To stiffen or smooth tulle, nylon and other fabrics you can't iron, put 1 tablespoon of uncoloured pure soap flakes into a spray bottle and mix with 1 litre of water. Shake the mixture until the soap flakes have completely dissolved and then spray the fabric. Pull the fabric straight and dry it with a hairdryer. Don't hold the hairdryer too close or the heat will melt the fabric. The mixture stiffens and irons at the same time.

Folding

The general principle for folding is to have as few folds as possible. Size up the space you have available and then work out the least number of folds for the greatest surface area of the shelf or drawer. Never put a fold down the front of a garment.

Fold socks by matching the tops together and folding three edges over your hand and the other edge over itself.

Then remove your hand. Another way is to lay the socks flat, fold them at the heels and pull the top edge over your hand. Then remove your hand.

Fold a tea towel in six squares. Fold towels in four or six depending on the size of the shelf. You can also fold towels in half and then roll them up. This helps them to stay fluffy and looks good.

To prevent creasing in good tablecloths, place a piece of acid-free paper along the middle line.

LINEN PRESS

Q 'I have a collection of my mother's 70-year-old hand-embroidered linen doilies and tea towels,' says Lynda. 'Some have dark rust-coloured spots on them. Can they be removed?'

PROBLEM: Rust-coloured stains on old linen.
WHAT TO USE: Non-iodised salt, lemon juice, sunshine.
HOW TO APPLY: Place a little mountain of salt over each spot and squeeze drops of lemon juice on top until the salt is just moistened. Leave in the sunshine to dry. Repeat if necessary. This can take up to 2 days but is a gentle solution that won't damage the fabric.
PREVENTION: Store items in acid-free paper or wrapped in an old cotton sheet. Add a couple of white chalk sticks to absorb moisture.

Q 'I must have put a damp towel in the linen cupboard,' says Gail. 'I think the mould spores must still be on the shelf. How do I fix it?'

PROBLEM: Mould on towels in linen press.
WHAT TO USE: Non-iodised salt, water, 9 litre bucket, stiff brush (towels); oil of cloves, water (shelves), 1 litre spray pack.
HOW TO APPLY: Mix 1 kg of salt with a bucket of water, add the towels and leave overnight to soak. Remove, gently wring (but don't rinse) and hang the towels on the clothesline. When dry, they'll be covered in a salt crust. Brush away the crust with a stiff brush. Wash the towels normally. To remove the mould spores from the shelves, put ¼ teaspoon of oil of cloves into a spray pack of water and lightly spray the shelves. Leave for 24 hours before wiping and re-stacking.

TIP
If there's rising damp in the rear wall of the linen press or the linen is sweating from lack of ventilation, place a tub of silicone crystals or a bouquet of white chalk sticks on the shelves.

Outside

The backyard used to be just a patch of lawn, a shed and a *Hills* hoist. These days it's generally a place for fun; be it hosting a barbie, digging about in the garden, jumping on the trampoline or kicking around a soccer ball. But there's also work to do including hanging out the washing, cleaning up after the barbie, mowing the lawn, sweeping the paths, looking after the compost and maintaining the pool. You might have to remove accidental spills from the car, caravan or boat as well. After you've dealt with spills and stains, you can play, entertain and tinker with ease and enjoy many a relaxing hour in your patch of paradise.

Don't paint in your good clothes: *Phil's story*

INCIDENT: *'I was helping a mate paint his fence. But I didn't change my clothes and, wouldn't you know it, I got paint on my shorts. The other complication is I don't know what kind of paint it is. Can I rescue the shorts? I really like them!'*

SOLUTION: To work out what kind of paint it is, get three small containers—one each of turpentine, methylated spirits and acetone. Dip a cotton bud in each one and apply it to the stain, then rub the stain between your thumb and forefinger. Whichever takes colour first is the solvent. Then dip two cotton balls in the solvent and place them on the top and bottom sides of the paint mark. Wipe the top cotton ball in circles until the paint is removed, working from the outside to the inside of the stain. If this doesn't work or if the paint mark is old, soak the painted part of the shorts in the appropriate solvent and then apply the cotton balls.

Rascally rabbits: *Kylie's story*

INCIDENT: *'We live on the edge of bushland and love the tranquillity. But our deck has become a bit of a haven for rabbits. The particular problem is rabbit urine staining the timber. How can we get it out?'*

SOLUTION: Remove by scrubbing with white vinegar on a stiff brush. If the urine has penetrated into the timber, mix plaster of Paris and water to form a paste the consistency of peanut butter. For each cup of mixture, add 2 teaspoons of white vinegar. Place a 1 cm thick layer over the stain. Leave to completely dry and brush away with a broom.

Timber Decking

A friend of Shannon's bought a beautiful house situated on top of an escarpment, with massive timber decks from which to enjoy the vista. But because the place hadn't been lived in for 10 years, lots of birds and animals had taken up residence on the decks and they were badly stained. The solution involved some methylated spirits, tea, and lots of scrubbing. Prevention is always better than the cure!

Whether you should seal timber depends on the wood. Some timbers such as teak, oak and treated cedar can handle exposure to the elements. But if you don't want it to wear or change colour, treat it with tung oil or a good outdoor sealant. If you have logs from the 1970s get rid of them because most were treated with copper and arsenic and are toxic. Remove them with great care.

There are some significant differences between cleaning sealed and unsealed timber and if you mix them up, you'll be in trouble. Clean sealed timber with 3 teaspoons of dishwashing liquid in a bucket of warm water. Use a broom rather than a mop because it can reach into all the crevices.

Don't use dishwashing liquid on unsealed timber because

it dries it out and causes splinters. Unsealed timber should be cleaned with 1 bucket of warm water and 1 cup of white vinegar and a couple of drops of eucalyptus oil. The eucalyptus oil both cleans and feeds the timber. But don't use eucalyptus oil on painted surfaces because it's a paint stripper. Rinse a pot of strong tea (use 4–5 tea bags) in a bucket of hot water and mop the timber. This will help prevent it going that silvery colour.

Q 'The oil surface on my 3-year-old pine timber decking has gone black and grimy,' admits Bob. 'How can I clean it?'

PROBLEM: Dirty timber.
WHAT TO USE: Dishwashing liquid, black tea, warm water, 9 litre bucket, stiff broom.
HOW TO APPLY: Mix 1 teaspoon of dishwashing liquid and 1 cup of black tea in a bucket of warm water. Sweep the mixture over the timber with a broom. Rinse with water, then re-oil the timber.

Q 'We love spending time on the outside deck,' reports Paul. 'But so do some kookaburras. What's the best way to deal with kookaburra poo?'

PROBLEM: Kookaburra poo on timber.

WHAT TO USE: Stiff scrubbing brush, cake of bathroom soap, cold water, deck scrubber.

HOW TO APPLY: Kookaburras eat a lot of protein. Remove as much poo as possible with a brush. Rub a cake of bathroom soap and cold water over the bristles of a deck scrubber or brush and scrub over the stain. If the area is exposed to sunlight, shade it with an umbrella while you're cleaning because heat sets kookaburra poo. If the poo has penetrated the surface, you'll have to scrub for longer.

Bricks, Cement and Brick Pavers

To clean bricks and pavers, sprinkle with a little bicarb followed by a little white vinegar. As the mixture fizzes, sweep with a stiff broom. If there's any mould, mix ¼ teaspoon of oil of cloves in a 1 litre spray pack of water and spray over the area. Respray after 24 hours.

Clean pathways with 2 cups of water and 1 tablespoon of dishwashing liquid in a bucket of sand. Mix thoroughly, spread over the path and sweep with a stiff broom. Collect the sand and reuse it.

PROBLEM: Masonry beetle in the mortar.
WHAT TO USE: *WD-40*.
HOW TO APPLY: Use the extension nozzle on the *WD-40* and spray into the holes dug by the masonry beetle. This kills them.

Q 'Is there anything you can do if you've spilled methylated spirits on spray-on faux brick?' asks Amanda. 'It's left white scaly marks between the bricks.'

PROBLEM: Methylated spirits on faux brick.
WHAT TO USE: Surface insecticide spray; or methylated spirits, shellac, cloth.
HOW TO APPLY: The white marks indicate there's shellac or a similar kind of sealant in the faux brick. To get rid of the marks, use surface insecticide spray on them. It contains kerosene and will remove the marks. To seal the faux bricks, mix 1 part methylated spirits to 1 part shellac and apply with a cloth.

Q 'When it rained, our new spotted gum decking oozed brown stains on the sandstone coloured concrete composite pavers,' reports Jamie. 'What can I do to fix this?'

PROBLEM: Brown stains on pavers.
WHAT TO USE: Glycerine, deck scrubber or stiff scrubbing brush, eucalyptus oil, old toothbrush, dishwashing liquid, 9 litre bucket, water.
HOW TO APPLY: The brown stains are tannin marks and can be difficult to remove. Scrub with glycerine on a deck

scrubber or brush, leave to soak for 20 minutes and scrub again. If there's gum sap (it looks shiny and resinous), remove with eucalyptus oil on a toothbrush. Add 1 teaspoon of dishwashing liquid to a bucket of water and scrub with a deck scrubber or stiff brush. Repeat if the stain remains. There is a proprietary product that removes stains from pavers which is available from hardware stores. Wear protective clothing when using it. Tannin stains become harder to remove with time so tackle them as soon as possible.

TIP

If there are gum leaf stains, use eucalyptus oil on an old toothbrush to remove them.

Q 'I've got oil and petrol from a lawnmower that's leaked onto pavers and stained them,' reports Sam. 'How do I remove them?'

PROBLEM: Oil and petrol on pavers.
WHAT TO USE: Plaster of Paris, water, dishwashing liquid, broom.
HOW TO APPLY: Mix plaster of Paris and water to form a paste the consistency of peanut butter. For every cup of mixture add 1 teaspoon of dishwashing liquid and stir.

Spread a 1 cm thick layer over the stains and leave to dry. Sweep away with a broom; the oil and petrol will be absorbed into the mixture.

Q 'I've got cooking oil on my brick pavers,' reports Keith. 'How can I get it out?'

PROBLEM: Cooking oil on pavers.
WHAT TO USE: Plaster of Paris, water, dishwashing liquid, broom.
HOW TO APPLY: Mix plaster of Paris and water to form a paste the consistency of peanut butter. For every cup of mixture, add 1 teaspoon of dishwashing liquid. Place a 1 cm thick layer over the stain and leave to dry. Sweep away with a broom.

Q 'Our umbrella stand has left rust marks on our pavers,' reports Rachel. 'How can I get it out?'

PROBLEM: Rust on pavers.
WHAT TO USE: Talcum powder, disposable rubber gloves, *CLR/Ranex*, water.
HOW TO APPLY: Cover the rust with a sprinkle of talcum powder and, wearing rubber gloves, moisten the powder with *CLR* or *Ranex*. Leave for 2 hours and rinse with water. You may need to repeat.

PROBLEM: Bore water stain on brick.
WHAT TO USE: White vinegar, water, bucket, stiff broom.
HOW TO APPLY: Because bore water is high in mineral salts, it causes white marks on bricks. To remove, mix equal parts white vinegar and water in a bucket. Sweep over the bore water stain with a broom.

> **Q** 'Help!' exclaims Michael. 'Eggs were thrown on the front brick wall of our home. How do we remove them?'

PROBLEM: Egg on brick.
WHAT TO USE: Cake of bathroom soap, stiff brush, cold water, glycerine.
HOW TO APPLY: If you get to it before the egg fries, rub a cake of bathroom soap and cold water over a stiff brush and scrub over the egg until it's removed. Don't use dishwashing liquid or spray products. If the egg has set, wipe with glycerine on a stiff brush. Leave for 20 minutes. Then use a cake of bathroom soap, cold water and a stiff brush as described above.

TIP

Don't use hydrochloric acid as a cleaner. It strips the top surface and leaves orangey marks. If you have used it, neutralise with equal parts bicarb and water.

Glazed Tiles

To clean tiles, lightly sprinkle with bicarb, spray with white vinegar and, while fizzing, scrub with a broom. Don't overuse the bicarb and vinegar or you'll get residue. If you do, wipe with a clean damp cloth. Seal terracotta or Spanish quarry tiles with a proprietary product or make your own temporary sealant with 1 part *Aquadhere* or *Multibond* to 20 parts water. Apply with a mop. (Make sure you wash the mop with soap and water afterwards or it will stiffen.) If the tiles are particularly slippery, mop the floor then scatter a small amount of sand over the surface, then mop again. I did exactly this at my doctor's surgery because I was worried someone would slip on the sloping tiled path. It lasts for about 3 months.

Q 'I've got some lovely camellia plants and palms in my courtyard,' reports Shirley. 'But the petals and leaves are leaving dark stains on the ceramic tiles. Is there a solution?'

PROBLEM: Plant stains on tiles.
WHAT TO USE: Effervescent denture tablet, wet cloth; or bicarb, white vinegar, brush, mop.
HOW TO APPLY: Place 1 effervescent denture tablet on the stain and then place a wet cloth over the top and leave overnight. Alternatively, sprinkle bicarb and splash white

vinegar over the area with a brush, scrub and leave for two hours. Then rinse with a mop and water.

Q 'We've been meaning to seal our terracotta tiles,' says Pat. 'But, of course, I managed to spill some two-stroke fuel on them before we did. Is there anything I can do?'

PROBLEM: Fuel on unsealed tiles.
WHAT TO USE: Mask, bucket, *Bacquicil* or chlorine, brush, white vinegar.
HOW TO APPLY: Put on a mask and in a large bucket of water, mix 10 per cent of the amount of *Bacquicil* or chlorine you would normally use in the pool each day (see the directions on the packet). Then scrub the stain with a brush to remove the oil. Rinse thoroughly. Make sure you still have your mask on when you neutralise the chlorine with a splash of white vinegar. Then seal the tile as described above. You can also buy commercial sealers.

Q 'What's the best way to remove bark and eucalyptus leaf stains from ceramic patio tiles?' asks Jim.

PROBLEM: Bark and leaf stains on tiles.

WHAT TO USE: Glycerine, broom, dishwashing liquid, 9 litre bucket, water; eucalyptus oil.
HOW TO APPLY: This is a tannin stain. Apply a little glycerine directly to the stain and scrub with a broom. Add 1 teaspoon of dishwashing liquid to a bucket of water and sweep backwards and forwards over the stain with a broom. If the leaves are eucalyptus, add 1 tablespoon of eucalyptus oil to the solution.

Unsealed Tiles

Q 'Our outside balcony has unsealed matt black ceramic tiles,' says Neil. 'But some of the tiles are turning white-ish. The house is near the coast so there's salt in the air. Any suggestions?'

PROBLEM: White marks on tiles.
WHAT TO USE: White vinegar, stiff broom; or sweet almond oil, stiff broom, cloth; tile sealer.
HOW TO APPLY: The white markings could be from salt, lime scale build-up or glass cancer. If it's from salt or lime scale, wash with white vinegar on a broom. If this doesn't work, it's glass cancer, which means the surface has been damaged. To deal with this, wipe with sweet almond oil on a stiff broom and polish with a cloth. Seal with a good quality tile sealer.

Stone and Sandstone

The best way to clean stone and sandstone is with the pool-cleaning product *Algene*. *Algene* is an alternative to chlorine and doesn't kill plants like chlorine does. Use 1 cap of *Algene* per bucket of water and apply with a broom. Leave it for a couple of hours then rinse with water. Add a couple of drops of oil of cloves to the rinse water to inhibit mould, or add yoghurt to encourage mould and mosses.

PROBLEM: Paint splashes on sandstone.
WHAT TO USE: Methylated spirits, stiff brush; or turpentine, stiff brush; or methylated spirits, cloth, brush; or cloth, soap.
HOW TO APPLY: If the paint is water-based, put methylated spirits on the end of a stiff brush and work out the paint. If the paint is oil-based, use turpentine the same way. If the stain is old, leave a methylated spirits soaked cloth on water-based paint for a while then scrub it with a brush. If the paint is oil-based, soak a cloth in hot water and soap and place it over the paint first.

Q 'I've got some purple droppings on my sandstone patio,' reports Shelly. 'I think it's from a bird. Can I get rid of them?'

PROBLEM: Bird or possum droppings on sandstone.

WHAT TO USE: White spirits, cotton ball, damp rag.
HOW TO APPLY: The droppings could be from a bird or possum and, in most cases, will fade in sunlight over time. The purple comes from berry juice and can be removed with white spirits. Dab it on with a cotton ball. Then rinse with a damp rag.

Q 'We moved our barbecue recently,' says Robin, 'but some of the fat from the drip tray fell onto our coloured sandstone pavers. How can we get it off?'

PROBLEM: Oil/fat on sandstone pavers.
WHAT TO USE: Mask, swimming pool chlorine, scrubbing brush, white vinegar.
HOW TO APPLY: The fumes are very strong so wear a mask. Mix ¼ tablet of swimming pool chlorine in a bucket of water. Apply this mixture to the stain and scrub with a brush. Neutralise with white vinegar, then rinse with water.

Concrete

Concrete is best cleaned with bicarb and white vinegar. Sprinkle the bicarb over the surface, splash the vinegar on top and scrub with a broom. Then rinse with water. Hydrochloric, or muriatic, acid is often suggested to clean concrete. I don't recommend this because it's toxic, difficult to use and can cause corrosion in bricks. To stop leaves staining the concrete and to make grease removal easier, seal concrete with a proprietary product or with a temporary sealant of 1 part *Aquadhere* to 20 parts water. Apply with a mop. Make sure you rinse your mop afterwards or it will stiffen.

PROBLEM: Ivy suckers stuck on concrete/brick.
WHAT TO USE: Heat gun, stiff brush.
HOW TO APPLY: Apply a heat gun to the suckers until they go hard. Allow them to cool and dry, then scrub them off with a stiff brush.

Q 'How can I remove battery rust stain from my concrete driveway?' asks Rob.

PROBLEM: Rust on concrete.
WHAT TO USE: White vinegar, deck scrubber or stiff broom, disposable rubber gloves, *CLR/Ranex*, water.
HOW TO APPLY: To remove battery acid (which is actually an alkaline), scrub with white vinegar on a deck scrubber or broom. Put on rubber gloves and sweep with *CLR* or *Ranex* on a broom and rinse with water.

PROBLEM: Fluorescent float paint on concrete.
WHAT TO USE: Non-iodised salt, water, cloth, ice-cubes, zip-lock bag, cake of bathroom soap, broom.

HOW TO APPLY: Mix 1 cup of salt with 1 cup of water and apply with a cloth. Place ice-cubes in a zip-lock bag and put on top of the stain and leave until the ice melts. Remove and rub a cake of bathroom soap over the bristles of a broom, add water and scrub over the stain. Repeat until removed.

Slate

Q 'I've got slate tiles,' says Harry. 'What's the best way to clean them?'

PROBLEM: Dirty slate.
WHAT TO USE: Bicarb, white vinegar, broom, water, non-iodised salt, marble wax.
HOW TO APPLY: Sprinkle on bicarb, followed by white vinegar and scrub with a broom, then rinse thoroughly with water. If mouldy, add 1 cup of salt to the rinse water. Seal with marble wax.

Stone

Q 'It looks as though wax has been splashed over my mother's headstone,' reports Valda. 'It's gone into the granite and left a grease mark on the stone about the size of a hand. Can you help?'

PROBLEM: Wax on granite.
WHAT TO USE: Tea tree oil, pantyhose, *Brasso*, cloth.

HOW TO APPLY: Scrub the wax stains with tea tree oil on a pair of pantyhose. You may need to repeat if the wax returns to the surface. If there are watermarks, rub with a little *Brasso* on a cloth. It will look worse before it looks better.

Q 'How do you remove graffiti on white marble?' asks Stephen.

PROBLEM: Graffiti on marble.
WHAT TO USE: White spirits, pantyhose; or plaster of Paris, methylated spirits; or rotten milk, damp cloth.
HOW TO APPLY: If the graffiti was applied with *Texta*, oil-based paint or spray paint, use white spirits polished on and off with a pair of pantyhose. If the graffiti is from water-based paint, mix plaster of Paris and water to the consistency of peanut butter. For every cup of mixture, add 1 teaspoon of methylated spirits. Paint a 1 cm thick layer over the stain and allow to dry, then brush away. If the graffiti is ink-based, place rotten milk solids over the stain. The ink will be absorbed into the solids. Remove and wipe clean with a damp cloth.

Metal

Q 'My powder-coated railings have become white and dullish,' reports Alan. 'What can I do?'

PROBLEM: Dull powder-coated rails.
WHAT TO USE: White vinegar, water, 2 x 1 litre spray packs, cloth, sunblock lotion, warm water.
HOW TO APPLY: The dullness is from sun damage. Mix equal parts white vinegar and water in a spray pack, spray over the stain and wipe with a cloth. Add 1 tablespoon of sunblock to a spray pack of warm water and lightly mist over the rail. The sunblock lotion protects the railing from further sun damage.

PROBLEM: Bird droppings on wrought iron.
WHAT TO USE: Glycerine, white vinegar, cold water, bucket, deck scrubber or stiff scrubbing brush, cake of bathroom soap.
HOW TO APPLY: Mix 1 teaspoon of glycerine, 1 teaspoon of white vinegar and 1 cup of cold water in a bucket. Scrub the mixture over the stains with a deck scrubber or brush and allow to dry. Rub a cake of bathroom soap over a deck scrubber or brush, dampen with cold water and scrub over the stain. Bird droppings are high in protein so use only cold water.

Doormats

I always have a mat at the front and back doors of the house. It's also a good idea to have mats on the inside to prevent dirt tracking into the house. If you don't want to use a mat inside, spray the carpet regularly with *Scotchgard*. It's also handy to have a shoe cupboard near the back door for dirty gumboots. Alternatively, go old-fashioned and use a boot scraper.

Outdoor Furniture

Most outdoor furniture is built to withstand the elements but, as with skin, it starts to look a bit shabby if damaged by the sun. When not in use, store underneath an umbrella or veranda.

Outdoor furniture can be made of sealed or unsealed timber, aluminium, glass, plastic, cane or polycarbonate.

To clean **sealed timber**, use a mild dishwashing liquid solution. Many outdoor settings are made of red cedar, which can be cleaned with water. Re-stain it every 3 years. Painted surfaces should be cleaned in a mild dishwashing liquid solution.

To clean **unsealed timber**, add 1 cup of white vinegar and a couple of drops of eucalyptus oil to a bucket of water and wipe with a cloth.

To clean **aluminium** settings, use bicarb and white vinegar. You could also try cold black tea! I discovered this recently when I accidentally spilt some tea over aluminium meshing and it came up like glass! Have one sponge with bicarb on it and another soaked in white vinegar. Press the vinegar sponge through the bicarb sponge and wipe. You can remove water marks the same way.

To clean **polycarbonate** or **plastic**, use a mild dishwashing liquid solution. Don't confuse polycarbonate with polyacetate. **Polyacetate** or **polyurethane** can be cleaned with *Brasso* but this cleaning method ruins polycarbonate. Don't risk it if you're not sure. If you have scratches, use whiting and glycerine. Mix them to the consistency of runny cream, then rub over the scratches with a silk cloth. It's best not to leave opaque polycarbonate in the sun because it becomes weak and a chair may collapse while you're sitting in it.

To clean **cane** and **wicker**, scrub with soap and water, leave in the sun to dry and seal with shellac or a good outdoor sealant. Spray the sealant on if possible with a plastic spray bottle. Clean the spray bottle with methylated spirits afterwards.

Some outdoor chairs are made of **shade cloth** and should be washed regularly with mild soapy water. Wash them after it rains because they collect mildew. Add a couple of drops of oil of cloves to the rinse water.

Where possible, keep outdoor cushions under cover when you're not using them. A potential hazard with outdoor furniture is the nasty surprises that take up residence under the table. Keep spiders away by regularly wiping some lemon oil on the underside of it.

PROBLEM: Outdoor furniture has gone grey in the sun.
WHAT TO USE: Strong solution of tea, varnish.
HOW TO APPLY: Wash it with a strong solution of tea before re-varnishing it.

PROBLEM: Rust on cast iron.
WHAT TO USE: White vinegar, wire brush, rust converter.
HOW TO APPLY: Loosen the rust with white vinegar then scrub with a wire brush. Then apply rust converter. This produces a hard surface that you can then repaint.

Q 'There's some salad dressing on our oil-finished table,' says Sandra. 'And I'm finding it difficult to remove. What can I do?'

PROBLEM: Salad dressing on oil-finished timber.
WHAT TO USE: Plaster of Paris, water, dishwashing liquid, broom, cold black tea, cloth.
HOW TO APPLY: Mix plaster of Paris and water to form a paste the consistency of peanut butter. For each cup of paste add 1 teaspoon of dishwashing liquid. Cover the stain with a 1 cm thick layer of paste, allow to dry and brush off with a broom. Before re-oiling, wipe the timber with cold black tea on a cloth and allow to dry.

Q 'Over time, the white vinyl cushions on our outdoor setting have turned a red-brown colour,' says Lisa. 'Is there anything you would recommend to clean them?'

PROBLEM: Stained white vinyl.
WHAT TO USE: *CLR/Ranex*, water, cloth, disposable rubber gloves; or glycerine, talcum powder, cloth.
HOW TO APPLY: The stain could be from mineral discolouration or sun damage. If it's been caused by mineral discolouration, wearing disposable rubber gloves, mix 1 part *CLR* or *Ranex* to 5 parts water, place on a cloth and wipe over the stains. If it's been caused by sun damage, it's difficult to repair. Reduce the staining by polishing with a paste of equal parts glycerine and talcum powder applied with a cloth. Rub off with a cloth.
PREVENTION: Keep outdoor cushions under cover when not using them.

Q 'We were entertaining outside,' says Sally, 'and managed to get both red wine and citronella candle wax on a cotton tablecloth. What can be done?'

PROBLEM: Red wine and wax on cotton.

WHAT TO USE: White vinegar, cloth, glycerine (red wine); freezer/ice-cubes, zip-lock bag, plastic knife, paper towel, iron, tea tree oil (wax).

HOW TO APPLY: Remove the wine stain first by wiping with a cloth wrung out in white vinegar. If the stain is stubborn, add 2 drops of glycerine directly to the stain, leave for 20 minutes, then wipe with white vinegar on a cloth. To remove the wax, place the tablecloth in the freezer. If it won't fit in the freezer, put ice-cubes in a zip-lock bag and place over the wax. When the wax is cold, remove as much as possible with a plastic knife. Put several layers of paper towel on either side of the stain and run a hot iron over the top. Repeat until all the wax is absorbed into the paper towel. If a greasy mark remains, wipe on tea tree oil with your fingers, then wash normally.

Umbrellas, Awnings snd Shade Cloth

These are essential in the Australian summer. The main issue with umbrellas, awnings and shade cloth is mould. Clean canvas with 2 cups of salt added to a small bucket of water and apply with a brush or broom. Leave to dry then rinse the salt away.

Clean plastic with water. If it's very dirty, add some dishwashing liquid to the water.

Raffia umbrellas attract bugs so hose or wash them regularly and spray with surface insecticide.

Metal poles can be cleaned with graphite. Rust can be cleaned with glycerine.

Plastic attachments should be cleaned with glycerine.

PROBLEM: Mildew on canvas.
WHAT TO USE: Strong salt solution, bucket, brush or broom, oil of cloves, spray pack.
HOW TO APPLY: Scrub the canvas with 2 cups of salt added to a small bucket of water and apply with a brush or broom. Leave it to dry. There should be a lot of salt on the surface. Scrub it again to help loosen any remaining mildew. Hose or wash it clean in a sunny spot. Then spray the canvas with a few drops of oil of cloves and water in a spray pack. This will prevent the mildew returning.

Caring for rubber

Never leave anything made of rubber sitting in the sunshine. This includes flippers, masks, trays or seats. To prevent rubber perishing, rub it with talcum powder after cleaning. If it has perished, rub some salt on the perished area then dust with talcum powder. The salt acts as a sander.

Barbecues

Barbecue hotplates are made of cast iron and should be cleaned after each use. It's preferable to do this while the barbecue is still warm. We know it's the last thing you want to do, but it's important—a grotty barbecue doesn't produce tasty food. Pour a little oil over it then wipe with a newspaper. Sprinkle some bicarb and splash over some white vinegar. Then scrub with a paper towel. Give the hotplate a light oiling once it's cooled, to prevent rusting. If the stains are really stubborn, try bicarb and white vinegar then apply sugar and white vinegar to a hot hotplate. Keep the heat on until the vinegar completely evaporates. Then oil the barbecue. Turn it off and wipe down with a paper towel. The reason sugar helps is that it bonds with the dirt and burns. The oil goes under the sugar and lifts it off. This is how they clean hotplates at McDonalds!

TIP

Spread barbecue ash around plants such as azaleas, camellias or citrus. They love it.

Before firing it up, sprinkle sand over pavers around the barbecue to absorb any oil splatter. If you do get oil splatter, see page 579.

To stop the oils in fish staining the barbecue and leaving a smell, place a piece of aluminium foil on the hotplate and cook the fish on top of it. Wrap aluminium foil around the fish to steam it.

Flyscreens

Flyscreens keep bugs out of your home but they can be dirt traps too, so clean removable ones on both sides with a vacuum cleaner using the brush attachment and wipe with lemon oil to keep spiders at bay.

To clean fixed screens, close the window or door, dampen the screen with water and sweep with a soft broom. With soft flyscreens, use a *Slurpex* instead of a broom.

To fix a ripped flyscreen, see page 250 in *How To Be Comfy*.

Under and Around the House

Q 'I live in an old house,' says Renee. 'When we have lots of rain, the house smells like wet carpet and is musty. How can I prevent the musty smell?'

PROBLEM: Musty smell in house.
WHAT TO USE: Bicarb, lavender oil, oil of cloves, water, 1 litre spray pack, long-nozzled spray pack.
HOW TO APPLY: The smell is from mould spores in the soil under the house. If you have carpet, sprinkle with bicarb before vacuuming. Add 1 teaspoon of lavender oil and

¼ teaspoon of oil of cloves to a spray pack of water and lightly mist over the carpet. Leave for 10 minutes and vacuum. If you can, pull up the carpet and replace it with floorboards. To get under the house, use a long-nozzled spray pack and add ¼ teaspoon of oil of cloves per litre of water. Spray through the vents at the side of the house to reach the soil underneath.

Q 'We get our water directly from the river,' reports Stuart. 'At the moment, the water has blue-green algae in it which has stained our vinyl-clad house. The cladding is a cream vinyl with a woodwork groove mark in the texture.'

PROBLEM: Blue-green algae on vinyl cladding.
WHAT TO USE: Bicarb, water, cloth, methylated spirits, glycerine, white vinegar, water, 1 litre spray pack; 3 per cent hydrogen peroxide, pantyhose, broom.
HOW TO APPLY: Mix equal parts bicarb and water and wipe with a cloth. Combine 1 cup of methylated spirits, 1 teaspoon of glycerine, 1 cup of white vinegar and 2 cups of water in a spray pack. Spray the mixture over the bicarb and, while fizzing, wipe with a cloth. If there's grey staining, add 1 teaspoon of 3 per cent hydrogen peroxide to the spray pack. For a large area, put pantyhose over the head of a broom and scrub the area after it's been sprayed with the mixture.

TIP

When cleaning hard-to-reach light bulbs, place a paper cup over the end of a broom handle and secure with masking tape. Place paper towel inside the cup and wipe over light bulbs.

The Garden

Shannon loves spending time in the garden. And she's particular about avoiding toxins. Her preference is for natural rather than chemical solutions. For example:

To keep birds away, hang old CDs in the trees.

To grow moss in the garden put a handful of moss into a bowl with 1 teaspoon of sugar and 1 can of beer and mix with a hand-cranked cake beater until all the ingredients resemble a chunky soup. Spread the mixture over rocks or any ground where you want moss to grow and don't water it for at least 24 hours. Then water it very lightly, making sure you don't wash the moss away. To encourage algae and lichen, paint everything with yoghurt.

PROBLEM: Aphids.
WHAT TO USE: Dishwashing liquid, cooking oil, water, spray bottle.
HOW TO APPLY: Thoroughly mix 1 tablespoon of dishwashing liquid and 1 cup of cooking oil. Add 2–3 teaspoons of this

mixture to 1 cup of water, put it into a spray bottle and spray your plants.

PROBLEM: Snails and slugs getting into pot plants.
WHAT TO USE: *Vaseline*.
HOW TO APPLY: Rub some *Vaseline* each month on the outside of pot plants.

PROBLEM: Mildew on terracotta pots.
WHAT TO USE: *Aquadhere*, water, oil of cloves.
HOW TO APPLY: To stop mildew forming on terracotta pots, seal with a mixture of 1 part *Aquadhere*, 3 parts water and a couple of drops of oil of cloves. It should be the consistency of runny cream. Paint it over the pots and let them dry inside and out.

Snail-proofing your vegetable patch

If slugs and snails are eating your vegetable patch, crush a whole clove of garlic and steep it in 1 litre of water for a couple of hours. Strain it, then spray the liquid on your vegetables. Another way to stop them is to put a circle of sand or sawdust around each vegetable. Snails and slugs don't like either so they won't cross them to eat the vegetables. To make a trap for snails, cut an orange in half, eat the flesh and half-fill the two orange skins with beer. Put these near the vegie patch and the snails will climb in and won't be able to get out. You could also persuade children to collect them in return for pocket money.

GARDEN PONDS

If you have a garden pond, stick water hyacinths in it. They clean the water, are easily pulled out with a rake and make a great fertiliser.

STATUES

Statues can be large or small. If you want to encourage moss to grow on them, paint them with a mixture of skim milk and yoghurt. If you can, use a yoghurt containing acidophilus. To inhibit moss and mould, paint with 1 part oil of cloves to 50 parts water.

GARDENING TOOLS

Leaf blowers are the jet-skis of the land—the latest gadgets to wake up the country on a Sunday morning. Along with the lawnmower, whipper snipper and other equipment, they should be stored in a cool, dark place. Protect all blades against rust by wiping them with machine oil applied with a cloth. Wipe the outside of the lawnmower, whipper snipper, etc, with a mild dishwashing liquid solution.

Don't throw old hedge clippers away. Pull them apart and recycle them into trowels, a hole digger or to cut grass edges around concrete.

WATER FEATURES

Q 'I have a glazed fountain', says David. 'And there's water staining on it. What should I do?'

PROBLEM: Water stain on glazed fountain.
WHAT TO USE: Bicarb, white vinegar, nylon brush.
HOW TO APPLY: Remove water from the fountain, sprinkle with equal parts bicarb then white vinegar and, while fizzing, scrub with a nylon brush. Refill fountain with water.

Q 'My water feature has a brown stain on it,' reports Kelvin. 'How can I get it off?'

PROBLEM: Brown stain on water feature.
WHAT TO USE: Glycerine, eucalyptus oil, old toothbrush.
HOW TO APPLY: It's likely to be a tannin stain from gum leaves. Remove water from the water feature. Mix 1 teaspoon of glycerine with ½ teaspoon of eucalyptus oil and scrub the marks with a toothbrush until removed.

Q 'We've got a fibreglass baptismal font at our church,' reports Ken. 'How can I clean the rust water marks from it?'

PROBLEM: Rust on fibreglass.

WHAT TO USE: Bicarb, white vinegar, old toothbrush; or glycerine, *Gumption*, old toothbrush.
HOW TO APPLY: Sprinkle with a little bicarb followed by a little white vinegar (equal parts) and, while fizzing, rub with a toothbrush. If the stain is really stubborn, mix equal parts glycerine with *Gumption* and scrub with a toothbrush.

Q 'How do I remove algae from a birdbath?' asks Val.

PROBLEM: Algae in birdbath.
WHAT TO USE: Pantyhose, non-iodised salt.
HOW TO APPLY: Remove water from the birdbath, then wipe over the algae with a rolled up pair of pantyhose. To prevent the problem, add a pinch of salt to each litre of clean water. The birds won't be deterred by the tiny amount of salt.

Swimming Pool

If it's hot and you've got a pool, everyone wants to be your friend. But despite the range of accessories, cleaning a pool can be painstaking. If it's all a bit too much for you, hire a professional pool cleaner.

There are a few things that need regular maintenance. Firstly, make sure the water level is high enough.

Maintaining the right pH level is also very important. You should already have a testing kit but if you don't, you can buy them. Be aware that chlorine is affected by the sun. The more sunny days there are, the more chlorine you'll need to use. If you don't like chlorine, try *Algene* or *Bacquacil*.

Skim the top of the pool regularly to collect leaves so they don't clog the filter. In fact, don't leave anything in the pool because it could get caught in the filter.

Clean the tiles with *Gumption* and a stiff brush. Create traction on slate surrounds by mixing 1 part *Aquadhere*, 20 parts water and 1 cup of sand. Clear potentially slippery moss from stones with chlorine or *Bacquacil*.

Make sure the pool is fenced and the lock childproof. Keep the lock oiled because chlorine can cause corrosion. It's a good idea to have a sign illustrating how to perform CPR in case of an emergency.

Keep sunscreen and spare towels near the pool. That way you won't have wet feet tramping through the house.

Q 'My swimming pool has a stain all around the wall edge,' reports John. 'The wall's made of pebblecrete.'

PROBLEM: Stain around swimming pool.
WHAT TO USE: Stiff brush, *Gumption*.

HOW TO APPLY: It's painstaking but it works. Get a stiff brush, put some *Gumption* on it and scrub the stain off bit by bit.

Q 'We've got a fibreglass-lined pool,' reports Tony. 'And there are rust marks. What can we do?'

PROBLEM: Rust marks on fibreglass.
WHAT TO USE: Biro eraser, disposable rubber gloves, *CLR/Ranex*, cloth.
HOW TO APPLY: Rub the rust with a biro eraser. If this doesn't work, you'll need to empty the pool and, wearing rubber gloves, apply *CLR* or *Ranex* to the rust with a cloth.

Spas and Saunas

Bacteria can thrive in spas. Backflush with white vinegar after every second use and change the water regularly. Maintain the right chemical level, which is generally higher than that for swimming pools. Check the manufacturer's instructions. If the spa has a timber surround, add a couple of drops of oil of cloves to the rinse water to keep mildew at bay.

Maintain the heating and filter units of a sauna by cleaning regularly according to the manufacturer's instructions. Add a few drops of oil of cloves to keep mildew away and add your favourite herbs to the hot stones for a super sauna.

> **TIP**
>
> *If there's sunblock clogging the spa filter, backflush with white vinegar.*

Sport and Camping

Many people have exercise bikes and treadmills at home and you can get your heart-rate up just cleaning them. Wipe regularly with a damp cloth, clean plastic surfaces with a little glycerine on a cloth and wipe rubber in a salt solution (1 cup of salt per 9 litre bucket of water) on a cloth.

Q 'How do I remove mould on leather boxing gloves?' asks Alicia.

PROBLEM: Mould on leather.
WHAT TO USE: Oil of cloves, baby oil, cloth.
HOW TO APPLY: Mix ¼ teaspoon of oil of cloves and 1 tablespoon of baby oil, dab a little on a cloth and rub over the gloves. Save the mixture for next time.

Q 'My white soccer boots are now covered in black stud marks,' says Frank. 'Can I get the marks off?'

PROBLEM: Black marks on leather.

WHAT TO USE: Glycerine, pantyhose, damp pantyhose.
HOW TO APPLY: Wipe a dab of glycerine over the marks with rolled up pantyhose. Remove with clean damp pantyhose.

Q 'Our tennis court has synthetic grass,' reports Anne. 'And there are big patches of mould in all the corners. What do you suggest?'

PROBLEM: Mould on synthetic grass.
WHAT TO USE: Swimming pool chlorine tablet, 9 litre bucket, warm water, stiff broom.
HOW TO APPLY: Wear protective clothing and be careful not to splash the mixture on your clothes. Add ¼ tablet of swimming pool chlorine to a bucket of warm water and allow to dissolve completely. Rub the mouldy area with a broom and leave for 15 minutes. Rinse with water. Don't use oil of cloves on synthetic grass because it can break it down.

Q 'Flying fox poo landed on my new canvas tent,' says Nathan. 'What should I do?'

PROBLEM: Flying fox poo on canvas.
WHAT TO USE: Cake of bathroom soap, cold water, stiff scrubbing brush; non-iodised salt, 9 litre bucket, water, cloth.

HOW TO APPLY: Flying fox poo is high in tannins and protein. Remove by dipping a cake of bathroom soap in cold water, rub over the bristles of stiff brush and scrub. When the stain is removed, make the canvas waterproof by mixing 1 cup of salt in a bucket of water. Wipe the salt solution over the canvas with a cloth.

Q 'On a recent camping holiday, I got diesel on my swag,' says Ron. 'What do you suggest?'

PROBLEM: Diesel on swag.
WHAT TO USE: Methylated spirits, cloth, bath, blood-heat water, dishwashing liquid, salt, sunshine.
HOW TO APPLY: Wipe the stain with methylated spirits on a cloth. Fill a bath with blood-heat water and 2 teaspoons of dishwashing liquid. Place the swag in the bath and walk up and down on it. Add 1 cup of salt to the water. Rinse in blood-heat water and dry in sunshine. Turn regularly to prevent clumping in the swag padding.

Pets

We know it's obvious, but make sure pet bedding is kept clean. Food bowls are easier to clean if you wipe them with a little cheap cooking oil on a cloth. Regularly change kitty litter and wipe the tray with bicarb before replacing kitty litter.

Pet baskets and kennels should be elevated so air can circulate. Put some bricks underneath or build some stilts. Hand wash all pet bedding regularly, adding no more than 2 drops of oil of pennyroyal to a bucket of water to prevent fleas. Note that oil of pennyroyal should only be used as directed as it can be harmful to pregnant women and pets. Remember one drop means one drop. Oil of pennyroyal kills existing fleas and deters new ones. You can also add no more than 2 drops to the pet's bath. Spray the inside of kennels and baskets with a mixture of 2 drops of oil of pennyroyal to 1 litre of water in a spray bottle. Again, this shouldn't be used by pregnant women or near pregnant pets.

To prevent cats coming into the yard, spread *Vicks VapoRub* onto a few stones. Turn them over to prevent sun and rain damage.

To stop dogs digging in a particular area, bury some of their poo in the spot and they'll stay away. To encourage digging, leave bones in a particular spot.

How to wash a cat

Do this regularly if there are people in the house who are allergic to cats. With this cleaning technique, you won't be left with scratch marks across your face! Secure a tea towel over the cat's head and front legs, wrapping it firmly. It won't be able to scratch and the darkness calms it. Clean the back with a pet brush. Then wrap the tea towel over the cat's back legs and wipe the front with a washer going from front to back. Don't use a brush because it irritates them. Use a pet shampoo over the entire cat and apply a mixture of no more than 2 drops of oil of pennyroyal mixed with 1 litre of water in a spray bottle. Note that oil of pennyroyal should only be used as directed as it can be harmful to pregnant women and pets. Remember one drop means one drop. Pamper the cat afterwards so it has a positive association with washing.

Q '**What's the best way to clean and deodorise a dog kennel?' asks Marina.**

PROBLEM: Smelly dog kennel.
WHAT TO USE: Oil of cloves, dried mint, hot water, 1 litre spray pack, pantyhose.
HOW TO APPLY: Mix ¼ teaspoon of oil of cloves, 2 tablespoons of dried mint and 1 litre of hot water. Allow to cool. Add to a spray pack and spray every surface. Wipe with pantyhose. The oil of cloves kills mould spores and the mint kills fleas. Do this once a month.

Pests

It's a bit harder to keep pests at bay in the outdoors. Here are some natural solutions to deter common barbecue stoppers.

MOSQUITOES

Lavender oil is a great mozzie deterrent. Add a few drops to a cloth and wipe around the chairs and table. Alternatively, place 1 teaspoon of lavender oil in a 1 litre spray pack of water and lightly mist around the area. You can also rub lavender oil directly over your wrists. Plant lavender, basil, pennyroyal, *Pelargonium citrosum* (citronella plant) and tansy around entertainment areas.

SPIDERS

Spiders hate lemon oil. Add a couple of drops of lemon oil or rub the outside of a lemon over the head of a broom and sweep over areas where spiders lurk. Don't forget bins, shed shelves and tools. Repeat every 3 months. To access spiders under the house, mix ¼ teaspoon of lemon oil in a 1 litre spray pack of water and squirt through vents and access areas.

FLIES

To kill flies, put white or black pepper (not red or green) onto a piece of paper painted with sugar and water.

The sugar attracts the flies and the pepper kills them. Pepper contains piperine which is a toxin to flies.

ANTS

Mix equal parts powdered borax and icing sugar for sweet ants or equal parts powdered borax and grated parmesan cheese for savoury ants. Or find the nest and pour boiling water down it. Warning: Borax is toxic and should not be placed where children or pets could eat it.

SNAILS/SLUGS

Wipe petroleum jelly (*Vaseline*) around areas where snails and slugs wander—they won't cross it. Renew every couple of months. Protect plants by crushing a clove of garlic in a 1 litre spray pack of water. Allow to steep for 2 hours, strain and spray over plants. To make a trap for snails, cut an orange in half, remove the flesh and half-fill the two orange skins with beer. The snails will be attracted by the beer, climb in and won't be able to get out.

FRUIT FLIES

Use a glass jar with a plastic or metal lid. Punch holes at 2 mm intervals on the lid and half fill the jar with 1 tablespoon of *Vegemite* and ½ cup of white vinegar. Tie string around the lip of the jar and hang from a tree or branch. Fruit flies are attracted to the yeast and acetic acid mix, fly into the jar through the holes and become trapped.

Garbage Area

When Shannon was at infants school, they had a goat that ate the garbage! With contemporary bins, deter flies, mosquitoes and dogs by adding a couple of drops of lavender oil to a paper towel and wiping it around the edge of the bin. To keep fleas and mites away, place no more than 2 drops of oil of pennyroyal on a cloth and wipe around the edge of the bin. Note that oil of pennyroyal should only be used as directed as it can be harmful to pregnant women and pets. Remember one drop means one drop. Lemon oil will keep spiders away. To preserve the environment, try to avoid using plastic bags. Instead, put rubbish directly into the bin or wrap it in newspaper.

Garage and Driveway

Two of the best ways to clean oil stains and other scum off a driveway or garage floor is to scrub with bicarb and white vinegar or spray it with diluted chlorine. Leave it until almost dry, then give it a good sweep with a nylon broom before hosing or washing it down. If you have plants nearby, substitute *Algene* or *Bacquacil* for the chlorine. You can also clean oil stains with the carbonated drink *Coca Cola*. If you do, wash the area well or ants will be attracted.

Cars

Cars are vulnerable to spills and stains especially if you allow food and drink in them. If you have to suddenly apply the brakes and that café latte goes all over the seat and floor, the milk will really begin to stink, so fix the spill as soon as you can. Clean upholstery and carpet in the car as you would the same fabrics in the house. To add another layer of protection, spray *Scotchgard* each time you vacuum. Clean plastics with glycerine on a cloth and keep an old pair of pantyhose in the glovebox to clean windows. To protect the heel of your shoe when you're driving, either fix a piece of towel to the mat, or have a dedicated pair of driving shoes.

PROBLEM: Scratches in the dashboard or on plastic surfaces.
WHAT TO USE: Glycerine, cloth.
HOW TO APPLY: Add 1 part glycerine to 5 parts warm water then wipe over the surface with a cloth. Glycerine will also give the surface a good sheen.

PROBLEM: Sticky adhesive on car window.
WHAT TO USE: Clingwrap, dishwashing liquid.
HOW TO APPLY: Tear off a piece of clingwrap larger than the size of the adhesive. Mix 1 part dishwashing liquid and 20 parts water and spray on the clingwrap then place this over the sticker. Leave it for about five minutes or until the

adhesive comes loose. Then peel off the cling wrap. The adhesive will peel off, too.

Q 'I've got the smell of mould in my car,' says Pete. 'I think the carpet must have got wet at some stage. What do you suggest?'

PROBLEM: Mould smell in car.
WHAT TO USE: Oil of cloves.
HOW TO APPLY: The smell comes from the bacteria and mould and the best way to fix it is with sunshine. If possible, take the carpet out of the car and leave it in the sun. If you can't, park the car on a funny angle or slope and leave the doors open so sun gets in. Or wipe the carpet with a little oil of cloves.

Q 'I managed to spill a cup of coffee in the car the other morning,' says Bev. 'There's a nasty sour smell now.'

PROBLEM: Coffee spill in car.
WHAT TO USE: Cake of bathroom soap, cold water, damp cloth, glycerine, cloth, talcum powder, vacuum cleaner.
HOW TO APPLY: Rub the stain with a cake of bathroom soap dipped in cold water, then wipe with a damp cloth. Rub with a dab of glycerine on a cloth and sprinkle with talcum

powder. Allow to dry, then vacuum. The soap will remove the milk, the glycerine will remove the coffee and the talcum powder will absorb the glycerine.

Q 'I need to change the electronic toll tag on my car window,' says Arthur. 'And I can't remove the plastic base. What do you suggest?'

PROBLEM: Glue/plastic base on windscreen.
WHAT TO USE: Tea tree oil, thin screwdriver (or similar), heat gun.
HOW TO APPLY: Work tea tree oil into the glue at the back of the plastic base and leave for 24 hours. Carefully work a screwdriver behind the base and lever it away from the glass. If it doesn't come away, aim a heat gun over the plastic. Only use the heat gun in short bursts or you could crack your windscreen.

Q 'Our newly acquired second-hand car has a very, very strong perfumed smell,' reports Meredith. 'It's giving me migraines. What can I do?'

PROBLEM: Perfumed smell in car.
WHAT TO USE: Black tea, cold water, lavender oil, 1 litre spray pack, cloth, bicarb, vacuum cleaner, damp tea bag.
HOW TO APPLY: Mix 1 cup of cold black tea, 2 cups of cold

water and ¼ teaspoon of lavender oil in a spray pack. Spray onto a cloth and wipe over hard surfaces. Lightly mist over the upholstery, dust with bicarb and leave for 20 minutes. Then vacuum thoroughly. If the perfume has been absorbed into the air-conditioning and venting system, hang a damp tea bag near the air intake. Deodorisers are often placed under seats (or hung from the rear-vision mirror), so check there and remove them.

Q 'What's the best way to remove the smell of cigarettes from a car?' asks David.

PROBLEM: Cigarette smell in car.
WHAT TO USE: Bicarb, vacuum cleaner, disposable rubber gloves, cigarette ash (yes, that's right), white vinegar, cloth, damp cloth.
HOW TO APPLY: Sprinkle bicarb over the upholstery, leave for 20 minutes, then vacuum. Put on rubber gloves and mix equal parts cigarette ash and white vinegar. Wipe the mixture over hard surfaces with a cloth and wipe clean with a damp cloth. You'll also need to remove smoke from the air-conditioning and venting system. To clean the filtration mat, wash with equal parts cigarette ash and white vinegar, leave for 5 minutes and rinse thoroughly with water. Allow to dry before replacing. If you can't remove it, see a specialist for a replacement pad.

Q 'How can I clean sweaty stains from the fabric of my car seats?' asks Jo.

PROBLEM: Sweat stains on car seats.
WHAT TO USE: Bran ball, vacuum cleaner.
HOW TO APPLY: Make a bran ball (see page 138), rub back and forth across the seats to remove the stains, then vacuum.

Q 'There's butter on the back seat of my car,' says Debbie. 'How can I get it out?'

PROBLEM: Butter in car.
WHAT TO USE: Dishwashing liquid, old toothbrush, damp cloth, paper towel.
HOW TO APPLY: Put a couple of drops of dishwashing liquid on your fingers and massage into the stain until it feels like jelly. If the stain is stubborn, scrub with a toothbrush, wipe with a damp cloth and dry with paper towel.

Q 'How do I fluff up woollen sheepskin car seat covers?' asks Jo.

PROBLEM: Cleaning sheepskin car seat covers.
WHAT TO USE: Unprocessed wheat bran, pillowcase, stiff hairbrush; or cheap shampoo, tub, blood-heat water, stiff hairbrush; or bran ball.

HOW TO APPLY: Place 1 kg of unprocessed wheat bran in a pillowcase and add the sheepskin covers. Secure the top and give a really good shake. Remove the sheepskin covers from the pillowcase and shake out the bran. Brush covers with a hairbrush. If they won't fit in a pillowcase, wash in 1 teaspoon of shampoo in a tub of blood-heat water. Rinse in blood-heat water and dry in the shade. As they dry, brush with a hairbrush. If the car seat covers can't be removed, rub with a bran ball (see page 138).

Q 'I'm a truck driver with a *BigFoot* ute,' says Joe. 'What's the best way to clean alloy wheels?'

PROBLEM: Dirty alloy wheels.
WHAT TO USE: Pantyhose, cold black tea.
HOW TO APPLY: Dip a pair of pantyhose in cold black tea and polish over the alloy.

TIP

To make your windscreen wipers last longer, mix 1 cup of salt in a 9 litre bucket of hot water and immerse the wipers for 5 minutes. Allow to dry and wipe with a dab of glycerine on a cloth.

Q 'How can I remove pizza smells from the car after collecting takeaway?' asks Brad.

PROBLEM: Pizza smell in car.
WHAT TO USE: Bicarb, vacuum cleaner.
HOW TO APPLY: The smell is from an oily residue in the steam which is absorbed by the upholstery. To remove, sprinkle bicarb over the upholstery, leave for 20 minutes and vacuum. To avoid the problem, put the piping hot pizza box in a paper bag so the steam can't escape.

Q 'How can I remove chocolate milk stains from my car seat?' asks Susie.

PROBLEM: Chocolate milk in car.
WHAT TO USE: Cake of bathroom soap, cold water, old toothbrush, paper towel.
HOW TO APPLY: Dip a cake of bathroom soap in cold water and scribble over the stain as though using a crayon. Scrub with a toothbrush and dry with paper towel. Chocolate milk contains protein so use only cold water.

Q 'A mouse died in the ventilation system of our car,' reports Trudy. 'We removed the mouse but can't get rid of the terrible smell. Help!'

PROBLEM: Dead mouse smell in car.
WHAT TO USE: 2 small containers or trays, bicarb, tea bag, lavender oil.
HOW TO APPLY: This is a tough one! Keep the windows open (when you can). Fill 2 containers or trays with bicarb and place under the front seats of the car. Dampen a tea bag with lavender oil and hang in front of the air-conditioning intake vents. Replace each day until the smell goes.

Q 'There's flying fox poo on my garage roller door,' reports Charlie. 'How can I get it off?'

PROBLEM: Flying fox poo on powder-coated steel.
WHAT TO USE: Dishwashing liquid, warm water, pantyhose, glycerine, cloth.
HOW TO APPLY: Apply a couple of drops of dishwashing liquid and a little warm water to the stain with a pair of pantyhose. Follow by wiping with a dab of glycerine on a cloth.

Caravans and Boats

Some caravans and boats could be considered houses in their own right. We won't include a comprehensive guide to their upkeep but here are a couple of real-life problems.

Q 'I've got a pop-top caravan and the nylon zippers have become stuck,' says Rick.

PROBLEM: Sticky nylon zippers.
WHAT TO USE: Glycerine; or lead pencil or graphite.
HOW TO APPLY: Wipe the zipper with glycerine. For metal zippers, use a lead pencil or graphite.

Q Val's husband and son are going away for a boys' holiday in their caravan. But they've left her with the job of fixing the scratches on the polycarbonate dome skylight. 'We were advised to clean them with a particular product, but it scratched them. Are there any solutions?'

PROBLEM: Scratches in polycarbonate.
WHAT TO USE: Whiting, glycerine, silk cloth or *Ceramicoat*.
HOW TO APPLY: It's very difficult to take scratches out. One option is to mix whiting and glycerine to a thin consistency, then rub it over the scratches with a silk cloth. The deep marks will be there permanently. Another option is to reglaze the surface. Try a product called *Ceramicoat*. Do a test patch first, and if it works, reglaze the dome in very thin coats. Spray one coat, leave it for 5 minutes, spray another coat and then leave for 24 hours. Repeat if necessary. To prevent scratching, use

car wax but make sure it doesn't have a cutting compound.

Q 'We've got a boat and the inside is covered with a white nylon carpet,' says Lynn, 'but it's starting to stain black and mildewy. What can we do? It's really hard to put new carpet in a boat!'

PROBLEM: Mildew in boat carpet.
WHAT TO USE: Pool chlorine, bucket, water.
HOW TO APPLY: Because the carpet is nylon, wash it with diluted pool chlorine. Use ¼ of a tablet of chlorine to a bucket of water.

Q 'How do I remove mould spots on orange synthetic life jackets?' asks Brad.

PROBLEM: Mouldy synthetic life jackets.
WHAT TO USE: Non-iodised salt, 9 litre bucket, water, stiff brush.
HOW TO APPLY: Mix 1 kg of salt in a bucket of water, add jackets and soak for 20 minutes. Remove and give a good scrub with a brush. Leave to dry without rinsing the salt off. When dry, brush the salt crust away and the mould will come with it.

Q 'I've got seagull droppings all over my canvas boat cover,' complains Jeff. 'What can I do?'

PROBLEM: Seagull poo on canvas.
WHAT TO USE: Cake of bathroom soap, cold water, stiff brush.
HOW TO APPLY: Dip a cake of bathroom soap in cold water and scribble over the stain as though using a crayon. Scrub with a brush and rinse in cold water.

Q 'I've got black sediment coming out of the water tank in my campervan,' says Karen. 'What can I do?'

PROBLEM: Black sediment in water tank.
WHAT TO USE: Salt, 9 litre bucket, water, glycerine.
HOW TO APPLY: Add ½ cup salt to a bucket of water and flush through the water tank. Combine ½ teaspoon of glycerine and a bucket of water, pour into the tank and leave for 12 hours. Empty and rinse with clean water.

Q 'We recently purchased a second-hand caravan,' reports Merv. 'The spare wheel was left on the vinyl floor for a long time and has left a mark. Can you help?'

PROBLEM: Tyre mark on vinyl.

WHAT TO USE: Non-iodised salt, talcum powder, glycerine, old toothbrush, damp cloth.

HOW TO APPLY: The colour from the tyre has leached into the vinyl floor. Mix 2 tablespoons of salt, 2 tablespoons of talcum powder and 1 tablespoon of glycerine and scrub into the stain with a toothbrush. Leave for 20 minutes, then remove with a damp cloth. Repeat if necessary.

Shed

When working in the shed, sweep up timber shavings and sawdust or you could be in for a nasty tumble. Remove glue and rust from tools and lightly wipe with machine oil. To remove sap and dirt from secateurs' blades, rub with lemon juice and an old cork coated in coarse non-iodised salt.

TIP

Don't stand on electrical leads. Not only could you get a nasty shock, it damages the leads. Wear goggles, masks and gloves, when required.

Formulas

This is a summary of the many cleaning formulas used throughout the book. We do advise, however, that you consult the detailed guidelines for dealing with your stain. Don't rush in and create another stain by using the wrong solution!

BLEACH
Mix 8 tablespoons of washing soda (sodium carbonate) and 2 cups of 3 per cent hydrogen peroxide.

BRAN BALL
Put 1 cup of unprocessed wheat bran in a bowl and add white vinegar, 1 drop at a time, until the mixture resembles brown sugar—it should be clumping but not wet. Place the mixture into the toe of a pair of pantyhose and tie tightly. Rub the pantyhose across a surface like an eraser. This mixture can be reused again and again. Add drops of white vinegar to re-moisten.

CAR WASH SOLUTION
Mix 3 cups of strong black tea, 1 teaspoon of tea tree oil, 1 teaspoon of dishwashing liquid in a 9 litre bucket of warm water.

CARPET CLEANER
Carpet steam-cleaning machines can be hired at supermarkets. They come with a bottle of chemicals but use only half the amount the manufacturer suggests and top up with 2 teaspoons of eucalyptus oil, 2 tablespoons of white vinegar, 2 tablespoons of bicarb and 2 tablespoons of methylated spirits. If you have mystery stains on your

carpet, add 2 teaspoons of glycerine. This solution is also a great multi-purpose spot cleaner so leave it in a 1 litre spray bottle and use as required.

GLYCERINE SOLUTION (TO REMOVE TANNIN STAINS)

Mix 2 tablespoons of glycerine to 2 cups of water in a 1 litre spray pack and lightly mist over areas. Leave for 20 minutes.

HARD SURFACE CLEANER

Do not use on marble.

Combine 1 teaspoon of lavender oil, 1 cup of white vinegar and 1 litre of water in a spray pack, lightly mist over hard surfaces and wipe with a clean cloth.

LAUNDRY DETERGENT FOR DELICATES AND SOFT WOOLLENS

Mix ½ cup of pure soap flakes, ¼ cup of cheap shampoo, 2 teaspoons of bicarb and 2 teaspoons of white vinegar in a clean relabelled detergent bottle. Add 2 litres of water, shake and it's ready to use. Add fragrance, such as 2 teaspoons of lavender oil, but be careful adding eucalyptus oil because it strips colour and oils from fabric. Adding ½ teaspoon of tea tree oil is a good disinfectant and antiviral. For a regular size lightly soiled

load, use 1 tablespoon of detergent for a top loader and
½ tablespoon for a front loader.

LAUNDRY DETERGENT FOR SENSITIVE SKIN

Combine 1 tablespoon of pure soap flakes, juice of 1 lemon and 2 tablespoons of bicarb in a large jar. Add 2 cups of warm water, mix well and label the jar. For a regular size lightly soiled load, use 1 tablespoon of detergent for a top loader and ½ tablespoon for a front loader.

MOULD REMOVER FOR FABRICS

Add 1 kg of non-iodised salt to a 9 litre bucket of water. Add item, soak, remove from salt solution but don't rinse or wring the item. Hang in sunshine until dry and scrub off the salt crust—the mould will come away with it.

MOULD REMOVER FOR HARD SURFACES

Mix ¼ teaspoon of oil of cloves in a 1 litre spray pack of water. Spray and leave for 24 hours before respraying. Wipe with a clean cloth.

RICE STARCH

Cook white rice in plenty of boiling water, drain and reserve the water. Add 1 cup of the reserved rice water to 2 cups of water and stir. To starch items, add ½ cup of rice starch to the rinse cycle of your washing machine.

ROTTEN MILK SOLIDS

Place an opened carton of milk in the sun and leave until it forms solids. The time it takes to rot will vary—up to a few days. Place the solids over biro ink stains and the ink will be absorbed into the solids. Wash normally. Warning: the rotten milk does smell and you might have to block your nose when using it. But once it's washed out, the smell disappears!

SEALANT DIAGNOSIS

Surfaces can be sealed with varnish, polyurethane, shellac or wax. To work out which sealant has been used, take a pin or needle, hold in a pair of pliers and heat on the stove. Touch the pin or needle to an inconspicuous part of the item and work out what smell it creates. If it smells like burnt plastic, it's coated in polyurethane. If it smells like an electrical fire, it's an oil-based varnish. If it smells like burnt hair, it's shellac. If it smells like a snuffed candle, it's wax. To repair polyurethane, apply a little *Brasso* with a lint-free cloth and rub swiftly over the mark in the direction of the grain. It will look worse before it looks better. *Brasso* partially melts polyurethane and allows it to refill the tiny air holes that create white water marks. Shellac, varnish and wax can be repaired using beeswax. Warm beeswax in a bowl in the microwave until it just softens and apply with the skin side of a piece of lemon peel. Rub in the direction of the grain using speed, not pressure.

SHAMPOO FOR BLONDES

Add 4 teaspoons of crushed maiden hair fern leaves to 3 cups of boiling water. Allow to steep for 5 minutes, then strain. Combine 1 tablespoon of this mixture with 1 tablespoon of brown sugar and use to wash your hair.

SHAMPOO FOR BRUNETTES

Place 4 teaspoons of chopped rosemary leaves in 3 cups of boiling water. Allow to steep for 5 minutes, then strain. Add
1 tablespoon of the rosemary mixture to 1 tablespoon of brown sugar and use to wash your hair.

SHOE FROU

Mix 2 tablespoons of bicarb (absorbs odours and moisture),
2 tablespoons of talcum powder (absorbs moisture and keeps a silky feel), 1 drop of tea tree oil (kills tinea), 1 drop of oil of cloves (kills mould spores) and 1 drop of lavender oil (adds fragrance and deters insects). Place the mixture in the centre of a small piece of muslin or cotton voile and tie with string or ribbon to enclose. Pat in smelly shoes.

SILK AND WOOL (BURNT/YELLOWED)

Chlorine-based bleaches burn silk and wool and turn them a yellowy brown. To repair burns, soak items in a 9 litre bucket of warm water with 2 cups of 3 per cent hydrogen peroxide and 8 tablespoons of washing soda. Immerse the items and cover with a plate to keep them in the solution. Leave for around 6 hours. Add 1 cup of white vinegar to a tub of warm water and rinse thoroughly. Hang in the sunshine to dry. If the fabric is too damaged, another option is to dye items with a quality silk dye in the colour of your choice.

SPIDER DETERRENT

Wipe 2 drops of lemon oil or the skin of a lemon over a broom head and sweep over areas where spiders lurk. Alternatively, mix ½ teaspoon of lemon oil with water in a 1 litre spray pack and mist over areas where spiders lurk. Lemon oil doesn't kill spiders, it just deters them.

TIMBER FLOOR WASH

Mix 2 cups of strong black tea, ½ cup of white vinegar with warm water in a 9 litre bucket.

TOWEL SOFTENER

For a large top loader, add ½ cup of bicarb to the wash slot and ½ cup of white vinegar to the conditioner slot of the washing machine. For a small top loader, add 2 tablespoons of bicarb and 2 tablespoons of white vinegar. For a large front loader, add 2 tablespoons of bicarb and 2 tablespoons of white vinegar. For a small front loader, add 1 tablespoon each of bicarb and white vinegar.

WARDROBE SACHET

Mix 2 bay leaves (deter moths), 5 whole cloves (kill mould spores and deter silverfish), 1 tea bag (kills dust mites), 1–2 heads of lavender (adds fragrance and deters flying insects), 2 cedar chips (deter moths), 1 tablespoon of bicarb (absorbs moisture and helps prevent mould) in a bowl. Place the mixture in the centre of a small piece of muslin or cotton voile and tie up with string or ribbon.

WINDOW CLEANER

1 cup of methylated spirits or 1 cup of white vinegar in a 1 litre spray pack of water.

WOOLLENS (HOW TO UNSHRINK)

Add 2 tablespoons (dark colours) or 4 tablespoons (light colours) of Fuller's Earth to 15 litres of blood-heat water. Immerse the garment for 15 minutes, remove, rinse in blood-heat water and gently wring out. Lay the garment on a towel flat in the shade to dry. As it dries, stretch back into shape.

Stain Diagnosis

Before tackling a stain, take some time to work out its components. Use your nose, fingers and eyes. The colour, pattern, smell and texture will help you identify the stain. And remember: there could be several parts to a stain that will need to be removed in a particular order. That order starts with proteins and finishes with resins. The order is important because what you use affects the chemical signature of the stain. If you've applied the wrong solvent, you must remove it before using the correct solvent.

Here are the five main types of stain:

PROTEINS these have a dark ring around the edge and include blood, semen, seeds, nuts, meat, cheese, milk, dairy and fish. To remove the stain, apply cold water and a cake of bathroom soap. Whatever you do, don't use warm or hot water or you'll set the stain.

CARBOHYDRATES these stains are darker in the centre, lighter around the edge and feel stiff. They include sugar, fruit juices, cakes, biscuits, lollies, soft drinks, alcohol, honey and many plants. They also include starches, such as potato, rice, corn, ground corn, wheat-based products (pasta and couscous), floury grain foods and wallpaper paste. To remove sugar stains, use warm water and a cake of bathroom soap. To remove starchy stains, use cold water and soap. If in doubt, use cold water first.

FATS AND OILS these stains spread evenly across a surface, feel greasy between your fingers and, when you wash the stained garment, they continue to spread—that's why a greasy chip mark on your T-shirt gets bigger every time you wash it. Stains include cooking oils (lighter in colour) and mechanical oils (darker in colour and more viscous). To remove lighter oils, rub dishwashing liquid into the stain with your fingers until it feels like jelly. For darker or thicker oils, use mineral oil (baby oil) to dilute the stain before emulsifying with dishwashing liquid.

PIGMENTS these stains include ink, paint, dye, rust and oxide and each requires a different solution. For ink stains, place rotten milk solids over the stain and the ink will be absorbed into the solids. Alternatively, rub with white spirits on a cotton bud. Permanent pen markers contain their own solvent, so write over the mark and while it's wet, wipe with white spirits on a cotton bud. For water-based paint, use methylated spirits on a cotton bud or cotton ball. For oil-based paint, use white spirits or mineral turpentine on a cotton bud or cotton ball. To remove rust, use *CLR* or *Ranex*. If a stain is vegetable based, wipe with white vinegar on a cloth. For an oxide stain, wipe with glycerine on a cloth and remove any remaining colour by exposing the stain to ultraviolet light. Protect the area around the ultraviolet light with cardboard.

RESINS these stains include sap, chewing gum, wax and glue and feel sticky to touch. For plant-based resins, such as tree sap, use a dab of glycerine or dab of tea tree oil. The solvent for shellac is methylated spirits. Glues used in children's crafts are made of carbohydrates, so use warm water and a cake of bathroom soap and scribble over the stain. To remove silicone, cut it using a utility knife.

Uses for essential oils

Fragrance	Properties	Where to use	How to use
Lavender Oil	Relieves headache, helps relaxation and smells clean. It's a great insecticide for mozzies and flies	Bedroom, living area, bathroom, cupboards, on your skin	1 teaspoon of lavender oil per 1 litre spray pack of water
Rose oil	Creates a cosy romantic feel	Bedroom, living area, on your skin	1 teaspoon rose oil per 1 litre spray pack of water
Cinnamon, vanilla and herbals	Encourage appetite	Kitchen, dining room	Use in satchets or simply wipe directly onto surfaces
Oil of cloves	Antibacterial, anti-mould. Has a festive scent	Anywhere you find mould	¼ teaspoon of oil of cloves per 1 litre spray pack of water. Lightly mist over mould and leave to dry. Mould spores will die and drop off in a couple of days
Cedar or pine chips	Clean scents that prevent insects	Particularly good for moths in cupboards and wardrobes. Great for sick rooms as they make breathing easier	Place in sachets or saucers

Fragrance	Properties	Where to use	How to use
Bay leaves	Kill pantry moths	Pantries, kitchen cupboards and wardrobes	Place a dry leaf on each shelf
Tea tree oil	Clean fresh smell and is a great disinfectant, antibacterial and antifungal	Just about anywhere	1 teaspoon of tea tree oil per 1 litre spray pack of water
Fruit oils	Warm welcoming fragrance, although apart from lemon they do encourage insects	Kitchen, dining room	1 teaspoon of fruit oil per 1 litre spray pack of water. Lightly mist as an air freshener
Lily, freesia, lily of the valley and the other srong floral oils	Good at temporarily masking very nasty odours and are wonderful on clothes	Anywhere there is a nasty pong or wardrobes and drawers to scent your clothes	¼ teaspoon of floral oil per 1 litre spray pack of water. Lightly mist as an air freshener
Bicarb	Absorbs gaseous smells	Anywhere there is a nasty pong	Place 2 tablespoons on a saucer near the offending odour

Index

A
acetone 7
adhesives *see* contact adhesives
air freshener (non-toxic) 113, 208
Akubra 445
algae 539, 543
allergies
    to dust mites 233
    laundry detergent for sensitive skin 571
    to washing powder 476
aluminium
    cleaning 167, 530
    corrosion in 43, 322
    paint on 324
angora shedding 427
ants
    killing 552
    in pantry 99–100
    in pot plants 211
appliances *see also* washing machine
    barbecue grill 45
    benchtop ovens 45
    dishwasher 47–48, 93
    entertainment systems 186–189
    espresso/coffee machines 41–42
    garbage disposal units 78
    juicers 54
    kettle/electric jug 40–41
    kitchen 39
    microwave 45–47
    mixers and blenders 42–43
    refrigerators 49–53
    sandwich maker 44
    stereos 188
    sticky labels on 49
    toasters 44
    TVs 186, 187
    water filters 53
Aquadhere 7–19
Araldite 258
artificial flowers 209
ashtrays 207
awnings 534–535

B
babies and young children *see* kids
baby oil
    on cotton 381
    described 7
    for hinges 259
baby packs 464–465
bags 433–436
Bakelite toilet seats 111–112
baking soda *see* bicarb (bicarbonate of soda)
bamboo floors 224–225
bamboo furniture 165–166
Band-Aids 453
barbecue grill 45
barbecues 536–537
bath 113–117
    bore water stain on ceramic 116
    essential oil on fibreglass 115
    liquid shoe polish on enamel 116
    resurfacing 114–115
    rust stains on sink ring 116
    scratch marks in fibreglass 117
    spa bath 117
bathroom 104–106
    bath 113–117

Index

drains 77–78, 134
handbasin and vanity 105
mirror 128–129
shower 117–121
taps 77, 125
tiles and grout 125–128
toilet 107–112
towels 132
bathroom walls 133–134
bay leaves 7, 97, 583
bed bugs 343
bedcovers 358–362
bedroom
   clutter bucket 350
   waterbeds, caring for 351
beds 342–351
bedside tables 367–372
beer
   on carpet 239–240
   on leather shoes 439–440
   stain removal 480
beeswax
   described 7
   on wardrobe 369–370
   wax finish 217
beetroot
   on carpet 240
   on cotton 382
   on laminate 59
   stain removal 480
benchtop ovens 45
benchtops 54–55
   Caesarstone/quantum quartz/*Silestone* 60–61
   Corian 61
   granite 65–67
   laminate/*Formica* 23, 56–60
   marble 61–65
   polishing 55
   stainless steel 67–68
   tiles and grout 68–69
   timber 69–71
   types of sealing 55
Betadine spots on carpet 240–241
bicarb (bicarbonate of soda) 7, 583
billiards 191

birdbaths 543
birds, deterring 539
biro *see* pen marks
bitumen *see* tar
black mould in silicone 75
black mud on carpet 271–272
black sediment in water tank 564
blackened copper 182
blankets 165, 363–366
   cat hair on 366
   cotton 365
   faux mink 365
   storing 365
   woollen 364–365
bleach
   on carpet 241–242
   described 7
   dioxins in 133
   solution 569
   in wool 428
blenders *see* mixers and blenders
blinds 326–329
   bee nectar on 329
   blue biro on 326
   cleaning cords 328
   dirty fabric 326
   food stains on 328
   food stains on plastic 327
   insect droppings on 327
   mildew on 327
   plantation shutters 329
   roman blinds 329
   venetian blinds 328
   wooden blinds 329
blood-heat water 3, 8
blood stains
   on carpet 242
   on mattress 344–345
   on sheets 354–355
   stain removal 481
   on timber 72, 219
Blu-Tack on carpet 243
boats 561–565
body oil 153
bone handles 90
books and bookshelves 203
boot polish on carpet 243
borax 8
bore water stain
   on ceramic 116

   on pavers 520
   on sheets 357
borer in furniture 170–171
bran *see* unprocessed wheat bran
bran balls 138, 569
brass
   cleaning 176
   tarnished 74
Brasso 8
brick mantlepieces 183
brick pavers 516
bricks 516
brocade 150
broken pot handle 39
bronze
   cleaning 176
   dirty fire screen 182–183
broom 8
bucket 8
bugs *see also* ants; cockroaches; flies; moths; spiders
   aphids 539–540
   bee nectar on blinds 329
   black bugs 106
   borer in furniture 170–171
   carpet beetles 279
   cobwebs 311
   in coir 295–296
   in computers 201
   in drains 77–78
   in drawers 367
   in dried flowers 210
   dust mites 233
   insect droppings on blinds 327
   insect stain on carpet 265
   on light bulbs 308
   masonry beetle in mortar 516
   millipedes 106
   mosquitoes 551
   mould-eating slugs 126
   under sink 73
   snail-proofing vegetable patch 540–541
   snails and slugs 540, 552

586 INDEX

burn marks *see also*
cigarette burns;
scorch marks
on carpet 281–282
on French polish 192
on glass 185
on iron 506–507
on laminate 58
on ovens 25
on timber 170
burnt pans 35, 37
burnt plastic 23–24
burnt popcorn in
microwave 46–47
burnt rice 36
bushfire smoke 334

C
Caesarstone benchtops
60–61
camphor 8, 251
candle wax
on carpet 290–291
on cooktop 29–30
on corduroy 415–416
on cotton 416,
533–534
on fabric 187–188
on granite 527–528
on polished timber
172
red wax on timber 224
on sheets 354
soot stains on wall
181–182
stain removal 488–489
on synthetics 417
on timber 171–172,
190
cane, cleaning 531
cane floors 224–225
cane furniture 165–166
canvas 535, 547–548
car wash solution 569
caravans 561–565
carbohydrates 579
carnauba wax, described 9
carpet
barbecue sauce on 239
beetroot on 240
Betadine spots on
240–241
black ink stain on 264
black mud on 271–272

black tea on cream
carpet 279–280
bleach on 241–242
blood stains on 242
Blu-Tack on 243
blue plumber's silicone
on 281
boot polish on 243
burn marks on
281–282
butter/margarine on
244
butter on 288–289
candle wax on
290–291
car grease on 260–261
chewing gum on 244
cleaning 229–230
coffee on 245–246
cordial on 246
cough mixture on
246–247
crayon on 247
cream on 247–248
DIY steam cleaning
233–235
dog poo on 249–252
dye on 252
egg on 253
Fanta on 253–254
fat-based food stain on
254–255
felt pad stains on 372
fluorescent pen on 255
fruit stain on 256
furniture indentations
on 257
glue on 272–273
glycerine on 257
graphite powder on
258–259
grass on 259
gravy on 259–260
green chicken curry on
248–249
hair dye on 252–253
hair gel on 261
hair serum on
261–262
ice-cream on 262–263
insect stain on 265
jelly beans on 266
jute in 237, 277, 280
lemonade on 266–267

lipstick on 267–268
lubricant on 268
make-up on 268–269
mayonnaise on
269–270
milk on 271
mould on 270
nail polish on 272–273
nappy rash cream
on 273
orange juice on
274–275
patching 238–239
plum jam on wool
carpet 265–266
pollen stain on
275–276
pot plants marks on
276
professional cleaning
280
professional steam
cleaning 235–236
red ink stain on
264–265
red wine stain on
276–277, 278
rubber marks on 278
rust stains on 278–279
scuff marks on 243,
282
shoe polish on enamel
282
soot on 282–283
sorbolene cream on
283
soup on 283–284
spaghetti bolognese on
284–285
strawberry daiquiri
stain on 255–256
sugar on 266–267
sugar stains on 282
suntan lotion on
285–286
tannin stains on
245–246
testing for
colourfastness 256
timber stains on 286
tomato sauce on 287
toner on 287
tree sap on 288
urine stains on 288

Index

using vacuum cleaner 230–233
Vegemite on 288–289
vomit on 289–290
water marks on 237, 290
zinc cream on 291
carpet beetles 279
carpet cleaner solution 569–570
carpet cleaners 9, 230
carpet protectors 451
carpet steam cleaner 9
cars 554–561
dirty allow wheels 559
windscreen wipers 559
cassette players 186
cast-iron bath 113
cast-iron chest 373
cast-iron furniture 532
cast-iron pots 34–35, 36
CD players 188
CDs 186
cedar chips 9, 582
ceilings 164, 334–337
cement pavers 516
Cera wax 9, 13
ceramic bath 116
chalk sticks 9
chamois 439
chandeliers 309–310
charcoal filters 33
chests of drawers 367–372
chewing gum
on carpet 244
on cotton 385
on leather 421
stain removal 481
chimneys 180–181
china cabinet 82
china ornaments, cleaning 177
chips
in crockery 84–85
in gilded frames 318–319
in glassware 95
in marble 63, 64–65
chlorine 235
chocolate
on carpet 245
on cooktop 30

on cotton 386
on sheets 355
stain removal 481
on wool 386
chopping boards 71–72
chrome furniture 167
chrome heaters 184
cider vinegar 3
cigarette ash 9
cigarette burns *see also* burn marks; scorch marks
on timber 219–220
on white plastic 73
cigarette smells
in cars 557
in furniture 149–150
in vinyl 164–165
cinnamon oil 582
on vinyl wrap 80
clay ornaments, cleaning 177
cleaners *see* solutions, summary of
clingwrap 9
clock radio 372
clocks 208
cloisonné, cleaning 177
cloth 10
clothes baskets 373
clothes lines 414, 501
clothing 379–433
collar grime 482
hanging 370
ironing shirt buttons 503
jackets 430–433
kids 454–460
making coloufast 458
quick stain removal guide 479–489
static in 409
stiff denim jacket 410
stiff new shirts 410
stretched cotton-knit 410–411
suits 430
cloudy shower screen 122
cloudy stain on timber 174–175
cloves 10
CLR (Calcium, Lime and Rust) 9–10
clutter bucket 350, 468

coat-hangers
hanging clothes 370
marks on clothes 371
Coca Cola 109, 553
cockroaches
in drains 78
dropping on books 203–204
in electrical appliances 40–41
in kitchen cupboards 78
poo on rubber-lined curtains 333
under refrigerators 50–51
coffee
in car 555–556
on carpet 245–246
on cotton 144–145, 386
on laminate 56
on mattress 344
on silk 422–423
stain removal 482
coir 295–296
Vicks VapoRub on 296
cold water 10
colour run 478–479
Colour Run Remover 10, 478
coloured marks *see also* pen marks; white marks; yellowing
black line on white tiles 127
black marks from carpet beetles 279
black marks on leather 546–547
black stuff in washing machine 490
brown marks on *Glomesh* 435–436
crepe paper on vinyl 298
discoloured billiard balls 191
foxing in books 204
green copper mark on basin 130
green dye on timber 195–196

green marks on shower
    head 124–125
red dirt in washing
    machine 492–493
coloured pencil *see* pen
    marks
colourfast
    making 458
    testing for 256, 478
columns 316–317
computer keyboards 200,
    201
computers 200–201
concrete
    cleaning 525–527
    paint on 526–527
    rubber marks on 278
    rust stains on 526
concrete floors 227–228
contact adhesives *see also*
        glues
    on appliances 49
    double-sided tape on
        walls 312
    on glass 554–555
    masking tape residue
        258
    old masking tape on
        glass 324
    removing 96, 258
    sticky label on wool
        409
    sticky tape residue 258
    on timber 218
    on vinyl records 189
    on walls 452
cooktops 29–32
    ceramic/induction
        30–31
    electric 31
    gas 31–32
copper 92
    blackened 182
    green copper mark on
        basin 130
cordial on carpet 246
Corian benchtops 61
cork floors 216–224
cornflour 10
corrosion in aluminium
    43, 322
cots 460–461
cotton 142–150 *see also*
    food stains

baby oil on 381
bird poo on 383
blankets 365
candle wax on 416,
    533–534
chewing gum on 385
coffee on 144–145,
    386
coloured pencil on
    146
crayon on 145–146
cricket ball marks
    on 458
dirt and sweat on 389
dirt on 389–390
dirty fringing 293
dye run in 457–458
eardrops on 147
fluorescent pen on
    391–392
grass and grease on
    393–394
hair dye on 395–396
lip balm on 397
lipstick on 398
Liquid Paper on 399
mascara on 363
mould on 196–197,
    496
oil on 146
red wine on 406,
    533–534
rust marks on valance
    348
scorch marks on 407
soil on 197
stretched cotton-knit
    410–411
sunscreen on 411
sweat on 411–412
tannin stains on 147
Tiger Balm on 361
tree sap on 414
Vaseline on 415
yellowing on 417–418
cotton ball 10
cotton bud 10
couches
    cleaning 138–142
    cleaning wool 158
    cushion covers 140
    food spills on 140
    nail polish on leather
        160

cough mixture on carpet
    246–247
CPR 544
cracked pot handle 39
cracks in timber veneer
    173–174
crayon *see* pen marks
creosote 10
crockery 76–77, 81–85
    chips in 84–85
    crystal bowls stuck
        together 83
    plates with discoloured
        crazing 84
    stained *Bessemer* plates
        83–84
    tannin stains 82–83
crystal bowls stuck
    together 83
Crystal Clear 309–310
cupboards 78–81
    cockroaches in 78
    grime in 79
    warped 26
curtains 329–334
    cat spray on 331–332
    chintz 330
    cockroach poo on
        rubber-lined 333
    cretonne 330
    dry-cleaning fluid smell
        in 333–334
    ironing 331
    stains on silk 332
    velvet 330–331
    yellowing in nylon
        331
cutlery 89–93
    knives 92–93

D

damask 506
damp cloth 11
Damp Rid on sisal
    294–295
decanters 205–206
deck scrubber 11
defrosting freezer 52–53
dents
    indentations on vinyl
        297–298
    in pans 38
    in timber 70, 219
denture tablets 11

deodorant
    on fabric 388
    on leather 420–421
    stain removal 483
deodorisers 557
desks 202
dining tables 191–196
    heat marks on French polish 192
    water marks on French polish 192
dishwasher 47–48, 93
dishwashing liquid 11
    on sealed granite 66
disposable rubber gloves 11
doonas 358–362
door handles 305
door jambs 305
door knobs 305
door locks 305
door mats 529–530
doors 305–307
drains 77–78
    blocked 78, 134
dried herbs 98
driveways 553
Driza-Bone 432–433
dry-cleaning 499
dry-cleaning fluid 3, 11, 19
    smell in curtains 333–334
dry cleaning symbols 493
dryers
    symbols 494
    tumble drying 501–502
drying racks 502
dust mites
    allergies 233
    how to kill 343
    kids and 450
DVDs 186
dye *see also* hair dye
    on carpet 252
    dye water 429
    green, on timber 195–196
    on leather 161
    on linen 141
    orange, on sandstone composite 316–317
    running 162, 457–458

E

eardrops on cotton 147
earrings 374
egg
    on brick 520
    on carpet 253
    on cotton 390
    in pan 37
    yolk on sheets 355
    yolk stain removal 483
electric blankets 365
electrical leads 565
electrical wiring 335
electronic games 467
embroidery, cleaning 177
enamel 25
enamel bath 116
enamel heaters 184
engine oil on timber 221
entertainment systems 186–189
ephemera, cleaning 177
epsom salts 11
eraser 11
espresso/coffee machines 41–42
essential oils
    on fibreglass 115
    uses chart 582–583
eucalyptus oil 11
exercise bikes 546
exfoliation 120
extractor fans 33–34

F

fabric softener 475
fabrics *see also* cotton; leather; linen; sheepskin; silk; synthetics; velvet; vinyl; wool
    brocade 150
    care symbols 493–494
    chamois 439
    chintz 330
    colourfast, making 458
    colourfast test 256
    corduroy 415–416
    cretonne 330
    damask 506
    denim 380, 384
    Driza-Bone 432–433
    embroidery 177
    HyVent 431–432
    ink stains on 143
    jacquard 154
    lace 178
    Lycra 458
    microsuede, macrosuede, supersuede and nubuck 151–154
    mohair 165
    nubuck 151–152, 437
    oily stain on 149
    ornaments 178
    pen marks 143
    quick stain removal guide 479–489
    raffia 535
    rust stains on 144, 406–407
    satin 399–400
    scuff marks on 147–148
    super suede 437
    tapestry 154–156
    tulle 459–460
    vacuum-cleaner marks 140
    velcro 441
    vinyl 164–165
    water marks in 150
    waterproof 431–433
Fanta on carpet 253–254
fats 2, 140
fats and oils *see also* grease stains
    barbecues 536–537
    butter in car 558
    butter/margarine on carpet 244
    butter on carpet 288–289
    on carpet 254–255
    cooking oil on timber 221–222
    cream on carpet 247–248
    cream on silk 387
    diagnosis 579
    essential oil on fibreglass 115
    fats on carpet 215
    heater oil on towels 185
    massage oil on towels 497

INDEX

oil and petrol on pavers 518–519
oil stains 403
oily stain on fabric 149
salad dressing on timber 532
on sandstone 525
on sheepskin 442
on shoes 441
stain removal 482
on suede 419
use by date 98
faux brick 517
faux mink blankets 365
fax machines 202
felt hats 444–445
fibreglass baths 115, 117
fibreglass, rust on 542–543, 545
filters
  in dishwashers 48
  in washing machine 475, 479
fireplaces 180–183
firescreens 182–183
flasks, stains on 44
flies
  fly speck 308
  fly specks on ceilings 335
  fly spray unit mark on wall 313–314
  fruit flies 552–553
  killing 551–552
floors
  bamboo, cane and palm 224–225
  concrete 227–228
  guide for cleaning 301–304
  marble/limestone 228
  rammed earth 229
  timber and cork 216–224
floral oils 583
flowers 208–209
  art of drying 210
  artificial 209
flyscreens 314, 537
flysprays 314
food stains *see also* beer; beetroot; chocolate; coffee; egg; fats and oils; ice-cream; milk; peanut butter; tannin stains; tomato
anchovy on denim 380
apple juice on cotton 380
baby milk vomit on jacquard 154
baked beans on cotton 381
banana 480
banana on cotton 381
banana sap on fabric 382
barbecue sauce 480
barbecue sauce on carpet 239
berry juice on sandstone 525
berry stains on cotton 382–383
black bean sauce on cotton 384
on blinds 328
carrot 481
chilli sauce 481
chilli sauce on cotton 385
on cotton 390–391
on couches 140
curry on cotton 387
custard on cotton 388
fruit juice on sheets 353
fruit juice stain removal 483
fruit stain on carpet 256
gravy on carpet 259–260
gravy on tablecloth 198
gravy stain removal 484
green chicken curry on carpet 248–249
green food colouring on sisal 294
ice-cream on cotton 457
inside microwave 47
jelly beans on carpet 266
lemonade on carpet 266–267
mayonnaise on carpet 269–270
mayonnaise stain removal 485
melted cheese on microsuede 152
mustard on cotton 401–402
oily noodles on silk 433
orange juice on carpet 274–275
pear on cotton 404
peas on timber 194–195
pizza in car 560
on plastic blinds 327
plum jam on wool carpet 265–266
pumpkin on wool 406
seafood on cotton 408
on sheets 352–353
soft drink stain removal 487
soup on carpet 283–284
soy sauce on cotton 408
soy sauce stain removal 487
spaghetti bolognese on carpet 284–285
squid ink on cotton 408
on suede 439
sugar on carpet 266–267
sugar stains on carpet 282
tuna in oil on cotton 415
turmeric 488
Vegemite on carpet 288–289
Vegemite stain removal 488
vinegar on sisal 294
watermelon 488
yoghurt on cotton 418
food storage
  canned food 97–98
  parmesan cheese 85

Formica benchtops 56–60
Formica, cleaning 168
foundation *see* make-up
French polish
    burn marks 192
    cleaning 193
    water marks on 192
fruit flies 552–553
fruit oils 583
Fuller's Earth 12
furniture
    borer in 170–171
    cane, bamboo, wicker and water hyacinth 165–166, 464
    gaps between bench and splashback 70–71
    glass tabletops 179
    for kids 463
    laminate coming away from chipboard backing 60
    marble tabletops 179
    metal-framed 167
    oriental 180
    outdoor 530–534
    sticking drawers 176
    timber 167–176, 180
furniture indentations on carpet 257
furniture polishes 167–168
furs 418–419

G
garages 553
garbage area 553
garbage disposal units 78
garden ponds 541
gardening tools 541, 565
gardens 539–543
    snail-proofing vegetable patch 540–541
gas heaters 184
gilded frames 318
    flaked or chipped 318–319
glass
    burn marks on 185
    contact adhesives on 554–555
    glass cancer 319
    leadlight cement on 322
    melted polyester on 184
    old masking tape on 324
    of paintings 318
    red wine stain in decanter 206
    saliva on 325
    scratch marks on 323
    sugar soap on 321
    windows 319
glass tabletops 179
glassware 76, 93–96
    champagne glasses 93–94
    chips in 95
    etched 94
    removing sticky labels 96
    scratch marks 94
    soap scum on 95
    whiteness on 95
gloves 442–443
glues *see also* contact adhesives
    on carpet 272–273
    craft glue on timber 193–194
    described 2
    removing *Araldite* 258
    removing contact adhesives 258
    removing craft glues 257–258
    removing gums 258
    removing paper glues 258
    removing PVA glues 257–258
    removing superglue 257
    removing two-part epoxy 258
    superglue on laminate 56–57
    on tulle 459–460
    on walls 312
    on windscreen 556
glycerine
    on carpet 257
    described 12
    solution 570
goanna oil, described 12
graffiti 528
granite benchtops 65–67
    dishwashing liquid on 66
    grease stains in 66–67
granite mantlepieces 183
granite, wax on 527–528
graphite powder on carpet 258–259
grass
    on carpet 259
    on cotton 393–394
    stain removal 484
grease stains *see also* fats and oils
    car grease on carpet 260–261
    on cotton 393–394
    diesel on polyester and cotton 388–389
    diesel on swag 548
    engine oil on timber 221
    on fabric 402–403
    on fabrics 394–395
    in granite benchtops 66–67
    on handbags 435
    on kitchen tiles 69
    on linen 141
    petrol on leather 440
    on plastic containers 88
    removing 260–261
    stain removal 484
    on tablecloth 197–198
    on velvet 156
    on wool 395
green copper mark on basin 130
grills 28–29
grout *see also* tiles and grout
    reapplying 126–127
    soap scum on 127–128
grout rake 12
guitar strings 190
Gumption 12
gums 258

H
hair brush 12
hair conditioner 12

Index   591

hair dryer 12
hair dye *see also* dye
    on carpet 252–253
    on cotton 395–396
    on laminate 59
    stain removal 484
    on timber 220
hair gel on carpet 261
hair serum on carpet 261–262
hair spray
    on linoleum 300
    on wool 396
hair, *Tiger Balm* in 131
halogen lights 308
hampers 373
hand basin and vanity
    cleaning 129
    green copper mark on basin 130
    mildew on vanity cupboard 131
    toothpaste and soap stains 105
    watermarks on sealed marble 129–130
hand washing
    delicates 498–499
    knives 93
    sweet-smelling hands 101
    washing up by hand 76–77
handbags 433–436
    brown marks on *Glomesh* 435–436
    dirty linings 434–435
    grease stains on 435
hanging out washing 500–501
hard surface cleaner 570
hard-water fur 109–110, 124
hard-water stain *see* bore water stain
hats 443–446
heat marks *see* burn marks
heaters 183–185
herbals 582
herbs 98
highchairs 463–464
hinges
    cots 460
    lubricating 259

    ovens 27
    rust in 306
holes
    bald patch in velvet 157
    in cane furniture 166
    in hot-water bottles 341–342
    patching carpet 238–239
    in sole of shoes 437
hydrochloric acid 520, 525
hydrogen peroxide (3%) 12

I

ice-cream
    on carpet 262–263
    icy pole on cotton 456–457
    stain removal 482
    on T-shirt 386
indoor plants 211
ingredients 7–19
ink in newspaper 319
ink stains *see also* pen marks
    on fabric 397
    on linoleum 299
    squid ink on cotton 408
insects *see* bugs
iron 13
ironing 502–507
    cleaning iron 504–505
    folding 507–508
    iron melt 506
    without iron 507
ironing-board covers 504
ironing symbols 493
ivory, cleaning 178, 374, 376

J

jacquard 154
jars 87
jewellery 374–376
    pearls 374
jewellery boxes 375
juicers 54
jute in carpet 237, 277, 280

K

kerosene 13
kerosene heaters 184

kettle/electric jug 40–41
key broken in lock 307
kids
    baby bottles 453
    baby vomit on sheets 461
    bed-wetting 453
    clothing 454–460
    cots 460–461
    hard furnishings 463
    highchairs 463–464
    nappies 462–463, 489
    oral thrush 450
    playdough liquid 466
    playdough on rug 452
    prams/strollers/baby packs 464–465
    routine house cleaning 450–452
    storing clothes 454–456
    toys 465–469
kitchen
    appliances *see* appliances
    chopping boards 71–72
    cooktops 29–32
    crockery 76–77, 81–85
    cupboards 78–81
    drains 77–78
    grills 28–29
    ovens 24–28
    pantry 96–100
    pots and pans 34–39
    range hood and extractor fan 33–34
    sinks 72–77
    splashbacks 32–33
    taps 77
    washing up by hand 76–77
kitchen drawers 79
kitty litter 13, 400
knives
    handwashing 93
    sharpening 92–93
    types 92

L

lace, cleaning 178
lacquer 168, 180

Index

laminate benchtops 56–60
laminate, cleaning 168
lamp bases 308
lamps 307–309, 326
laundry detergent 13
   for delicates and soft
      woollens 570–571
   for sensitive skin 571
lavender oil 13, 582
LCD screens 187
leadlight cement on glass
   322
leadlight windows
   325–326
leaking pipes under sink
   74–75
leather 158–164
   beer on 439–440
   biro on 161
   black marks on
      546–547
   chewing gum on 421
   deodorant on
      420–421
   dirty 442–443
   dye on 161
   fluorescent pen on
      392–393
   ink stain on 202
   leather-bound books,
      preserving 203
   mould on 401, 546
   nail polish on 160
   paint on 163
   petrol on 440
   plaster powder in 164
   repairing hole in
      419–420
   scratch marks in 162
   shoes 436–437
   sweat marks on 432
   white-out on 162
leather conditioner 13
leather dew 13
lemon juice 13
lemon oil 13
lice comb, metal 13
lichen 539
light bulbs
   broken in socket 309
   bugs on 308
   cleaning 308
   hard-to-reach 539
light shades 307–309

light switches
   cleaning 310–311
   greasy fingermarks 315
lime scale
   on coffee machine 42
   in kettle/electric jug
      40–41
   scaling in kettle 41
limestone floors 228
linen 142–150
   dye on 141
   grease stains on 141
   red wine on
      upholstered linen
      145
   rust stains on 508
linen press 508–509
linoleum 296–300
   ballpoint ink on 297
   hairspray on 300
   ink stain on 299
   rust stains on 299
lint 479, 502
lipstick *see* make-up
Liquid Paper on cotton 399
liquid soap 476
lock, key broken in 307
lounges *see* couches
lubricant on carpet 268
lunch bags 89
Lycra 458

M

macramé 315–316
macrosuede 151–154
make-up
   on carpet 268–269
   foundation on
      synthetics 393
   lip balm on cotton 397
   lipstick on carpet
      267–268
   lipstick on cotton 398
   lipstick on fabric 148
   lipstick on plastic 398
   liquid foundation on
      towels 132
   mascara on cotton 363
   on quilt cover 360
   removal 120
   on sheets 353
   stain removal 484, 485
   using a mirror tile
      367–368

mantlepieces 183
marble
   dull in shower
      119–120
   graffiti on 528
   mantlepieces 183
   marks on 194
   polymarble showers
      118
   protective coating 130
   water marks in 179
   watermarks on sealed
      marble 129–130
   windowsills 320
marble benchtops 61–65
   chips in 63
   polyurethane finish on
      61–62
   rust on 63–64
   stains on 63, 64
   tannin stains on 62–63
   white, chalky-looking
      chips in 64–65
marble floor wax 9, 13
marble floors 228
marble vanity top 105
marks *see also* burn marks;
   coloured marks;
   pen marks; rubber
   marks; rust; scorch
   marks; scratch
   marks; scuff
   marks; smoke;
   stains; sweat
   marks; water
   marks
   dirty marks on fabric
      148–149
   on marble 194
   ring marks on electric
      cooktop 31
   tile marks 226
   vacuum-cleaner marks
      on fabric 140
mats *see* rugs and mats
mattress
   airing and turning 342
   ballpoint ink on
      345–346
   blood stains on
      344–345
   coffee on 344
   cots 460–461
   freshening up 349–350

594 INDEX

mould in 350
red wine on 346–347
semen stain on 346
smells 347–348
spillages on 343
tannin stains on 343–344
urine stains on 346, 453
mattress protector 342
melamine
   stains on 83–84
   yellowing on 80–81
metal
   frames 318
   rust on 309
metal-framed furniture 167
metal lice comb 13
metal residue on tiles 227
metal, tarnished 178–179
methylated spirits
   described 14
   on faux brick 517
mice and rats
   dead mouse smells 81, 560–561
   rat poo in ceiling 336
   snake poo to deter 336–337
microsuede 151–154
microwave 45–47
   burnt popcorn in 46–47
mildew *see also* mould
   on blinds 327
   in boat carpet 563
   in books 203
   on canvas 535
   on satin 399–400
   under sink 73
   on terracotta 540
   on vanity cupboard 131
   in washing machine 490
milk
   baby milk vomit on jacquard 154
   in car 560
   on carpet 271
   rotten milk 15, 399
   rotten milk solids 572
   stain removal 485
millipedes 106

mineral oil *see* baby oil
mirrors 128–129, 317–319, 373–374
   cleaning 318
   using a mirror tile 367–368
mixers and blenders 42–43
mohair shedding 165
moss 539
mothballs 251
moths
   in pantry 97, 99, 100
   in wardrobe 371
   in wool 424–425
mould *see also* mildew
   in bags 434
   on bath toys 467
   in car 555
   on carpet 237, 270
   on ceilings 335
   on cotton 196–197, 496
   damp in linen press 509
   damp in wardrobes 369
   on laminate 58
   on leather 401, 546
   in life jackets 563
   on lingerie 379
   in mattress 350
   on outdoor shades 534–535
   on painted walls 133–134
   on pavers 516
   on pram 465
   on rubber seals 491
   in showers 118
   in silicone 75, 123
   on silk 400
   smells 270–271
   solution for fabrics 571
   solution for hard surfaces 571
   on suede 436, 443
   on synthetic grass 547
   on towels 509
   on wallpaper 314
   on walls 311
mouse and mouse mat 201
mud stain removal 271–272, 485
muriatic acid 520, 525

Murlex see dry-cleaning fluid
musical instruments
   guitar strings 190
   pianos 189–190

N

nail polish
   on carpet 272–273
   on leather 160
   on microsuede 153–154
   on sheets 341
   stain removal 485
   on timber 222–223
naphthalene flakes 336
NapiSan Oxyaction Max 14
NapiSan Plus 14
NapiSan, removing 360
nappies 462–463, 489
nappy bucket 463
nappy rash 462–463
nappy rash cream on carpet 273
newspaper 319
non-iodised salt 14
nubuck 151–154, 437
nylon brush 14

O

odours *see* smells
office equipment 200–201
oil of cloves 14, 270, 494, 582
oil of pennyroyal 14, 99
oils *see* fats and oils
ointment on sheets 357
orange oil 235–236, 497
oriental furniture 180
Oriental rugs 292–293
ornaments 176–179
outdoor furniture 530–534
ovens 24–28

P

paint
   on aluminium 324
   on clothes 513
   on concrete 526–527
   on fabric 403–404
   on leather 163
   on sandstone 524
   stain removal 485
   test 513

Index   595

painted windowsills
    320–321
painting a room 317
paintings 317–319
    acrylic 317
    cleaning glass 318
    gilded frames 318
    oil 317–318
    water colours 318
palm floors 224–225
Panama 446
pantry 96–100
pantyhose/stockings 15
paper
    cleaning 178
    crepe paper stain on
        vinyl 298
    musty 205
paper glues 258
paper towel 15
paste 3
pathways 516
pavers
    bore water stain on
        520
    brick 516
    cement 516
    mould on 516
    oil and petrol on
        518–519
    protecting 536
    rust stains on 519
    tannin stains on
        517–518
    tree sap on 518
peanut butter
    on cotton 404
    jam, margarine and, on
        wallpaper 315
    on timber 215
pearls 374
peg bags 501
pen marks
    Artline 405, 486
    ballpoint ink on
        linoleum 297
    ballpoint ink on
        mattress 345–346
    biro on leather 161
    biros 263
    black ink stain on
        carpet 264
    blue biro on blinds
        326

coloured pencil on
    cotton 146
on couches 142
crayon on carpet 247
crayon on cotton
    145–146
crayon on microsuede
    152–153
crayon on walls 311,
    452
crayon stain removal
    483
felt pen on carpet 451
felt-tip pen on nubuck
    151–152
fine-point liners 263
fluorescent pen 405,
    486
fluorescent pen on
    carpet 255
fluorescent pen on
    cotton 391–392
fluorescent pen on
    leather 392–393
gel pens 263, 405, 486
ink stain on leather
    202
ink stains on fabric 143
permanent markers
    263, 405, 486
permanent pen on
    fabric 143
red ink stain on carpet
    264–265
removing from
    whiteboard 203
on sheets 356
stain removal 484, 486
Texta on cotton 455
Texta on microsuede
    151
treatment of 142
whiteboard marker
    405, 486
pencil *see* pen marks
pepper shakers 85
permanent pleating 505
pests *see* bugs
petroleum jelly (*Vaseline*)
    15
pets
    bedding 548–550
    cat hair on blankets
        366

cat spray on curtains
    331–332
cat urine on timber
    223
deterring cats 366, 549
deterring dogs 549
dog poo on carpet
    249–252
dog poo on stroller
    wheels 464–465
dog urine/poo on tile
    grout 226–227
fur and hair on
    couches 139
killing fleas 549
mothballs to deter
    cats 251
pet urine smell 251
preventing scratching
    163
rabbit urine on timber
    513–514
scratch marks in
    leather 162
smelly dog kennel 550
washing cats 549–550
pewter 90
photocopiers 202
pianos 189–190
pictures 317–319
pigments 580
pillow protector 362
pillowcase 15
pillows 362–363
pine chips 582
plantation shutters 329
plants
    ants in 211
    barbecue ash on
        536–537
    indoor plants 211
    ivy suckers on
        concrete/brick 526
    pot plants 208–209
    snails and slugs 540
    stains on tiles 521–522
plasma screens 186, 187
plaster of paris 15
plaster powder 164
plastic
    burnt 23–24
    cigarette burns on 73
    cleaning 531
    frames 318

on laminate 57
lipstick on 398
Plexus plastic cleaner 187
removing sticky labels 96
scratch marks in 554
stains on sink 498
plastic bag 15
plastic chopping boards 72
plastic containers
  greasiness in 88
  recycling 100–101
  sticky *Tupperware* 88
  tomato stain in 88
plastic, self-levelling 296–300
pleats 504, 505
Plexus plastic cleaner 187
pollen stain on carpet 275–276
polyacetate, cleaning 531
polycarbonate
  cleaning 531
  frames 318
  glasses 77
  scratch marks in 562–563
polymarble showers 118
polyurethane
  cleaning 168, 531
  finish on marble 61–62
  scald marks in 167
  scratch marks on 169
  tannin stains in 62–63
  timber and cork floors 216–217
poo stains
  bird 480
  bird on cotton 383
  bird on wrought iron 529
  bird or possum on sandstone 524–525
  dog on carpet 249–252
  dog on stroller wheels 464–465
  dog on tile grout 226–227
  dog, stain removal 483
  flying fox on canvas 547–548
  flying fox on powder-coated steel 561
  kookaburra on timber 515–516
  seagull on canvas 564
pot plants 208–209
  marks on carpet 276
pots and pans 34–39
  burnt 35, 37
  cast-iron pots 34–35, 36
  lid replacements 35
  rust in 38
potter's plaster 15
powder-coating
  flying fox poo on steel 561
  on playpens and security gates 464
  on railings 528–529
  on taps 77, 125
prams 464–465
printers 202
proteins 2, 140, 579

Q
quantum quartz benchtops 60–61
quilts 341–342, 360

R
raffia 535
rammed earth floors 229
Ranex 15
range hoods 33–34
rapeseed oil 98
recycling containers 100–101
refrigerators 49–53
resins 2, 580
respirators, dirty mask and straps 361–362
rice
  burnt 36
  starch solution 571
  starches from 352, 477
roman blinds 329
rose oil 582
rotten milk 15
rubber
  caring for 535
  mould on seals 491
  perishing 112, 189, 320
  preserving 466–467
  soiled shoes 437, 440
rubber marks
  on carpet 278
  on concrete 278
  on quilt cover 341–342
  on shower tiles 120
  stain removal 486
  on timber 188
  on towels 132
  tyre on vinyl 564–565
  on vinyl 298–299
rugs and mats *see also* carpet
  coir 295–296
  dirty cotton fringing 293
  dirty flokati rug 292–293
  lifting edges 292
  Oriental rugs 292–293
  sisal 293–295
Runaway see Colour Run Remover
rust *see also* rust stains
  in cast-iron 36
  on cutlery 91
  on fibreglass 542–543
  in hinges 306
  in marble vanity top 105
  on metal 309
  in pots and pans 38
  removing from painted wrought iron 167
  removing from screws 306
  on sandstone composite 316–317
  on shower tiles 119
  on sink ring 116
  on stainless steel 68
  on unsealed marble 63–64
rust stains
  on carpet 278–279
  on cast iron 532
  on cast-iron chest 373
  on concrete 526
  on cotton valance 348
  on fabric 144, 406–407

on fibreglass 545
on linen 508
on linoleum 299
on pavers 519
on shower tiles 119
stain removal 486
in toilet 109–110
on wool 455
Rustyban 406–407

S

saddle soap 15
saline solution 16
saliva
    to clean mirrors 128
    on glass 325
salt 16
salt on metal zippers 429–430
salt shakers 85
sandstone cleaning 524
sandstone composite 316–317
sandstone mantlepieces 183
sandstone windowsills 320
sandwich maker 44
saunas 545–546
scald marks *see* scorch marks
scaling *see* lime scale
scanners 202
scorch marks *see also* burn marks
    on cotton 407
    from ironing 504
    on laminate benchtops 23
    on oven glass 26
    in polyurethane 167
Scotchguard 139
scraper 16
scratch marks
    in fibreglass 117
    in glassware 94
    in leather 162
    in old *Bakelite* canisters/handles 38–39
    in plastic 554
    in polycarbonate 562–563
    on polyurethane 169
    on splashback 33
    on stainless steel 68, 74, 91
    in timber 169, 349
screws, removing rust from 306
scuff marks
    on carpet 243, 282
    on cotton 147–148
    rubber, on vinyl 298–299
    on shoes 438
sealant diagnosis 572–573
seals in ovens 27
semen stain
    on mattress 346
    on sheets 355
septic toilets 110
sequins 423
sewing machine oil 259
shade cloth 531, 534–535
shampoo
    for blondes 573
    for brunettes 573
    described 16
sheds 565
sheepskin
    cleaning car covers 558–559
    shoes 442
    washing 365, 366, 465
sheets 351–357
    ballpoint ink on 356
    blood stains on 354–355
    bore water stain on 357
    candle wax on 354
    chocolate on 355
    egg yolk on 355
    flannelette 492
    food stains on 352–353
    fruit juice on 353
    make-up on 353
    nail polish on 341
    ointment on 357
    semen stain on 355
    starches from rice 352, 477
    tannin stains on 352
    vomit on 461
shellac
    cleaning 168
    described 16
    removing 175–176

shoe polish
    on carpet 282
    on enamel 116
    stain removal 487
shoelaces 437
shoes 436–442
    boot scraper 530
    nail heads 438
    sheepskin 442
    shoe cupboard 530
    shoe frou 573
    squeaky 438–439
    stretching 438
    ugg boots 442
shower 117–121
    dull marble in 119–120
    rubber on tiles 120
shower curtain 123–124
shower head 124–125
shower screen 121–123
    cloudy 122
    streaky 122–123
shutters 329
Silestone benchtops 60–61
silicone 16
    black mould in 75
    blue plumber's, on carpet 281
    joins 74
    on mirror 129
    mould in join 123
    on tiles 127
silk
    coffee on 422–423
    cream on 387
    mould on 400
    oily noodles on 433
    red wine stain on 422–423
    solution 574
    stains 332
    stains on 332
    washing 421–422
    in washing machine 360–361
    water marks on 422
    white lines on 422
silver
    cleaning 86–87, 178, 199
    cleaning silver plate 207
    polishing 90

598 INDEX

shadow on tray 206–207
tarnished 199, 376
singe marks *see* burn marks
sinks 72–77, 498
  mildew under 73
  rust stains on sink ring 116
sisal 293–295
  Damp Rid on 294–295
  green food colouring on 294
  vinegar on 294
slate 527, 544
slugs 126
Slurpex 16
smells
  in bags 434
  in books 204
  cigarette smells in furniture 149–150
  cigarette smells in vinyl 164–165
  dead mouse 81, 560–561
  in dog kennel 550
  dry-cleaning fluid in curtains 333–334
  in fridge 51–52
  fumes from heaters 184
  garlic odour in jar lid 87
  incense in drawers 369
  in jar linings 87
  in kitchen 55
  locating using ultraviolet light 251–252
  in mattress 347–348
  mould 270–271
  musty clothes 402
  musty paper 205
  musty smell in house 537–538
  naphthalene flakes 336
  nappy bucket 463
  perfume 556–557
  pet urine smell 251
  pizza in car 560
  salmon juice in lunch bags 89
  in sink drain 75
  smoke in house 27–28
  stinky teddy bear 449
  sweet-smelling hands 101
  urine in shoes 449
  urine in toilet 108, 112
smoke
  from bushfires 334
  fireplaces 180–183
  heaters 183–185
  mantlepieces 183
  marks on splashback 32
  smells in house 27–28
  soot in chimneys 180–181
  soot on carpet 282–283
  on splashback 32
  stains on ceilings 335
snail-proofing vegetable patch 540–541
snails and slugs 540, 552
soap
  cake of bathroom soap 8
  scum in soap holder 120–121
  scum on clothes 495
  scum on glassware 95
  scum on grout 127–128
  stains on timber 105
soap holder 120–121
soap powder 476
socks 459, 507–508
soil on cotton 197
solutions, summary of 569–575
soot *see* smoke
sorbolene cream on carpet 283
soundproofing 306–307, 358
spa bath 117
spas 545–546
spider webs
  on ceilings 311
  under couches 139
spiders
  deterring 313, 531, 551
  solution 574
splashbacks 32–33
sports equipment 546
spray pack 16
squeaky floorboards 217–218
squeaky shoes 438–439
squeegee 16
stainless steel
  benchtops 67–68
  furniture 167
  rust on 68
  scratch marks on 68, 74
stains *see also* blood stains; food stains; grease stains; marks; poo stains; rust stains; tannin stains; urine stains; wine stains
  around swimming pool 544–545
  on *Bessemer* plates 83–84
  diagnosis 579–580
  on fabrics 148–149
  felt pad stains on carpet 372
  on flasks or thermos 44
  in marble 63, 64
  on melamine 83–84
  on ovens 25
  stain removal guidelines 2, 5–6
  on timber benchtop 71
  toothpaste and soap on timber 105
  from washing machine 491–492
starches
  from rice 352, 477
  spray 503
static in clothes 409, 479
statues 541
steam cleaning
  DIY 233–235
  professional 235–236
steel wool 52, 76
stereos 188
sticking doors 306
sticking drawers 176, 368
sticky floors 300
sticky labels *see* contact adhesives
sticky nylon zippers 562
sticky zippers 429

stiff brush 17
stockings 441–442
stone
    cleaning 524
    wax on granite 527–528
straw hats 444
strawberry daiquiri stain on carpet 255–256
streaky shower screen 122–123
streaky *Silestone* 60–61
strollers 464–465
suede
    dirt marks on 430–431
    food stains on 439
    mould on 436, 443
    oily stains on 419
    shoes 437, 438
sugar containers 98
sugar soap 17
sugar soap on glass 321
sunscreen
    on cotton 411
    stain removal 487
suntan lotion on carpet 285–286
super suede 437
superglue
    on laminate 56–57
    removing 257
supersuede 151–154
swags 548
sweat marks
    on car seats 558
    on cotton 389, 411–412
    on leather 432
    on nubuck 153
    on Panama 446
    stain removal 487
sweet almond oil 17
swimming pools 543–545
synthetic grass 547
synthetics
    candle wax on 417
    diesel on polyester and cotton 388–389
    foundation on 393
    mink blanket 473
    mould in life jackets 563
    polyester melted on glass 184
    removing stains from 379
    stretched fabric 494

T
tablecloths 196–198, 508
talcum powder 17
tannin stains
    bark and leaf stains on tiles 522–523
    black tea on cream carpet 279–280
    on bone china 82–83
    brown stains on pavers 517–518
    on carpet 245–246
    on cotton 147
    on crockery 85–86
    on flasks or thermos 44
    glycerine solution 570
    from jute in carpet 237, 277
    on marble 62–63
    on mattress 343–344
    on sheets 352
    stain removal 482
    on strainers 86
    on teacups 84
    on teapots 84, 85–87
    toothpaste and soap on timber 105
tapestry 154–156
taps 77, 125
tar
    on denim 384
    on fabric 412–413
    stain removal 487
    in washing machine 495
tarnished metal 178–179
tarnished silver 199
tea bag 17
tea leaves 217
tea stains *see* tannin stains
tea tree oil 17, 450, 583
teapots
    cleaning silver 86–87
    stains on 84, 85–87
telephones 200
terracotta tiles
    in brown sugar 98
    as coolers 53
    mildew on pots 540
    sealing 225, 521

thermos, stains on 44
throws 165, 363–366
Tiffany lamps 326
Tiger Balm
    on cotton 361
    in hair 131
tiles and grout 521
    in bathrooms 125–128
    in benchtops 68–69
    black line on white tiles 127
    cleaning 225
    dog urine/poo on 226–227
    fuel on unsealed tiles 522
    glazed tiles 521–523
    metal residue on tiles 227
    reapplying grout 126–127
    rust marks on shower tiles 119
    sealing terracotta tiles 225, 521
    sealing unglazed Spanish quarry tiles 225, 521
    silicone on 127
    slippery tiles 521
    soap scum on 127–128
    tile cleaner on carpet 237–239
    tile marks 226
    unsealed tiles 523
timber *see also* dining tables; timber decking; timber floors
    benchtops 69–71
    blood stains on 72, 219
    burn marks on 170
    candle wax on 171–172, 190
    chopping boards 71–72
    cigarette burns on 219–220
    cleaning 178
    cleaning sealed 530
    cleaning unsealed 530
    cloudy stain on 174–175

600 INDEX

cooking oil on 221–222
craft glue on 193–194
dents in 70, 219
frames 318
furniture 167–176
green dye on 195–196
hair dye on 220
kookaburra poo on 515–516
mantlepieces 183
nail polish on 222–223
peanut butter on 215
peas on 194–195
red wax on 224
removing shellac 175–176
rubber marks on 188
scratch marks in 169, 349
sticky labels on 218
toothpaste and soap stains 105
urine stains on 217, 223
water marks on 174
wax on polished timber 172
white markings on 373–374
white stain on 171
windowsills 320–321
timber decking 514–516
timber floors 216–224
sealed 217
squeaky floorboards 217–218
timber stains on carpet 286
unsealed 217
wash solution 574
timber veneer
cleaning 169
cracks in 173–174
lifting or bubbling 173
peeling away 79–80
tint film on windows 322–323
tinware, cleaning 178
tissues 17
toasters 44
toilet
cleaning 107–109
cleaning septics 110
dirty seats 111–112

non-toxic air freshener 113
ping-pong ball technique 109
rubber perishing 112
rust in 109–110
urine smells 112
urine stains 108
water stains on 111
toilet paper 112
tomato
sauce on carpet 287
sauce on cotton 413
stain removal 487
stains in plastic containers 88
on tablecloth 197–198
tomato stains
in plastic containers 88
on tablecloth 197–198
tomato sauce on carpet 197–198
toner on carpet 287
toothbrush 17
toothpaste
on timber 105
on wool 413–414
towels 132
heater oil on 185
massage oil on 497
mould on 509
scratchy 496
softener solution 574–575
tea towels 508
toy cleaning 468–469
toy storage 468
toys 465–469
trays 206–207
treadmills 546
tree sap
bark and leaf stains on tiles 522–523
on carpet 288
on cotton 414
gum leaf stains 518
on pavers 518
stain removal 486
tumble drying 501–502
symbols 494
tung-oil 217
Tupperware 88
turpentine 18
TV screens 186, 187

two-part expoxy glues 258
two-sponge method 3

U
ugg boots 442
ultraviolet light 18, 251–252
umbrellas 534–535
unprocessed wheat bran 8, 18
bran balls 138, 569
urine stains
on carpet 288
cat spray on curtains 331–332
dog urine/poo on tile grout 226–227
on mattress 346, 453
neutralising acid in urine 108
pet urine smell 251
rabbit urine on timber 513–514
rat, in ceiling 335–336
in shoes 449
stain removal 488
on timber 217, 223
in toilet 108, 109–110

V
vacuum cleaner
cleaning 233
described 18
finding lost objects 233, 451
marks on fabric 140
using 230–233
vanilla 582
vanilla essence 18
vanity *see* hand basin and vanity
varnish 168, 217
Vaseline (petroleum jelly) 15, 415
vases 210
VCR heads 186
velcro 441
velvet 156–157
bald patch in 157
cleaning 423
curtains 330–331
water marks on 157
veneer *see* timber veneer
venetian blinds 328

VHS tapes 186
Vicks VapoRub
   on coir 296
   on cotton 456
vinegar 3, 18
vinyl 296–300
   blue-green algae on 538
   buckled 196
   cinnamon oil on warp 80
   cleaning 164–165
   crepe paper stain on 298
   indentations on 297–298
   rubber scuff marks on 298–299
   shoes 436–437
   stains 533
   sticky floor 300
   tyre mark on 564–565
Viraclean 18
vomit
   on carpet 289–290
   on sheets 356, 461
   stain removal 488

W

wall hangings 315–316
wallpaper 311, 314–315
   mould on 314
   peanut butter, jam, margarine on 315
walls 310–317 *see also* bathroom walls
   candle soot stains on 181–182
   crayon marks on 311
   double-sided tape on 312
   fly spray unit mark on 313–314
   glue on 312
   mould on 311
wardrobes 367–372
   beeswax on 369–370
   damp in 369
   hanging clothes 370
   moths in 370
   sachets 575
washing
   babies' clothes 454
   sheepskin 365, 366, 465

washing gloves 77
washing, hanging out 500–501
washing machine
   cleaning 489–493
   general principles for using 474–476
   hot *versus* cold water 476
   shrunken jumper 426
   soaking 477–478
   spot cleaning 477
   starches from rice 352, 477
   starches, spray 503
   tissues in 473–474
   washing pillows in 363
washing soda 18
washing symbols 493
washing up by hand 76–77
water features 542–543
water filters 53
water hyacinth furniture 165–166
water marks
   on carpet 237, 290
   damaged ceilings 334
   in fabric 150
   on French polish 192
   on glazed fountain 542
   in marble 179
   on sealed marble 129–130
   on silk 422
   on timber 174
   on toilet 111
   on velvet 157
   on water feature 542
   yellow, on basin 130–131
water saving 108
water tanks 564
waterbeds, caring for 351
wax *see* candle wax
WD-40 18
weevils in pantry 97
wet-and-dry 19
white marks
   fleck from iron05 504–505
   on plastic 51
   on silk 422

   on tiles 523
   on timber 171, 373–374
   white-out on leather 162
   whiteness on glass 95
white spirits *see* dry-cleaning fluid
white vinegar 3, 19
white washing 494
whiteboard markers 405, 486
whiteboards 203
whiting 19
wicker 165–166, 464, 531
window frames and sills 320, 321
windows 319–334
   blinds 326–329
   leadlight 325–326
   old tint film on 322–323
   putty in 320
   window cleaner 575
wine coolers 53
wine stains
   red wine in decanter 206
   red wine on carpet 276–277, 278
   red wine on cotton 406, 533–534
   red wine on mattress 346–347
   red wine on tablecloth 198
   red wine on upholstered linen 145
   on silk 422–423
   stain removal 489
witch-hazel 19
wooden blinds 329
wool
   angora shedding 427
   berets 444
   caring for 427–428
   chocolate on 386
   cleaning 424
   cleaning lounge 158
   grease stains on 395
   hair spray on 396
   ironing 503
   mohair shedding 165

moths in wardrobe 424–425
plum jam on wool carpet 265–266
pumpkin on 406
rust stains on 455
shrunken jumper 426
solution 574
sticky label on 409
toothpaste on 413–414
what not to do 428
woollen blankets 364–365
woollens 424–428
woollens (how to unshrink) 575
yellowing on 456
woolwash 19, 156
wrought iron 167, 529

Y

yellowing
  on clothes 454–455
  on cotton 417–418
  ivory 376
  on melamine 80–81
  in nylon curtains 331
  on oven doors 26–27
  of sheets 356–357
  silk and wool solution 574
  on wool 456
  yellow water marks on basin 130–131

Z

zinc cream on carpet 291
zip-lock bag 19
zippers 429–430, 562

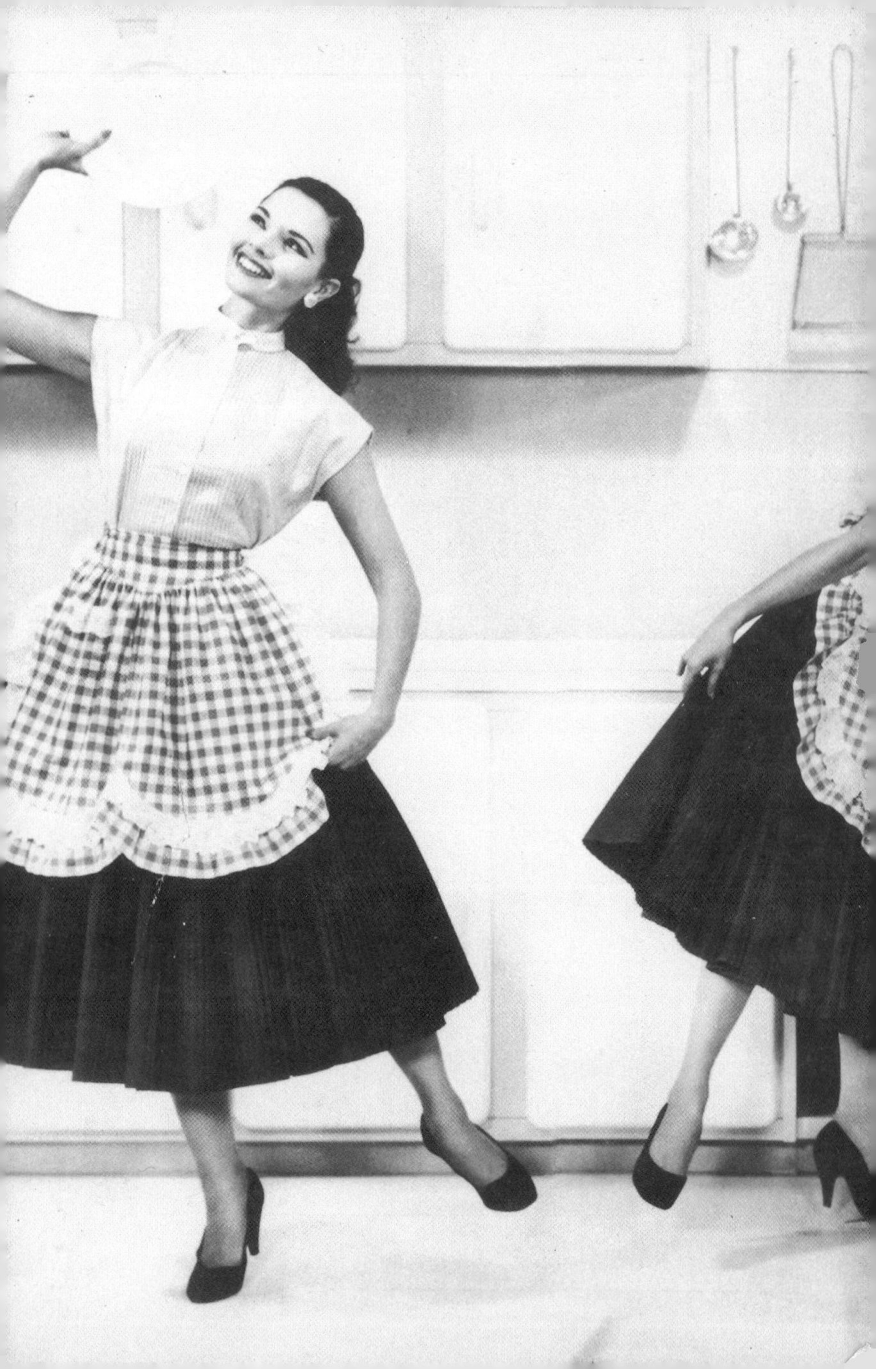